# THE
# BATTLE OF
# BRITAIN

## The Greatest Air Battle
## of World War II

RICHARD HOUGH
AND
DENIS RICHARDS

W. W. NORTON & COMPANY
New York   London

Library of Congress Cataloging-in-Publication Data

Hough, Richard Alexander, 1922–.
The Battle of Britain : the greatest air battle of World War II /
Richard Hough and Denis Richards.— 1st American ed.
p. cm.
Includes bibliographical references (p. ) and index.
ISBN 0-393-02766-X
1. Britain, Battle of, Great Britain, 1940. I. Richards, Denis. II. Title.

D756.5.B7 H67 1989
940.54'211—dc20
89012697

ISBN 0-393-30734-4 pbk.

W. W. Norton & Company, Inc.
500 Fifth Avenue, New York, N.Y. 10110
www.wwnorton.com

W. W. Norton & Company Ltd.
Castle House, 75/76 Wells Street, London W1T 3QT

1 2 3 4 5 6 7 8 9 0

# Contents

*List of Illustrations*                                    vii
*Abbreviations and Code-Names Used in Text*                xiii
Preface                                                     xv
Carnage at Noon                                              1

PART ONE: BEFORE THE BATTLE

  1  No Longer an Island                                     7
  2  Groundwork                                             17
  3  The Bomber Won't Always Get Through                    31
  4  Late Spurt                                             52
  5  Bonus of Time                                          66
  6  Surviving the Storm                                    81
  7  Battle Order                                          101

PART TWO: THE BATTLE

  8  British Day One: 10 July 1940                          121
  9  Channel Fight: 11 July–11 August                       129
 10  Clearing the Way: 12 August                            140
 11  Eagle Day – and After: 13–14 August                    154
 12  Enter – and Exit – *Luftflotte* 5: 15 August           167

13  The Assault Continues: 16 August                                      186

14  Respite and Re-engagement: 17–18 August                               197

15  Desperate Days: 19 August–6 September                                 219

16  Strategic Turning-Point                                               242

17  The New Target: 7 September                                           252

18  'Ominous Quiet!': 8–14 September                                      267

19  'The odds were great; our margins small; the stakes
    infinite': 15 September                                               274

20  The Scent of Victory: 16–30 September                                 284

21  The Battle Fades: October                                            298

PART THREE: AFTER THE BATTLE

22  Retrospect                                                           307

23  Scrambles                                                            335

APPENDICES

I     Chronology of the Battle                                            357
II    Basic Statistics of Fighter Command and Luftwaffe Aircraft
      Engaged in the Battle of Britain                                    371
III   Higher Command, Summer 1940                                        372
IV    Air Defence Higher Formations, July–September 1940                 373
V     Operational Chain of Command in the Luftwaffe                      374
VI    Equivalent Commissioned Ranks: RAF and Luftwaffe                   375
VII   Fighter Command Order of Battle, 8 August 1940                     376
VIII  Luftwaffe Order of Battle against Britain, 13 August 1940          379
IX    Anti-Aircraft Defences: Number and Location of Heavy
      Guns, 21 August 1940                                               380
X     The Balloon Defences, 31 August 1940                               382
XI    Fighter Command Order of Battle, 7 September 1940                  384
XII   100 Octane Fuel                                                    387

Source References                                                        388
Acknowledgments                                                          395
Index                                                                    399

# List of Illustrations

*Between pages 142 and 143*

Air Chief Marshal Sir Hugh Dowding (portrait by Sir Walter Russell) (*Imperial War Museum*)

65 Squadron Spitfires at Sawbridgeworth, Herts., August 1940 (painting by Eric Ravilious) (*Imperial War Museum*)

Bombing the Channel ports, September 1940 (painting by Eric Ravilious) (*Imperial War Museum*)

Air fight over Portland, September 1940 (painting by Richard Eurich) (*Imperial War Museum*)

A heavy anti-aircraft battery about to open fire (painting by C. W. Nevinson (*Imperial War Museum*)

The Battle of Britain (painting by Paul Nash) (*Imperial War Museum*)

Junkers 87 Stukas en route to England (*Robert Hunt Library*)

Messerschmitt 110 flying above the white cliffs of South-East England (*Robert Hunt Library*)

Messerschmitt 110 crews at an outdoor briefing (*Robert Hunt Library*)

Messerschmitt 109s in 'finger four' formation over St Margaret's Bay (*Robert Hunt Library*)

Group Captain Peter Townsend's decorations (*Sotheby's*)

Civil Defence control room (painting by John Piper) (*Imperial War Museum*)

*Between pages 46 and 47*
Early London bomb damage from Zeppelin raid in 1915 (*Popperfoto*)
Zeppelin L31 (*RAF Museum*)
Gotha GIV of 1917 (*E. F. Cheesman*)
Staaken 'Giant', just airborne (*E. F. Cheesman*)
Hendon airshow, 1936 (*RAF Museum*)
The German Aviation Monument in Berlin, 1935 (*US National Archives*)
Sir Hugh Trenchard (*RAF Museum*)
Sholto Douglas (*Imperial War Museum*)
The Luftwaffe hierarchy on 19 July 1940 (*Weidenfeld Archives*)
R. J. Mitchell, creator of the Spitfire (*Popperfoto*)
Willy Messerschmitt, responsible for the Me 109 and 110 fighters (*Robert Hunt Library*)
Sir Robert Watson-Watt (*Imperial War Museum*)
Sir Henry Tizard (*Popperfoto*)
Lord Hives (*Rolls-Royce*)
A CH radar tower (*Imperial War Museum*)
A Remote Reserve aerial (*Imperial War Museum*)
Merlin engine (*RAF Museum*)
Heinkel 111s in the standard 'stepped vics' formation (*Imperial War Museum*)
Messerschmitt 109E (*Heinz Nowarra*)
Junkers 87 Stuka dive-bombers (*Imperial War Museum*)
Dornier 17s (*RAF Museum*)
First prototype Hurricane in flight (*Popperfoto*)
First prototype Spitfire (*RAF Museum*)
Gloster Gladiators in tight vic (*Popperfoto*)
Bristol Blenheim IVs in stepped-up echelon (*Imperial War Museum*)


*Between pages 206 and 207*
Winston Churchill (*Imperial War Museum*)
Lord Beaverbrook and Sir John Anderson (*Popperfoto*)
Hurricane assembly (*Tom Graves*)
Sir Cyril Newall, Chief of the Air Staff (*D. Bateman*)
Keith Park, AOC 11 Group (*Imperial War Museum*)
Sir Quintin Brand, AOC 10 Group (*RAF Museum*)
Trafford Leigh-Mallory, AOC 12 Group (*Imperial War Museum*)
Werner Moelders, the Luftwaffe's greatest fighter pilot (*RAF Museum*)
Reichsmarschall Hermann Goering with Adolf Galland (*Weidenfeld Archives*)
Sir Frederick Bowhill, AOC-in-C Coastal Command (*Imperial War Museum*)

Sir Charles 'Peter' Portal, AOC-in-C Bomber Command (*Imperial War Museum*)

H. A. V. 'Harry' Hogan, CO 501 Squadron (*courtesy of Air Vice-Marshal Henry Hogan CBE, DFC*)

John Hannah VC (*Imperial War Museum*)

Flight Lieutenant R. A. B. Learoyd VC (*Imperial War Museum*)

Josef Frantisek (*Imperial War Museum*)

Alan Deere (*Imperial War Museum*)

A. G. 'Sailor' Malan (*Imperial War Museum*)

Johnny Kent (*Imperial War Museum*)

Spitfire pilots of 610 Squadron recovering from yet another operation (*Imperial War Museum*)

German pilots off duty (*authors' collection*)

The Duke of Kent talking to pilots of A Flight 302 (Polish) Squadron (*authors' collection*)

Three US pilots: 'Andy' Mamedoff, 'Red' Tobin and 'Shorty' Keogh of 609 Squadron (*Imperial War Museum*)

A birthday cake for the flight commander of 41 Squadron, E. N. Ryder (*by courtesy of Robert Beardsley DFC*)

Goering and his staff study a troop-landing exercise (*Imperial War Museum*)

Personnel of an Army Airfield Defence Unit (*Imperial War Museum*)


*Between pages 270 and 271*

The filter room, RAF Fighter Command, Bentley Priory (*D. Bateman*)

Bofors light anti-aircraft guns and crew (*Imperial War Museum*)

Balloons over London (*Imperial War Museum*)

Observer Corps post (*RAF Museum*)

Sound locators for the guns being inspected by King George VI, 14 August 1940 (*D. Bateman*)

Pilots of A Flight 607 Squadron relaxing (*courtesy of William Blackadder DSO, DBE*)

610 Squadron pilots at Biggin Hill (*RAF Museum*)

Ground crews servicing guns: bombing up in France (*RAF Museum*)

Refuelling in England (*RAF Museum*)

Sergeant Elizabeth Mortimer, Corporal Elspeth Henderson and Sergeant Emily Turner (*Air Historical Branch*)

Me 110 under attack (*RAF Museum*)

'Near miss' between attacking Spitfire and He 111 (*Keystone*)

'Bombs away!' – from a Heinkel (*RAF Museum*)

Crew away – from a ditched Me 110 (*RAF Museum*)

Local Defence Volunteers as viewed by Edward Ardizzone (*Imperial War Museum*)

Home Guard on duty over a wrecked Dornier (*RAF Museum*)

Aircraft salvage dump (*Imperial War Museum*)


*Between pages 334 and 335*

He III, flying north over Millwall, London (*Imperial War Museum*)

Sir Hugh Dowding with the King and Queen at Bentley Priory, 6 September 1940 (*Imperial War Museum*)

Peter Townsend with two of his ground crew, Kenley (*RAF Museum*)

Five Czech sergeants of 310 Squadron (*authors' collection*)

James Nicolson of 249 Squadron (*Imperial War Museum*)

George Barclay of 249 Squadron (*courtesy of A. R. F. Thompson DFC*)

Roland 'Bee' Beamont of 87 Squadron (*courtesy of R. Beamont CBE, DSO and Bar, DFC and Bar, US DFC*)

Biggin Hill photographed during an evening raid on 30 August (*Crown copyright*)

Some of the pilots of 249 Squadron in September (*Air Historical Branch*)

Low-level Dornier attack on Kenley (*RAF Museum*)

The end for one more Dornier (*courtesy of Bruce Robertson*)

Two captured German crew survivors, 11 September 1940 (*Imperial War Museum*)

London's dockland burns, 7 September 1940 (*RAF Museum*)

The 'blitz': a heavy rescue team and helpers (*RAF Museum*)

Shelterers in the London Underground, 1940 (*Imperial War Museum*)

The Battle fades; the 'blitz' continues (*Cecil Beaton photograph, courtesy of Sotheby's Belgravia*)


MAPS

| | |
|---|---|
| 1 The Air Defences of Great Britain, August 1940: The South | 72 |
| 2 The Air Defences of Great Britain, August 1940: The North | 74 |
| 3 15 August: The Northern Thrust | 172 |
| 4 Ordeal of the Airfields: 15 August | 177 |
| 5 'Sealion': The German Invasion Plan – Final Version, September 1940 | 246 |
| 6 One Target: London, 7 September, Daylight | 257 |
| 7 The Culmination: 15 September | 279 |


LINE ILLUSTRATIONS

| | |
|---|---|
| 'Careless Talk Costs Lives' | 107 |
| Front page of the *Daily Telegraph*, 16 August 1940 | 183 |
| *Punch* cartoon, 4 September 1940 | 240 |

Front page of the *Daily Telegraph*, 7 September 1940　　　　　247
Production and Wastage of Hurricanes and Spitfires, July–October
　1940　　　　　249
B Flight at dawn readiness　　　　　253
Front page of the *Daily Telegraph*, 9 September 1940　　　　　264
One of Group Captain Vincent's combat reports　　　　　281
Front page of the *Daily Telegraph*, 16 September 1940　　　　　283

# Abbreviations and Code-Names Used in Text

| | |
|---|---|
| AA | Anti-aircraft |
| AAF | Auxiliary Air Force |
| AASF | Advanced Air Striking Force |
| AC2 | Aircraftman 2nd Class |
| *Adlerangriff* | 'Eagle Attack': German air offensive against Britain |
| *Adlertag* | 'Eagle Day': first day of *Adlerangriff* |
| AI | Air Interception: airborne radar |
| AMES | Air Ministry Experimental Station: radar station |
| AOC | Air Officer Commanding |
| AOC-in-C | Air Officer Commanding-in-Chief |
| ARP | Air-Raid Precautions |
| BE | British Experimental – early aircraft |
| BEF | British Expeditionary Force |
| CAS | Chief of the Air Staff |
| CH | Chain Home: standard radar stations |
| CHL | Chain Home Low: low-reading radar stations |
| CO | Commanding Officer |
| 'Cromwell' | Code-name to bring British forces to highest degree of readiness, September 1940 |
| DF | Direction Finding |
| Do | Dornier |
| 'Dynamo' | Code-name for evacuation from Dunkirk |
| Enigma | German encoding machine |
| *Erpro* | *Erprobungsgruppe* |
| G, *Geschwader* | = RAF Group |

| | |
|---|---|
| GCI | Ground Controlled Interception: ground radar used in conjunction with AI |
| Gr, *Gruppe* | = RAF wing |
| He | Heinkel |
| HF | High frequency radio |
| IFF | Identification Friend or Foe – device to identify British aircraft |
| JG, *Jagdgeschwader* | Fighter group |
| Ju | Junkers |
| KG, *Kampfgeschwader* | Bomber group |
| *Knickebein* | 'Crooked leg': wireless beam system for navigation |
| LAC | Leading Aircraftman |
| LDV | Local Defence Volunteers – later Home Guard |
| Me | Messerschmitt |
| MT | Mechanical transport |
| OKW | Oberkommando der Wehrmacht – High Command of the German Armed Forces |
| Ops room | Operations room |
| OTU | Operational Training Unit |
| PAC | Parachute and Cable – defence device for airfields, etc. |
| RDF | Radio Direction Finding – British name (till 1943) for radar |
| R/T | Radio telephony |
| 'Seeloewe' | 'Sealion': code-name for projected German invasion operation |
| Sigint | Intelligence derived from signals |
| *Staffel* | = RAF squadron – 9 aircraft |
| StG, *Sturzkampfgeschwader* | Dive-bomber group |
| Stuka | Dive-bomber (Ju 87) |
| Ultra | Highest grade of secrecy – decrypts of messages encoded on the Enigma machine |
| Vector | Compass bearing |
| Vics | V formations |
| WAAF | Women's Auxiliary Air Force |
| W/T | Wireless telegraphy |
| VHF | Very high frequency radio |
| Y | Listening or interception service, W/T and R/T |
| ZG, *Zerstoerergeschwader* | Destroyer (Me 110) group |

# *Preface*

'Fifty years on' is a good moment for reappraising, and where appropriate celebrating, any great event. Sufficient time has elapsed for it to be seen in historical perspective; nearly all the preserved documentation is usually available; and there are enough of the participants still alive to furnish detail and informed criticism.

There are two further reasons which apply especially in the case of the Battle of Britain. The first is that the passing years have only confirmed, what was hoped and thought at the time, that the Battle was one of the great turning-points in World War II – a defensive victory which saved the island base and so, once Russia and the United States became involved, made future offensive victories possible. The second reason is that within these fifty years fresh generations have been born to whom much of the story is unfamiliar. There are indeed already many excellent books concerned with the Battle which they might read with profit, but as many of these are personal memoirs, or relate to particular episodes, or are intended mainly for the scholar or aficionado, it seemed to us that there was still a place for a new narrative intended for the general reader.

There are two points of emphasis within the book which may need explanation. The British victory resulted primarily from the fact that when the German threat materialised, there were the means to deal with it. How the RAF managed to survive at all in the 1920s, how an efficient air defence system was created over the years, how modern fighters were developed and brought into service, and how the strength of

Fighter Command was painfully built up and preserved amid many competing claims, are therefore a substantial part of our story.

Similarly there is a perhaps unusual concentration within the Battle itself on seven of the sixteen weeks for which it officially lasted. The official duration, decided by the Air Ministry after the war, was based on the operations as seen from the British side and was promulgated primarily to define the limits within which aircrew would qualify for the Battle of Britain clasp. Nothing else would explain the choice of a sheer calendar date, 31 October, as the termination. But it seems to us that in as much as invasion was the proposed next step if the Luftwaffe succeeded, the heart and soul of the Battle was very much the period between the 'Eagle' attacks in the second week of August and the closing days of September, by which time Hitler had postponed the invasion indefinitely and the British had sensed the relaxation of his preparations. We have accordingly treated these vital weeks in considerably greater detail than the fighting of July and October.

In the course of our narrative we have made many references to the strength of opposing forces, and to numbers of aircraft participating in an operation or shot down. The reader should not expect any complete exactitude in these figures. Strength is notoriously difficult. Take so apparently simple a matter as a British fighter squadron at some typical and favourable time. In theory, initial equipment sixteen aircraft, immediate reserve held by squadron five aircraft, number of pilots twenty-eight. But the squadron is not expected to put up more than twelve aircraft at a time; and within a few hours, after an operation, half the aircraft may be unserviceable. The immediate reserve may turn out in practice to be only two aircraft: and if at the same time there are only about twenty pilots and several of these are more or less untrained operationally, what then is the strength? All we can say is that we have taken what seem to be the most accurate of the various figures available, and tried to keep the basis of comparison consistent. Combat victories and losses are as determined in the light of post-war research: a note of this appears in Appendix I (Chronology of the Battle). Where claims are mentioned, they are stated as such.

The writing of this book would naturally have been impossible without the generous co-operation of a number of organisations and individuals, and we should like to acknowledge this and thank them warmly for their help. Among them were Dr John Tanner CBE, creator and lately Director of the Royal Air Force Museum, and his staff; Dr Alan Borg, Director of the Imperial War Museum, and his staff; Air

Commodore Henry Probert MBE, Head of the Air Historical Branch of the Ministry of Defence, and his staff; Mr Denis Bateman, who assisted us with picture research; the Librarians of Adastral House Library; and the helpful staff of the Public Record Office, Kew.

We owe a very special debt to the Battle of Britain Fighter Association, to its Chairman Air Chief Marshal Sir Christopher Foxley-Norris GCB, DSO, OBE, RAF (Retd), and its Honorary Secretary and Treasurer, Wing Commander N. P. W. Hancock DFC, RAF (Retd). The members of this Association, from all over the world, were liberal in the time and trouble they expended in answering our questions and offering us reminiscences, both in writing and in the course of conversation. Among those who were particularly generous with their time were: Group Captain W. D. David CBE, DFC, AFC, RAF (Retd); Air Vice-Marshal A. D. Deere OBE, DSO, DFC, AFC, RAF (Retd); Sir Hugh Dundas Kt, CBE, DSO, DFC, RAF (Retd); Air Vice-Marshal A. V. Hogan CB, DFC, RAF (Retd); and Air Commodore J. A. Leathart CB, DSO, RAF (Retd).

We are also very grateful to numerous former ground crew and members of the auxiliary services and civil defence organisations who wrote to us about their experiences in response to a letter printed in the *Daily Express* and the *Daily Mirror*. Their names, together with those of the Battle of Britain Fighter Association who helped us, are listed in the latter part of this volume. Among those on the ground side who gave us particularly valuable help were Mr W. Eslick, Mr J. R. Hearne, Mrs E. Kup and Mr P. O'Connor.

Finally we should like to thank Mrs Barbara Richards for her help in dealing with these communications, and our editor-publisher, Mr John Curtis, together with the directors and staff of Messrs Hodder and Stoughton, for so harmonious and enjoyable a collaboration.

R.H. and D.R.
February 1989

# Carnage at Noon

The convoy code-named 'Peewit' was picked up during the night of 7–8 August by German radar as it attempted to slip through the Straits of Dover. There were twenty merchantmen in all, escorted by a number of light naval craft. Protective balloons floated above this prime target; but these were of no help when the first German E-boats raced in at dawn, sinking three of the merchantmen with their torpedoes and damaging three more.

The first Stuka dive-bombers appeared out of the sky soon after the withdrawal of the E-boats; above them little clipped-wing Me 109 fighters darted to and fro like lethal mayflies. Every sailor knew that this was no more than the threatening first note of the overture. On land, seasoned RAF controllers awaited word of the inevitable appearance of big blips on the radar screens before scrambling their fighter squadrons.

The first great air attack on the hapless merchantmen by more than 100 dive-bombers and escorting fighters closed in at noon. The Hurricanes and Spitfires of 145, 257 and 609 Squadrons were ready for them, and three Hurricanes of 145 Squadron were among the first to dive out of the sun, slicing through the Me 109s to grapple with the Stukas in their own near-vertical dives.

Pilot Officer James Storrar,* with five enemy aircraft already to his credit, opened fire at close range at one of the crank-winged, fixed-undercarriage dive-bombers and sent it out of control straight into the sea.

*Later Wing Commander DFC, AFC, AE.

Two more Stukas and four German fighters followed it. Others staggered home, crippled, some with dead or wounded aircrew, to crash on French soil. But the price they had exacted was four blown-up merchantmen and two Hurricanes shot down.

The midday dogfight off the Sussex coast had been one of the biggest so far of the Battle, with the sky alight with flaming balloons and aircraft, the white circles of parachutes contrasting with the sinister black spotting from the anti-aircraft fire. But the day's destruction was not over. Soon General Wolfram Freiherr von Richthofen,* at his Deauville headquarters, ordered another attack on the convoy on an even bigger scale.

As this massive force of dive-bombers and twin- and single-engined fighters headed north across the glass-like grey waters of the Channel, the German pilots could see the umbrella of RAF fighters over the convoy, which was now off the Isle of Wight. And they knew that their arrival would be like the sudden contact between two live high-tension cables.

James Storrar's CO, Squadron Leader John Peel, had already led 145 Squadron on a breakfast-time attack over Weymouth, claiming nine enemy aircraft for the loss of two Hurricanes. So this was their third big fight, and another chance for the surviving pilots to add to their score, Storrar already with a Me 109 as well as the earlier Stuka to his credit. Almost fifty years later he recalled this last battle of 8 August:

'The squadron split up when we engaged the enemy aircraft which had just bombed the convoy. I saw a Ju 87 Stuka at sea level on its own heading back across the Channel. I attacked from astern and soon became aware that I had silenced the rear-gunner. As I finished my ammunition with little obvious effect I suddenly became aware that there was a flame round his right undercarriage leg. I came up alongside. There was no sign of the rear-gunner but the pilot was looking at me and I was no more than twenty or thirty yards away. I could see his face clearly and could virtually see his hand on the stick. The flame suddenly burst over the top of the wing. We both looked at it for what seemed like seconds, when the Stuka's wing suddenly buckled – it turned over into the sea and exploded.

'I circled the smoke a couple of times, and was then joined by another Hurricane from 145 Squadron, who headed back with me towards the English coast. I could see as we pulled back our hoods he was giving me a thumbs-up sign. It was Sub-Lieutenant Smith.

*A nephew of the great World War I ace.

2

'I had a sudden feeling to look back over my other shoulder and saw two 109s pulling in behind us. I yelled over the R/T and broke hard into a turn towards them. As I got round to engage I pressed the button and it just hissed – of course, no ammunition. So I kept turning to avoid them and they disappeared. Sub-Lieutenant Smith failed to return.'

It had been a hard day for 145 Squadron, and a bloody day, with five of their twenty-two pilots killed. Four more of their Hurricanes were shot down a few days later, including Squadron Leader Peel's, although – thank the Lord – he was only injured, and three more pilots of 145 were killed on 12 August. And these were only early days of the Battle: twelve more weeks of fighting lay ahead – fighting for the airfields, fighting over London, fighting by night as well as by day. How could that frail screen of RAF fighters hold out against the German onslaught? The work of twenty-five years lay behind the answer.

# PART ONE

# BEFORE THE BATTLE

*Rearmament*

I have heard the sullen howl of madness
rising, falling, from afar;
I see the desperate hate of nations
boiling up; it reeks of war.

I have dreamed of joy, unmeasured gladness,
planned my joys – for I am young;
England was weak, and dreams were broken;
England meet the day – be strong!

FLYING OFFICER A. N. C.
WEIR DFC, SHOT DOWN AND
KILLED NOVEMBER 1940

# I

## No Longer an Island

In the late hours of Sunday, 1 October 1916, one of the present authors was aroused from his youthful slumbers, inserted into a dressing-gown, and brought downstairs for greater safety. The Zepps were over again, and a six year old could happily look forward to the pleasures of cherry cake and a glass of milk in the middle of the night.

On this occasion there was soon greater excitement. To the banging of the north London guns was added the news, brought in by a neighbour, that the searchlights were 'holding' one of the raiders. A rush into the street followed. The night was starlit between the clouds, and away to the north a Zeppelin was indeed clearly visible, trapped in a cone of light. Suddenly there was a burst of flame, which swiftly spread along the entire length of the huge machine. 'Blazing from end to end like an enormous cigar,'[1] the Zeppelin canted over and sank nose-down towards the earth. Sounds of cheering came over the air. Then a final flash, sudden darkness and an afterglow in the sky.

The next day a visitor to the wreckage, luckier than the thousands who crammed the trains to Potters Bar but were denied a close view, observed two large heaps of twisted metal widely separated in a field, a pile of charred corpses, and indentations in the ground made by one of the crew who had presumably jumped to avoid incineration: 'a round hole for the head, then a deep impression of the trunk, then the widely separated legs – a most uncanny sight'.[2]

The destruction of L31 by the bullets of Second Lieutenant W. J. Tempest flying a BE2$^c$ was the fourth combat-loss to be inflicted on the German airship services within a month. After a year and a half in which the Zeppelins had made thirty-seven raids without a single loss over British soil, they had suddenly become prey to the defences. The shooting down of two more on 27 November 1916, and the dwindling of further Zeppelin effort into a mere dozen raids during the rest of the war, only confirmed that the first assault on Britain from the skies had been decisively defeated.

'When did the Battle of Britain really begin? A not unreasonable answer is that the Battle of Britain began when the Wright brothers flew.' So wrote the American historian Alfred Gollin, who went on to show that of all the governments to express an interest in the Wright brothers' achievement, Britain's was the first.[3]

History is indeed a continuum, and there is a chain of progression between the innocent half-minute hops in the sandhills of North Carolina in 1903 and the deadly encounters at 350 mph 18,000 feet above the chequered counties of southern England thirty-seven years later. Of the many links in this chain, few are more important than the experiences of 1914–18, a glance at which will show how victory in 1940 stemmed at least in part from developments more than twenty years earlier.

The threat to Britain from an enemy in the skies was appreciated from the earliest days of flying. The story is well known of how the newspaper magnate Lord Northcliffe was angered to read in his *Daily Mail* only a brief factual report of Alberto Santos Dumont's pioneer aeroplane flight in Europe in 1906 – a mere 722 feet. The news, Northcliffe told the offending editor, was 'not that Santos Dumont flies 722 feet, but that England is no longer an island. It means the aerial chariots of a foe descending on British soil if war comes.'[4] The lesson became clearer still when Louis Blériot flew the Channel in 1909 and the German Army and Navy began to interest themselves in the dirigible balloons or airships invented by Count Ferdinand von Zeppelin.

The British response to this new danger was to create the Royal Flying Corps (RFC), with naval and military wings, in 1912. This, however, raised as many questions of responsibility for air defence as it solved – questions of the utmost importance, since intelligently allocated and clearly recognised spheres of authority and lines of command are a prime requisite for military success. The historic roles in the defence of the United Kingdom were reasonably clear: it was the duty of the Royal Navy to prevent invaders approaching Britain, and the duty of the Army to throw them back, or out, if they got there. Now, by extension, it was the duty of the Army to deal with enemy aircraft which crossed British coasts. But air attack was likely at first to fall on ports and naval bases, so the Navy was soon busy providing aircraft and air stations for their defence. With the Army concentrating purely on reconnaissance tasks for aircraft, and the Navy, under the energetic and adventurous Mr Churchill at the Admiralty, much more aware of wider possibilities like attacking Zeppelins in their sheds, the two wings of the RFC rapidly grew apart and finally separated. Meanwhile, at the outbreak of war in 1914, the Army sent almost its entire strength in operational aircraft – four squadrons of the RFC – over to France to reconnoitre for the British Expeditionary Force (BEF). This produced the situation aptly described by Churchill: 'The War Office . . . claimed that they alone should be charged with the responsibility for home defence. When asked how they proposed to discharge this duty they admitted sorrowfully that they had not got the machines, and could not get the money. They adhered, however, to the principle.'[5]

In the face of the facts of the situation, principle had to go out of the window. In September 1914 the Admiralty was formally charged with the air defence of the United Kingdom, the role of the Army being to co-operate with guns and any aircraft awaiting despatch overseas. But as the Army soon had more men and guns available than the Navy, it was quickly given the task of defending most of the strategic points outside London. No military aircraft were set aside to protect any particular place, but when available they were to co-operate with the naval aircraft. Under arrangements of this sort it was not surprising that, despite many advances in the provision of aircraft, airfields, high-angled guns, searchlights and other elements of defence, including training for night flying, the defences succeeded in damaging only one of the thirty-seven Zeppelins and none of the four German aeroplanes which crossed the British coasts during 1915.[6]

With more resources available, in February 1916 the Army resumed responsibility for air defence over Great Britain – though not in advance of its shores. The next few months, with Field Marshal Lord French as Commander-in-Chief Home Forces, saw much progress. Height-finders were introduced for the guns; the gun and searchlight defences of London and other centres were thickened up; and five RFC squadrons – increased to eleven by the end of the year – were allocated specifically to Home Defence. In an 'Ever-Ready' zone aircraft stood by and flew regular night patrols. A 'barrage-line' of air stations and searchlights was developed inland parallel with the east coast. For air-raid warning, dependent on reports from thousands of observer posts and not yet generally communicated to the public, the military took over from the chief constables and operated a much more effective system with control areas based on the main telephone centres. At the sharp end of things, incendiary and explosive bullets began to replace the previously ineffective machine-gun ammunition and the attempts to bomb Zeppelins from above. After a preliminary success in April 1916, the result was seen six months later in the virtual ending of the 'Zeppelin menace'.

On 28 November 1916, only a few hours after the destruction of two Zeppelins, some bombs fell on London in broad daylight from an unseen German aeroplane. It was the first episode of its kind, but a portent. The Zeppelins, for all their advantages in range, ceiling and bomb-load, had proved highly vulnerable to the defences and still more so to the weather. Aeroplanes were a different story.

For the next six months enemy air activity was slight and two of the Home Defence squadrons were sent over to France. Then, with the better weather, the Germans struck in force. On the afternoon of 25 May 1917 twenty-three Gothas, sturdy twin-engined bombers from what came to be unofficially known as the *Englandgeschwader*, set off from their bases in Belgium to attack London. Thwarted by cloud, most of them dropped bombs on Folkestone instead, killing ninety-five people. On 13 June – 'the Wednesday' of Londoners' later memories – fourteen Gothas in clearer weather then penetrated to the heart of the capital. Flying high in formation like a flock of white birds, and watched in fascination by thousands of people below who at first mistook them for 'friendlies', they calmly unloaded their bombs on Liverpool Street Station and the neighbouring areas, killing 162 persons. Until heading home they met no challenge from the ninety-odd British fighters ordered into the air. Three weeks later the pattern was repeated when eighty-three fighters failed to intercept, or even see, Gothas bombing Harwich. Then on 7 July – 'the Saturday' – came the second big daylight raid on London. Again the Gothas rode the skies, undisturbed by ineffective gunfire. But this time, after dropping their bombs on the City, they paid a price – two shot or forced down on the flight back, three more wrecked in landing.[7]

This second daylight raid on London had profound effects. The public outcry against the weakness of the defences led to the setting up of a Prime Minister's Committee on Air Organisation and Home Defence against Air-Raids. It consisted only of Lloyd George and General Smuts, with the latter doing all the work. Criticising 'the dispersal of Command' in the Home Defence Force under Lord French as between the RFC, the artillery and the Observation Corps, Smuts recommended on 19 July that all such forces should be placed under the control of an airman, responsible to French but 'charged with the duty of working out all plans for the London Air Defence'.[8]

The institution of the London Air Defence Area, covering in fact south-east England, swiftly followed. To command it, a brilliant combination of airman and artillery officer was brought back from France in the person of Brigadier-General E. B. Ashmore. With naval fighters on the coast, a gun-belt planned to extend twenty-five miles round London, an RFC fighter patrol zone between the gun-belt and the capital, and finally gun defences within the capital itself, the whole defensive system became coherent. More and better British fighters, too, became available, as Sopwith Pups, Camels and Bristol fighters gradually replaced the slow, old BEs, and as daring pilots demonstrated that such inherently unstable aircraft could be successfully flown and landed at night. To direct the pilots towards the enemy in the air – there was as yet no radio telephony – a system of white arrow pointers was devised. 'The great principle of air defence', in Ashmore's later words, was becoming recognised: 'that although aeroplanes are the first means of defence, they are ineffective unless supported by a control system on the ground'.[9] All told, the defenders could soon look forward to giving the raiders a hotter time.

So, indeed, it proved. During August 1917 the combination of better defences and strong north-westerly winds made the task of the Gothas much more difficult. Their losses on 22 August – three out of ten which attacked – spelt the end of German daylight raiding. The second phase of Germany's air assault on the British homeland had ended, like the first, in favour of the defenders.[10]

For the *Englandgeschwader*, however, there was still the unexploited cover of night. Navigation in the dark would be difficult for the Gothas – unlike the Zeppelins they carried no wireless for direction-finding fixes – but at least they could hardly have an easier target to find than London. After an experimental raid on Chatham which took the defences completely by surprise, eleven Gothas set out the following night – 4 September 1917 – to attack the capital. Only five got through, but the damage they inflicted caused the British to estimate their numbers at twenty-six.

Again there was a public outcry, to which Ashmore was swift to respond. Fighter patrols were reorganised within a broader zone free from guns but with more searchlights, work was begun on sound locators, guns were brought in from outlying areas, and barrage fire became more accurate as the raiders were more accurately plotted from square to square in the gun zone. It was found, too, that single-seat fighters – Camels – could be successfully flown at night. In addition, balloon nets or aprons – steel wires suspended from groups of three or four barrage balloons yoked together with steel cables – were installed at points along the northern and eastern approaches to the capital. Flown at up to 10,000 feet, they were intended to force the raiders to a height which was more predictable for the gunners, and from which bomb-aiming would be less accurate.[11]

The Gothas' most sustained night assault came in late September 1917. Between 24 September and 1 October they attacked London on no fewer than six nights – 'the week of the harvest moon'. They were joined by half-a-dozen Riesen (Giants), huge multi-engined aircraft nearly as big as a World War II B29 Superfortress. With a crew of eleven, a bomb-load of two tons and a range of nearly 600 miles, they carried every known refinement of the time from wireless, an intercom system and electrically heated clothing for the crew to a wide selection of instruments including an artificial horizon.

This series of raids caused little physical damage by World War II standards, but nevertheless had big effects. Each night, thousands of Londoners poured into the underground railway stations: as the song of the time had it:

> When the moon shines bright
> Ma red-faced Rube,
> Put your little hand in mine
> And hop it for the tube.

Others took to the western suburbs or the countryside. In the East End of London the psychological trauma was deep. Despite earlier experiences in the war civilians still did not expect to be bombed, and least of all in a proud island which had successfully resisted intrusion for centuries. On all sides arose the cry not only for further strengthening of the defences, but for retaliation.

The organisation to make this possible had already been proposed in the second part of Smuts's report, completed on 17 August 1917. Smuts suggested that the Air Board, a co-ordinating body of great achievement in the fields of aircraft production and allocation, should be replaced by a fully fledged Air Ministry 'to control and administer all matters in connection with aerial warfare of all kinds whatsoever'. At the disposal of this Air Ministry would be a unified air force, co-equal with the Army and the Royal Navy, to be formed from the amalgamation of the RFC and the Royal Naval Air Service. Only by freeing this service from the direction of the Admiralty and the War Office, in Smuts's opinion, could the resources be found for air operations independent of the Navy and the Army. By these he meant the proper protection of Britain against air attack and the bombing of the enemy homeland. In prophetic words he wrote of 'the day . . . when air operations with their devastation of enemy lands and destruction of industrial and popular centres on a vast scale may become the principal operations of war'.[12]

Once it was known that the Giants were operational and had been in action, Smuts's recommendations were accepted and swiftly implemented. The Air Ministry came into being in January 1918, and the two air services became the Royal Air Force (RAF) on 1 April 1918. No great change in air defence arrangements immediately followed, but the other half of Smuts's 'independent' air operations, the bombing of Germany, received a great impetus. RFC units in eastern France, which began bombing Germany regularly in October 1917, grew from a wing into a brigade into the RAF's Independent Force, which in turn was meant to be the nucleus of the projected Inter-Allied Independent Air Force. When the Armistice came, the RAF was planning to bomb Germany the following year with a force of forty squadrons based in France and eight in England – four-engined Handley Page V1500s, capable of reaching Berlin. The cries of 'give it 'em back' which greeted Churchill in London's bombed East End in 1940 had already resounded with equal vehemence in 1917.

Meanwhile, there was the battle against the German night raiders. They did not come very often – two or three times a month during the autumn and winter of 1917–18, and then not at all between 17 March and a final big fling on 19 May 1918. But their losses were greater; and on the last raid of 19 May, when less than half of the attacking force of forty-two got through to London, the defenders had their best night ever – three Gothas to the guns, three to the fighters, another Gotha down in England from engine failure and three more crash-landed in Belgium.

And there, apart from one fatal Zeppelin approach to Norfolk in August, the raiding ceased. One cause was undoubtedly the increased effectiveness of the defences; but the Allied bombing of western Germany, and still more the enemy's need to concentrate all his resources on the desperate struggle in France and Belgium, also contributed powerfully to the German change of policy.

Was this another clear-cut victory for the defences? The answer must be 'no', as it was to be again during the German 'night blitz' of 1940–41. The verdict would seem to be a draw, though the official historian of the RAF in World War I, H. A. Jones, was in no doubt that the raids – even the Zeppelin raids – had been effective for Germany in terms of allocation of military resources.[13] In operating the *Englandgeschwader* the Germans lost sixty Gothas – twenty-four shot down, thirty-six in crashes – and inflicted what was in reality insignificant damage. The effect of the raids on production was demonstrable but in total small, and on civilian morale was partial and very temporary. But during the last six months of the war the mere threat of raids, after the raiding had actually ceased, caused Britain to retain at home some 200 fighters which would have been invaluable on the Western Front, to say nothing of over 450 guns and over 600 searchlights.[14]

Whatever the balance sheet of the raids, there can be no doubt that they forced the United Kingdom to develop, from nothing, an admirably coherent and well-organised system of air defence. During the final months of the war Ashmore, unhappy that out of every eighteen pilots sent up to intercept only one usually got so much as a sight of an intruder, concentrated on some obvious weaknesses. To improve early warning, a beginning was made with installing a few sound locators; and a big new telephone network, independent of the public service, was set up throughout the system of control. To lessen night-flying accidents, there was better training and better equipment in cockpits and on the ground. To communicate with the pilots in the air, the radio telephone was developed. For day fighters, this became standard equipment by May 1918; for night fighters, it was restricted to the patrol leaders.[15] In the Home Office sphere of public warning, general by 1917, the firing of maroons by day (and later at all hours) replaced earlier methods such as police wearing 'Take Cover' placards and blowing their whistles as they bicycled through the streets. Bugles, usually sounded by Boy Scouts, proclaimed the 'All Clear'.*

The British victory in 1940, then, was very far from an improvisation. It rested on, among other things, the solid foundations of a system which had been largely evolved from experience in an earlier conflict. Here is Cecil Lewis, author of that wonderful account of a young man's flying, *Sagittarius Rising*, describing proceedings at Hainault Farm in 1917: 'Each squadron had a telephone operator constantly on duty. When raid warnings came through, he pressed a Morse Key close to hand sounding three large klaxon horns set up on the roof of the men's quarters and the officers' mess. The men swarmed into their kit and warmed up their engines. If the raid warning was followed by the action signal, machines were off the ground within a minute.'[17]

And here is Major-General Ashmore in 1918: 'A deep zone of country surrounding London, and extending to the sea on the south-east and east, was already covered with defence units under my command – gun-stations, searchlights, aerodromes, balloon aprons, emergency landing grounds, coastal and inland watching posts. Each of them was now treated as an observation station and was connected up by telephone to a sub-control. The sub-controls (there were twenty-five of them) were in their turn connected to the central control in the Horse Guards. This central control consisted essentially of a large squared map fixed on a table, round which sat ten operators (plotters) provided with headphones; each being connected to two or three of the sub-controls. During operations, all the lines were kept through direct: there was no ringing up throughout the system.

'When aircraft flew over the country, their position was reported every half-minute or so to the sub-control, where the course was plotted with counters on a large-scale map. These positions were immediately read off by a "teller" in the sub-control to the plotter in the central control, where the course was again marked out with counters. An ingenious system of coloured counters, removed at intervals, prevented the map from becoming congested during a prolonged raid.

'I sat overlooking the map from the raised gallery; in effect, I could follow the course of all aircraft flying over the country, as the counters crept across the map. The system worked very rapidly. From the time when an observer at one of the stations in the country saw a machine

---

*Characteristically, the Home Office declined to accept responsibility for compensation if Scouts were killed on duty, since they were non-combatants.[16]

over him, to the time when the counter representing it appeared on my map, was not, as a rule, more than half a minute.

'In front of me a row of switches enabled me to cut into the plotter's line, and talk to any of my subordinate commanders at the sub-controls.

'The central control, in addition to receiving information from outside, constantly passed it out to the sub-controls concerned: so that the commander, say, of an anti-aircraft brigade would know, from moment to moment, where and when hostile aircraft would approach his guns.

'By my side, in the gallery, sat the air force commander . . . with direct command lines to his squadrons, and a special line to a long-range wireless transmitter at Biggin Hill. This transmitter was used for giving orders to leaders of defending formations in the air during day time, in accordance with the movements of the enemy as shown on the control map.

'In order to leave me and my staff free for the defence work, a representative of Scotland Yard was present in the central control during operations, and was responsible for keeping the public and fire brigade informed of events. . . .'[18]

As yet, of course, there was no radar to pick up swiftly flying raiders fifty miles out from shore; but in so many other essentials, how like 1940!

# 2

## Groundwork

The Battle of Britain was fought when the RAF was but twenty-two years old. A glance at its adolescence will perhaps explain how, despite the best efforts of admirals to dismember it and governments to run it on the cheap, it grew strong enough to triumph in 1940.

In the first few months after the Armistice the Coalition Government of Lloyd George, 'the man who won the war', swiftly dismantled one of the instruments of victory – the largest air force in the world. There had earlier been counsel to the contrary, for General Smuts's great report of August 1917 had ended with these words:

We should not only secure air predominance, but secure it on a very large scale; and having secured it in this war we should make every effort and sacrifice to maintain it for the future. Air supremacy may in the long run be as important a factor in the defence of the Empire as sea supremacy.[1]

As soon as the guns fell silent, any thought of following Smuts's advice vanished like smoke. In November 1918 the RAF had an operational strength of 188 squadrons (excluding seaborne units) backed by another 199 training squadrons. Eighteen months later it was down to twenty-five operational squadrons, mostly in India or the Middle East, and eleven training squadrons.[2] The air defence of Great Britain, about which there had been such frenetic concern two years earlier, for a time rested on two half-squadrons.[3]

★　★　★

There were, of course, good reasons for a rapid run-down, if not for wholesale slaughter. Complete demobilisation of the non-professional forces was expected, and demanded; economy was the order of the day; the nation, sickened with four years of slaughter, was in unmilitary mood; and the late enemy had been comprehensively disarmed and forbidden to maintain military aviation. All the same, the reduction was so drastic that in some matters its effects could never, in the later years of rearmament, be overcome in time for the next conflict.

Small though the thinned-down RAF was, its mere existence affronted the heads of the two older Services. From 1919 to 1923 the War Office and the Admiralty waged a relentless campaign to dismember the new Service in the hope of recovering for themselves what they regarded as lost component parts.[4] All their efforts, however, failed in face of the resolute defence put up by Sir Hugh Trenchard, Chief of the Air Staff from 1919 to 1929.

There are many reasons why Trenchard, whom it has become fashionable to depict only as a rather dim-witted enthusiast for strategic bombing, should rank as one of the progenitors of victory in the Battle of Britain. The first and most important is that by beating off the repeated assaults of the other Services he preserved a separate air force. Independence, theoretically justified by the economy and flexibility of centralised air power, was in practice essential at the time not only for the development of strategic bombing, in which context it is usually considered, but also for the sustained study of, and wholehearted commitment to, the air defence of Britain. General Lord Ismay, Churchill's closest military confidant, gave his heartfelt verdict on this in his *Memoirs* (1960): 'One shudders to think what would have happened in the Second World War if the Admiralty and the War Office had had their way and the Air Arm had again become a mere auxiliary of the older Services.'[5]

Trenchard won these battles largely by accepting, and making a virtue of, the concept so dear to the politicians of the time – economy. Early in 1919 he undercut the imaginative but probably impractical proposals of Sir Frederick Sykes, then Chief of the Air Staff, for a permanent Imperial Air Force. Trenchard's much more modest ideas attracted Churchill, at that time combining, ominously, the portfolios of War and Air. Having displaced Sykes, Trenchard outlined his proposals in a remarkable memorandum published in December 1919 as a White Paper, price one penny. Its principles were accepted, and Parliament gave approval for a peacetime independent air force of some

30,000 officers and men and thirty-three operational squadrons – of which only twenty-five existed.[6] Small as this was, it was better than the complete extinction as a separate Service for which the naval and military leaders hankered.

Trenchard and Churchill then soon found an additional role for the RAF which actually saved money. In 1922 the new Service was entrusted with responsibility for the internal security of the British mandated territories first of Iraq and then of Palestine and Transjordan. Its occasional warning and punitive operations, conducted at much less cost in lives and cash than the previous military expeditions, were brilliantly successful. 'Air control', extended later to Aden, became a further justification for an independent air force.

Although official investigations and reports by A. J. Balfour and the formidable Sir Eric Geddes again came down in favour of a separate air force in 1921, it was another two years before Trenchard's post-war creation became reasonably secure. What doubts still surrounded its existence after the fall of the Coalition may be seen from the words with which the new Conservative Prime Minister, Bonar Law, offered Sir Samuel Hoare the Secretaryship of State for Air in November 1922:

Will you take it? But before you answer I must tell you that the post may be abolished within a few weeks. Sykes tells me that the Independent Air Force and the Air Ministry cost much too much, and that there is everything to be said in peacetime for going back to the old plan of Navy and Army control. I agree with him. I shall therefore expect you, if you take the post, to remember that it may very soon cease to exist. There will be an immediate enquiry into the whole question by the Cabinet and the Committee of Imperial Defence. . . . I ought to add that the post will not be a Cabinet post.[7]

The reviewing body set up by Bonar Law was a sub-committee of the Committee of Imperial Defence under Lord Salisbury. Within this, a sub-sub-committee under Lord Balfour conducted a separate investigation into the special question of the squadrons, both ship-borne and shore-based, which worked with the Navy.* The climate of opinion at the time these committees were appointed may be judged from the later account of Hoare, who was to prove an able lieutenant to Trenchard in all his struggles. Referring to his speech in connection with his first Air Estimates of March 1923, Hoare wrote:

*The shore-based squadrons intended primarily for naval co-operation were entirely administered and controlled by the RAF. Operationally they normally worked in accordance with naval wishes, but they could be required to undertake other tasks. The ship-borne squadrons, known after 1924 as the Fleet Air Arm, were trained, manned and maintained by the RAF, but operationally were under complete naval control.

I told the House that we had only sixteen first line machines equipped and ready for Home Defence, and that all the squadrons in India had been grounded for lack of spares. If I had not wished to avoid a quarrel with the Government of India, I would have amplified my Indian story by telling the House that the squadrons had received no new engines for seven years, and that they were buying bits and pieces in the bazaars for patching up their obsolete equipment. Members were mildly surprised by my statement rather than seriously shocked. They were bent on economy. . . .[8]

By the time, however, that Salisbury and Balfour had begun their deliberations, the international climate had changed. Economy, as personified in the previous Government by Sir Eric Geddes, wielding a far sharper axe than any remotely contemplated in later days by Mrs Thatcher, had suddenly lost its charm when Britain fell out with France over reparations policy towards Germany. Could it be that the strongest air force in the world, the French, situated only a few miles across the water, might have to be reckoned as hostile? The prospect was unlikely, but disturbing. In its last days the Coalition Government had already, reviewing the defences of the country, approved the creation of further squadrons.[9] Now, with the vastness of Britain's imperial commitments also in mind, the Salisbury committee quickly recommended not only the retention of a separate air force, but also a further measure of expansion.[10] At the same time Balfour's sub-committee came down in favour of leaving the maritime squadrons, ship-borne and shore-based alike, within the RAF.[11] At the time, this was a vital victory; for had the Admiralty won its case, the War Office would have fought still harder, and the residual air force would have been too small to survive.*

These judgments infuriated the Admiralty, where Admiral Lord Beatty had already tried to sway the issue by a threat of resignation if the verdict went against him, and where the First Lord, L. S. Amery, with difficulty now prevented the whole Board of Admiralty from resigning. Little less aggrieved was the War Office, whose political head, Lord Derby, when informing the Prime Minister of his 'grave apprehension' about the ability of the RAF officers to run a separate Service, wrote thus: 'After Trenchard, who is a first-class man, there is nobody . . . really the calibre of the young officers who are taken in now is very low, worse even than many of those who were taken in during the war, and we know what their standard was, and you cannot expect to make a good staff out of such men.'[12] Such opinions, held at a time when

---

*By 1937, when the Fleet Air Arm went over to the Admiralty, the RAF was strong enough to survive the amputation.

the RAF's senior officers included men like Sefton Brancker, Robert Brooke-Popham, Frederick Bowhill, John and Geoffrey Salmond, John Higgins and John Steel (and at a more junior level Christopher Courtney, Hugh Dowding, Edgar Ludlow-Hewitt, Wilfrid Freeman, Cyril Newall, Charles Portal, Arthur Harris, John Slessor and Arthur Tedder), did not facilitate the task of the new Service in establishing itself.*

One of the principles enunciated by the Salisbury Committee, and accepted by the Cabinet, was that Britain should maintain 'a Home Defence Air Force of sufficient strength adequately to protect us against an attack by the strongest air force within striking distance of this country'.[13] In practical terms its main recommendation, announced by Bonar Law's successor Stanley Baldwin in the summer of 1923, was that the Home Defence Force should consist of fifty-two squadrons (including thirteen non-regular).[14] This Force comprised bombers as well as fighters – in fact, roughly two bombers to every fighter, since in the prevailing conditions of the time counter-attack was considered the prime element in defence. The programme was to be completed 'with as little delay as possible', later defined as within five years. Thenceforth, until 1934, a fifty-two-squadron Home Defence Force was to be the prescribed – but always unattained – goal.**

At least, however, the principle had now been confirmed of a separate air force containing a strong home defence element – though part of this was soon scheduled to double as a strategic reserve for India. With a victorious conclusion to yet one more enquiry in 1925, Trenchard had now won his basic battle. But before he retired at the end of 1929 he also had to his credit other achievements without which his Service would never have been strong enough to withstand the strain in 1940.

Many of these stemmed from his original memorandum on the creation of the permanent air force in 1919, the basic principle of which was 'first and foremost the making of a sound framework on which to build'. In this spirit he set up RAF institutions which provided admirable training for possible future commanders (the Staff College at Andover), for entrants to permanent commissions (the Cadet College at Cranwell) and for technicians (the Apprentices' Schools at Halton and

*One of the present authors heard a good specimen of this kind of pronouncement as late as 1943 in a conversation with Brigadier General Sir James Edmonds, the official military historian of World War I. Edmonds informed him that the early officers of the RFC were largely 'bad hats – fellows with debts from Ascot, and so on'.

**The Home Defence Force constituted by far the greater part, but not the entirety, of the Metropolitan Air Force, which also included some squadrons for naval and army co-operation.

elsewhere). He also gave a prominent place to special establishments for research into aircraft, wireless, armaments and aerial photography. To build up a reserve on a minimum budget he limited permanent commissions to fifty per cent and introduced the revolutionary idea of short-service commissions – four years, followed by five on the reserve – and had no difficulty in finding suitable entrants. With the same object in mind he founded the Auxiliary Air Force (AAF) on the analogy of the Territorial Army and with its assistance, though perhaps aiming more at a corps d'élite; and this outstanding creation he followed with the first of the University Air Squadrons.* In the sphere of aircraft provision, he spread the tiny permitted orders among a variety of firms, to help keep them alive against the day when much larger orders might descend upon them. On the personnel side, he spotted much youthful talent – Portal, for instance – and saw that it was groomed for future command.

Above all, perhaps, by means such as the Hendon airshows, the long-distance record flights, the pioneer carrying of air mail (including all the official mail and the *British Gazette* during the General Strike), the opening up of new air routes to be subsequently exploited by Imperial Airways, and the winning of the Schneider Trophy races, Trenchard captured public attention and affection for his Service and built up for it a fund of popular goodwill. At the same time he instilled throughout its ranks a high regard for technical proficiency, a determination to keep abreast of the times (and if possible a bit ahead), and a buoyant morale compounded of high spirits, courage and aggressive intentions towards any enemy. All this gave the youthful RAF a strength not to be measured only in numbers and was to be of profound importance in 1940.

There was a further way in which the Trenchard period contributed to the outcome of the Battle. In the demobilisation of 1919 the air defences so painfully built up in response to the German raids had been utterly swept away. The observer posts ceased to exist, the guns were mostly dispersed, all the Home Defence squadrons except three were disbanded or sent overseas. When Parliament approved a modest expansion in 1922 and the much bigger fifty-two-squadron Home Defence scheme in 1923, Trenchard and his staff had to start on home air defence almost from scratch. Beginning by securing in 1922 – for the

*The AAF squadrons, at first equipped with bombers, were converted to fighters from 1934 onwards, and in 1940 made up nearly a quarter of Fighter Command's first-line strength. The University Air Squadrons were sometimes criticised as a minor element of doubtful use. Their value quickly became apparent in September 1939 when the Oxford Squadron alone provided nearly 500 officers.[15]

first time – recognition of the Air Ministry as the authority primarily responsible for the air defence of the country – 'only the Air Force', wrote Balfour, 'can protect us from invasion by air' – they went on, in full co-operation with the War Office, to provide a coherent and well-thought-out system.

Since France was then the only potential enemy, defensive measures were basically devised to meet an attack on southern England from across the Channel. Naturally much of what had existed in 1918 was revived, such as ops rooms with visual displays of hostile and friendly forces. Details of the system included the installation of acoustical mirrors – of very limited range and useless against low-flying aircraft – on the south coast, the recreation (after new experiments by Major-General Ashmore) of observer posts and observer group centres, and the establishment of a fighter zone beginning thirty-five miles inland. After some extension, this ran roughly across England from the Thames Estuary to the Bristol Channel. Directly in front of the fighter zone was the Outer Artillery Zone, with the function of breaking up and indicating enemy formations, and behind the fighter zone was the Inner Artillery Zone, mainly for the protection of London. Three fighter squadrons were located beyond the fighter zone, and there were also isolated batteries for the defence of the ports.[16]

Operational control of this whole system rested with an airman, but full co-ordination with the Army-manned guns and searchlights was effected by locating the GOC Ground Troops in headquarters adjoining those of the air commander. Direct telephone links – the laying of which by the Post Office was a vast task in itself – fed the observer tracks both to the air command and to the ten fighter sector stations, each with one or two squadrons. By 1926 all this was controlled from Fighting Area headquarters, one of the two subordinate operational formations – the other being for the bombers – which together made up a new overall command entitled the Air Defence of Great Britain (ADGB).

Put to the test of war at that time, the system would doubtless have given only poor protection, since the fighting area had to be so far back from the coast for lack of good early warning out to sea, and because the fighters of the day needed fifteen minutes or so to reach 14,000 feet – the height around which raiders were expected. Put to the test of war in 1940 against much faster bombers, it would, as it stood, have been utterly hopeless. Nevertheless, it provided much of the ground plan for the later greatly extended and improved system which defeated the Luftwaffe.

Many things which were to prove essential for Britain's survival in 1940 could not, of course, be provided in the Trenchard era. Disregarding technical developments beyond the capacity of the time, the most important of these was a force large enough to sustain a big expansion quickly when the moment came. The fifty-two-squadron Home Defence scheme of 1923 should have been completed by 1928. But the application of the Cabinet's Ten Years Rule – that defence estimates should be framed on the assumption that Britain would not be engaged in a major war within the next ten years – though sensible enough when it was introduced in 1919, was by assumption moved forward year by year in the 1920s and then formally from 1928 as international relations became more settled. The resolution of the reparations–Ruhr crisis, the Locarno treaties of 1925, the extended preparations for the great Disarmament Conference, capped by the onset of a world depression at the end of 1929, all provided reasons for the politicians to pare down or even defer defence measures already agreed.

So it came about that in 1924 the completion date for the fifty-two-squadron Home Defence scheme was moved forward from 1928 to 1930. Then in 1925 it was moved forward from 1930 to 1935–6. Then in 1929, under the second Labour Government, it was moved forward from 1935–6 to 1938[17] – by which time it had long been superseded. So Trenchard never got his fifty-two Home Defence squadrons. When he retired in 1929 he had brought the total up to thirty-eight, but with the world recession and with the Disarmament Conference due to meet in 1932 progress then became slower still. By 1933, ten years after the first approval of the scheme, and a year after the dropping of the Ten Years Rule on account of accumulated deficiencies and developments in the Far East, the total was still ten squadrons short of the original target figure. Moreover by that time, such had been the stranglehold of economy, many of the aircraft were not up to the best contemporary standards: some American, Italian and German airliners were faster than the most modern British bombers.

How tight the financial constraints were in the years up to 1934 may be seen from two examples drawn from Trenchard's own creation of the Cadet College at Cranwell. The first is the simple fact that the College, opened in 1920, had to exist in wood and iron huts and a galvanised iron mess for thirteen years before it got proper buildings.[18] The second concerns the Sword of Honour awarded annually to the outstanding cadet. The year it was instituted, the Treasury approved an expenditure of £10 for the purpose. The Air Ministry ordered a sword for this sum, but forgot to provide for the inscription – which brought the total up to nearly £12. To cover this, the Air Ministry felt obliged to seek Treasury approval for the expenditure of a further £2.[19]

Without the developments in Britain's air defence before 1934, it would have been difficult to defeat the Luftwaffe in 1940. Without those from 1934 onwards, it would have been impossible.

The year 1934 is a landmark because, for the first time since 1923, the theme of expansion was heard alongside that of economy. The events of 1933 – the advent to power of Hitler, the Japanese notice of departure from the League of Nations, the German walk-out from the League and the Disarmament Conference – coupled with the realisation that Germany was not only producing exceptionally large numbers of civil aircraft but also building up a secret air force, spurred Britain's leaders into action. The result for the RAF was Expansion Scheme A, approved in July 1934.[20]

Scheme A set up a new target of seventy-five Home Defence squadrons within five years instead of the old unachieved objective of fifty-two squadrons. It had scarcely got going when, in March 1935, Hitler officially acknowledged the existence of the Luftwaffe and went on to inform the astonished Sir John Simon and Anthony Eden that this was already as strong as Britain's air force and would soon equal the Metropolitan and North African Air Forces of France. Within two months the RAF had a new target in its sights – Scheme C,[21] intended to bring the Home Defence Force up to 112 squadrons by March 1937. According to Baldwin, this was designed to achieve 'parity' with Germany at that date – an objective which posterity has understandably viewed as over-modest.

Scheme C, like Scheme A, was basically intended to impress Hitler. Nearly all the additions were to the front line, the provision of reserves being deferred and therefore totally inadequate for serious fighting purposes within the next five years. It soon became apparent that something more must be done – especially when Italy invaded Abyssinia and Home Defence squadrons had to be sent out to Egypt and Aden. But a general election was looming in Britain, public opinion was still deeply suspicious of rearmament, and Baldwin dared not risk letting in a Labour government opposed to all the progress thus far made. Only when the election of November 1935 was safely over did a further expansion scheme – F, approved in February 1936 – become possible.[22] Designed to produce by March 1939 a Home Defence Force of 107 squadrons (five fewer than in the previous scheme, but with fourteen aircraft instead of twelve in all the fighter squadrons), it was a well-rounded project and ran its full course. Among its features were provision for full aircraft reserves, medium instead of light bombers, and the 'shadow factory' scheme for the aircraft industry (providing factories for certain firms, mostly motor manufacturers, to make aircraft components or later complete aircraft, under the guidance of a specialist airframe or aero-engine firm).

Expansion and the hypothesis of Germany rather than France as the enemy soon created a need for reorganisation. What was delicately termed the 'reorientation' of the air defences began. The existing Fighting Area, running from the Thames Estuary thirty-five miles inland across to the Bristol Channel, had Duxford in Cambridgeshire as its most northerly station. It was France-facing and would obviously not serve against Germany. Any part of England, it now seemed, would soon be within range of German bombers flying either directly across the North Sea or overflying the Low Countries, or else operating from captured bases in Belgium. (No one remotely thought of captured bases in western France or Norway.)

The solution, produced by a joint Air Ministry–War Office committee, was a new continuous defended zone twenty-six miles wide, running from Portsmouth eastwards of London up to the Tees. The first six miles of this, the coastal strip, became the new Outer Artillery Zone and the next twenty miles the new Fighting Area. Further inland were the Inner Artillery Zone protecting London, and ground defences at various important points outside the Zones. By this extension the Midlands and most of the north-east were brought within the ADGB system. At the same time, as the purely defensive element began to face towards Germany, so did the offensive part. Most of the bombers had thus far been stationed on southern and central airfields, in Oxfordshire and thereabouts. Now they began to be based on new airfields built in East Anglia, and as they moved, so fighter squadrons could occupy the vacated stations.[23]

The full implementation of these changes, involving extension of the Observer Corps network to new regions, took some years.* The slowest progress was in ground defence. The recommended total of guns and searchlights was nothing like achieved by the time war broke out.

The growth of the Home Defence squadrons from an actual forty-two

---

*In 1929 the War Office had relinquished control over the observer system, and the observers had become a civilian corps under Air Ministry aegis.

in 1934 to a projected 107 in 1939 was accompanied by all the problems of construction, recruitment, equipment and training inherent in the task of nearly trebling an air force within five years. It also brought with it problems of command. During 1935 the Air Ministry decided that the task of commanding the enlarged Home Defence Force – all the home-based bombers and fighters – would be too much for one man. In 1936 the ADGB Command which had existed for the past eleven years was accordingly broken up. In its place appeared a division of command by function: Bomber Command, Fighter Command, Coastal Command, Training Command and a Maintenance Group, later Maintenance Command. With two additions – Balloon Command in 1938 when the barrage was extended outside London, and Reserve Command in 1939 to handle the new Volunteer Reserve centres and the civil elementary flying schools – this formed the basic structure of RAF Command organisation at home at the outbreak of war.[24]

Since there was no longer an overall operational commander at home, the Air Officer Commanding-in-Chief at Fighter Command, as at Bomber Command, became directly responsible to the Chief of the Air Staff at the Air Ministry. In practice, the AOC-in-C would run his own Command without any day-to-day control from above, but within the context of any major policy decisions emanating from Whitehall. Co-operation with other Commands would be achieved by mutual agreement or Air Staff directive. In practice, it would depend heavily on goodwill.

Fighter Command headquarters opened on 14 July 1936 at Bentley Priory, a late eighteenth-century mansion in extensive grounds at Stanmore – once a village in Middlesex but by this time virtually an outer suburb of London. The house, where the dowager Queen Adelaide had resided in the 1840s, had later declined into an hotel and a girls' boarding-school before falling into the hands of the Air Ministry in 1926. Since then it had been the headquarters of Inland Area, responsible for training in the ADGB organisation.

A few days before Fighter Command set up its headquarters, its main subordinate formation, No. 11 (Fighter) Group, whose task was the defence of south and south-east England, had opened in the old ADGB headquarters at Hillingdon House, Uxbridge. The other main subordinate formation, No. 12 (Fighter) Group, formed in accordance with the decision to extend the continuous belt of protection to the Midlands and beyond, opened the following April at Watnall in Nottinghamshire. To these two Groups, and to their counterparts farther north and west which came later, would be entrusted the detailed conduct of operations, acting under the higher strategic control of Fighter Command.

The man chosen as the head of Fighter Command, Air Marshal Sir Hugh Caswall Tremenheere Dowding CB, CMG, had no exceptional wealth of operational or command experience behind him. Not very happy as a schoolboy at Winchester, where his father had excelled, he had entered the Army Class to escape classical studies and then proceeded through the Royal Military Academy at Woolwich. After a dozen years' service as an artillery officer in the outposts of the Empire he had been admitted to the Staff College course at Camberley and had rounded off his final year by taking flying lessons at Brooklands at his own expense – unless he should qualify, in which case the War Office would meet the cost. He did qualify – in a total time, passenger, dual and solo, of one hour forty minutes. Having then attended the Central Flying School and got his 'wings', he found himself swept into the RFC at the outbreak of war in 1914. Service in France followed, with command first of squadrons and then a wing, specialising for the most part in the development and use of wireless communication for purposes of artillery observation from the air. In 1916 he was posted home on promotion to colonel and spent most of the next two years doing good work in training. At the end of the war he was aged thirty-five and a brigadier general.

Dowding received a permanent commission and was soon posted to command a Group at Kenley. There, among other duties, he organised the second and some subsequent RAF displays at Hendon – a most exacting and nerve-racking task. Later he was Chief of Staff at Headquarters Inland Area, Uxbridge, dealing with training and reserves, and then for two years Chief of Staff in Iraq. Other work included a spell as Director of Training at the Air Ministry, where he found himself working harmoniously with Trenchard and almost receiving an apology, presumably for the employment at home in 1917–18: 'Dowding, I don't often make mistakes about people, but I made one about you.'

All this led up to the experience which particularly qualified Dowding for his new post. In 1929 he commanded Fighting Area for some months. Then, in 1930, he was invited to join the Air Council, the governing hierarchy in the Air Ministry, as the Air Member for Supply and Research. In this position, and after January 1935 as Air Member for Research and Development – a new Department having been created for Supply and Organisation – Dowding had greater responsibility than any other person for fostering technical progress within the RAF.

Not all Dowding's decisions between 1930 and 1936 turned out well. Within a few weeks of his first appointment, trusting to the experts, he cleared the airship *R101* for her maiden flight to India. The disaster at Beauvais made him very wary in future of trusting experts without strong proofs of their correctness. Among the aircraft he sponsored which did not properly justify themselves were the Battle light bomber – it could be produced fairly quickly, and there was the call for quantity – and the two-seat Defiant fighter. He also sanctioned some aircraft of poor performance for the Fleet Air Arm – though in doing so he was only striving to satisfy the desire of the Naval Staff for aircraft which would meet a multitude of inherently conflicting requirements. Perhaps his worst mistake, which he was later bitterly to regret, was in connection with aircraft petrol tanks. Trying to develop tanks which would be crash-proof, he overlooked the much greater need, far easier to satisfy, to produce tanks which by means of a suitable coating would seal themselves when penetrated by bullets.

But if Dowding as the Service head of research made some errors, he also made some decisions of supreme importance which were to help win his Battle a few years later. Among these, two stand out. Perceiving the need for much faster fighters, he took a lead in plumping for metal monoplanes instead of wooden biplanes, and supported at every stage the development of the Hurricane and the Spitfire. Perceiving also the need for much earlier warning of the approach of hostile aircraft, he backed radar wholeheartedly from the moment of the first experiments (see pages 48–51).

It must have been above all with these two dawning achievements in mind that Dowding approached his task as he settled in at Bentley Priory in 1936. A realist, he knew that the revolution in air defence was only just beginning, and that he might have very little time to translate it into Hurricanes, Spitfires, radar stations and communications before the enemy was upon him. Whatever he might lack in material resources or personal glamour, however, this tall, pale-faced, serious-minded, kindly man of unmilitary bearing and distant manners, who had acquired long ago at the Army Staff College the lasting nickname 'Stuffy', would never lack the fearless determination, the devotion to duty and the integrity to see his tasks through to the best conclusion he could possibly reach. Fighter Command needed a fighter at its head, and in Stuffy Dowding it had one – a quiet fighter, but one of the greatest obstinacy and singleness of purpose. Because he had been born in Dumfriesshire, where his Wiltshire-bred father ran a preparatory school, he was sometimes referred to as 'a dour Scot'. He was no Scot, but fortunately for his country he could certainly be dour.[25]

# 3

## The Bomber Won't Always
## Get Through

When Dowding arrived at Bentley Priory in July 1936 the Luftwaffe was officially only sixteen months old. How did it ever come about that within four years this parvenu could be strong enough to crush the air forces of Poland, Holland, Belgium and France, and be ready to launch itself against Britain?

Such astonishing and deplorable progress could not have been achieved without much surreptitious spade-work before the advent of Hitler. The principal pioneer was General Hans von Seekt, Chief of the Army Command and creator of the new Reichswehr.* As the Service chief within the Defence Ministry in the early 1920s, von Seekt was able to plan a clandestine air force, endow it with higher staff and set up, by agreement between the Weimar and the Moscow Governments, a secret military flying school and aircraft testing station for German use in Soviet Russia.

This base was at Lipetsk, 220 miles south-east of Moscow. Between 1924 and 1932 some 240 German fighter pilots and air observers graduated from Lipetsk under the direction of, among others, Hugo von Sperrle, later to command *Luftflotte* 3 against Britain, and Kurt Student, later to command the airborne invasion of Crete. During the same period staff at Lipetsk tested the prototypes or early models of

*The German Armed Forces, 1920–35.

31

nine military or semi-military aircraft; ironically, the Napier Lion engines used for the Fokker XIII D fighters had at first to be sent for repair to England under the guise of coming from Holland. Secrecy also enveloped the corpses of the very few German airmen to be killed at Lipetsk during training. They were returned to Stettin by sea from Leningrad in crates marked 'spare parts'.[1]

Lipetsk was for the military elite. On a broader level, and in this case consistent with the Treaty of Versailles, the Weimar regime encouraged the youth of Germany to take up sports aviation. Scores of light aeroplane and glider clubs sprang into existence, and by 1929 the *Luftsportsverband* boasted no fewer than 50,000 members.[2] Well before that time, however, and much more significantly, von Seekt's Defence Ministry had established a vital link with another government department. In 1924 his nominee, Ernst Brandenburg, former commander of the *Englandgeschwader*, became head of the civil aviation branch of the Transport Ministry.

Though the secret air force was born within the Defence Ministry, the civil aviation branch of the Transport Ministry provided most of its upbringing. When the Allies in 1926 cancelled all restrictions on the size and number of Germany's civil aircraft, the Transport Ministry lost no time in helping to create a largely state-owned airline, Lufthansa, with monopoly rights in Germany. This made control from the centre easy. The chairmanship went to another wartime pilot, Erhard Milch, who soon endowed Lufthansa with ground facilities and pilot-training sessions well beyond its commercial requirements. Lufthansa training schools ran secret courses for officers of the armed services. Some of Lufthansa's new airliners were readily convertible to bombers.[3]

By the time Hitler became Chancellor in January 1933, the seeds had thus already been sown for the rebirth of German air power. Thereafter, growth was spectacular. With Hermann Goering, the Nazi's show airman from World War I, at the head of a newly created Air Ministry, and with Milch as his deputy, plans were drawn up for a large air force independent of the older Services – as von Seekt had always intended. On Milch's advice this was conceived as a force in depth, well balanced, to be created over eight to ten years.[4]

The new Air Ministry, existing officially at first only for civil purposes, soon sprouted all the necessary military departments. A military command structure in the regions came into being under the guise of civil air-traffic control. Secretly, the training facilities multiplied. When Hitler and Goering unveiled the whole creation in March 1935 it almost seemed – though not to the British Government, which had read the signs aright and begun rearmament the previous year – that Greek legend was being updated. Warriors – in this case trained pilots in military aircraft – were springing fully armed from the soil.

Under Hitler's frenetic impulse the pace then became faster still – too fast, in fact, for his own ultimate benefit. Milch's plans were speeded up, the rapidly growing German aircraft industry was stimulated, and the expansion of the Luftwaffe became geared not to sound long-term development but to the need to produce an intimidating weapon quickly.[5] Hitler could not wait to begin his Greater Germany programme – the absorption of Austria, the break-up of Czechoslovakia and Poland, the winning of *lebensraum* in the East. The Luftwaffe had to be ready to help enforce it.

So the numbers grew apace. At the end of 1934, before the existence of the Luftwaffe was declared, Germany possessed 584 combat aircraft with a monthly production of about 180 machines of all types, including trainers.[6] By the outbreak of war she had a fully formed and trained first-line of 3,609, plus 552 military transports, and her monthly output exceeded 700.[7] No double or treble working shifts were required for this near-miracle: only plentiful government orders and generous subsidies to the aircraft industry. Secrecy also continued to play a helpful part. No government budgets were published in Germany after 1936.[8]

How Germany was able to produce experienced airmen as well as a wealth of new aircraft may be seen from the career of the eminent fighter commander, Adolf Galland. In 1927, while still at school, Galland became well known as a glider pilot. Determined to fly with Lufthansa he took rigorous tests lasting ten days and was one of eighteen applicants chosen from several thousand. In the course of his Lufthansa training in 1932 he was required to master aerobatics and handle very high performance aircraft – in his own words 'real fighter pilot training, including formation flying . . . only the guns were missing'. The following year, when the Nazis took over and the collaboration with Russia ceased, he was sent off to Italy – in Italian uniform – to train with the Regia Aeronautica. As a fully qualified Lufthansa pilot in 1934 he was then asked if he wished to be 'on the active list'. Having agreed, he received six months' infantry training and a commission in the Army before being promptly discharged and sent back to Lufthansa to join what was in effect a specialised fighter school. There, a few weeks before the existence of the Luftwaffe was announced, he and his fellow pupils were treated to an oration by Goering and a preview of the new Service uniform.

Something more was needed to turn skilled pilots like Galland into veterans of combat. The Germans found it in the Spanish Civil War. Having tested their military transports by flying some 10,000 Nationalist troops from Morocco to Spain at the outbreak of hostilities in 1936, they went on to help Franco with their *Legion Kondor* – a mixed group of aircraft and ground forces. Relays of German pilots received their blooding in this, with Galland serving a longer term than most. Having travelled to Spain in a group purporting to be a 'Strength Through Joy' holiday excursion, he put in fifteen months with the *Legion*, gaining invaluable operational experience. To his grief, this was on the slower He 51 fighters relegated to ground attack and not on the new, fast Me 109s reserved for air combat.

Like the other squadron commanders of the *Legion Kondor* Galland faithfully recorded all details of developing techniques for transmission to the German Air Ministry. Eventually replaced by Werner Moelders, later to become the Luftwaffe's leading fighter pilot, he was recalled to Germany in 1938 to be on call during the Sudetenland crisis. A year later he was on the eastern frontier, ready for action against Poland.[9]

In the five years preceding the outbreak of war both the Luftwaffe and the RAF acquired the aircraft with which they fought the Battle of Britain.

'The heart of an aeroplane', wrote the first official historian of the RAF, 'is the engine, but the pilot is its soul.' Here we are concerned with the engine – on the British fighter side, the product in the main of a single firm. Rolls-Royce were never remarkable for their innovation: as with their motor-cars the chief quality of the product stemmed from development and refinement from a sound base. In 1926, a year after Richard Fairey, breaking with the long tradition of air-cooled, radial engines, had imported American Curtiss D-12, liquid-cooled, in-line engines to power his Fairey Fox light bomber, Rolls-Royce unveiled their own liquid-cooled, in-line F.XI, remarkable for its low weight and high output. This was the excellent Kestrel engine, which was developed in size and power until it rated 950 hp. Eventually, by 1934, under the paternal guidance of Sir Henry Royce and through the engineering genius of A. J. Rowledge, A. G. Elliot and Ernest Walter Hives,* this became the PV 1200 Merlin, the most famous aero-engine

*Later the first Baron Hives, who worked for Rolls-Royce from 1908 to 1957.

of all time. It was to power both the Hurricane and the Spitfire, and indeed the majority of Britain's front-line aircraft throughout the war. Built under licence by Packard in America, the Merlin was also to power the American Air Force's most successful fighter of World War II, the P51 Mustang.

Improvements to the Merlin were introduced while still only a handful of Spitfires had reached the squadrons of Fighter Command. Stanley Hooker of Rolls-Royce worked on improving the supercharger in 1938–40, increasing the boost pressure from six to twelve psi for short periods and boosting output from 990 to 1,310 hp.

But this dramatic increase could only be obtained by the use of 100 octane in place of 87 octane fuel in order to avoid detonation.* Even today, very few people have heard of the development by Esso and Shell of this high octane aviation fuel which had such a dramatic effect on performance. Shell used a base petrol from Borneo crude, which was especially high in aromatics and blended with imported American 'mixed octane', but was unable to produce this in sufficient quantity for RAF needs. Reliance was therefore placed on Esso with its refineries in Baton Rouge and the Dutch colonies, although early in the war, and for a brief time only, the US Neutrality Act prohibited the export of aviation petrol entirely.

By March 1940 Fighter Command was beginning to convert its Merlin-engined Hurricanes and Spitfires to accept 100 octane fuel.** Hurricanes in France during the brief French campaign were still running on blue 87 octane, and it came as a considerable shock to Me 109 pilots in particular who witnessed the startling improvement in the performance of both the Hurricane and Spitfire from July 1940 onwards. Adolf Galland confessed that he was puzzled by the improvement of the enemy's performance until late in August when fuel from a crashed RAF fighter was analysed. The Luftwaffe operated throughout on 87 octane fuel.

The airframes, so far at least as the British single-engined fighters were concerned, were largely the work of two brilliant designers, Sydney Camm and Reginald Mitchell. In 1928 Sydney Camm was thirty-five and had been with the Hawker Engineering Company for five years, three of them as chief designer. The first evidence of his genius was revealed in 1929 in the Hawker Hart biplane light bomber,

*See Appendix XII.
**By 1943 there were some fifty alkylation plants operating in the USA, Canada and the Caribbean meeting the colossal need for 100 octane aviation fuel and the higher 115/145 grade.

powered by Rolls-Royce's Kestrel, giving it a maximum speed of 184 mph, far superior to that of any contemporary fighter. But this anomaly was quickly corrected by Camm's Hawker Fury, a fighter version of his Hart, which in 1931 gave the RAF a 200+ mph fighter for the first time.

The Hawker Fury marked the fine flowering of the biplane, in-line engined, single-seat fighter, graceful, manoeuvrable, a delight to fly. Foreign air forces queued up to order it. But, like any far-sighted designer, Camm was already at work on the next generation, and by 1933 the first hint of rearmament was in the air. The early months of 1934, with plans actually developing for RAF expansion, spelt the end of the traditional biplane fighter, represented in its final form by the Fury and the new radial-engined Gloster Gladiator – yet to come.

From then on, events moved rapidly towards the birth of Britain's first series of high-speed, multi-gun, monoplane, single-seat fighters – fighters for the war with Germany which no one wanted but which seemed increasingly probable.

For many years Hawker's had used a system of metal tubular construction with fabric covering. It had the merits of simplicity and was capable of taking a lot of punishment. This system was continued in the Hurricane. Very advanced for 1934, the undercarriage of the new fighter was to be retractable; and, in view of the high speed envisaged, the pilot was given a sliding canopy above his cockpit for protection.

These features, and the monoplane configuration, were not the only novel elements in Camm's new fighter. Equally revolutionary was the armament. This had come a long way since the days of 1914 when the young Sholto Douglas,* having been fired on from a reconnaissance aircraft with a revolver, 'afterwards, just for safety's sake, always carried a carbine in the air'. But it had not come much beyond the standard fighter equipment of 1918 – one or two fixed forward-firing guns, sometimes augmented by a third gun operated by an observer/gunner. In the RAF the most common of these guns were the Vickers and the Lewis. The first was particularly liable to stoppages; but these could often be cleared manually – usually with a good biff with a mallet specially carried for the purpose.

In 1934 this Neanderthal period of fighter armament gave way to a more sophisticated age. At an Air Ministry conference in July, it was shown that, in the second or two a fighter pilot could expect to keep a

*Later Marshal of the RAF Lord Douglas of Kirtleside (1893–1969).

36

bomber in his sights, he would require six or preferably eight guns, firing at 1,000 rounds a minute, to destroy it. The propounder of this disturbing thesis was Squadron Leader Ralph Sorley of the Supply and Research Department – and he had the full backing of his chief, Dowding.

Early plans for the new Hawker monoplane fighter had called for two Vickers guns in the fuselage and two more guns in the wings. After the new Air Ministry requirement Camm took his design a stage further to incorporate the unprecedented armament of eight machine-guns in the wings, all of them beyond the mallet reach of the pilot and therefore needing to be reliable. This became possible with the completion of negotiations between BSA in Britain and Colt in America for the manufacture of the magnificent Browning machine-gun, bored out from .3 to .303 inches. Besides being reliable, the Browning was extremely economical in weight and size, the complete battery of eight guns, accessories and over 2,500 rounds of ammunition weighing little more than 400 pounds.

Fitted with a fixed-pitch, two-blade, wooden propeller, the Hawker Hurricane made its first flight on 6 November 1935, piloted with impressive insouciance by chief test pilot P. W. S. 'George' Bulman, who refused to remove his trilby hat for the event. Like the Dreadnought battleship of thirty years earlier, the Hurricane was by a wide margin the most heavily gunned and fastest of its kind in the world. Thanks to sound and steady development from the earlier Hawker biplanes, the Hurricane revealed no major flaws.

Formally tested three months later, this prototype showed a speed of 315 mph at 16,200 feet, a service ceiling of 34,000 feet and a startling rate of climb of 8.4 minutes to 20,000 feet. Without waiting for Air Ministry orders, T. O. M. Sopwith of Hawkers arranged tooling-up for 1,000 machines. Within a few weeks the first official order for 600 was in the company's hands.

It was not until 3 May 1938 that the existence of the Hurricane was made public. The following day, the air correspondent of *The Times* wrote, 'The fastest 'plane in service in any air force in the world was yesterday removed from the Air Ministry's semi-secret list. . . . The Hurricane is outstanding in its class in respect of duration as well as speed.' But as the correspondent pointed out, the circumstances of the announcement were anomalous, as the Hurricane had already 'made itself famous by covering the 327 miles from Edinburgh to Northolt at a speed of 408 mph'. This sensational achievement was brought about with the aid of a strong tailwind, and the pilot, John Gillan, was promptly nicknamed 'Downwind'.

Five hundred Hurricanes had been delivered to the RAF by the outbreak of war on 3 September 1939. A number of improvements had already been introduced by then, including the installation of a more powerful Merlin engine and the introduction of stressed metal wings. The fuselage retained its fabric covering for all its long life and total output of 14,000.

To a pilot coming to the Hurricane for the first time after flying Kestrel or Bristol-engined biplanes, it was a revelation of speed without any loss of manoeuvrability. The absence of a second wing, far from being a deprivation, was a liberation offering much superior all-round visibility. Roland Beamont, who flew early Hurricanes in France in 1939–40 and only recently retired as a famous test pilot, wrote: 'To a new pilot the Hurricane was an immensely powerful but not excessively demanding aeroplane. Its wide track undercarriage, stable and responsive flying characteristics and reliable engine and hydraulic system resulted in a general atmosphere of confidence in the squadron, so that the newcomer had no reason to become apprehensive.'[10]★

The genesis of the Spitfire was interestingly different from that of its stouter cousin, the Hurricane. Unlike Hawker's, the Supermarine Company of Southampton had no tradition of designing and building fighter aircraft. The company was, appropriately, associated more closely with the sea than the land, and had a sound reputation for building large flying-boats, which they launched directly into the Solent from their own slipway. In 1916 a twenty-one-year-old engineer, Reginald Joseph Mitchell, had joined this company as a designer. 'R.J.', as he came to be known, showed immediate promise of brilliance. One of Supermarine's test pilots described him as 'sandy-haired, of slightly florid complexion, and a man of few words', though 'not taciturn'.[11]

In the 1920s the company became deeply involved in the construction of high-speed seaplanes for the Schneider Trophy, which it won

★This writer vividly recalls climbing into the cockpit of a Mark 1 Hurricane for the first time on a dirty afternoon in Scotland and being awed by the overall size of the machine by contrast with the claustrophobic effect of the enclosed cockpit. The power, after training machines, was heady, one's back pressing hard against the seat as the 1,000 hp sent the aircraft racing down the runway, and then into a climb so steep and swift that it was hard to credit the truth of the instrument figures. Though I later flew faster machines, nothing could equal the joy of handling the utterly predictable and vice-free responsiveness of the Hurricane. But its most enduring memory is the song of the Merlin, deep-noted without harshness, accompanied by an unobtrusive and steady pulsation. R.H.

outright for Britain in 1931 with the elegant, Rolls-Royce engined S.6B. Shortly afterwards, this also took the world air-speed record at 406.99 mph.* By this time the company had been taken over by the industrial giant, Vickers, who were anxious to extend the repertoire of their new acquisition into fighters for the RAF.

With the benefit of his experience with the S.6s, Mitchell sat down at his drawing-board, using a fuselage of similar configuration to the racing seaplanes but creating an entirely new elliptical wing of great strength, narrow depth and memorable grace, which made the fighter immediately recognisable to the millions who saw it in the air during its twenty-year-long service life.

Structurally, the Spitfire was more advanced than the Hurricane, its fuselage being not only slimmer but of light alloy monocoque construction. The wings, too, were of single spar type, again with a stressed metal skin covering, except for the fabric-covered control surfaces. It was, without question, the most beautiful single-seat fighter of its day, and (as the old engineering slogan goes) 'what looks right is right'. But this was not always the view of first-time pilots, who found the close-set wheels of the outward retracting undercarriage tricky, especially on rough grass surfaces. Moreover, early models required manual pumping to retract the undercarriage after take-off, a distracting operation when full attention should be given to flying the machine, which resulted in a certain amount of longitudinal oscillation. More serious were the aileron problems in high-speed dives. To manoeuvre the plane laterally at full speed was a two-handed business, requiring some strength.

Like any fighter plane, the Spitfire was only as good as its engine and armament, and both Spitfire and Hurricane owed their success – after the triumph of their designers – to the light, powerful, reliable Merlin engine and the light, small, reliable Browning machine-gun.

The prototype Spitfire's first flight took place, in the hands of J. 'Mutt' Summers, the chief test pilot, on 6 March 1936, four months after the Hurricane took to the air. It carried no armament, was unpainted and, for safety, was fitted with a full-fine, fixed-pitch airscrew. The Spitfire took off after a very short run, Summers checked the flaps and slow stalling characteristics, and landed back within a few minutes. His first words of comment have gone down in aviation

*Amid growing economic difficulties, Ramsay MacDonald's Government had declined to make funds available for a British entry. The eccentric and ardently patriotic philanthropist Dame Lucy Houston came to the rescue with a gift of £100,000.

history: 'I don't want anything touched', which has mistakenly been interpreted as a reflection of the machine's perfection. It was nothing of the kind. There were numerous snags to be ironed out, but the test pilot wanted nothing altered until his next flight.

A week or two later, Jeffrey Quill flew this prototype, fitted now with a fixed coarse-pitch airscrew, for the first time. Settling himself into the cockpit, he found it narrow without actually being cramped, and with the seat in the up position, very little headroom. 'I primed the Merlin engine carefully and it started first time. I began taxiing out to the north-east end of the airfield. . . . Never before had I flown a fighter with such a very long nose . . . so I taxied slowly on a zig-zag course in order to ensure a clear path ahead.'

Quill experienced a little difficulty with the torque effect of the big prop, which tended to roll the Spitfire on its narrow undercarriage: 'However, once fully airborne and "tidied up", the aircraft began to slip along as if on skates with the speed mounting up steadily and an immediate impression of effortless performance was accentuated by the low revs of the propeller at that low altitude. The aeroplane just seemed to chunter along at an outstandingly higher cruising speed than I had ever experienced before.'[12]

The test pilot confined himself to some steep turns and a few rolls on that first flight. On the approach to land he experienced for the first time the trouble which every Spitfire pilot had to contend with – 'nonexistent view': 'As I chopped the throttle on passing over the boundary hedge the deceleration was hardly discernible and the aeroplane showed no desire to touch down – it evidently enjoyed flying – but finally it settled gently on three points and it wasn't until after the touch-down that the mild aerodynamic buffeting associated with the stalling of the wing became apparent. "Here", I thought to myself, "is a real lady."'

Two years later, Quill was to take in hand the first squadron pilots to convert from their biplanes to the first production Spitfires at Duxford. Among these was Pilot Officer Robert Stanford Tuck, who fell in love with the fighter from his first flight and who found it 'an understanding and intelligent creature that responded instantly to the most delicate suggestive pressures of its master's hands and feet'. His biographer wrote: 'He had never dreamed that flying could be like this. He knew that with a little time he could make this 'plane almost a part of him – like an extension of his own body, brain and nervous system.'[13]

Flying a Spitfire, which many still enjoy today, has been described in many ways, but there is no account on record that is not favourable, even those of German pilots who flew captured examples during the war. But a great deal of work had been done between Quill's first flight and his first instruction of squadron pilots like Tuck. The first official speed trials had been disappointing, showing a top speed of only 335 mph, hardly a respectable superiority over the Hurricane, which had a head start in development anyway. One of the earliest modifications, to the propeller, resulted in a significant increase of speed and made the Spitfire the 350 mph fighter Mitchell had hoped for.

Trials, and modifications, moved fast, in unison with the worsening international situation. Within a few weeks of Hitler's marching his troops into the demilitarised Rhineland, the first production order for 310 Spitfires was given by the Air Ministry, which with the 600 Hurricanes promised to multiply many times over the front-line strength of the nation's fighter force. By the outbreak of war three years later, over 2,000 Spitfires were on order. Supermarine had long since been forced to subcontract on a large scale, and the first of numerous shadow factories was working on the fighter.

The Hurricane and the Spitfire each had their proponents, roughly divided between the squadron allocations, the Hurricane in the Battle of Britain being more numerous in the ratio of about five to three Spitfires, even though it is still popularly believed that the Spitfire 'won the battle'. Certainly the Spitfire attracted the most immediate admiration, as befitted its glorious appearance, by contrast with the hump-backed Hurricane. The Spitfire by 1939 was also significantly faster and with a faster rate of climb. In handling there was little to choose between the two. The Hurricane was a superior gun platform and its twin batteries of four Brownings closely grouped in the wings was preferred to the more widely scattered guns in the Spitfire's wings. Moreover, the Hurricane offered a better forward view in the air and *felt* capable of taking greater punishment than the Spitfire, and was certainly easier to repair.

In the run up to war, both fighters took a heavy toll among pilots brought up on biplanes with a much lower performance. The loss of these pilots was to be felt severely when the fighting was at its hottest, more severely (from a strictly military point of view) than the losses sustained during training on them during the war.

Mitchell, alas, died of cancer before the first production Spitfires were delivered, but he was comforted in the knowledge that he and his staff had produced a winner. Camm went on to design the Typhoon and Tempest, and, at the end of an amazingly productive life, the first VTO

Harrier jump-jet, which in its small way won control of the air over the Falkland Islands in 1982, just as his great masterpiece helped to tame the Luftwaffe in 1940.

In addition to the Hurricanes and Spitfires two other kinds of aircraft were in Fighter Command's front line by 1940, though in much smaller numbers. The first of these, the two-seat Defiant, was something of a hybrid. A two-seat fighter had proved successful in World War I in the form of the superb Bristol Fighter, and the idea of a gunner able to give his whole attention to his task instead of flying and aiming a high-speed aircraft at the same time certainly had its appeal. Moreover, by the mid-1930s such a gunner could swiftly traverse through 360 degrees, since in the new four-gun, enclosed, hydraulically operated turret he could bear on the target effortlessly while protected from the elements.

When, therefore, the Air Ministry issued a specification in 1935 calling for a two-seat fighter with main armament in a revolving turret and a speed around the 300+ mph of the future single-seat fighter, several designers applied themselves to this formula. The only company that brought it to fruition and the production stage was Boulton and Paul, who had a special interest because they had themselves perfected a powered four-gun turret.

The Defiant of 1939, powered by the same Merlin fitted to the Hurricane and Spitfire, looked every inch as modern as its contemporaries with lines more reminiscent of the Hurricane than the Spitfire, but spoilt by the massive four-gun turret set into the fuselage behind the pilot's cockpit. In spite of this burden, the Defiant handled pleasantly and without any vices. Its virtues were loudly extolled at the time, and the press wrote of 'the fighter with the sting in its tail'. But, as one critic later wrote: 'Its biggest shortcoming and the most serious error in its concept lay in the division of responsibility between pilot and gunner. The Defiant possessed no fixed forward-firing armament, and while the pilot had to think in abstract terms of his gunner's likely line of sight, it was all too easy for an enemy fighter to creep in under cover of the blind spot beneath the tail and deliver the coup de grâce.'[14] This, however, was to become plain only after the fighting had begun.

The other aircraft in Fighter Command's front line in 1940 were the six squadrons of twin-engined Blenheims converted from the light bomber role. These Bristol-designed machines had been as much a sensation in their class as the Hurricane, and for the same reasons: their high speed and revolutionary configuration, with retractable undercarriage. In fighter form, intended mainly for night work, Blenheims were capable of close on 300 mph and had an armament of up to seven .303 machine-guns, four of them in a fuselage belly-pack fitted just to the rear of the wing leading edge. But on any unfortunate occasion when they might be obliged to contend with enemy day fighters, they were likely to stand little chance, and as night fighters they would have a hard task to catch the German bombers even when they were fortunate enough to locate them.

Meanwhile, what of developments on the other side? Some six weeks before 'George' Bulman took off in the prototype Hurricane from Brooklands, Flugkapitaen 'Bubi' Knoetsch conducted the first flight of what was to become the new German Air Force's most numerous and famous fighter, the Messerschmitt Bf 109.* By 1935 the rearmament of Germany was in full swing and the most important event in the expansion of the Luftwaffe's fighter force took place in October: the trial of four competing machines for the order, and honour, of providing Germany with a mass-production front-line fighter.

The four competitors were from Arado, Focke-Wulf, Heinkel and BFW (later Messerschmitt). The first two were quickly discarded, being too crank or too slow, narrowing the choice down to the two low-wing, all-metal Messerschmitt Bf 109s and the Heinkel He 112. The Heinkel was one of the lost causes of military aviation. By all accounts it handled beautifully, and the later production V9 series, which attracted a number of export orders, was favourably compared with the Messerschmitt by those who had flown both types. But a combination of superior salesmanship and swifter development won the day for the Augsburg company. Just possibly, this was a blessing for the RAF.

The design team at Augsburg, under the direction of Professor Willy Messerschmitt, had set out to create the smallest possible, single-seat, monoplane fighter that could accommodate the most powerful engines under development in Germany, notably at Daimler-Benz, although ironically the trials prototype, like the Heinkel, was powered by a Rolls-Royce Kestrel imported for the purpose. The 109, again like the Heinkel, was a low-wing, all-metal monoplane with a flush-riveted duralumin skin, the fuselage being an oval-section monocoque structure. But the pilot was less thoughtfully cared-for than in Heinkel's machine, his cockpit being cramped and visibility much inferior.

*Bf 109 stood for the name of the works – Bayerische Flugzuegwerke – and was at first the official abbreviation. After 1938 this became Me 109.

The 109 was sharply purposeful in appearance and lacked the grace both of its competitor at the trials and its chief British antagonist in future combat. By 1939 the developed 'E' series of the 109 was being delivered to the Luftwaffe's squadrons contemporaneously with Supermarine's Spitfire to the RAF. This production 109E was powered by the DB601 engine, a power unit only marginally inferior to the Rolls-Royce Merlin and in some respects – the fuel injection system, for example – manifestly superior. It produced 990 hp at 2,400 rpm by contrast with the Merlin's similar output at 2,600 rpm. The straight-and-level performance, with 311 mph obtainable at sea level to 354 mph at 16,500 feet, was remarkably similar to the Spitfire's.

Numerous armament permutations were worked out for this new Luftwaffe fighter, from four heavy calibre (roughly .5 inch) machine-guns, two mounted in the fuselage and two in the wings (109E1), to the more popular twin heavy machine-guns augmented by the much more lethal and longer-ranging 20 mm cannon, one in each wing (109E2). The most recently delivered 109s in the Battle of Britain were armed with a single cannon firing through the airscrew hub, supported by four heavy machine-guns (109E3). But RAF pilots were most likely to have to face a 109 armament of two-wing cannon and two 7.9 mm (.3 inch) machine-guns sited on the engine crankcase and firing through the upper nose decking. All these combinations, except the first, were potentially more lethal than the eight .303s of the British fighters, the cannon not only permitting the pilot to open fire at a greater range but having no difficulty in piercing the British armour, whereas the Browning .303 was incapable of penetrating the German bomber armour which later became increasingly common.

The 109 was a superb fighting machine which attracted strenuous pilot loyalty, even after the advent of the Focke-Wulf 190 when the Battle of Britain was over. But the pilots had to overcome more inherent faults than those faced by RAF pilots. At high speeds the controls, and especially (and critically) the ailerons, were even heavier than the Spitfire's, and many pilots got into trouble struggling for purchase with the near-immovable ailerons within the confines of a tight cockpit. They also suffered from the absence of a rudder trimmer, which added to the difficulty of banking to port at high speeds. But the aircraft's most significant weakness, as the Battle of Britain was to show, was its short endurance. A single fuselage fuel tank following the contours of the pilot's seat (but best forgotten by him!) accommodated eighty-eight imperial gallons, sufficient for only marginally over one hour's flying at maximum continuous power.

A few months after Willy Messerschmitt had settled at his drawing-board to conceive his successful single-seat fighter, he learned that the Luftwaffe was also planning a long-range escort plane – 'the strategic fighter' – to protect its bombers on deep penetrations into enemy territory. For this purpose some air forces were venturing into the unexplored field of the twin-engined fighter. The trouble here, however, was that a heavy twin-engined *fighter* was a contradiction in terms and function. It was not possible to design such a machine to match in manoeuvrability a nimble little Spitfire or Bf 109.

The Messerschmitt Bf 110 twin-engined fighter, with a crew of two, achieved no such manoeuvrability, but it was as good a compromise as could be expected, and in its configuration, speed and armament made impressive material for Dr Joseph Goebbels's spine-chilling propaganda machine. It was a slim, low-wing, all-metal, cantilever monoplane with twin fins and rudders, the pilot and gunner-navigator sharing a long plexiglass enclosed cockpit, which gave them both excellent visibility. The first prototype flew in May 1936 and, for what it was, proved highly satisfactory, being faster straight-and-level than both the early 109 and the Hurricane. In 110C production form, with the same DB601 engine as the 109, the '*zerstoerer*' or destroyer (as Goering liked to call it) was capable of 350 mph at 23,000 feet and had a range of 565 miles – formidable figures indeed, especially when complemented by an armament of two cannon and four machine-guns in the nose and another machine-gun firing to the rear. But in the Battle of Britain the 110s were to prove no match either for the Hurricanes (when they could catch them) or the Spitfires.

Mercifully for Britain, and later her allies, the Luftwaffe failed to produce a heavy bomber force in any way comparable to the American Eighth Air Force in Europe or RAF Bomber Command. The German bombers were all single- or twin-engined machines with a strictly limited bomb capacity.

The type that became most familiar to Britons during the Battle and the subsequent night bombing, both for its readily identifiable silhouette and the irregular beat of its unsynchronised engines, was the Heinkel He 111. Like its stablemate from Dornier, this Heinkel was designed ostensibly as a high-speed transport although its more lethal role was intended from the start. It dated from the early days of German rearmament (1934) when Hitler still wished to proceed with some degree of caution. But, even under the colours of Lufthansa, the potential of this 240+ mph machine was at once evident.

There was no more pretence after the Luftwaffe flew some thirty 111s in bomber form to Spain to gain experience in the Spanish Civil War. The Heinkel proved highly effective and possessed the considerable advantage of outpacing enemy fighters (except the latest from Russia). Like the Bf 109, it gained useful experience in combat before the more serious battles of 1939 and 1940.

The 111 was a low-wing, all-metal, twin-engined machine with a crew of four, a bomb-load of 4,400 pounds, a speed just short of 250 mph at 16,000 feet and a defensive armament of three 7.9 mm machine-guns. This was to prove inadequate against eight-gun British fighters. The types most used in the Battle of Britain were the 111P and H, the second with slightly more powerful engines. Armour-plate was increasingly added. This was a comfort to the crew but also made the bomber more vulnerable by reducing its speed.

The Dornier Do 17 – the 'flying pencil' – had more authentic civil origins, having been originally designed in 1933 to meet a Lufthansa requirement for a fast mailplane with accommodation for half-a-dozen passengers. Three prototypes of this shoulder-wing, all-metal, twin-engined monoplane were built, with single fin and 660 hp BMW engines. The new venture gave all the speed expected – around 250 mph – but failed its tests as passengers would have had great difficulty in getting in or out, or, if there were six of them, in all sitting down. The prototypes were then put into store until someone had the idea of converting them into bombers. With the cockpit area glazed and enlarged, the fuselage shortened, the single fin and rudder converted to twin, and a dorsal gun blister fitted, the Dornier became a fast light bomber. Despite a bomb-load of only 2,200 pounds it was to give useful service, but to prove as vulnerable as its stablemate to the Hurricane and Spitfire.

The third twin-engined Luftwaffe bomber, and the best, was the Junkers Ju 88, which had no mixed ancestry and, like the Messerschmitt fighter, was the winner of a competition. Just as a German took the major part in the design of the best American fighter,* so the American Alfred Gassner was the co-designer of Germany's best bomber.

*Edgar Schmued, late of Fokker and Messerschmitt: the North American P51 Mustang.

Early London bomb damage from Zeppelin raid in 1915.

Zeppelin L31. This Navy 'Super Zeppelin' met its end, witnessed by one of the authors of this book, over Potters Bar on the night of 1/2 October 1916.

Gotha GIV of 1917. Maximum speed 87 mph. Normal bomb-load six 50 kilo bombs.

Staaken 'Giant', just airborne: the photograph much mutilated by censor.

Hendon airshow, 1936, with the first prototype Hurricane in the foreground. It was first flown by Hawker's chief test pilot, 'George' Bulman, on 6 November 1935.

The German Aviation Monument in Berlin, 1935, with, above, evidence of the Luftwaffe's rebirth.

Sir Hugh (later Lord) Trenchard – defender and builder of the post-1918 RAF.

Sholto Douglas, Deputy Chief of Air Staff during the Battle and afterwards successor to Dowding at Fighter Command.

Marshals all: the Luftwaffe hierarchy on 19 July 1940 after Hitler's promotion ceremony. *Left to right:* Milch, Sperrle, Hitler, Goering and Kesselring.

*Top:* R. J. Mitchell, creator of the Spitfire, and Willy Messerschmitt, responsible for the Me 109 and Me 110 fighters.

*Middle:* The 'boffins': Sir Robert Watson-Watt and Sir Henry Tizard.

*Bottom:* Lord Hives of Rolls-Royce.

CH radar tower and the smaller Remote Reserve aerials, which proved their worth.

A Merlin engine.

*Frontline Luftwaffe aircraft in July 1940:*

Messerschmitt 109E. Some 35,000 109s in all were built.

Junkers 87 Stuka dive-bombers, deadly when there were no hostile fighters around.

Dornier 17s rehearsing for their occasional low-level role.

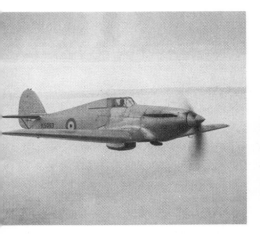

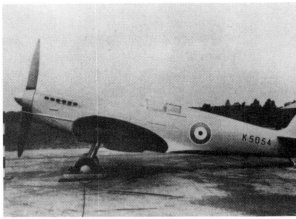

*British fighters in July 1940*:

*Above left:* First prototype Hurricane in flight.

*Above:* First prototype Spitfire, with Merlin 'C' engine and two-blade fixed-pitch airscrew.

*Left:* Gloster Gladiators in tight vic: nimble and beautiful but almost obsolete before they went into service.

*Below:* Bristol Blenheim IVs in stepped-up echelon: a light bomber converted to day and night fighter, but inadequate in both roles.

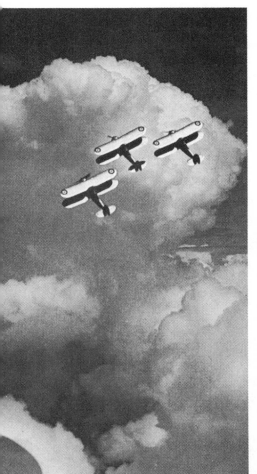

Like the He 111, the Ju 88 was a cantilever low-wing, twin-engined monoplane, built with flush-riveted stressed skin and a single fin. It was powered by twin Daimler-Benz 600 engines. This bomber at once proved its exceptional qualities, in handling, capacity, speed and potential versatility. A specially 'souped up' prototype, now fitted with two Jumo 1,200 hp engines, carried a 4,400 pound load over 600 miles at an average speed within a closed circuit of over 320 mph.

In production form, with the characteristic Luftwaffe glazed nose and armed with three machine-guns, the Junkers could still achieve 286 mph at 16,000 feet with a 4,000 pound bomb-load. As many who suffered during the Battle of Britain bore witness, the 88 was equally formidable as a dive-bomber, diving at sixty degrees and releasing its load at just above 3,000 feet. Because of its high speed, the 88 was to prove all too often capable of getting away from the Hurricane.

The other Junkers aircraft to participate in the Battle, the Ju 87 Stuka (*Sturzkampfflugzueg*, dive-bomber), was unique in being single-engined and with a fixed undercarriage. It was intended exclusively for dive-bombing. It was also immediately distinguishable in the air by its single inverted gull wing, which had prominent dive-brakes fitted to the trailing edge to control the plane's speed in a near-vertical dive. It was notorious for its screaming siren, the sole purpose of which was to demoralise even further anyone in the line of flight of its bombs.

The 87 carried a crew of two, and was protected by one rear-firing and two wing-mounted machine-guns. It normally carried during the Battle a single 1,100 pound bomb under the fuselage and a selection of lighter bombs beneath the wings.

In the role for which it was intended – pinpoint bombing in support of ground troops – the 87 was to prove very effective in Spain, Poland and France. It was also very accurate against ships. But its low speed – little over 200 mph – and poor manoeuvrability made it an easy target for modern fighters, and only heavy, close escort was likely to give it much chance of survival against well-co-ordinated attack.

In November 1932 Stanley Baldwin, who had a habit of blurting out uncomfortable truths and half-truths, delivered himself of one of his most memorable pronouncements. Impressed by the potential horrors of air warfare to the point of wishing to abolish aeroplanes altogether, he pronounced, in the course of a Commons debate on disarmament, his famous warning to the British public:

I think it is well also for the man in the street to realise that there is no power on earth that can protect him from being bombed. Whatever people may tell him, *the bomber will always get through.* The only defence is offence, which means that you have to kill more women and children more quickly than the enemy if you want to save yourselves.[15]

The reality of the situation in 1932 could not, in fact, be expressed quite so crudely. Even with completely inadequate warning of attack, even with resort to an utterly wasteful and inefficient system of flying standing patrols, the defences would still have shot down *some* of the bombers. And though attack was indeed considered the main element in defence, it was not, in 1932, conceived in terms of killing more of the enemy's women and children than the enemy could kill of ours.

Nevertheless, allowing for exaggeration, Baldwin was not too far from the mark. The fighters of 1932 had little edge over the bombers; the anti-aircraft guns, limited in range and number, could not do much more than keep the bombers high; and, above all, the warning of enemy attack, derived from observer posts and a few unreliable sound locators on the coast, would be far too short to permit effective defence of London and other vital areas.

How the development of the Hurricane and the Spitfire from 1934 onwards helped to redress the balance of advantage earlier enjoyed by the bomber has already been indicated – to redress it, that is, as long as the bomber came by day and not by night (when it could anyway do much less military damage). But no transformation in the performance of the British fighters could have made effective defence possible without a corresponding transformation in the means of receiving warning of attack.

With every increase in the speed of aircraft – and of the approaching bomber – the problem of securing good early warning of attack became more and more acute. In the early 1930s it seemed unlikely that anything could provide the RAF in Britain with warning before, as in 1918, the enemy came within sight and sound – a crippling handicap to the defence of the coastal regions and the capital. But, just as the press of crisis – the rise of Nazi Germany – led to the flight of the 300+ mph eight-gun Hurricane in 1935, so in that same year of renaissance began an equally revolutionary improvement in the early-warning system.

During the early 1920s sound locators of intermittent performance and a range of eight miles or so had been installed on Britain's south coast, and later there were experiments with outsize locators, curved concrete rectangles dubbed 'acoustical mirrors'. Construction in series would have been a major task – the 'prototype' at Hythe was 200 feet long. All sound locators, however, gave only the most limited help. Quite apart from their short range, in some conditions they did not work at all, and at all times they suffered from the interference of general noise – anything from seagulls and breaking waves to the human voice and passing cars.

More fruitfully, it had been noted from time to time that passing aircraft sometimes interfered with radio signals. A somewhat wild hope was also being expressed that radio waves might detonate the bombs of enemy aircraft before they reached their target, or that some form of electro-magnetic 'death-ray' might kill the aircrew. To examine such theories and the general application of science to air defence, the Air Ministry towards the end of 1934 set up a small body officially entitled the Committee for the Scientific Survey of Air Defence. The Air Ministry members were two scientists from within Dowding's Research and Development Department – the Director of Scientific Research, H. E. Wimperis, and his assistant, A. P. Rowe, who had initiated the idea of bringing in outside help and who acted as secretary. The outside members, entirely unpaid, were three scientists of great distinction: Henry Tizard, Rector of the Imperial College of Science and Technology and Chairman of the old-established Aeronautical Research Committee, Professor A. V. Hill of University College, London, and Professor P. M. S. Blackett, who had recently discovered the positive electron.

In the mind of the public, the formation of a committee immediately suggests deputation, procrastination and bureaucratic delay. All these characteristics might have been manifested in this small group which had its first meeting on 28 January 1935. But under the chairmanship of Tizard, a pilot of World War I, the very reverse was the case. Well aware of the vital importance of their task, and perhaps sensing that they were on the brink of epochal discovery, these men were like Sir Walter Scott's black dogs – 'unmatch'd for courage, breath and speed'.

At once they called in Robert Watson-Watt, a brilliant, forty-two-year-old, Scottish-born scientist who headed the Radio Research branch of the National Physical Laboratory. Confirming their own thoughts, he swiftly brushed aside as boys' science-fiction stuff any ideas of a death beam – the amount of radiant power required was too 'fantastically large'. But following suggestions by his assistant, A. F. Wilkins, by the time of the Committee's next meeting a month later

Watson-Watt was able to produce a paper showing the possibilities of using radio waves not to destroy aircraft, but to detect them. This described lines of research ten years earlier in which the height of the ionosphere above the earth's surface had been measured by the transmission of radio waves. This had been achieved by noting the length of the interval between the emission of a radio pulse and the return of its 'echo', as registered by a cathode-ray oscillograph. 'Why not see if we can bounce radio emissions back off aircraft?' Watson-Watt asked.

Within a fortnight the Committee had acted on his suggestion. A bomber pilot, who had no idea of the historical nature of his flight, flew his machine up and down above a fixed line corresponding to the lateral centre of the beam transmitted by Daventry's BBC radio station, while Watson-Watt, Rowe and Wilkins huddled round a receiver to which was attached a cathode-ray oscillograph. As soon as the bomber entered the path of the beam, its presence was registered by the oscillograph. Electro-magnetic energy, it was now proven, was reflected from an aircraft.

By 4 March Wimperis was able to write an astonishing minute to Dowding, which began: 'We now have in embryo, a new and potent means of detecting the approach of hostile aircraft, one which will be independent of mist, cloud, fog or nightfall.'[16]

In the rapid advances that then followed two figures apart from the scientists stood out. The first was Dowding, Air Member of Research and Development. He had needed the proof just vouchsafed that this new idea was worth pursuing before he could seek resources from the Treasury; and having had the proof, he threw all the weight of his influence and position into translating the idea into an actual early-warning system. The second figure was Sir Philip Cunliffe-Lister, soon to become Viscount Swinton, who was appointed in June 1935 to succeed Lord Londonderry as Secretary of State for Air. He was already chairing the Air Defence Committee, a sub-committee of the Committee of Imperial Defence embracing ministers, Service leaders and scientists. In his new post at the Air Ministry he now rapidly proved to possess all the intelligence, the drive and the spirit of urgency which the times (and these new developments) demanded.

The first step was to set up experimental equipment. This was done at a radio research station at Orfordness, on the Suffolk coast. Transmission and receiving aerials of modest size were erected, and serious trials using aircraft began in the summer. Though Watson-Watt, in charge of the work, had to overcome many difficulties, within a few weeks aircraft were being tracked at forty miles range. 'RDF' (radio direction finding, as it was named with misleading intent) had been born.*

Less than nine months after the Tizard Committee's first meeting, the Air Council was recommending the construction of a chain of stations to cover the coast from Southampton up to Newcastle. A beginning had to be made slowly with three stations – the first at Bawdsey Manor, near Orfordness, purchased by the Air Ministry to permit larger aerials and greater scope for experiment. Watson-Watt, in charge at Bawdsey, ran into great constructional and administrative difficulties, but all were overcome. By the outbreak of war the planned chain of twenty stations at home – the Chain Home (CH) stations – had been completed, as well as three overseas. Their mysterious soaring transmitting (350 feet) and receiving (240 feet) towers soon became a feature of the landscape. Such installations, termed for security's sake Air Ministry Experimental Stations (AMES), could detect aircraft up to 100 miles away, and could give the bearing and an approximate indication of the height and number of an approaching formation. Already, too, by the outbreak of war they were being supplemented by another series – Chain Home Low (CHL) – specially designed to detect aircraft flying below 3,000 feet. A further element in the system was, of course, necessary – a device to distinguish friendly aircraft from hostile. It was provided during 1939 and 1940 by a small transmitting device – IFF (identification friend or foe) – which was fitted to RAF aircraft and operated when within British radar range. It gave a distinctive periodic elongation to the blip produced on the radar screen by an approaching aircraft.

Much had still to be done before the outbreak of war to produce more aircraft, to integrate the new radar into the basic defensive lay-out, and to improve and complete the system of fighter control. But, in essence, within the short space of four years, the revolution had been completed. New fast fighters. Greatly extended early warning. No need, inland, for wasteful standing patrols. Effective defence against fast-flying raiders at last possible. The bomber *won't* always get through!

---

*RDF remained the official term until 1943, though when its existence was officially acknowledged in 1941 it was called radiolocation. In 1943, to harmonise with the Americans, it became 'radar' (radio direction and ranging).

# 4

*Late Spurt*

B y 1936 the crucial innovations in Britain's air defence – radar and the eight-gun, monoplane fighter – augured well. Quality seemed assured, but what of quantity? An aggressive move by Germany, the Foreign Office thought, might now come within three years. Conversely, it might never come at all. In an uncertain situation, how much of the new defensive equipment should (or, for that matter, could) be provided, and by what date?

The decision to construct a chain of twenty radar stations – a very bold one, in view of the technical problems outstanding – was taken in the summer of 1937. They were to be ready by 1940 and were estimated to cost £1 million.[1] This seemed a lot at the time, but could in fact be readily afforded. More difficult to finance would be another large increase in the number of squadrons, with their big demands for airfield space, station accommodation and trained manpower. Such an increase, moreover, would involve questions of priority. In any further expansion, should the emphasis be on the RAF overseas (to counter Italy and Japan) or on the RAF at home (to counter Germany)? And within the RAF at home, should the emphasis be on fighters or on bombers?

During 1937 and 1938 these problems were confronted, if not exactly solved. Alarmed at the information coming from Germany, in January 1937 the Air Ministry put forward a new scheme to equal Germany's estimated first-line strength by the spring of 1939. Most of it was rejected by Neville Chamberlain and his ministers – he succeeded

Baldwin as Prime Minister in May – on grounds of expense. Armed with fresh evidence, the Air Ministry tried again in October. Its proposals this time visualised, among other things, building up the RAF overseas and adding 440 bombers and 132 fighters to the already approved target strength of the Metropolitan Air Force, all at an additional cost of £270 million. But – the Air Ministry pointed out – this could be achieved by 1939 only if the Cabinet abandoned the principle on which Britain's rearmament had so far been conducted: that there must be 'no interference with the normal course of trade'.

Chamberlain and his ministers, however, had as yet no intention of forgoing peacetime practices. They had no wish to direct labour, forbid 'strategic' exports such as aircraft, pre-empt materials or introduce any of the government controls which could step up aircraft production. In Parliament Churchill, since 1934 intent on goading the Government and the Air Ministry into faster rearmament, was by now demanding exceptional measures such as the setting up of a Ministry of Supply. Most of the ministers, however, remained unmoved. They had steered the ship of state into calmer waters after the storms of 1931 and they were convinced that, if a war had finally to be fought, the best chance of winning it would be from a sound financial base – 'the fourth arm of defence'. Huge peacetime expenditure on arms beyond the unprecedented total of £1,500 million for the years 1937–41 already agreed, direction of manufacture and labour – all this might cancel out their hard-won gains and plunge the country into a new financial crisis. Also, though this was less clearly enunciated, it would greatly annoy employers and unions and cause much trouble for the Government.

Though determined to maintain 'business as usual' the Cabinet hesitated to turn down the Air Ministry's new proposals flat. It was Sir Thomas Inskip, Minister for Co-ordination of Defence – a post established in 1936 – who showed his colleagues a way out. The extra £270 million could, he pointed out, be cut to £110 million if all proposed increases overseas were omitted, and if the proposed increase in the home bomber force was substantially reduced. The proposed increase in the home fighter force could then stand.[2]

These amendments Inskip justified not only on financial grounds but on strategic. Even a British bombing force inferior to the Luftwaffe's could, he argued, prove a useful deterrent. And as long as Britain had a strong fighter arm, she could defend her home base should attack come, build up resources under a wartime economy once hostilities started, and then in the fullness of time move over to the offensive.

This prescription scandalised the Air Staff, who had for so long regarded offence as the number one weapon in defence. As a strategy it was, in fact, just becoming tenable – because of the promise shown by radar and the new eight-gun fighters. Was Inskip's strategic insight, then, keener than that of the Air Staff? Did it need, as some have averred, a lawyer-politician to call back to reality airmen lost in impractical visions of strategic bombing – to point out to them the importance of 'defensive' defence, and impose on them a decision which helped to win the Battle of Britain?

It may be doubted whether the answer to these questions should be 'yes'. Had the Air Staff been blind to the demands of 'defensive' defence they would scarcely have shown such vigour in backing the Hurricane, the Spitfire and radar. In essence, Inskip was offering the Air Staff all the extra fighters they had requested for home defence, but not all the extra bombers. Fighters were much cheaper than bombers and required a single crew member instead of four or five; and his proposals, consonant with the continuation of 'business as usual', accordingly commended themselves to the majority of the Cabinet.

Did this decision, as has been claimed, make a substantial contribution towards the victory of 1940? If so, the feather in Inskip's cap would indeed be a big one. But in fact, though many have lauded Inskip's sense of priorities, no one has yet shown that the scaling down of the Air Ministry's bomber proposals in 1937 produced more Hurricanes and Spitfires in 1940.

Certainly, however, the adoption of Inskip's proposals became one more factor in committing Britain to a completely defensive posture at the start of the war. It helped to delay the beginning of any significant British bombing offensive, and to confirm in Hitler's hands the strategic initiative – an initiative which was to result in the collapse of France and the installation of the Luftwaffe just across the English Channel.

During 1938 financial considerations at last fell into second place. In February the Chiefs of Staff, pointing out alarming deficiencies in planned production, advised that these could be remedied only by exceptional industrial measures.[3] They had scarcely sounded their warning when, on 11 March, Hitler's columns rolled into Austria to the frenzied applause of the home-bred Nazis. With Mussolini firmly in the German camp since the abortive Anglo-French efforts to restrain him over Abyssinia, nothing could now be done about Austria. But could

Britain and France avert further moves towards a Greater German Reich? Very quickly Chamberlain asked the Chiefs of Staff to advise on the practicability of Allied military action if Hitler threatened Czechoslovakia.

The Chiefs of Staff did not mince their words. 'No pressure', they reported, 'that we and our possible allies can bring to bear, either by sea, on land, or in the air could prevent Germany from invading and overrunning Bohemia.'[4] They added that only by the defeat of Germany in a long war could Czechoslovakia be restored, and that for a long war the British land and air forces were as yet entirely unfitted. The Army was far too small, and the RAF could not operate in a major war for more than a few weeks. Many months would elapse after the outbreak of hostilities before the aircraft industry would become capable of replacing wastage in a major conflict.

Lacking comfort in this direction, Chamberlain went on to place his faith in his powers of negotiation and to give a new shade of meaning to the word 'appeasement'. But, meanwhile, his Government no longer gambled on Hitler's unwillingness or inability to commit aggression. On 22 March 1938 the Cabinet formally abandoned 'no interference with the normal course of trade' as the basis for rearmament,[5] and during April, in virtually approving a new RAF expansion scheme, it gave the Air Ministry authority to accept as many aircraft as could be produced within the following two years up to a total of 12,000 – 4,500 more than previously authorised.[6] For the RAF, this was at last a clear green light. Events had decisively overtaken 'business as usual'. In two or three years, the resources would be there. But would they be there in time for the moment of truth?

After the rape of Austria, rearmament became almost respectable. On the Labour side, politicians who four years earlier had denounced the Government's first modest proposals as immoral now began to inveigh against its failure to keep pace with Germany. Allied to constant harrying by Churchill this produced difficulties for Chamberlain, who responded in May 1938 by dropping the Secretary of State for Air, Lord Swinton. This was no help at all. As a peer, Swinton had been unable to defend his Ministry's record in the Commons, but he had been an outstandingly able political chief, a minister whose drive and vision had been a potent force behind all the new developments, especially radar and the shadow factories.

Most of the shortcomings in the RAF to which Swinton's critics pointed had, in fact, stemmed either from shortages in manufacture under 'business as usual' or else from the difficulty of training large numbers of men to the required skilled standard when the trainers themselves were so few. The business of trying to treble so technical a service as an air force within five years was an immensely difficult one. If the Luftwaffe seemed to be more successful than the RAF, that was partly because Germany's Government was setting a hotter pace, but also because its own shortcomings, which were real enough, were not yet apparent to the outside world.

Meanwhile, the build-up continued of the defence organisation which was to withstand the Luftwaffe in 1940. Early in 1937 the Air Defence of Great Britain Committee, chaired by Dowding, had produced an 'ideal' air defence scheme to counter attacks from an estimated German bomber force of 1,700 aircraft by the spring of 1939. (The scheme was 'ideal' in the sense that current manufacturing, financial and recruiting limitations were not taken into account.) The scheme had been prefaced by three general principles: that 'passive defence' (air-raid precautions) was as important as active; that no system could give complete security; and that 'it is the air offensive which, if successful, will contribute most to a successful outcome of the war'.[7] (The last of these may surprise those who think of Dowding only as a 'fighter' enthusiast.)

Among the features of the scheme had been that the Aircraft Fighting Zone should be extended north from the Tees to beyond Newcastle; that it should be widened in the West Riding and the Midlands; and that new defences should be set up for the Forth–Clyde, Bristol and South Wales areas. With the advent of radar and the possibility of forward interception, the old Outer Artillery Zone had now been abolished and fighter activity would be carried to the coasts and beyond. For the new extensions and a general thickening up of the defences further radar stations and many more observer centres and posts would be required, together with twenty-four more fighter squadrons to add to the twenty-one then in place. The eleven existing fighter sectors would need to be supplemented by another four, and the resulting fifteen sectors would then contain three squadrons apiece. Communications must be provided to tie in all the new developments with the rest of the system.

With regard to ground defences the Committee recommended that the existing approved (but far from provided) number of searchlights and heavy anti-aircraft guns needed to be virtually doubled – the lights to a total of 4,700, the guns to a total of 1,264. Large numbers of light anti-aircraft guns, possibly amounting to some 1,200 barrels, would be required as a defence against low-flying aircraft at airfields and other key points. In addition, balloon barrages, already approved for London at 450 balloons, should be provided for the ports and other major centres.[8]

Though this scheme was accepted 'in principle' during 1937, action was at first sanctioned only for an 'intermediate' stage. In general this meant that the Air Ministry got on with forming more fighter squadrons and stations to the extent approved under its current expansion scheme, and the Air Ministry and the Home Office between them saw to the expansion of the Observer Corps. During 1937 the Home Office also initiated several Civil Defence measures, placing on local authorities the burden of providing shelters and attracting volunteers as air-raid wardens and auxiliary firemen. The War Office part of the scheme, however, hung fire. Without suitable models already in production, the provision of anti-aircraft guns lagged far behind required totals.

As the summer of 1938 wore on, it became clear that Hitler had indeed got Czechoslovakia in his sights. The annexation of the Sudetenland and other disputed areas, with their three million inhabitants of German origin, had become, as expected, Hitler's next objective. Behind the shrieking propaganda about Czech ill-treatment of the German-speaking minority lay, obvious enough to some but not to all, Hitler's desire to demolish an outpost of the French security system and open up the way to *lebensraum* in the East. In this growing crisis, Britain's formal interest was that of a League of Nations member pledged to concert measures against aggression; but France had the direct commitment of a military ally.

The possibilities, however, of saving Czechoslovakia from being overrun were as negligible as the British Chiefs of Staff had indicated six months earlier. Only Soviet Russia, committed to protect Czechoslovakia if France moved to her aid first, might have brought effective help; but Russia had no common frontier with the threatened state. With her armies shaken by Stalin's purges, and their transit dreaded by Czechoslovakia's neighbours, Russia seemed of doubtful military value. In any case Chamberlain, intent on averting the horrors of war by helping to remove what many felt to be Germany's legitimate grievances, was not interested in military combinations. Declining to guarantee armed support to France, he hoped to minimise Hitler's demands and induce the Czechs to accept them. Terrified of honouring their treaty commitment, France's ministers quickly and gratefully followed Chamberlain's lead.

Few of mature age who lived in Britain during the crisis of September 1938 can have forgotten that appalling week when Chamberlain, having flown to Germany – daring stuff for an elderly prime minister; Baldwin had never been in an aeroplane – and agreed in principle but not in detail to Hitler's claims, found himself on his second visit cheated and affronted when the German dictator suddenly insisted on instant occupation instead of investigation and orderly transfer. The agony of the days when it seemed that Britain and France, however reluctantly, might stand behind Czechoslovakia – 'a far-off country of which we know nothing', in Chamberlain's immortal phrase; the sudden ghastly imminence of war confronting the deeply pacific British people; the mobilisation of the Royal Navy, part of the AAF, the Observer Corps and anti-aircraft units; the distribution of gas masks to the regions, the makeshift plans announced for evacuation of the big cities, the hasty digging of shelter trenches (soon to be waterlogged) in the London parks; and then the ecstasy in the House of Commons as another 'invitation' to Germany cleared the way for the Munich 'Agreement' – all these, together with Chamberlain's waved scrap of paper and 'peace with honour' on his return, were to become engraved on the national memory.

Only those concerned with the Services, however, knew the true weakness of Britain's land and air defences at that time. In the RAF, everything was still in the throes of an expansion which would produce impressive results in a year or so, but was meanwhile greatly restricting operational availability. In terms of Dowding's 'ideal' scheme only twenty-nine of the forty-five fighter squadrons deemed necessary for March 1939 were formed and in place during the crisis of September 1938, and of these only five were as yet equipped with the new monoplane fighters – Hurricanes whose guns, being not yet heated, could not function properly above 15,000 feet.[9] None of the new promised balloon barrages was yet in place, and of the heavy anti-aircraft guns approved only a third were available. Modern light anti-aircraft artillery was virtually non-existent. Good progress was being made with the radar chain, but only five of the planned CH stations, those guarding the Thames Estuary, together with three mobile outfits, were as yet reasonably complete. They were brought into operation during that memorable month and remained on watch until the war with Germany was won.

As for the other arms of defence whose importance Dowding had stressed, civil defence under a voluntary system as run by local authorities of varying degrees of competence and enthusiasm was a thing of shreds and patches; and the offensive arm, as represented by Bomber Command, was in a far worse state of preparedness and availability than Fighter Command. The general picture, as described to his Cabinet colleagues shortly afterwards by Swinton's successor, Sir Kingsley Wood, was that, at the anticipated rate of loss, 'We had less than one week's wastage behind the squadrons.'[10] Fighter Command's front line of some 400 aircraft was, in fact, backed by only 160 aircraft in reserve.[11] Of the RAF's reserve pilots, less than ten per cent were operationally fit. Fighter Command's ops room, and those of its Groups, were not yet underground.

It was scarcely an inducement to go to war.

After Munich the Air Ministry conducted a grand inquest into the state of the RAF during the emergency. Apart from known shortages, the most common deficiencies were found to be in communications and administration. Landline communications were still far too centralised through London, but here action was already in train; during the next eighteen months the completion of the GPO's new Ring Main system brought great improvements. During the same period lines from the radar stations, connected at first to Bawdsey and then to the filter room at Fighter Command headquarters, were also laid down to the Groups and the Fighter sector stations. In administration, it emerged that some of the hard-pressed staff at Group headquarters during the crisis had taken days to deal with matters needing action within minutes. A remedy was found by redeploying most of the staff of the supporting services – equipment, engineering and signals – from Command head-quarters, where they had been largely concentrated, out to the Groups, which had to conduct the operations and needed more supporting staff to do so.[12] Had this not been done, the system would inevitably have broken down under the pressures of 1940.

Munich also gave rise to yet one more expansion scheme (M) for the RAF. It was the last of the pre-war programmes, due for completion in 1942. It now recommended a total of eighty-five squadrons for Bomber Command, mainly of the new 'heavies' (four-engined Stirlings and Halifaxes, and twin-engined Manchesters) specified in 1936. The Cabinet in November 1938, with the Chancellor of the Exchequer still urging financial caution, sanctioned this part of the programme only in principle: actual orders for bombers were only to be such as to utilise existing manufacturing capacity and 'avoid dismissals'. The fighter element of the new scheme, however, the Cabinet once more approved in full.[13] Of the 3,700 additional fighters required, half were to be ordered immediately, and Fighter Command was now to be brought up – by April 1941 – to a strength of fifty squadrons, including four for a possible move abroad with the Field Force. This total of fifty squadrons at once became Dowding's fixed requirement – an imperative for now, never mind 1941.

On 15 March 1939, having stirred the Slovaks into declaring their independence, Hitler completed the dismemberment of Czechoslovakia. German columns poured into Bohemia, the Luftwaffe – two days late because of bad weather – roared menacingly above Prague, and the Munich Agreement was revealed for the sham it always was. In angry reaction, Chamberlain instantly reversed tracks and guaranteed the integrity of Poland, Hitler's next potential victim. With the junior partner in the Rome–Berlin Axis invading Albania a week later, the British Government then hastily extended guarantees to two other possible victims of aggression – Greece and Romania. All this made it virtually certain for the first time that if trouble with Germany flared up again, Britain would be involved from the start.

The effect of this was only marginal on the RAF, which was already in the throes of all practicable expansion, but it was revolutionary on the British Army. Up to this point there had been no positive commitment to send an expeditionary force to fight alongside the French, and no steps had been taken to provide a Field Force of more than four divisions. Now, on 29 March 1939, the Cabinet agreed to double the Territorial and strengthen the Regular Army, to a total of thirty-two divisions.[14] A month later, greatly daring, it announced a first feeble instalment of conscription. Extremely limited though this was, it was too much for the parliamentary opposition. A. J. P. Taylor records that Clement Attlee spoke of the 'danger of giving generals all they want', and that Aneurin Bevan exclaimed, 'Hitler has won.'

Conscription helped the RAF, very late in the day, to make good some of the deficiencies in the ground trades. But the main immediate effect of the decision to build a large army for service overseas was to increase the problem of close home defence. An army of thirty-two divisions would need large supporting forces in the air; and even an army of five divisions, which is what was now promised to the French as a first step, must be able to call on considerable help from bombers, reconnaissance aircraft and fighters. Above all, from fighters – fighters to protect the reconnaissance aircraft, and possibly the bombers, and to restrict the enemy's air assaults on the Army and its communications.

The number of fighter squadrons earmarked to accompany a BEF had long been four – which would come from Fighter Command. In May 1939, following the decision to create a much larger army, the Air Ministry agreed to put six more fighter squadrons on a mobile basis so that in case of need, and if the situation at home permitted, they too could be sent abroad.[15] Such plans were anathema to Dowding. Though by no means blind to broad strategic requirements, he deplored commitments which might send any fighter squadrons at all to the continent until he was assured of his projected total of fifty. On 7 July 1939, in a letter to the Air Ministry, he made his position abundantly clear: 'If this policy is implemented and ten Regular Squadrons are withdrawn from this country, the air defence of Great Britain will be gravely imperilled.'[16] It was a warning which he was to sound incessantly in the months that lay ahead.

To add to Dowding's anxieties, three further tasks were laid on Fighter Command before war broke out. One was the defence of Belfast, which was outside the continuous system and was now given separate radar cover, ground defences and a locally based fighter squadron. Another was the defence of Scapa Flow, which the Admiralty decided late in the day to use as a main fleet base. Far beyond the continuous system, this Orkneys anchorage was now to have the protection of separate radar cover and two fighter squadrons based near Wick, on the mainland.

The third task was the most onerous. During 1939 it was decided that not all British shipping could be diverted to west-coast ports, and that east-coast convoys must be sailed with air protection between the Forth and Southampton. In consequence, Fighter Command was required on the outbreak of war to institute regular patrols with four squadrons specially allocated to this task. Since four squadrons could not be spared from the general defensive system, they had to be specially formed on Blenheims withdrawn from bomber resources and converted to fighters.[17]

Though Dowding's cares multiplied, the last year of peace saw great progress in his Command and in supporting structures. The AAF, earlier equipped in the main with obsolescent bombers, completed its conversion to modern fighters: by September 1939 it could show fourteen squadrons in the line – more than a third of the strength of Fighter Command. The balloon squadrons of the AAF, too, inaugurated in 1938, grew rapidly in number: in September 1939 Balloon

Command, formed the previous year when it became necessary to create a second Balloon Group, deployed 624 out of its approved total of 1,450 balloons.[18] In September 1938 only London, with about 150 balloons for which there were crews, would have had this form of protection. A year later, barrages, mostly small, were also available for a dozen of the major ports and industrial areas.

With aircraft production, and particularly fighter production, moving into higher gears, steps were also taken to enlarge facilities for maintenance and repair. To deal with repairs beyond the capacity of the squadrons and to obviate sending damaged aircraft back to the factories, a new upper formation, Maintenance Command, with two Groups and many subordinate units, was formed during 1938. And to man the new depots and fly the new aircraft there was now the intake of the RAF Volunteer Reserve, started in 1937, and gratifyingly swollen by a rush of recruits during the September 1938 crisis. By September 1939 some 5,000 pilots, trained or under training, were becoming available from this source alone. For Fighter Command, however, the number of fully trained VR pilots, most of them not too generously accorded the rank of sergeant, was around 200.

Other new formations were also promising well. The Civil Air Guard, founded belatedly in 1938 to encourage activity in flying clubs, was producing skilled pilots, women as well as men, who later as the Air Transport Auxiliary would perform invaluable service in ferrying aircraft from factory to maintenance depot or squadron. And the future held few limits – on the ground – for the air companies of the Auxiliary Territorial Service, detached in June 1939 to become the Women's Auxiliary Air Force (WAAF). Enrolled for only five trades in September 1939 they were quickly in demand for many more – not least to act as operators in the radar stations.

On the ground defence side there was more limited progress. Enough anti-aircraft forces became available to warrant the formation of Anti-Aircraft Command – with headquarters at Stanmore adjacent to Dowding's, and placed, like Balloon Command, under Dowding's higher operational control. All the same, the deficiencies in this arm of defence remained appalling. Though about two-thirds of the approved number of searchlights were available, the number of heavy anti-aircraft guns deployable was only 695 out of the newly approved total of 2,232, and about a third of these were obsolescent. Light anti-aircraft guns were even more scarce – 253 towards the approved strength of 1,860.[19]

Civil defence, however, so rudimentary in September 1938, was a year later in a vastly more efficient state. The 1938 crisis had produced thousands of volunteers, and by the outbreak of war over 1.5 million men and women were enrolled as air-raid wardens or as auxiliaries in the local fire and ambulance services. Hundreds of street shelters had been prepared by local authorities and nearly 1.5 million 'Anderson' shelters – steel contraptions to be dug into the garden and covered with earth, hard work to install but each capable of holding six persons – had been distributed free to the less well-off sections of the population in the more vulnerable areas.

As the crisis deepened through August 1939, with Hitler clamouring for Danzig and concluding his deal with Russia to divide Poland, British mobilisation unobtrusively began. On the civil defence side, the gas masks were distributed, the women and children from the threatened urban centres began their strange adventure of evacuation into the 'reception areas', and the blackout fastened its eerie grip on the life of citizen and serviceman alike. And in the hospitals thousands of beds were emptied of their occupants to make room for the 140,000 or so casualties expected from the initial German air-raids.

But the dreaded 'knock-out blow' from the air, the possible opening gambit by Germany which had haunted British politicians in 1937–8, was not to be launched. In fact, the British Chiefs of Staff, their advisers, had never thought an actual 'knock-out' possible – rather that a massive opening blow from the air could cause fearful damage and dislocation. But after Hitler in 1938 revealed his preoccupation with expansion to the East, the possibility that Germany might begin a European war with an all-out air assault on Britain, though still powerfully entertained by the civil population, was seen in military circles to be much less likely. In truth, it had not featured among the German plans: the Luftwaffe, though an independent service, had been built up and conditioned since the Spanish Civil War to work closely with the German Army. In a major strategic role, without concurrent operations by the German land forces, the Battle of Britain, together with the ensuing 'night blitz', was to be its first – and last – venture.

When the disillusioned Prime Minister broken-heartedly informed the nation on 3 September 1939 that his hopes had all collapsed and that the country was at war, Britain's defences were in every way stronger than they had been a year before. Though still far short of their approved totals of equipment, Fighter Command and Anti-Aircraft Command were much more capable of taking on the enemy, and armament production was increasing fast. Above all, there had been heartening progress with the most vital elements in the defensive system – the radar chain, the eight-gun fighters and the system of fighter control.

In September 1938 radar cover had extended only from Dungeness to the Wash, with a mobile outpost for Scapa Flow. By September 1939, having meanwhile also improved greatly in performance, the main chain gave continuous cover from Southampton to beyond the Forth. In addition, by September 1939 many new fighter airfields had been built, the sector organisation had been completed and control from the ground had been perfected.

To achieve accuracy in control had been a problem, but during 1939 'Pipsqueak' had provided the answer. One fighter in each section of three switched his R/T on to this device, which produced periodic signals picked up by D/F (direction-finding) ground stations. Cross-bearings from these fixed the fighters' position, which could be continuously plotted. Armed with this information, and with knowledge of the enemy's course derived from the radar and observer plots, a controller on the ground could give his pilots over the R/T a 'vector', or compass bearing, which would – it was hoped – bring them to within sight of the enemy. This 'controlled interception', as yet unknown to the Luftwaffe, was to be the basis of Fighter Command's operations in the forthcoming Battle.

On top of these developments, by September 1939 a new fighter Group – No. 13 – had been opened with headquarters at Newcastle for the defence of the north, and a further fighter Group – No. 10 – had been projected for the defence of the south-west. Most striking of all, however, was the change in the composition of the fighter force itself. In September 1938 Fighter Command had mustered twenty-nine squadrons, of which only five had Hurricanes. All the rest had biplanes. In September 1939, after four squadrons had left for France, no more than thirty-five were available for home defence – but seventeen of these were on Hurricanes and twelve on Spitfires. The difference in fighting power was immense.

So the inevitable question arises – did Munich buy the time which, wisely used, made victory possible in the Battle of Britain two years later? It is tempting to draw the apparently obvious conclusion. But there is no certainty that in 1938, if France had intervened against a much less well-prepared Germany, she would have collapsed as ignominiously as she did in 1940. Had France not collapsed, Fighter Command would not have had to face, as it did in 1940, attacks by escorted bombers from bases close at hand. Instead, it would have been dealing with unescorted attacks from much more distant bases – a task not entirely impossible for the older biplane fighters.

Such speculations, however interesting, are only the 'ifs' and 'buts' of history. What seems much more certain, to those who lived through that month of crisis and bitter controversy, is that had Britain gone to war in September 1938 it would have been in disregard of the convictions of a large part of the population. By September 1939 Hitler's cumulative aggressions had convinced all but a tiny minority that he must somehow be stopped – that it was really the case, as the uninspiring Prime Minister put it in his broadcast, that Britain would be fighting against 'evil things – brute force, bad faith, injustice, oppression and persecution'. Deeply though Chamberlain had offended many by the combination of 'appeasement' and an air of self-satisfaction, he finally took into war a united nation. Of that, the inestimable benefit was to be reaped in the summer of 1940, when the zeal and ardent toil of the many helped to make possible the brilliant achievements of the few.

# 5

# *Bonus of Time*

T he Prime Minister's broadcast had barely faded from the air when – as Churchill termed them – the 'banshee wailings' of the air-raid sirens struck a chill into several million hearts. An unidentified aircraft had crossed the Kent coast, and three of the civil defence regions had been put under raid warning 'red' – which should have been 'yellow'. In Whitehall, brass hats and mandarins trooped obediently down to the cellars, on local initiative a few fighters in the south took off to investigate, and one of the authors of this volume, conditioned like most of his contemporaries to expect instant air attack, gazed apprehensively at the skies as he motored off to snatch an hour or two – possibly his last hour or two – with his betrothed. He, and the others, need not have worried. For the time being, the Luftwaffe was under orders to confine its attacks in the West to retaliatory action against naval targets;[1] and the intruder was only a friendly 'civil' from France, flight plan unfiled, heading happily for the aerodrome at Croydon.

Within the same half-hour similar false alarms scared the inhabitants of Edinburgh and Newcastle, also without dire consequences. But three days later, on 6 September, a much more serious incident occurred. Soon after dawn a searchlight battery on Mersea island, in the Thames Estuary, reported to 11 Group some incoming aircraft that it suspected were hostile. Group swiftly alerted sector at North Weald, and sector sent off Hurricanes of 56 Squadron to investigate. But the radar station at Canewdon, in the Estuary, was – according to Dowding – malfunctioning. The screening to block off echoes from the landward side, where the Observer Corps was responsible for raid reporting, seems to have been ineffective, so that when blips from the Hurricanes appeared on the cathode-ray tubes they were taken as indicating, in the usual way, approach from the sea.* Also they may have suggested a larger force than 11 Group had ordered up: the Group had asked for six aircraft, but sector had allowed the squadron, in excess of zeal, to put up fourteen. At all events they were taken for 'hostiles', and further squadrons – 151 (Hurricanes) from North Weald, and a squadron and two flights of Spitfires from Hornchurch – were ordered up and vectored into the same area. Amid a whirling confusion of aircraft, to which local anti-aircraft batteries contributed by shooting freely despite the firing of recognition signals, a section of Spitfires from 74 Squadron, sun-dazzled, mistook a section of 151 Squadron for Me 109s and shot two of them down, killing one of the pilots. Worse would doubtless have followed had not the CO of 151, Squadron Leader E. M. Donald-son,** one of three well-known brothers in the RAF, shouted out over his R/T: 'Do not retaliate. They are friendly.'[2]

This tragic shambles, hushed up at the time, was dubbed in the RAF 'the Battle of Barking Creek' – a place several miles from the shooting-down but one which, like Wigan Pier, was a standing joke in the music halls.

These incidents told all too plainly of raw nerves, inexperience and technical imperfections. Fortunately there was ample opportunity, in the absence of serious enemy air attack, for improvement during the next few months. Flying Officer Alan ('Al') Deere,† a New Zealander with 54 Squadron at Hornchurch, who had spent an hour during the 'Barking Creek' episode trying to join up with his squadron 'which was receiving so many vectors that it was impossible to follow them', later recalled that five of his next six training flights were devoted to tactical exercises in co-operation with the reporting and control organisation.[3] The fact of the matter, not surprisingly, was that controllers, filter-room plotters, radar operators, pilots, gunners and members of the Observer Corps all needed much more practice, and that the last three groups also needed basic training in aircraft recognition. Thanks to the

---

*Watson-Watt had another explanation – that a British fighter had originally been on the seaward side. IFF sets for British aircraft had been devised and ordered, but not yet generally fitted.

**Later Air Commodore E. M. Donaldson CB, CBE, DSO, DFC.

†Later Air Vice-Marshal A. C. Deere OBE, DSO, DFC, AFC.

enemy's very restricted activity in the air, they were able to get it more or less in peace.

For this reason the period which American journalists, impatient for action, dubbed the 'Phoney War' was of vital importance for future success in the Battle of Britain. As the British and French had decided to defer all offensive action, except at sea, until they grew stronger, and as Hitler, having failed to pull off a profitable peace after the defeat of Poland, was husbanding his resources for an attack on France, nothing happened between September 1939 and April 1940 to disrupt either the British air defences or British war production. Enough, however, happened to give many of the defenders useful experience.

During the autumn of 1939 much of this experience arose from the Luftwaffe's operations against the Home Fleet. On 16 October, for instance, when nine Ju 88s struck at naval vessels in the anchorage at Rosyth, on the Forth, pilots of 602 (City of Edinburgh) and 603 (City of Glasgow) Squadrons had an early taste of combat and enjoyed the distinction of shooting down the first two German aircraft to be destroyed over Britain since 1918. They came down in the Firth of Forth after what was described as 'a roof-top chase over Edinburgh'. This was first blood to the Auxiliaries – and equal scoring between Hurricanes and Spitfires! But again there was trouble with the reporting system. Wireless intercepts had given good advance warning of the raid, and an extra fighter squadron – 607 (County of Durham) – had been brought up in readiness, only for the local radar to become ineffective through a power failure. So the attackers were able to inflict serious damage on two cruisers and a destroyer, and would doubtless also have crippled the recently docked battleship *Hood* had they not been forbidden to drop bombs which might fall on land.[4] All told, the day's work was scarcely a success for the defences. According to the Ministry of Home Security's report the following day, 'no general warning was given, and great indignation has been expressed by the local populace, who crowded into the streets to watch under the impression that a practice was in progress'.[5]

Coming on top of the episode two days earlier on 14 October, when U-boat 47 had penetrated the waters of Scapa Flow and sunk the battleship *Royal Oak*, this raid caused the main fleet to retire to the west coast, where it was poorly placed for speedy intervention in the North Sea. But by great exertions the defences approved for Scapa Flow in the summer of 1939, including a balloon barrage and two fighter squadrons on a newly built airfield, were completed, together with new underwater defences, months ahead of schedule, and by March 1940 the Home Fleet could safely return to the Orkneys.

Among the combats resulting from the Luftwaffe's interest in British warships two left valuable legacies. On 28 October 1939 a He 111 was brought down in the Lammermuir Hills, north of Edinburgh. Months later its Lorenz blind-landing set yielded to Dr R. V. Jones, the brilliant young Assistant Director of Scientific Intelligence at the Air Ministry, the secret of how the Germans were able to use a radio beam system (*'Knickebein'*) for night bombing (see page 268). Equally satisfactory, another Heinkel, forced to land near North Berwick on 9 February 1940, suffered so little damage that it could soon be flown and systematically evaluated. When 111s began operating against Britain in force six months later, their strengths and weaknesses were thoroughly well known to the defenders.

The other main type of operational experience at this time was the usually wearisome and uneventful business of flying patrols to protect east-coast merchant shipping. This work, shared by Fighter and Coastal Commands, from time to time also produced combats, and usually successful ones – such as that on 29 October 1939, when 46 Squadron destroyed four He 115B reconnaissance-bombers out of nine in an encounter off the Humber Estuary. Similarly 43 Squadron, while protecting another convoy off Yorkshire on 3 February 1940, shot down three He 111s. At that stage in the war the chivalry of the air still prevailed. One of 43's victorious pilots, Flight Lieutenant Peter Townsend, visited a badly injured member of the German crews in hospital; and at the burial of two others there was a wreath bearing the message: 'From 43 Squadron, with sympathy'.

Most of the German attacks, with the resulting combats, took place off the east coast, and it was not until 21 March 1940 that the Luftwaffe achieved a sinking in the English Channel. On that occasion the merchant ship *Barn Hill*, sailing alone, was hit by a bomb during the hours of darkness and set on fire. At fearful risk from the heaving vessel and from explosions, men of the Eastbourne lifeboats rescued most of the crew, while others of the Eastbourne fire brigade, brought out in the lifeboats, fought the flames. This was experience of a different sort, involving civilian services – and an early instance of that widespread courage and concern for others which was to be such a source of strength to the country later in 1940. Not everyone, however, was as yet fully imbued with this spirit. The Ministry of Home Security's report next day recorded: 'Twenty-eight survivors are now in hospital and in the Grand Hotel, Eastbourne, the management of which has asked for their removal today.'[6]

All told, the Luftwaffe directed some 400 reconnaissance or bombing sorties towards or over Britain's coasts before the end of March 1940. In the course of these operations, it lost forty aircraft, but during the same period Fighter Command suffered no combat losses at all. Such a contrast augured well for the more strenuous days ahead and suggested, comfortingly but also correctly, that against the defences now built up in Britain unescorted daylight raiding from Germany would not be – for the Germans – a profitable operation of war.

On 3 April 1940 a pilot of 41 Squadron, in dealing successfully with an He 111, was himself fired on and compelled to ditch. This was the first time that a home-based fighter pilot was brought down through enemy action. Obviously, Dowding was not worried by losses during this period. Several other matters, however, worried him greatly. The shipping patrols took up long flying hours which otherwise would have been devoted to operational and combat training; the Germans were increasingly attacking shipping off coasts north and west of the defence system proper; and some of the great technical improvements in progress or in prospect, notably those affecting radar reporting, fighter control and aircraft performance, might not be fully achieved before the storm broke. But Dowding's greatest worry of all, or at least the one about which he was most vocal, was that his Command was gravely short of the number of squadrons agreed to be necessary for his supremely important task.

Some of these worries lessened as time went on. Fighter Command's responsibilities at sea became confined to a belt extending five miles from the coast, Coastal Command looking after everything farther out. To counter German attacks beyond the existing defence system, Dowding pressed for the creation of a new Fighter Group (No. 14) covering Scotland north of the Tay – a recommendation accepted but impossible to implement before the autumn of 1940. For the west, where another Group (No. 10) had already been approved before the war to cover the area between Portsmouth and Bristol, but was not yet formed, Dowding recommended, and got, an extension into Devon, Cornwall and South Wales. The full defence organisation would thus shortly cover all but the most remote parts of the country – the parts least accessible to the Luftwaffe. The problem, however, still remained of equipping the new parts of this organisation with all the necessary fighters, guns,

searchlights, balloons, airfields, communications, radar stations, observer posts and centres.

The improvements which the Air Ministry and Dowding were able to
make within Fighter Command during the quiet months of the war
were crucial to its later success. First and foremost there was the
addition of more squadrons, discussed later. Next in importance came
the re-equipping of Blenheim and Gladiator squadrons with Hurricanes
or Spitfires. Beyond this, there were the modifications made to the
Hurricanes and Spitfires themselves – notably the fitting of constant-
speed airscrews, which gave a dramatic increase in take-off speed, rate
of climb and ceiling. Also, for the Hurricanes and Spitfires as yet
without them, there was the addition of bullet-proof windscreens and
armour-plate behind the pilot's seat. No one as yet, alas, thought of
coating the petrol tanks with a dope which would seal bullet holes.

Even more important were the new developments in the radar
reporting system. During the 1938 trials it had become clear that the
standard CH stations could not be relied on to detect aircraft coming in
low. Special sets and aerial arrays to detect intruders below 5,000 feet
had accordingly been developed just before the war and began to appear
along the coasts from September 1939. These subsidiary stations, thirty
in number, the CHL, were all in place by July 1940 – a vital element in
the defensive system. Vital, too, was the fact that between September
1939 and June 1940 all British operational aircraft were fitted with IFF,
so that no episode of the 'Barking Creek' kind ever occurred again.

All these matters progressed fast during the 'Phoney War' – and still
faster after Germany broke the stalemate in April 1940. But for
Dowding the supreme task, even more than speeding up these improvements, was how to get, and keep, his full quota of squadrons. This
problem was bound up with another vitally affecting Dowding's Command, but not within his sphere of responsibility – how to provide
fighter protection for the BEF on the continent. Herein lay a conflict of
requirements which gnawed at Dowding's heart from the very first days
of the war.

In the final defence plans of 1938 and 1939 it had been agreed between
Dowding and the Air Ministry that forty-six modern fighter squadrons
were needed to protect the country against an estimated first-line
strength by April 1940 of the 1,750 German bombers. Peace, it was
thought, might not last beyond 1941, and Dowding's force was to be
brought up to the recommended level during 1940 and 1941. It was

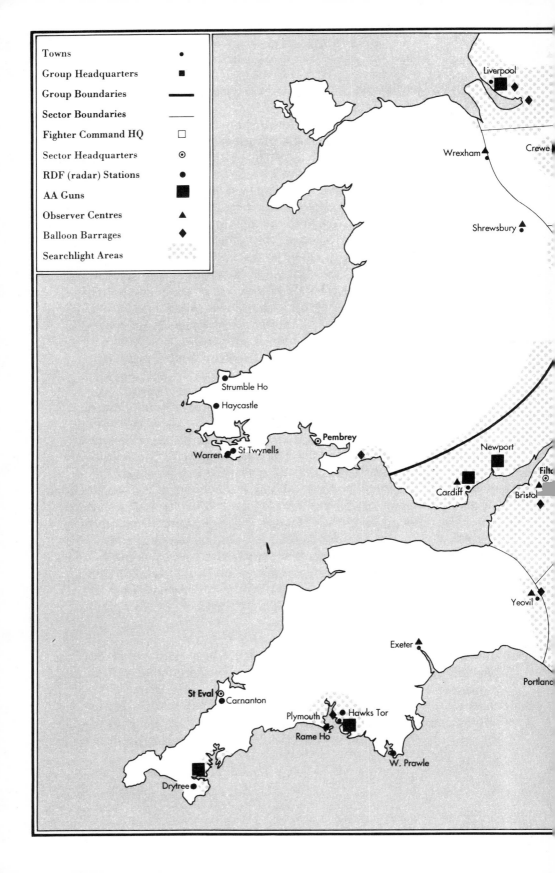

Towns •

Group Headquarters ■

Group Boundaries ▬▬▬

Sector Boundaries ───

Fighter Command HQ □

Sector Headquarters ◉

RDF (radar) Stations ●

AA Guns ■

Observer Centres ▲

Balloon Barrages ◆

Searchlight Areas

Liverpool

Wrexham

Crewe

Shrewsbury

Strumble Ho

Haycastle

Pembrey

Newport

Warren • St Twynells

Cardiff

Filto

Bristol

Yeovil

Exeter

Portland

St Eval • Carnanton

Plymouth Hawks Tor

Rame Ho

W. Prawle

Drytree

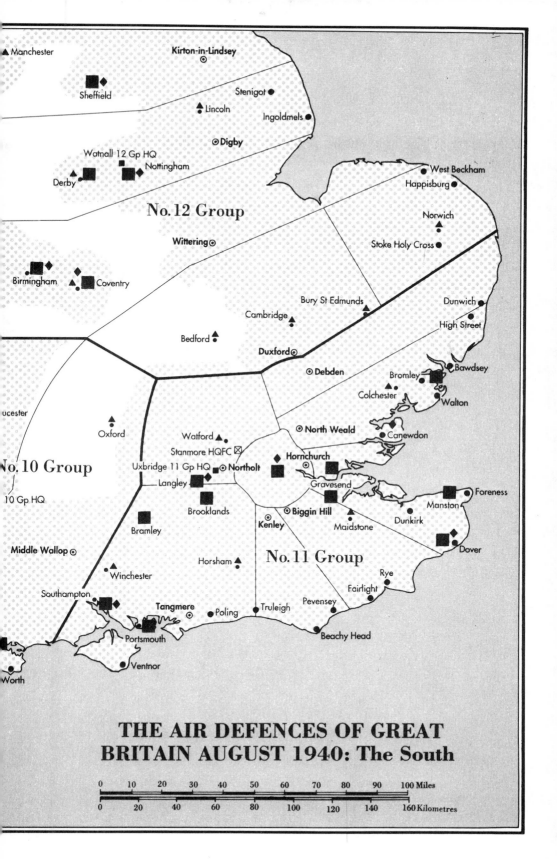

THE AIR DEFENCES OF GREAT
BRITAIN AUGUST 1940: The South

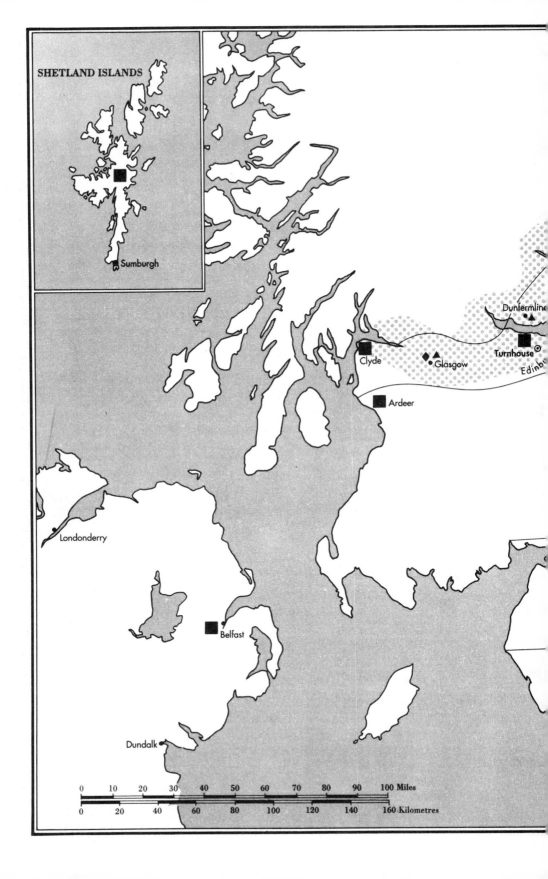

SHETLAND ISLANDS

Sumburgh

Dunfermline

Clyde

Glasgow

Turnhouse

Edinb

Ardeer

Londonderry

Belfast

Dundalk

0    10    20    30    40    50    60    70    80    90    100 Miles

0      20      40      60      80      100      120      140      160 Kilometres

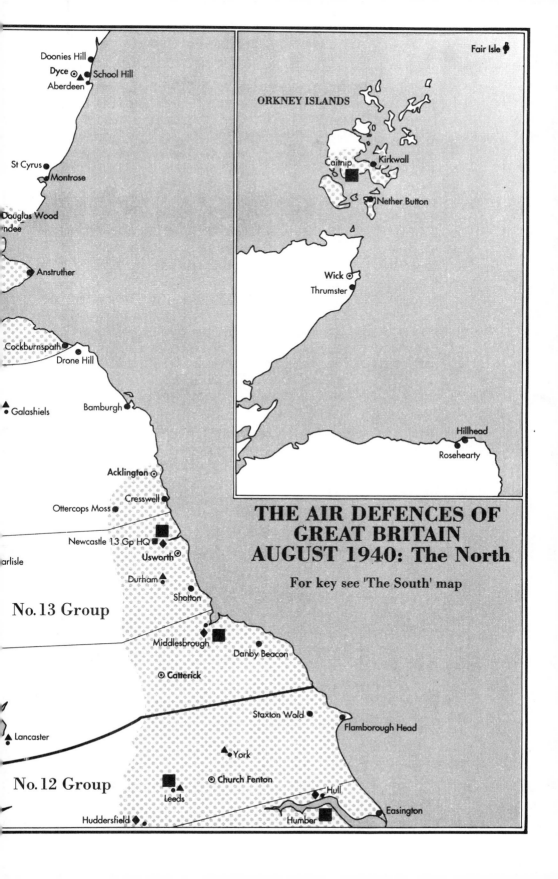

Doonies Hill
Dyce ◉ ▲
Aberdeen ● ● School Hill

St Cyrus ●
● Montrose

Douglas Wood
ndee

● Anstruther

Cockburnspath ●
Drone Hill ●

▲ Galashiels
●

Bamburgh ●

ORKNEY ISLANDS

Fair Isle ⚓

Caitnip
■
Kirkwall ●

● Nether Button

Wick ◉
Thrumster ●

Hillhead ●
Rosehearty ●

Acklington ◉

Cresswell ●

Ottercops Moss ●

Newcastle 13 Gp HQ ◆ ●

■

Usworth ◉

arlisle

Durham ● ▲

Shotton ●

**No. 13 Group**

Middlesbrough ◆ ■

Danby Beacon ●

◉ Catterick

Staxton Wold ●

Flamborough Head ●

▲ Lancaster

▲ ● York

◉ Church Fenton

**No. 12 Group**

■ ▲
Leeds ●

Hull ◆

Huddersfield ◆ ●

Humber ■

Easington ●

# THE AIR DEFENCES OF GREAT BRITAIN
# AUGUST 1940: The North

For key see 'The South' map

reckoned that these forty-six squadrons could ensure that losses of thirteen to sixteen per cent were inflicted on raiders operating from Germany, and that the Luftwaffe – like any other air force – could not sustain a regular casualty rate of this order.

During the last months of peace, as indicated earlier, arrangements had been made to send a BEF to France and to implement the long-standing plan by which four Field Force squadrons from within Fighter Command should accompany it. These four squadrons were accordingly not counted as part of the forty-six. But last-minute requirements had also arisen for Fighter Command to defend Northern Ireland (one squadron), Scapa Flow (two squadrons) and shipping in the North Sea (four squadrons). At the outbreak of war the total number of squadrons projected for Fighter Command was thus four for despatch to France and fifty-three for duties at home.

Towards this total of fifty-seven squadrons Dowding on 3 September 1939 had in fact thirty-nine, of which one or two were non-operational. Of these thirty-nine squadrons, twenty-five were regular and fourteen auxiliary – the latter soon to be indistinguishable in competence, if not in character, from the former. Only twenty-six of the thirty-nine, however, had Hurricanes or Spitfires: the rest were on outdated biplanes (Gladiators, Gauntlets, even a few Hinds) or the makeshift fighter adapted from the Blenheim bomber. And when four Hurricane squadrons – 1, 73, 85 and 87 – left England to form part of the Air Component of the BEF in France, as they did on 8 and 9 September 1939, Dowding's Command was reduced to twenty-two squadrons of first-class fighters out of the agreed requirement of fifty-three. No wonder he was worried.

Several accounts of this situation have assumed that in this the Air Staff had let Dowding down – that they had defaulted on their 'promised' totals, and that it took a long campaign by Dowding, more or less single-handed except for a boost in the final months from Lord Beaverbrook, to get matters right in time for the Battle. This, of course, is nonsense. The full fifty-three squadrons were 'promised' – if that is the right word: 'planned' would be better – for the financial year 1940–41, not September 1939; and twenty-two modern squadrons could not suddenly become fifty-three simply because Hitler plunged the world into war rather earlier than the British Government (or his own generals or Mussolini) had allowed for. It is certainly true that Dowding now waged a vigorous, sustained and absolutely justified campaign to bring his Command up to the fifty-three squadron total as soon as possible; but in this, though he often seemed unaware of it, he had the Air Staff with him all the way.

Commanders and others in the field have a frequent tendency to see their battles as waged against two enemies, the foe in front and their own Service bosses behind. If everything is not provided which seems necessary, it is common to impute the deficiency to the stupidity, sloth or ill-will of those sitting at desks in Whitehall. The fallacy in this thesis, little noticed, is that the officers in the field and the officers in Whitehall are usually the same set of people at different stages of their career. Dowding, for instance, had been 'Air Ministry' from 1930 to 1936, and would willingly have become so again had he been appointed, as he once thought he would be, to succeed Sir Edward Ellington as Chief of the Air Staff. He did not suddenly develop new qualities of energy, wisdom and good will by going out to a Command, nor would he have lost these qualities by returning to Whitehall. Differences between staff in a Service Ministry and commanders in the field in fact usually arise not, as those at the sharp end commonly think, from complacency and obstruction at the centre, but from the different nature of their responsibilities. The commander needs to stress only one set of needs – his own; senior staff at the centre have to decide between or balance competing needs. It is in this light, rather than in the one somewhat luridly cast by his more extravagant champions, that Dowding's dealings with the Air Ministry should be seen.

Dowding's first shots in his campaign to get his fifty-three home-based squadrons before the scheduled date were fired at the Air Ministry within a few days of the outbreak of war. He requested that twelve more fighter squadrons should be formed immediately – which he knew could not be done with Hurricanes or Spitfires, since the output of these was needed to re-equip the Blenheim and biplane squadrons. The Air Staff were already determined on all possible fighter expansion, and after discussion Dowding reduced his request from twelve to eight. But in doing so, in a letter on 16 September, he described the situation in a way which can hardly have failed to give offence. He asserted that the four squadrons which had left his Command during the first week of the war to support the BEF had been sent despite the fact that he had been 'repeatedly told that these squadrons would never be despatched until the safety of the Home Base had been assured'. This claim was far-fetched, to say the least. Dowding had known for months that the BEF would be going to France at the outbreak of war, and that the four squadrons must go soon afterwards unless Britain was under air attack. To maintain in effect that the BEF should receive no RAF fighter protection at all until the Luftwaffe had attacked Britain and been defeated, or until the full total of Home Defence squadrons planned for 1941 was in place, was distinctly overplaying his hand.

Moreover, Dowding went on to refer to recent orders that he should put six more Hurricane squadrons on a mobile basis by 1 January 1940 in case they too were needed in France. 'Although I received assurances', he wrote, 'that these would never be withdrawn from the Defence unless this could be done with safety, I know how much reliance to place on such assurances.'[7] A more tactful man would have avoided impugning his colleagues' good sense and good faith, but tact was not a weapon in Dowding's armoury. He went on to observe that once the squadrons in France had begun to operate intensively they would inevitably suffer much wastage and that in his opinion 'the despatch of the four Field Force squadrons had opened a tap through which will run the total Hurricane output'. This, too, was an exaggeration, but one which displayed percipience. The same could be said of his characteristically forthright conclusion: 'The home defence organisation must not be regarded as co-equal with other Commands, but . . . should receive priority to all other claims until it is firmly assured, since the continued existence of the nation, and its services, depends on the Royal Navy and Fighter Command.'[8]

The combination of Dowding's pressure and the Air Staff's parallel concern soon led to highly important developments. The Chief of the Air Staff, Air Chief Marshal Sir Cyril Newall, an attractive and able leader who had guided the RAF's expansion and presided over the Chiefs of Staff Committee skilfully during the last two years of peace, conferred with Dowding and arrived at acceptable solutions. The eight new squadrons requested by Dowding were to be created. According to the Supply and Organisation Department, aircraft output would permit at that moment the formation of only two, and those on Blenheims; but by dint of utilising these, upgrading and splitting a training squadron, and forming a number of other half-squadrons, all on Blenheims, Dowding's eight could be created in nucleus form for future growth.

Within a few days Newall took still more radical action – action which would upset all previous notions of the correct balance between defence and offence in the RAF, and give it for the first time more fighter than bomber squadrons. On 17 October 1939 he called a meeting of Air Members and Air Staff. He did not begin by discussing how new fighter squadrons could be formed in the absence of any surplus of suitable aircraft. He began by baldly stating that the eight nucleus squadrons he had recently promised Dowding must be formed by the end of the month and that ten more must be formed by the end of November. He then invited discussion on how this could be done.[9]

Like the decision to build a radar chain while technical problems still abounded, this was a decision of flair and courage, which was a vital ingredient of success in the Battle of Britain. These eighteen new squadrons brought Dowding's force, on paper at least, and for the time being, up to the target figure of fifty-three. They could, of course, be formed only on inadequate aircraft mostly taken from bomber resources – Blenheims and even the appallingly vulnerable Battles – and with crews consisting largely of novices. Yet because they were formed in the autumn of 1939, on the wrong aircraft, most of them were operating in the line of battle on the right aircraft – Hurricanes and Spitfires, as the production of these increased – weeks earlier than if their formation had been deferred until the correct equipment came along. In the summer of 1940 those weeks – weeks of extra training and experience – were to prove precious beyond measure.

Though Dowding now seemed assured of his fifty-three squadrons in 1940 instead of 1941, there soon proved to be nothing hard and fast about this total. In February 1940 the four 'trade defence' squadrons formed on Blenheims in 1939 were, by Dowding's wishes, handed over to Coastal Command, so relieving Fighter Command of any responsibility for maritime protection beyond five miles from the coast. This brought Fighter Command's approved objective down to forty-nine squadrons; but during March and April 1940, in view of the thinness of the defences in the extreme north and west, the fact that more squadrons might be needed for France, and an anticipated rise in the German bomber force to 2,250 aircraft, the Air Staff began to contemplate a new target of sixty squadrons for September 1940 and eighty squadrons for April 1941.

Meanwhile, Dowding had in fact lost two of his fully operational squadrons. Signs of a forthcoming German attack in the West in mid-November 1939 – an attack projected but cancelled – had resulted, in the continued absence of serious air attack on Britain, in the despatch of two AAF Gladiator squadrons – 607 and 615 – to join the Air Component of the BEF. By the end of March 1940, however, all the approved new squadrons had formed, and, with the loss of the four to Coastal Command and the extra two to the Air Component, Dowding had under his command, in one condition or another, forty-seven squadrons. This was twelve more than six months earlier. Moreover, inside another two months the number of Hurricane and Spitfire squadrons within his force, twenty-two in mid-September, had risen to thirty-eight. This considerable feat of supply and organisation on the part of the Air Ministry, the factories and Maintenance Command has not received the recognition it seems to deserve.

The 'Phoney War' could not last for ever. In the early hours of 9 April 1940 Hitler's forces seized Denmark and the main ports and airfields of Norway. The bonus of time, so productive for Britain's air defences, was at last running out.

# 6

*Surviving the Storm*

As if Dowding were not worried enough at six of his squadrons going to France before he had his full fifty-three at home, in the spring of 1940 he had to satisfy a further demand: to provide fighter support for the Allied expeditionary force intended to occupy the iron-ore fields of north Sweden (under cover of helping the Finns against the Russians – what Chamberlain called 'killing two birds with one stone'). When the Finnish resistance, mercifully for the Allies, collapsed and the Germans, eager to acquire offensive bases for war against Britain, seized the ports and airfields of Norway, part of the projected expedition was employed on the new task of trying to expel the invaders. Fighter protection was to come from one of Dowding's Gladiator squadrons – 263.

Intended to support the troops who had landed south at Trondheim it attempted, for lack of other landing grounds, to operate from a frozen lake. Much of its equipment, meant to be sent up in advance from the nearest port, had not arrived. There was no petrol bowser, no acid for the uncharged accumulators in the starter trolleys, no spare oxygen supply, no mobile radar set, and no ground defences other than two light guns. And the Luftwaffe was established within comfortable flying distance.

The squadron flew in from the carrier *Glorious* during the evening of 24 April. The next morning wheels were frozen to the ice, controls were locked and engines refused to start. By heroic efforts the CO, Squadron Leader J. W. ('Baldy') Donaldson, Flight Lieutenant Stuart Mills* and

*Later Group Captain R. S. Mills DFC.

81

a few others got airborne and took toll of the repeatedly attacking enemy. But by evening the bombs of the Ju 88s and He 111s had reduced the snow-cleared runway to ruins and most of the Gladiators to shattered wrecks. The next morning the five surviving aircraft, operating from a tiny plateau near the coast, fought till all but one were out of action – and for that there was no petrol. The pilots, preserved for a while, reached home a few days later by sea. The whole affair had been a glaring example of what Dowding most feared: having to waste his squadrons overseas in circumstances far removed from his carefully planned scientific air defence system at home – circumstances almost inviting disaster.

Worse was to follow. Driven from central Norway, the Allies still hoped to hold the north and to recover the isolated port of Narvik. But when Germany invaded France and the Low Countries on 10 May, and things began to go badly, this hope disappeared. Instead, the Allies now planned only to take Narvik, a key port for the iron-ore trade to Germany, destroy the harbour facilities and then depart. To protect the attacking Allied forces Dowding now had to provide two squadrons – the unfortunate 263, with a fresh supply of Gladiators, and 46 (CO Squadron Leader K. B. Cross),* on Hurricanes.

This time things had been better prepared, including two landing grounds. In a fortnight of hectic and heroic endeavour the two squadrons flew over 300 sorties, fought ninety-five combats and accounted for two dozen or more enemy aircraft. The Allies duly took the port, wrecked it and left. Then came the final tragedy: all the aircraft safely aboard the *Glorious* on 7 June – including the Hurricanes, officially deemed unsuitable for deck landing and flown on now after a spirited plea by Cross – only for the fatal encounter next day with the *Scharnhorst* and *Gneisenau*. A few pilots, mostly wounded, had sailed in other ships. Of those with the *Glorious*, Cross and Flight Lieutenant P. G. Jameson alone survived – after three days in an open float during which all but seven of the twenty-nine occupants died.

At a time when he was moving heaven and earth to build up his forces at home, the Norwegian fiasco cost Dowding three whole squadrons of valuable fighters and almost two squadrons of invaluable pilots. And this on top of what had happened, and was happening, in France.[1]

During the 'Phoney War' the six fighter squadrons in France had experienced, to their disappointment, only occasional encounters with

*Later Air Chief Marshal Sir Kenneth Cross KCB, CBE, DSO, DFC.

the enemy. Nos 1 and 73 Squadrons, which left the Air Component in October to work with the Advanced Air Striking Force (AASF) (of Battle and Blenheim bombers) east of Reims, had a far busier time than their comrades who remained in the north. Even so, weeks elapsed before, on 30 October 1939, 1 Squadron drew first blood by shooting down a Do 17. Not until 23 November was there a multiple combat, with six 17s – an episode in which, after his crew had jumped, one of the German pilots climbed into the navigator's seat and shot down his assailant. In the best tradition of the time he was retrieved from French captivity and honourably dined in 1 Squadron's mess.

The first serious encounter with German fighters, on 22 December, was unpromising. Four Me 109s jumped a section of 73 Squadron, on patrol near Metz, and shot down two of the Hurricanes. Among the lessons drawn were the need for clearer identification markings – one of the British pilots had not known friend from foe – and for the new constant-speed airscrews to be fitted as quickly as possible to improve Hurricane performance. More satisfactory was the shooting down on 29 March 1940 of one of Goering's vaunted new 'destroyers', when a section of 1 Squadron got in among nine Me 110s on escort duty near the Franco-German frontier. The victorious pilots told the commander of British Air Forces in France, Air Marshal A. S. Barratt,* at a celebratory dinner he gave them in Paris, that the big twin-engined fighters were faster than their Hurricanes and had a higher ceiling, but were less manoeuvrable. Up to 10,000 feet, the pilots reported, a Hurricane could easily turn inside a 110, whose rear-gunner had a hard job bringing his guns to bear on an attacker.

During the eight months of comparative quiet little was accomplished in the sporadic air fighting but much was learnt. Among other things, 1 Squadron found out the advantage of painting the underside of wings light blue, like the Luftwaffe, to hinder detection from below. The same squadron also soon discovered that the standard recommended harmonisation of the Hurricane's eight guns to achieve converging fire at 400 yards was useless against the enemy fighters: harmonisation at 250 yards, which of course required the pilot to go in closer, achieved far more lethal results.

Equally important was the change in the Hurricane's propeller. The need had long been appreciated to improve on the original fixed-pitch, two-blade, wooden version, but now experience in France lent

*Later Air Chief Marshal Sir Arthur Barratt, KCB, MC. BAFF was the overall Command responsible for both the AASF and the Component.

additional urgency. As output permitted the variable pitch (fine and coarse), de Havilland airscrew, or later and better the Rotol, adjustable pitch, constant-speed airscrew, was fitted to all the Hurricanes in France, manufacturers' parties flying from England to do the work (and incidentally instruct the squadron ground crews) on the spot.

Together with the fitting of armour-plate behind the pilot's seat, and the re-equipment of the two Gladiator squadrons with Hurricanes – still in progress when the Germans struck – all these improvements, coupled with relative immunity during the long hours of patrol, gave the six fighter squadrons in France the confidence that they could hold their own with the Me 109s, outmanoeuvre the Me 110s and have a field day with unescorted Do 17s.

But actual experience in combat, so crucial, remained thinly spread. Several of the pilots of 1 and 73 Squadrons, with the AASF, had it, but hardly any of the pilots with the Component. From 10 May 1940 all alike were to get more than enough.[2]

A German invasion of France or the Low Countries was the agreed signal for four more British fighter squadrons to reinforce the six already in France. Nos 3, 79 and 501 (County of Gloucester) Squadrons duly flew across on 10 May, 504 (County of Nottingham) two days later. They at once found themselves in a hornet's nest as the Luftwaffe struck against the Allied airfields. No. 3, joining the Component in the afternoon, was in combat three times before nightfall. No. 501, sent down to the AASF, was in action within half an hour of landing. By that time most of the squadrons already in France had been frantically busy since first light. Aircraft of 607 Squadron fought nine separate engagements during the day. Many pilots flew three or four sorties, some six or seven.

Equally active that day, though in a less dangerous sphere, were the politicians in London. Chamberlain having resigned that morning after a battering in the House over Norway, Churchill, 'walking with destiny', was forming a National Coalition. By midnight his success was assured, and Britain had a government fit to face the perils ahead.

For more than a week the air operations continued at maximum pitch, while the BEF moved swiftly forward into Belgium – and slowly back. During the first seven days, though a far greater number of the Luftwaffe perished, at least fifty Hurricanes were lost. But the attrition in France of what he inevitably still regarded as 'his' squadrons was not Dowding's only worry. He had also to provide support direct from

England. On the very first day, aircraft of Fighter Command flew forty-four sorties to protect the French Seventh Army in its forward dash along the coast to the mouth of the Scheldt, escorted a bombing raid against Ju 52s on the beaches near The Hague and tried to shoot up German bombers on the aerodrome at Waalhaven. Six Blenheims of 600 (City of London) Squadron attempted this unenviable task, the War Cabinet having ruled out the use of bombers for fear they might kill Dutch civilians. A dozen Me 110s were patrolling high above the airfield. Five of the six Blenheims 'failed to return'.[3]

Within twenty-four hours Dowding's forces were thus being sucked into the battle across the Channel even more completely than he had feared. But far greater agonies lay ahead. Within another twenty-four hours pleas began to pour in from all quarters – from the King of the Belgians, the Queen of the Netherlands, the French, the BEF, Air Marshal Barratt, the Component – for more fighter support. From only one source could it possibly come: Fighter Command.

In response, and to avoid detaching complete squadrons, the War Cabinet agreed on 13 May to send over an extra thirty-two Hurricanes and pilots, taken from different units. They instantly became replacements, not reinforcements. The French Air Force, hopelessly inferior to the Luftwaffe in numbers as in most of its equipment, tried valiantly but could do nothing to stem the tide. The cry for more fighters redoubled, and on 14 May reached a climax. That evening the French Premier, Paul Reynaud, informed London that the Germans had broken through south of Sedan and asked for ten more fighter squadrons to be sent over immediately – if possible that day.[4] The following morning he phoned Churchill, told him the battle was lost and repeated his request.[5]

To Reynaud's appeal were added further pleas from Lord Gort, Commander-in-Chief of the BEF, and from Barratt. The British pilots, too, conscious that they were inflicting losses in combat far exceeding those they were suffering, longed for help. Paul Richey* of 1 Squadron, in one of the earliest (and best) accounts of those desperate days, described their feelings: '. . . we hadn't wanted this bloody awful war . . . we had been forced to fight. "And now that we are fighting," we thought, "we'll teach you rotten Huns how to fight. We'll make you wish to Christ you'd never *heard* of the aeroplane! We'll teach you the facts of war!" And we knew we could – *if we were reinforced*. . . . We

---

*Later Wing Commander Paul Richey DFC.

were sure we had the measure of the Germans. . . . We knew the Huns couldn't keep going indefinitely at that rate, but we also knew we couldn't keep it up much longer without help. We were confident that help would soon come. *We reckoned without Dowding.*[6]

Though the hard-pressed pilots, perhaps fortunately, could not know it at the time, Dowding was indeed moving heaven and earth to stop more fighters going to France. Since he was several squadrons short of the number considered necessary for the defence of Britain, it was his duty to try to hold on to those he had – just as it was the duty of Gort, Barratt and the French to plead for them. On 14 May, trying to help in some other way, he wrote to the Air Staff giving his opinion – it had been requested – that Bomber Command should immediately open an offensive against oil targets in Germany, which might have the effect of drawing German air attack away from France and on to Britain. He bitterly opposed any idea of supporting France by sending more fighter squadrons. He wrote:

The Hurricane tap is now turned full on and you will not be able to resist the pressure to send Hurricanes to France until I have been bled white and am in no condition to withstand the bombing attack which will inevitably be made on this country as soon as our powers of resistance fall below a level to which we are already perilously close.[7]

That same day Dowding saw Newall, who fully shared his anxieties but also had responsibilities to the BEF and the British Air Forces in France, and asked if he might put his views before the highest authorities. This was arranged for the following morning, 15 May, when he was taken into a Chiefs of Staff meeting with Churchill in the chair. So came about the famous episode, much written of as stemming the flow of fighters to France and thereby making victory possible in the Battle of Britain. Though it was important, it was not in fact as immediately decisive as that. Nor was it the scene of A. J. P. Taylor's imagination in which Dowding, having produced a graph of the fighter wastage and told Churchill that not a single fighter more should go to France, gently lays down his pencil on the table in a way that indicates he will resign if his views are not accepted. 'The War Cabinet cringed,' writes Taylor, in this instance more poet than historian, 'and Dowding's pencil won the Battle of Britain.'[8] What spoils this story is that Dowding, as he made clear to his biographer Robert Wright, was far too conscientious and aware of his awesome responsibilities to have the slightest intention of resigning.[9]

What undoubtedly happened was that Dowding produced figures with a forward intimation of nil reserves, and speaking with great firmness expressed his belief that with his existing force the RAF and the Navy could protect Britain from invasion. But only with his existing force: he was 'absolutely opposed to parting with a single additional Hurricane'.[10] He also urged opening up the bombing war against Germany, to draw retaliation on Britain and take pressure off the French. His statements, he felt, were well received – though he later expressed disappointment that Newall, who was doubtless worrying about Barratt, added nothing in support.

A meeting of the War Cabinet then followed immediately, at which it was agreed to send no further fighter squadrons to France. It was also agreed to bomb targets in the Ruhr that night. Dowding had carried conviction on both points.

On the very next day, however, other counsels prevailed. Barratt had again spoken to Newall and thought he could 'stop the rot' if he were sent four additional fighter squadrons at once. Newall accordingly told the Chiefs of Staff that despite the previous day's decision he felt he must recommend the despatch of further fighters to the extent of four squadrons – in the form of eight half-squadrons, to minimise the damage to Fighter Command. His fellow Chiefs of Staff agreed, as did the War Cabinet later in the day.[11] Churchill was all for sending six squadrons rather than four, but failed to budge his colleagues. Within twenty-four hours the eight half-squadrons were with the desperately hard-pressed Component.

Of these momentous days there is an account in Churchill's war history in which a truly astonishing statement appears. 'Air Marshal Dowding', wrote Churchill, '. . . had declared to me that with twenty-five squadrons of fighters he could defend the Island against the whole might of the German Air Force, but that with less he would be overwhelmed.'[12] Throughout this account Churchill implies that though he thought more fighters should be sent to France, he and his colleagues would never have permitted Fighter Command to fall below Dowding's twenty-five-squadron minimum. But Dowding, as he informed Robert Wright, cannot possibly have made any such statement to Churchill:[13] he might have said forty-five squadrons, or even under pressure thirty-five, but not conceivably twenty-five. If this was more than a lapse of memory on Churchill's part, if in fact Churchill really believed in May and June 1940 that the safe minimum for the air defence of Great Britain *was* twenty-five squadrons, there were clearly even greater dangers at the time than has customarily been thought.

Be that as it may, the pressure from France still mounted. Late at night on 16 May Churchill, after attending a meeting of the Supreme War Council in Paris, signalled to London urging that another six fighter squadrons should go to France, so making (with the eight half-squadrons sent that day) the ten for which Reynaud had asked. But here Newall rescued matters. At the War Cabinet meeting called at 11 p.m. to discuss Churchill's message, he pointed out that the RAF bases in France, under constant air attack and with limited servicing facilities, could not possibly operate more than three extra squadrons. To meet Churchill's views and sustain the French, but at the same time to limit the loss to Fighter Command, he recommended that three squadrons should fly from England each morning and operate from bases in France, returning home afterwards, and that three more should do the same in the afternoon. This was agreed by the War Cabinet and put into practice from the following day, 17 May.[14] Meanwhile, the squadrons in France continued their heroic struggle against hugely greater forces. One of the replacement pilots, Flight Lieutenant Ian ('Widge') Gleed,* sent out to join 87 Squadron, was credited with two kills on his first day of action, 18 May, and four kills and a probable on his next.[15]

But by that time the whole Allied position in the north was collapsing as Guderian's panzers, exploiting the breakthrough they had made in the Ardennes with the help of the Luftwaffe's dive-bombers, cut a swathe across France and headed for the English Channel. The BEF, attacked frontally and at the same time cut off from the French forces south of the German advance, could only retire. Meanwhile, the Component lost its forward landing grounds and suffered incessant air attack on its bases farther back. For all it could now achieve, it could operate just as well from England. On 19 and 20 May the remnants of its battered reconnaissance and fighter squadrons flew home. The lasting impression of Flying Officer M. M. Stephens, of 3 Squadron, was of 'chaotic conditions, a fight against overwhelming odds and appalling communications – or none at all. One's memory is of the desperate, untiring efforts of our gallant ground crews to keep the aircraft airworthy – cannibalising damaged aircraft, improvising and working all hours of the day and night.'[16]

In their ten days of intensive operations the Component fighter pilots

*Later Wing Commander Gleed DSO, DFC.

88

had taken a magnificent toll of the enemy. Of the 250 Hurricanes they used during that time, however, only sixty-six returned. No more than seventy-five had been lost in combat; the rest, damaged or otherwise unserviceable, were unfit to fly back. For Fighter Command, this was tantamount to losing nearly half its entire strength in this vitally important aircraft. The 'Hurricane tap', as Dowding had foreseen, had indeed been 'turned full on'.

Up to this point Dowding had had ample reason, despite the War Cabinet decision he had helped to secure on 15 May, to fear that his squadrons would continue to be drawn into the maelstrom of France. In a letter written after that meeting to his principal commander, Keith Park at 11 Group, he had said, 'I do not know how this morning's work will stand the test of time'; and in this spirit he had followed up his appearance before the Chiefs of Staff with a letter the following morning to the Air Ministry.[17] It has become the most famous letter in RAF history. In it he reminded the Air Council that fifty-two fighter squadrons – he could have said fifty-three – had been considered necessary to defend Britain, and that his force was now down to the equivalent of thirty-six. Very cleverly, he asked to be told what the War Cabinet and the Air Ministry regarded as the minimum fighter strength on which they were 'prepared to stake the existence of the country'; and he went on to seek an assurance that once this level had been reached 'not one fighter will be sent across the Channel however urgent and insistent the appeals for help may be'. He ended by expressing his belief

that if an adequate fighter force is kept in this country, if the Fleet remains in being, and if Home Forces are suitably organised to resist invasion, we should be able to carry on the war single-handed for some time, if not indefinitely. But if the Home Defence force is drained away in desperate attempts to remedy the situation in France, defeat in France will involve the final, complete and irremediable defeat of this country.

This was powerful stuff which Newall, who had that day recommended the despatch of the eight half-squadrons, quickly used to good effect. The day after receiving it he circulated Dowding's letter to his fellow Chiefs of Staff with a note asking them to support his views in the War Cabinet.[18] The views for which he sought support were almost identical with those in Dowding's letter. He stressed that the Home requirements had been assessed at fifty-three fighter squadrons for defence against bombers operating from Germany, and that Fighter Command was now down to thirty-seven squadrons and liable to be faced with attacks also from bases in occupied Holland and Norway. Of these thirty-seven squadrons, many had already suffered losses over the continent and six had just begun to operate daily from bases in France. 'In the light of the foregoing considerations', Newall continued, 'I can reach no other conclusion than that we have already reached the absolute limit of the assistance that we can afford to France. . . .'

Newall then went on to raise the issue, 'grave to the last degree', which had been tormenting him and his colleagues for the last four days – that if further help were denied, 'then it is not beyond the bounds of possibility that the French Army may give up the struggle'. Meeting this dilemma squarely, he concluded:

I do not believe that to throw in a few more squadrons whose loss might vitally weaken the fighter line at home would make the difference between victory and defeat in France. . . . It can, however, be said with absolute certainty that while the collapse of France would not necessarily mean the ultimate victory of Germany, the collapse of Great Britain would inevitably do so.

Coming on top of the ever worsening situation in France, this decided matters. The Chiefs of Staff and the War Cabinet accepted Newall's views. The next day, 19 May, Churchill minuted General Ismay: 'No more fighters will leave the country whatever the need in France.'[19] And a few hours later the flow was reversed: the remains of the Component began to fly home.

In view of the narrow margin by which the Battle of Britain was won, it is clear that these decisions were a key factor in that victory. Had the flow of fighters to France continued, Fighter Command could have been weakened to the point of failure in the great test to come. Desperately needed though they were, and great as were their achievements in destroying enemy aircraft despite the lack of adequate warning and control systems, the British fighters in France could not possibly make up for the Allied inferiority on the ground. Of the Armée de l'Air, which by 16 May was reported in the Supreme War Council to have lost 500 of its 650 fighters,[20] one of its most brilliant officers, Antoine de St Exupéry, wrote: 'Crew after crew was being offered up as a sacrifice. It was as if you dashed glassfuls of water into a forest fire in the hope of putting it out.'[21] Dowding's metaphor was similar about the British effort: 'Water in the desert sand.'

The credit for stopping the flow of fighters to France – and for stopping it after only a few days of operations – has traditionally been assigned to Dowding, with the implication that if Churchill had had his way all would have been lost. The reality was rather more complicated. Dowding's influence on the decision was unquestionably great: his singleness of purpose and clarity of vision, his effectiveness of exposition in his letters and in his meeting with Churchill and the Chiefs of Staff, his absolutely sustained, unwavering opposition from first to last – from even before the fighting began – made his contribution unforgettable. He stood rock-like amid swirling currents. But Newall, who had responsibilities to the British land and air forces in France as well as to Fighter Command, had the harder task; and it was his opinion, and his advocacy, which produced the final decision, only eight days after the opening of the German offensive, to send no more fighters to France 'whatever the need'.

So it was Dowding and Newall between them, then. But perhaps the sheer onrush of events was a still more potent factor. Imagine the Belgians, the BEF and the French in the north holding their forward positions only a little longer – say a fortnight – than they did. What pressures then might not have mounted to give such heroic resistance more protection in the air from the Luftwaffe – protection which would surely have made not the slightest difference in the end? Not only the firmness and good sense of Dowding and Newall, but also the unprecedented, unimaginable swiftness of the German advance saved the main strength of Fighter Command for the Battle of Britain.

By 21 May Guderian's tanks had reached the mouth of the Somme at Abbeville, completely severing the main French forces to the south of the advance from the Allied armies to the north. Mercifully the order to Gort (dictated by Churchill on behalf of his bemused colleagues) to move southwards to join up with the main French armies could not possibly be carried out: Gort tried, but was far too closely engaged in front and too well aware of crumbling Belgian support on his left to move his main forces anywhere except backwards and northwards in the direction of the coast. Within a few days the BEF was withdrawing towards its last main link with England – Dunkirk.

The call to Fighter Command was now to give all possible support from England. This included a new duty. On 12 May five AASF Battles out of five had been lost in a single bombing operation, on 17 May eleven out of twelve Bomber Command Blenheims. In flat contradiction to all pre-war assumptions, British bombers in daylight could neither look after themselves nor survive with only the help of offensive sweeps by half-a-dozen fighters intended (but often failing) to coincide with the approach of the bombers to the target area. From 20 May Fighter Command was regularly required to supply close escort to daylight bombing.

This, however, was only part of the Command's involvement. Its main task, for which Dowding had now to use his Spitfires and Defiants as well as his Hurricanes, was to fly offensive patrols over the Channel ports, the Belgian coast and as much of the diminishing BEF area as could be covered. It was already heavily engaged on this before the BEF's full evacuation began, when only the 'useless mouths' were being brought home. Such famous names in the RAF canon as A. G. 'Sailor' Malan and Bob Stanford Tuck registered successes over France as early as 21 and 22 May. On 23 May 11 Group, which provided the forces for all these operations,* flew 250 sorties and lost ten pilots. The following day, when 54 Squadron (Spitfires) fought its first big battle against seventy escorted bombers near Dunkirk and then three hours later took on twelve Me 109s near Calais, 11 Group claimed fifteen enemy aircraft destroyed but had to post another ten pilots missing. Four returned later, but the loss was still sixteen skilled pilots in two days.

It was during this critical period, when the German armour had just reached the Channel, that an event occurred which was later to be of untold benefit to the Allied cause. On 22 May the cryptographers at the Government Code and Cypher School, Bletchley Park, who had already enjoyed similar success during the Norwegian campaign, cracked the new key used by the Luftwaffe two days earlier for their top-secret wireless messages enciphered on the Enigma machine. From then on, during the rest of the campaign in France, something like a thousand messages a day emanating from the Luftwaffe in their highest security codes were intercepted and read by the British intelligence services, in addition to all the signals in lower grade cipher which were already part of their standard fare. For a number of reasons this breakthrough did not produce great results straight away: Luftwaffe Command orders were usually sent by landline, which was secure, and by the time the multifarious fragments of information from the wireless intercepts had been translated, collated and interpreted it was usually too late to make immediate operational use of them. Nevertheless, the information soon helped the Air Ministry to build up a more complete and reliable picture

*The provision of reconnaissance and the co-ordination of bomber, fighter and coastal operations during the evacuation was the responsibility of an improvised 'Back Component' headquarters at Hawkinge.

of the Luftwaffe's organisation, methods and order of battle than ever before. In the days ahead this was to be of significant, though far from decisive, importance in the Battle of Britain; and in the forthcoming evacuation it enabled some of the shipping movements, some of the more successful air patrols, and the jamming of communications between the German dive-bomber units, to be undertaken with the foreknowledge of the Luftwaffe's intentions.[22]

'Operation Dynamo', the full evacuation from Dunkirk, was set in motion during the evening of 26 May. The next day the air fighting grew hotter still. Goering had claimed the final destruction of the BEF as his prerogative, much to the dismay of General Albert Kesselring, whose by now depleted *Luftflotte* 2 was denied the recuperation it sorely needed. Hitler had agreed, according to Goering, partly because the German Army would round up the British prisoners in too gentlemanly a fashion: the Luftwaffe would teach them a lesson they would not easily forget.[23]

From bases in Holland and France, but also from Germany – a limiting factor – the Luftwaffe set to work against Dunkirk, the shipping and the troops awaiting evacuation. To thwart its activities 11 Group, which had also to make sweeps inland and escort bombers, tried at first to supply continuous cover: every fifty minutes throughout the entire day its aircraft patrolled the Calais–Gravelines line. But with only sixteen squadrons made available by Dowding, this meant that the patrols were at single-squadron strength and could be heavily outnumbered. According to Major Kreipe of KG2, whose unit lost eleven out of its twenty-seven Dorniers on 27 May, the British pilots 'attacked with the fury of maniacs';[24] but though 11 Group sent over 287 sorties that day and claimed thirty-seven enemy aircraft for the loss of fourteen, the Luftwaffe began its task impressively. It sank only two small vessels but made life hell for the waiting troops and virtually destroyed the port of Dunkirk.

In the following days Park was able to strengthen his patrols, but only by leaving gaps between them. On 28 May, by which time Dowding had allowed him an extra two squadrons, he arranged the patrols at two-squadron strength, and from 29 May, after a suggestion to Dowding from the Air Staff, at up to four-squadron strength. But Dowding, his eye as ever on his main task, gave him no more squadrons – so Park made the patrols stronger, with longer intervals – up to an hour – between them. The British pilots enjoyed the bigger formations, the Luftwaffe the gaps.

Each day 11 Group flew some 300 sorties, leading on most days to major combats. On 29 May, when the Defiants of 264 Squadron had their first and last big success, the British fighters beat off three big raids, but failed to intercept two others, during which the Luftwaffe played havoc with shipping. Poor visibility during the next thirty-six hours kept the Luftwaffe largely grounded, but by the afternoon of 31 May it was up in force again. In one of the biggest combats, when 213 Squadron reported an enemy formation of 100 bombers and fighters, the British lost five Hurricanes, three Defiants and a Spitfire. In the turmoil of another engagement, Spitfires fired on Hurricanes.

Taking advantage of the gaps between patrols, on 1 June the Luftwaffe enjoyed its greatest success since 27 May. Instructed now to concentrate on the shipping – bombs on the beaches were losing their impact in soft sand – it sank among other vessels three destroyers and two big transports. The Ju 87s, with their pinpoint accuracy, scored heavily. Together with the installation of German artillery commanding the central approach to Dunkirk, this caused Vice-Admiral Dover, in charge of 'Dynamo', to restrict evacuation to the hours of darkness. This was a blessing in disguise: Fighter Command could now concentrate its patrols for the vital periods of dusk and early morning, as the Allied shipping approached and left Dunkirk. At around 8 a.m. on 2 June, the biggest patrol that Park had yet sent over, five squadrons strong, met some sixty bombers, dive-bombers and fighters. In a desperate mêlée, during which the evacuation ships escaped all damage, the British pilots claimed twenty-two enemy aircraft for the loss of seven Spitfires. Later in the day the Luftwaffe three times attempted major attacks on shipping. Three times the patrols successfully intercepted.

That night the evacuation of the BEF was completed, but many thousands of the French 1st Army had still to be taken off. Mercifully on 3 and 4 June mist blanketed the Channel and the chief danger to Park's pilots came not from the Luftwaffe but from the difficulty of landing back in Britain. On 4 June 72 Squadron, returning to Manston, nearly hit the cliffs. After trying Hawkinge and Littlestone, where the conditions were no better, three of the Spitfires got down at Shoreham, one finished up in a field and four crashed in renewed attempts to land at Manston. But what was bad for flying was good for the evacuation, which went ahead until German pressure made it pointless for the French forces still heroically holding the Dunkirk perimeter to offer further resistance. When 'Dynamo' finally ended during the afternoon of 4 June over 338,000 troops, two-thirds of them British, had been snatched – minus all equipment – from what threatened to be the biggest military disaster in the history of Great Britain.

The many factors that made possible this 'miracle of deliverance' included the brave resistance on the perimeter, the two-and-a-half day delay imposed on the German armour by Hitler and Rundstedt, Commander of Army Group A, the poor visibility on four of the days and, of course, the supreme efforts of the naval vessels, the merchantmen and the 'little ships'. But no list of contributors should omit the RAF, which during the nine days of the evacuation flew 171 reconnaissance, 651 bomber and 2,739 fighter sorties directly connected with it, and in the process lost ninety-eight of the Hurricanes and Spitfires intended for the defence of Great Britain. Though Dowding never allowed Park more than eighteen squadrons on any one day, by the end of the nine days every Hurricane and Spitfire squadron in Fighter Command except three had taken part in the fighting. The gain in experience was immense – more than one squadron learnt to harmonise its guns at 250 yards instead of 400 yards and to forget about text-book forms of attack – but the wear and tear on Fighter Command, and for that matter on Coastal Command and the daylight forces of Bomber Command, was also immense.

On 4 June, as the evacuation finished, Churchill told the Commons that there was a 'victory inside this deliverance – gained by the Air Force'. He went on to say that the Luftwaffe had 'paid four-fold' for any losses they inflicted, and that 'all of our types and all our pilots have been vindicated as superior to what they at present have to face'.[25] These last two statements were typical, and sincerely believed, exaggerations of the time; but without question the RAF had frustrated many of the Luftwaffe's attacks and inflicted on it severe losses – some 200 aircraft and over 300 aircrew[26] – which weakened it for the struggle ahead. Adolf Galland, commenting after the war, said that Dunkirk 'should have been an emphatic warning to the leaders of the Luftwaffe'.[27] And the morale-boosting optimism that Churchill purveyed in his speech of 4 June had more than enough basis in fact to justify his inspired prophecy:

When we consider how much greater would be our advantage in defending the air above this Island against an overseas attack, I must say I find in these facts a sure basis upon which practical and reassuring thought may rest. I will pay my tribute to these young airmen. The great French Army was very largely, for the time being, cast back and disturbed by the onrush of a few thousand of armoured vehicles. May it not also be that the cause of civilisation itself will be defended by the skill and devotion of a few thousand airmen?[28]

In view of the great effort that had been made it was distressing that so many of the rescued soldiers should have been unaware of it. Bombed on their retreat to Dunkirk, on the beaches or on the ships, they had been fully conscious of the presence of the Luftwaffe, but not of the RAF, which had often operated at some distance and above cloud. A bomb falling close at hand is, of course, a far more memorable experience than the faint chatter of a distant fighter's machine-guns. In the resulting bitterness soldiers jeered at airmen in the streets of Dover; and Sir John Dill, newly appointed Chief of the Imperial General Staff, felt it necessary to visit Army camps and explain that the RAF really had done something.

One with painful experience of all this was Group Captain Victor Goddard,* among the last of the Component officers to leave France. He attributed the Army's hostility in part to the extreme inability, even reluctance, of Allied anti-aircraft gunners to distinguish friendly from hostile aircraft. Goddard records an incident on 26 May, when a British soldier yelled at him: 'Where's your bloody air force?' ' "Shot down by your bloody ack-ack," I retorted, with a resentment as futile as his.' Goddard goes on to comment: 'What a terrible training failure this was. . . . Speaking generally, the Army at that time – and for that matter the Navy too – fired at every aeroplane that came near enough to be shot at. . . .'[29]

Another witness at first hand was Alan Deere, whose experiences during these days vividly illustrate the strain that Dunkirk imposed on the pilots of Fighter Command. After flying uneventful patrols with 54 Squadron on the Calais–Dunkirk line from 16 May, interspersed with long boring hours at readiness in his cockpit at Hornchurch, Deere got into serious action on 23 May. His first patrol, a fruitless one, was at dawn. While breakfasting he was then called upon, with a fellow pilot, to cover a two-seat trainer on a mission to pick up the stranded CO of 74 Squadron from Calais-Marck airfield. In the midst of the rescue Me 109s intervened, but Deere shot two down, and all three British aircraft got home safely. Then came lunch, after which Deere was up again, on a squadron patrol inland of Dunkirk–Calais. Spotting some bombers, the squadron moved into one of the prescribed attack patterns ('No. 5') only to be immediately set upon by 109s, which gave

*Later Air Marshal Sir Victor Goddard KCB, CBE.

Deere the opportunity for another 'kill'. But his day's work was not yet done: after another meal at Hornchurch there was still an evening's patrol to fly over Boulogne, with a landing in the dark on return. So for Deere that day it was duty from 3.30 a.m. to nightfall, four patrols, seven-and-a-half hours' flying and a very satisfactory 'bag' of three of the enemy.

The next day, 24 May, Deere flew another three patrols and was again in combat. Two days after that, by which time 54 Squadron was reduced to 'eight aircraft and twelve very tired pilots', he shot down two Me 110s during an early patrol, only to suffer the shock of a cannon shell from a 109 hitting his starboard wing. Despite the gaping hole and a punctured tyre, he made Hornchurch safely.

'After the ground crew, for whom no praise, however much, is too great, had managed to get eight Spitfires serviceable,' Deere was off again the following morning, 27 May, patrolling near Dunkirk and viewing with dismay the huge pall of smoke and flame from the bombed oil tanks. But the evening of 28 May at length brought promise of relief. After his last patrol, by which time 'the surviving pilots in 54 Squadron were literally on their last legs', he heard that the squadron was to do one more patrol the following morning, at dawn, and then change places with 41 Squadron, at Catterick.

That final patrol, flown as part of a wing of three squadrons, proved one too many. Bullets from a Do 17 that Deere was chasing hit his engine and smashed the coolant system. Through a mist of glycol spray and white smoke he managed to put down on one of the beaches, hitting his head violently on the windscreen and gashing his forehead as he did so. A few minutes after he had recovered consciousness and scrambled out, his Spitfire burst into flames.

Helped by local people Deere then set off for Ostend, but was soon caught up in a flood of refugees moving the opposite way towards Dunkirk. A bus, a 'borrowed' bicycle, a lift in an Army lorry and the last mile or two on foot got him to this new destination, where he joined the bedraggled thousands awaiting evacuation. One of his first acts was to attempt, in vain, to stop British gunners shooting at a Spitfire. Knowing how badly pilots were needed back in action, he then tried to beat the queues to a waiting destroyer, only to be turned away by an Army major who told him that for all the good the RAF was doing, it might as well stay on the ground.

Eventually taken off in another destroyer, Deere met a chilly silence in the wardroom from the Army officers already there – until near misses from German bombs shook everyone up. With relief he found himself called to the bridge to help with aircraft recognition, a naval lieutenant explaining: 'We think the last chap we had a go at was a Blenheim.' Safe at last at Dover, he boarded a train and at once fell asleep, only to be aroused by the guard and told that as he had no ticket and no money he would have to get out at the next station. Fortunately a brigadier in the compartment, 'who obviously hadn't heard about [the supposed failure of] the RAF at Dunkirk', intervened. From Charing Cross, in the normal manner of airmen who live between death in the skies at one moment and almost civilian comfort on the ground at the next, Deere then took the tube to Elm Park and walked into the mess at Hornchurch nineteen hours after he had left it. The next day he flew up to Catterick to join his now 'resting' squadron. Three days later they were all back again at Hornchurch, in the hot seat.[30]

The completion of 'Dynamo' lessened, but by no means ended, the strain on Fighter Command. On 26 May Barratt had asked for two or three more fighter squadrons for his new bases near Rouen, and on 31 May the French Air Force Commander-in-Chief, General Vuillemin, put forward a demand for 'massive' reinforcement. The whole British fighter force, or at least half of it, he urged, must intervene if the Germans now launched an offensive across the Lower Somme – and preparation should be made for at least twenty squadrons to operate in other areas.[31] Considering this on 3 June, the British Chiefs of Staff advised: 'no additional fighters should be sent to France. Every fighter withdrawn from the country increases the risk of a decisive air attack on, or a successful invasion of, this country.'[32] The War Cabinet, fortified by the presence of Dowding, who had gone so far as to ask for the recall of the three fighter squadrons still in France, immediately accepted this recommendation.[33] But both Barratt and Vuillemin persisted, Barratt suggesting either an additional ten squadrons or else complete evacuation, Vuillemin asking for ten squadrons at once, and ten more if the next attack fell on France rather than Britain.

By 5 June there could be no further doubt about the direction of the next German attack. It opened that day – the Battle of France – against the French positions on the Somme. By that time Barratt's three fighter squadrons were down to eighteen serviceable aircraft. In the new situation, the War Cabinet agreed on 7 June that two more fighter squadrons should go to France and that four more should 'visit' daily, refuelling on landing grounds south of the Seine.[34] The following day 17 and 242 Squadrons duly flew over to join the AASF.

This decision came none the easier from the fact that the preceding nights, 5/6 and 6/7 June, had seen the Luftwaffe attempting reconnaissance and probing missions for the first time in any numbers over England. Over 100 aircraft had been plotted in scattered and ineffectual raids, many apparently directed against aerodromes and steel works. But behind the decision to send over the two more squadrons there was a consideration apart from the need to support the French. They would be useful in covering any further evacuation – an eventuality all too likely, to judge from the information now pouring in from decoded wireless intercepts.

By 11 June Fighter Command was again coming under strain. That day, mainly to support the 51st (Highland) Division as it marched towards St Valéry and a frustrated evacuation, Dowding's squadrons flew 147 sorties over northern France – seven patrols at an average strength of twenty-one aircraft. The following day they flew nine patrols totalling 180 sorties. But no amount of patrolling by Fighter Command could make the slightest difference to the general picture: the regrouped German forces crossed the Somme with ease, and the new French Commander-in-Chief, Weygand, was soon pressing Reynaud to sue for peace. In a desperate attempt to bolster up resistance, Churchill in Tours on 13 June promised that ten squadrons of Fighter Command should operate over France from British bases, and for a day or two this was done.[35] But soon the battle passed beyond such possibilities, and the final fighter tasks became the protection of the last British forces as they congregated at Cherbourg and the west-coast ports.

With the French requesting an armistice on 17 June, all the remaining British units now got out as quickly as they could. Fighter Command aircraft and 17 and 501 Squadrons from the AASF successfully covered Cherbourg and St Malo, while 1, 3 and 73 Squadrons from the AASF supplied protection over Brest, Nantes, La Rochelle and St Nazaire. Despite much local chaos the British departures went extremely well, with one tragic exception – the loss of some 3,000 troops in SS *Lancastria*, bombed off St Nazaire. Their task completed, nothing now remained for the five AASF Hurricane squadrons, or what was left of them, to regain England and, in the weeks to come, to recover strength in preparation for their next, and greatest, assignment.

Though the biggest danger to Britain's safety, the draining away of the greater part of her fighter force to France, had been averted, and though the Luftwaffe had lost around 1,300 aircraft, or nearly a third of its strength employed in the campaign, the RAF had suffered appalling damage. Over 950 of its aircraft based in France or England had been lost, or roughly half its entire first-line strength at the outset of the German offensive. Among these destroyed or abandoned aircraft, 386 were Hurricanes and sixty-seven Spitfires – the very types Dowding so sorely needed for home defence. Fighter Command itself had lost no fewer than 219 Hurricanes, Spitfires, Defiants and Blenheims. In addition, large quantities of vital spares had been left behind in France – the equivalent, Maintenance Command estimated, of four complete Air Stores Parks. The task of rebuilding the battered squadrons would be immense, and the time in which to complete it desperately brief.[36]

But it was not only the fighter force which needed rebuilding. The daylight bomber squadrons, the spearhead of defence against invasion, were in a far worse state. Those which had been based in France, before they were mercifully relegated to night bombing, had suffered most of all. It was of them that Paul Richey, after meeting the CO of a squadron which had lost twenty-six complete crews and had only six of its original pilots left, memorably wrote: 'These Battle and Blenheim boys of the AASF were the real heroes. We fighter chaps had a deadly aeroplane in our hands and had the consolation of hitting back and chalking up a score. But the bombers had none of the thrill, none of the fast aerobatics, and twice the dangers. They knew every time they took off they didn't stand much chance of coming back, but they never shirked a job and never hesitated. We all admired and respected them, and it was our greatest sorrow that we were physically unable to protect them as planned.'[37]

As he was flown home, wounded, on 14 June, Richey saw beneath him wrecked aircraft, smoking villages and streams of refugees. His thoughts on crossing the Dorset coast were more than understandable: 'I looked down on the calm and peaceful English countryside, the smoke rising, not from bombed villages, but lazily from cottage chimneys, and saw a game of cricket in progress on a village pitch. My mind still filled with the blast and flame that had shattered France, I was seized with utter disgust at the smug insular contentedness England enjoyed behind the sea barrier. I thought a few bombs might wake those cricketers up, and that they wouldn't be long in coming either. . . .'[38]

# 7

## Battle Order

Early in May, after the German attack on Norway, the British Chiefs of Staff had addressed themselves to the problem of Hitler's next move. He would aim, they thought, to finish off the war that year. Would he move against France, or would his assault, at first from the air, fall on Britain? Deciding that the likelihood favoured attack on Britain, they made recommendations which the Cabinet largely accepted on 9 May.[1] The following day Hitler struck at Holland, Belgium, Luxembourg and France.

This spectacularly wrong guess had at least one merit. Approval of the Chiefs of Staff recommendations – to speed up the supply of fighters, bombers and Bofors guns, heighten the efficiency of civil defence, prepare for the diversion of shipping to west-coast ports and overhaul the plans against invasion – was obtained before it emerged that France, not Britain, was the next on Hitler's list. But in any case a new German offensive on the continent was still a signal for maximum vigilance at home. On 10 May orders went out to bring civil defence, home forces and coastal defences to the highest pitch of readiness.[2]

Four days later, following the surprises sprung by German airborne troops in Holland and Belgium, came the call for Local Defence Volunteers. Broadcasting an appeal for recruits up to the age of sixty-five, the new Secretary of State for War, Anthony Eden, struck a note to which the public eagerly responded. Patriots old and young, delighted with the thought of potting at parachutists, began arriving at the police stations to enrol even before Eden had finished speaking, and within six days the recruitment figure stood at over a quarter of a million.[3]

Among the immediate measures taken by Churchill was the creation in mid-May of the Ministry of Aircraft Production. This was done by severing Air Chief Marshal Sir Wilfrid Freeman's Department of Development and Production from the Air Ministry, recalling it from its wartime home at Harrogate, and installing it as the nucleus of the new Ministry in London under the direction of the dynamic owner of the *Daily Express*, Lord Beaverbrook. Within twenty-four hours the Minister and the Air Staff took an important decision – to give top priority (1A) until September to the production of five types of aircraft. Three of these were bomber types, to maintain offensive capability, not least against any attempted invasion. The other two were the Hurricanes and Spitfires which waged and won the Battle of Britain.[4]

Simplistic notions have sometimes been entertained about this decision. Plants making one type of aircraft could not, of course, suddenly switch to making another. And the restriction of priority 1A to five aircraft types was so narrow as to be impossible to sustain for anything like the proposed time: after only a fortnight other bombers and fighters had also to be included, and after a month training aircraft as well – or the training organisation would have broken down. But the aircraft industry as a whole now had undisputed first call on the raw materials it needed, and the favoured types would suffer far less delay from lack of components manufactured elsewhere and common to other aircraft. Merlin engines, R/T sets, Browning guns, oxygen tubes – the Hurricane and Spitfire output became much more assured of these and other essentials.

The fighter production figures for the summer of 1940 tell their own story and are one reason why it was possible for Dowding to win the Battle of Britain. When Beaverbrook became Minister of Aircraft Production on 14 May, the planned production of fighters for that month was 261 machines. The actual output for the month was 325. For June the planned programme was 292; the actual output was 446. In July and August the improvement still continued: total planned production 611, total output 972.[5] Already by early July the supply of fighters had become so satisfactory that it was decided to allocate an additional four aircraft to each of thirty Hurricane and six Spitfire squadrons – though, unfortunately, there were not the pilots to go with them.[6]

It has been customary, particularly in Lord Beaverbrook's newspapers, to ascribe all or most of this to the Minister's genius, energy and powers of inspiration. The long extended working week, the telephone calls at all hours, the slashing of red tape, the consignment of closely planned programmes to the waste-paper basket (behind the Minister's desk was the notice: 'Organisation is the Enemy of Improvisation') – these well-known features of the Beaverbrook technique have been extolled on many a page. Dowding himself in his *Despatch* endorsed this heroic view of the Minister by describing the effect of the appointment as 'magical' – an adjective which, in conjunction of course with his great achievements, earned the Fighter Chief permanent front-row status in the Beaverbrook Press hall of fame.

It is certainly a fact of history that Beaverbrook seized all possible priorities, turned on the heat, and by personal interventions and appointments helped at a critical time to galvanise the aircraft industry into efforts far beyond previous norms. But justice must also acknowledge that in this he was immensely aided by a sudden realisation on the part of the British workforce that the moment indeed cried out for supreme efforts. The end of the dismal Chamberlain regime, the débâcle in France, the escape from Dunkirk, Churchill's eloquence and honesty – offering only 'blood, sweat, toil and tears' – created a mood in which, for a time at least, cherished trade restrictions could be swept aside and willing labour work its heart out in long hours of overtime. Nor should another factor in the great surge of production escape recognition. Sir Wilfrid Freeman, his Director of Production (Sir) Ernest Lemon (who had inspired the development of subcontracting), Lemon's successor Sir Charles Craven of Vickers Armstrong, and many others in the Air Ministry who had now become the core of the Ministry of Aircraft Production, had in fact done their work well. Indeed, the highest percentage increase in the production of fighters – about forty-five per cent – came in April 1940, before Beaverbrook took over. Long-standing difficulties in production were at last easing: there was already a growing momentum. The Minister and the general sense of crisis added the decisive extra push.

In harmony with the new mood in the country Churchill's Government on 22 May sought and received from Parliament emergency powers beyond those granted at the outbreak of war. These gave it, in deputy Prime Minister Clement Attlee's words, 'complete control over persons and property . . . not just some persons . . . but of all persons, rich and poor, employer and workman, man and woman, and all property'.[7] In virtue of these powers the new Minister of Labour and

National Service, Ernest Bevin, became responsible for controlling the supply of labour to all industries. He could theoretically direct anyone to any task, and set for it whatever conditions of work and pay he thought fit. The old liberal easy-going British ways, so many of which had persisted through the first eight months of hostilities, were at last giving way to the rigorous state direction regrettably necessary for the efficient waging of large-scale war.*

Five days later, on 27 May, with the escape from Dunkirk only just beginning, the Cabinet substantially approved a Chiefs of Staff paper on 'British Strategy Relating to a Certain Eventuality'. The eventuality so coyly referred to was, of course, that France might soon collapse. The Chiefs of Staff paper accordingly reviewed the prospects for a war in which the British Commonwealth and Empire would be fighting alone. It emphasised that with Britain exposed to air attack from bases anywhere on a semi-circle from Brest to Trondheim, the first essential was 'to prevent the Germans achieving such air superiority as would enable them to invade this country'. If the Germans once got ashore with their armoured vehicles, the British ground forces were unlikely to be able to drive them out. British fighter defences, and to a lesser extent the bomber force, must therefore be built up with all possible speed, and every step taken to improve civil defence. If this were done, the Navy and the RAF between them would be able to prevent any actual invasion.

On the assumption that British civilian morale did not crack under the night bombing which would inevitably follow if daylight attacks failed – and against which there was as yet little effective defence – the Chiefs of Staff then proceeded to examine how such a war could actually be won. They concluded that, though Italy was bound to join with Germany and make trouble in the Mediterranean, the prospects were not discouraging. As long as the United States (whose influence would cancel out Japan's) was willing to give full economic support, the British Commonwealth and Empire might ultimately expect to win the war by a combination of economic blockade, air attack and resistance in the German-occupied countries.[9]

This remarkably sanguine appraisal, in which it was merely said of Russia that she was unlikely to look favourably on German successes,

---

*Bevin was not among those dazzled by Beaverbrook's reputation. Churchill once said to him, referring to Beaverbrook's achievement at the Ministry of Aircraft Production: 'Max is a magician – positively a magician.' Bevin replied: 'You're quite right, Prime Minister – I was always taught when I was young that magic is nine-tenths illusion.'[8]

had its counterpart in the optimism of the British public as a whole. Once the troops were safely back from Dunkirk, any thought of defeat seemed to disappear from the general consciousness. Being 'alone' brought exhilaration to many, and was certainly welcomed by Dowding and King George VI. The latter wrote to his mother, Queen Mary: 'Personally, I feel happier now that we have no allies to be polite to and pamper.'[10]

On the highest plane, the tone was set by Churchill. On 4 June, as the Dunkirk evacuation ended, came his classic expression of defiance: 'We shall defend our island, whatever the cost may be. We shall fight on the beaches, we shall fight on the landing grounds, we shall fight in the fields and in the streets, we shall fight in the hills: we shall never surrender. . . .' Then, on 18 June, after the French had sought an armistice, came a call equally famous and stirring:

What General Weygand called the Battle of France is over. I expect that the Battle of Britain is about to begin. Upon this battle depends the survival of Christian civilisation. . . . Let us therefore brace ourselves to our duties, and so bear ourselves that, if the British Empire and the Commonwealth last for a thousand years, men will still say 'This was their finest hour.'

Such words may have become dulled nowadays by familiarity, or may by some be dismissed as rhetoric, but to the embattled British nation of 1940 they were a true inspiration, a potent factor in helping to bring about the victory that was to come.

At a lower level, the popular joke of the time proclaimed: 'We're in the final now, and we're playing on the home ground.' But this light-heartedness only concealed a new and stronger sense of purpose. By June, war expenditure had risen two-thirds above the figure for April. With the new purchase tax, and the top rate of tax for big incomes at eighteen shillings in the pound, the spectre of the war profiteer of 1914–18 was firmly laid. Rationing, already introduced for some articles, became more stringent and now affected even that bulwark of British morale, the cup of tea. Wherever there were arrangements for collective bargaining, strikes and lock-outs became illegal. With the Whitsun and August Bank Holidays cancelled, the aircraft factories, on Beaverbrook's insistence, working twenty-four hours a day, including Sundays, and only the female sex limited to a sixty-hour week, the phenomenon emerged of a Britain at last utterly and wholly committed to the war effort.

On 3 July Britain's new fierceness of resolve was shown to the world in 'Operation Catapult' – in Churchill's words, 'the simultaneous seizure, control, or effective disablement or destruction of all the available French Fleet'. At Plymouth and Portsmouth, at Alexandria and Dakar and – very bloodily – at Mers-el-Kebir, the deed was done. The Royal Navy's superiority remained intact, and the USA took the incidental message: Britain meant to win.

Meanwhile, as the splendid summer days wore on, the authorities in Britain took every conceivable step against the invasion which now seemed inevitable. The Navy laid minefields, and in the ports from Harwich to Plymouth held ready its destroyers and lighter warships. RAF Coastal Command scoured the seas and flew high-level photographic reconnaissance of the possible invasion ports. RAF Bomber Command, besides planning a massive assault with other Commands against any invading forces, strove to disrupt the Luftwaffe's preparations by attacking airfields. And the Army, with the help of 150,000 civilians full-time and thousands more part-time (including schoolboys, among them one of the authors of this book), festooned the beaches and cliffs with barbed wire, dug tank traps, set up concrete 'dragon's teeth' and pill boxes, and arranged for fire to engulf suitable stretches of shore and roadway as the enemy appeared. And behind the Army stood the unpaid Local Defence Volunteers, their number swollen by the end of June to one-and-a-half million. 'A People's Army officered by Blimps', in the eyes of George Orwell, they were still largely without rifles or uniform (other than a brassard bearing the letters LDV), but their enthusiasm and ingenuity would doubtless, at great cost to themselves, have created difficulties for any invader.*

From the coastal districts most vulnerable (and in June proclaimed 'protected areas' forbidden to ordinary visitors), a new wave of evacuation now began. Any civilians who remained were under orders to 'stay put': they must not become refugees cluttering the roads, as had happened in France. Among those required to stay were members of local authorities, lifeboat crews, employees of banks, water, sewage, gas and electricity undertakings and workers on the land. These last had the heavy responsibility of obstructing their larger fields with barbed wire, disused farm machinery, tractors, commandeered old cars – anything that would make landing of airborne troops hazardous.

There was also intense preoccupation with the danger of the Fifth

---

*They acquired a new name – Home Guard – during July and, more importantly, rifles and uniforms during the succeeding months.

"Of course there's no harm in *your* knowing!"

CARELESS TALK
COSTS LIVES

Column,* who, as in France, were held to lurk everywhere. Rumour-mongering was strenuously discouraged and the citizen was everywhere reminded that 'careless talk costs lives'. In one of the most vexatious orders since the imposition of the blackout, road signposts were removed and place names obliterated, or reduced to minuscule size, on railway stations, buildings and even war memorials. In London the district references on street names were removed or obscured – all to confuse and delay the invader.

The list of precautions and restrictions was almost endless. Church bells were to be rung only on the news of landings: one unfortunate cleric was *sent to prison* for failing to maintain the silence. During July, BBC newscasters for the first time identified themselves by name, lest enemy agents surreptitiously usurp their place. Motor vehicles, when left unattended, had to be immobilised: for open cars, removal of the rotor arm was enjoined, but in emergency a large nail could be hammered into the petrol tank. Newspapers grew strangely thin, and

*An expression derived from the boast of General Mola in the Spanish Civil War, that he had four columns outside to besiege Madrid and a fifth column (of secret helpers) within.

juries were reduced from twelve to seven (except in murder cases) to save manpower. Iron railings, splendid or otherwise – even the presentation gates outside Baldwin's Worcestershire home – were torn down for scrap.* Lord Beaverbrook called on housewives, needlessly, to surrender their aluminium saucepans. Grouse-shooting was advanced from the Glorious Twelfth to 5 August, causing great mystification and – in more limited circles – indignation.

As part of the new ruthlessness, from May onwards several hundreds of pre-war Fascist sympathisers, including Sir Oswald Mosley, were imprisoned without trial under Defence Regulation 18B, and some 27,000 inhabitants of alien stock, mostly German and Austrian refugees from Hitler, were rounded up and interned. Britain, as never before, was making ready for all-out war in defence of the homeland. And whether any of these restrictions and preparations would prove to be necessary would depend now, above all, on the skill and strength of the Luftwaffe, and of Fighter Command.

The view has often been put forward, even by military men of the standing of Kesselring and Milch, that 'if only' the Germans had mounted an assault on Britain after Dunkirk, instead of deciding to finish off the French, they could have followed their air attacks with an almost unopposed landing. This ignores the need of the Luftwaffe to recuperate and regroup, and the fact that invasions across a stretch of water like the English Channel cannot be 'improvised' within a few days when the defenders have an enormous superiority in naval strength: especially not, too, when the very idea of invading Britain was a novelty to most of the German staffs, whose wildest dreams had been exceeded by the swiftness of their triumph in France.

The first planning for an invasion of Britain was undertaken in the autumn of 1939 by Grand-Admiral Raeder and the German naval staff. Raeder seems to have initiated this not from any enthusiasm for such a project, but because he was anxious for the German Navy to be prepared if Hitler's mind moved that way. Some desultory naval and military study followed, to be discontinued as the German plans matured for the attacks on Norway and France. No further mention of invasion was recorded until 21 May 1940, when Guderian's panzers reached the Channel coast and Raeder, more anxious than ever not to be

---

*One MP, with the slow pace of rearmament in 1934–6 in mind, cruelly enquired in the Commons whether these gates were not needed to save Baldwin from the wrath of a justly incensed populace.

caught napping, raised the subject directly with Hitler. No fresh decision was taken, but as a result the naval staff resumed planning, this time more intensively.[11]

Meanwhile, Hitler's views for, at minimum, an air attack on Britain were taking shape. He had already, on 29 November 1939, issued a directive which looked forward to the occupation of the Belgian and north French coasts in order to pursue the 'blockade' of Britain by sea and air. The main targets under this directive were to be British ports and aircraft factories.[12] Now, on 24 May, a new directive stated that as soon as sufficient forces were available – i.e. after the defeat of France – the Luftwaffe should start independent operations against the British homeland. These should begin with 'a crushing attack in retaliation for the British raids in the Ruhr area'.[13] Two days later Hitler specified the aircraft industry in Britain as the prime object of attack.

Apart from exploratory night raids on Britain on 4 and 5 June, no further important step occurred until the complete defeat of France, when regular small-scale night raiding of Britain was resumed. Though hoping that Britain would come to terms, Hitler at the end of June then decided that he must at least initiate contingency planning for an invasion. On 2 July Feldmarschall Wilhelm Keitel, Chief of the OKW,* noted: 'The Fuehrer has decided that a landing in England is possible, providing that air superiority can be attained. . . . All preparations to be begun immediately.'[14] This proviso about air superiority was to remain constant, from first to last, throughout all the German invasion preparations of the following two months.

While the German Navy and Army got down to serious if far from harmonious planning, the Luftwaffe was busy occupying aerodromes in northern France and the Low Countries, bringing up stores, and establishing communications and anti-aircraft defences. Goering himself seems to have taken little interest in the inter-Service deliberations. The Luftwaffe was in any case regarded as the key to the whole invasion project, which must obviously begin with intensive air attack. In Goering's view, this was almost certain to be sufficient in itself. Any subsequent military action would be in the nature of a virtually unopposed occupation.[15]

Though the British officially date the beginning of the Battle of Britain from 10 July, with the heavy air fighting over one of the Channel convoys, Hitler at that time was, in fact, still partly hoping for a

*Oberkommando der Wehrmacht – i.e. High Command of the Armed Forces.

bloodless culmination to his victories in the West. With his eyes always on the Soviet Union, which in June reacted to his successes by taking over Estonia, Latvia, Lithuania, Bessarabia and northern Bucovina, he would have been glad to reach agreement with Britain – naturally on his own terms. He was not so set on peacemaking, however, that he neglected to follow up the invasion alternative. Another meeting with Raeder elicited the Admiral's view that invasion should be a 'last resort', undertaken only under conditions of complete air supremacy, and that the immediate strategy should be the blockade of Britain by U-boats and aircraft: but when Hitler conferred with the Army chiefs Walter von Brauchitsch and Franz Halder, during the second week of July, he found them far more optimistic. If the German Navy could get the troops across and the Luftwaffe protect the beachheads, they were confident that the Army could readily overcome any opposition from the British ground forces.[16]

The outcome was the issue on 16 July of Hitler's Directive No. 16, the keynote of which was struck in the opening sentence: 'As England, in spite of the hopelessness of her situation, has shown herself unwilling to come to a compromise, I have therefore decided to begin to prepare for, and if necessary carry out, an invasion of England.'[17] To this provisional operation OKW gave the code-name 'Sealion'.

Three days later Hitler made a clumsy and half-hearted attempt to determine whether 'Sealion' would be really needed. On 19 July at a special meeting of the Reichstag with senior commanders and officials, at which promotions were liberally handed out for the good work recently done in France, he made what he called 'a final appeal to reason and commonsense'. Characteristically he accompanied it with threats. Referring to Bomber Command's attacks on west Germany – which however ineffective had evidently angered and embarrassed him – he promised a reply which would bring the British people (but 'of course, not Mr Churchill, for he no doubt will already be in Canada') 'unending suffering and misery'.[18] The British Government saw nothing in this to alter the situation, and on 22 July the Foreign Secretary, Lord Halifax, in a broadcast dismissed the so-called 'peace offer' as 'a mere summons to capitulate'. Churchill himself declined to make any reply on the grounds that he was 'not on speaking terms' with 'Herr Hitler'.

Meanwhile, and until the plans for 'Sealion' could be agreed, Luftwaffe units now established in northern France, the Low Countries, Denmark and Norway concentrated much of their attention on British shipping. Their attacks were designed both to restrict British trade and to wear down RAF Fighter Command, which would be drawn into battle in difficult circumstances well away from home.

So the operations began which the RAF would later see as the opening of the Battle of Britain and the Luftwaffe as the *Kanalkampf*. On the German side about four-fifths of the entire operational strength of the Luftwaffe was by 20 July arrayed for action. Under Goering as a largely absentee Commander-in-Chief – he was also, among other things, Hitler's official deputy, Air Minister, President of the Reichstag and the Prussian Council, and Reich Master of Hunting – the German forces were organised in three *Luftflotten*, or air fleets. The smallest of these, *Luftflotte* 5, under General Hans-Juergen Stumpff, a former soldier and Chief of the Air Staff, was in Norway and Denmark. It deployed about 130 bombers (He 111 and Ju 88), about thirty-five long-range fighters (Me 110), nearly fifty reconnaissance aircraft and a force of Me 109s for local defence. Any daylight attacks against Britain would have to be escorted – a job for the 110s, which had the range but had already proved vulnerable to Hurricanes and Spitfires. Nevertheless, *Luftflotte* 5, in addition to mining British waters, could pose a constant threat to convoys in the North Sea, the naval bases in the Orkneys and the Forth, and the whole relatively lightly defended north-east of England and Scotland.

The main forces assigned to the struggle were the two *Luftflotten* facing Britain across the English Channel. *Luftflotte* 3, in western France, was led by Feldmarschall Hugo von Sperrle, a World War I airman who had directed this *Luftflotte* in the French campaign and had earlier commanded the *Legion Kondor* in Spain. With his square head, jowls, weighty figure, monocle and lavish display of decorations, Sperrle resembled a British caricature of a Prussian officer, but his appearance belied his abilities, which were considerable. His Command's zone of operations would normally be west and north-west of a line from Le Havre through Selsey Bill to the Midlands. Operating for the most part east of that line would be *Luftflotte* 2 based in France north of the Seine and in Belgium, Holland and north Germany. Its commander, Albert Kesselring, now a feldmarschall, was a tough, ebullient and efficient professional soldier who had been transferred to the Luftwaffe in 1933. He had already with great success directed *Luftflotte* 1 in Poland and *Luftflotte* 2 in France and the Low Countries.

Together *Luftflotten* 2 and 3 on 20 July officially controlled, in addition to about 150 reconnaissance aircraft, forces amounting to

1,131 long-range bombers (Ju 88, He 111 and Do 17), 316 dive-bombers (Ju 87), 809 single-engined fighters (Me 109) and 246 twin-engined fighters (Me 110). All told the three *Luftflotten*, leaving aside reconnaissance planes, disposed for operations against Britain a strength of about 1,260 bombers, 316 dive-bombers and 1,089 single- and twin-engined fighters. The general level of serviceability at that date was around three-quarters of strength.[19]

On the British side, all three of the RAF's home operational Commands – Bomber, Fighter and Coastal – would be involved in contesting any German invasion. So too would be no fewer than 660 operational-type aircraft brought in from the training units and manned largely by instructors. All would attack invading forces, but Coastal Command would also fly repeated reconnaissance and Bomber Command would also strike farther back along the line – especially at ports of assembly, communications and aircraft plants. But in the preliminary struggle for air superiority – the essence of the Battle of Britain – the contribution of these two Commands would be much more restricted. During June and July Bomber Command could, and did, raid German-held airfields in France and the Low Countries and aircraft plants in Germany to reduce the striking power of the Luftwaffe; but as the main force of the Command was still inaccurate by night and the small daylight force of 2 Group needed heavy fighter escort, which took fighters away from home defence, its effectiveness in this role was very limited. In practice the RAF's battle for air superiority against the Luftwaffe would depend overwhelmingly on Fighter Command, backed up by the ground defences.

In reckoning the force opposed to the 1,576 bombers and dive-bombers and 1,089 fighters of the three *Luftflotten* in the preliminary air battle before an invasion could be launched, the 1,200-odd aircraft of Bomber and Coastal Commands can thus scarcely be included. What mattered above all in this particular context was the strength of Fighter Command, where Dowding by early July at last had fifty-two of the fifty-three squadrons planned for the previous spring – with three more forming during the month. By mid-July his force stood at around 800 aircraft, with a high rate of serviceability. Nearly 100 of these, however, were Blenheims, unable to hold their own with single-engined fighters and increasingly being relegated to night fighting. In practice, the 700-odd Hurricanes and Spitfires would be the force withstanding the 1,576 long-range bombers and Ju 87s and the 1,089 Me 109s and Me 110s. These odds sound, and were, extremely formidable; but the

German bombers, and still more the dive-bombers, were vulnerable to modern fighters and would need escort. The air fighting was thus likely to turn on how well the 700 Hurricanes and Spitfires performed against the nearly 1,100 Me 109s and 110s – a different way of computing the odds and one less daunting for the British side.

At the head of Fighter Command Dowding, the most senior serving officer in the RAF, had recently reached the age of fifty-eight. Scheduled for retirement a year beforehand, he had three times received short extensions owing to the outbreak of war and the developing crisis, and was now due to retire at the end of October. As the Air Member for Research and Development who had fostered the eight-gun fighter and radar, and as the head of Fighter Command since its inception in 1936, he was supremely experienced in his post and had a firm grasp of technical matters – though apparently not, as it turned out, of the most recent developments in the tactics of air combat. In his complete and dedicated professionalism, as in his quiet tastes and demeanour, he was the very antithesis of Goering.

Upon Dowding at Stanmore also rested responsibility for the static defences and the issuing of public air-raid warnings. The anti-aircraft guns defending the cities, dockyards, airfields and special targets (such as the Rolls-Royce works at Derby and the Supermarine plant outside Southampton) were, like the searchlights, under the direct command of Lieutenant-General Sir Frederick ('Tim') Pile, a tank enthusiast who had been sidetracked into anti-aircraft artillery. An Anglo-Irish baronet, able and popular, he was to be the only officer to hold the same major Command throughout the whole war. His task was no easy one. In July 1940 radar for gun-laying or searchlight direction was a promising development for the near future, as yet available only for a few guns at Dover; in general, reliance still had to be placed on sound locators to pick up unseen targets. Moreover aiming, as Pile himself wrote, was 'based on the assumption that the enemy would fly at a constant height and a constant speed'. 'It may be said', continued the General, 'that that assumption was purely a false one, but with the equipment in existence, it was not possible to engage targets on any other assumption.'[20]

Anti-Aircraft Command being operationally under Dowding's control, Dowding and Pile had adjacent headquarters at Stanmore. In practice, discussion sufficed, and Dowding gave no orders; the two were mutual admirers and friends, who worked together in perfect harmony. In mid-July 1940 Pile deployed about 1,700 heavy guns –

including old 3 inch to supplement the modern 3.7s and 4.5s. This was out of an approved schedule (in 1938) of over 2,200 and was vastly better than at the outbreak of war. In addition, for the protection of special targets and airfields he could muster about 600 light guns, mainly 40 mm, out of a recommended total of nearly 1,900. Old 3 inch guns swelled this total for the time being; and for defence, mainly of airfields, against very low fliers there were some 3,000 machine-guns. He also deployed, more nearly up to establishment, some 4,000 searchlights.

Also at Stanmore was the headquarters of the Observer Corps,* the body responsible for tracking aircraft once they had crossed the coast. By mid-1940 there were thirty-one Observer Corps Groups in Britain, each containing thirty to fifty observer posts. Manned entirely by volunteers, the Corps had acquired a morale and enthusiasm unsurpassed by that of any other civilian service. In July 1940 the standard of competence, in many places not yet enhanced by much experience of the enemy, was varied but fast improving. Not surprisingly, aircraft flying at great heights or in cloudy conditions often made accurate reporting difficult, if not impossible.

At Stanmore, too, was the headquarters of Balloon Command, under the direction of Air Vice-Marshal O. T. Boyd. By July 1940 the total of 'gas bags' under his control had risen to some 1,400, of which about 450 were disposed for the protection of London. Like the guns – until these became more scientifically controlled – their main function was to keep the raiders at heights from which their bombing would be less accurate. Flown up to a maximum of 5,000 feet, the balloons discouraged low-level attacks and presented a special hazard to the dive-bomber.

Though Dowding had complete responsibility for Fighter Command, unlike the more limited jurisdiction he possessed over the other elements in the air defence system, in practice this did not extend to any day-to-day, still less hour-to-hour, control of operations. During the Battle he would exercise higher control by, for instance, moving squadrons to meet the needs of rest or reinforcement, but – since swiftness of local reaction was vital – all detailed operational decisions remained devolved to the Fighter Groups and the sectors within them, as planned from the inception of the Command.

By mid-July 1940 these Groups had become four in number.** Each

---

*Royal from 1941.
**After the Battle they would become six, with the formation of further Groups (9 and 14) to cover lightly defended areas in the north-west and north.

worked in close co-operation with one or more of the seven Anti-Aircraft Divisions. Pride of place went to 11 Group (HQ Uxbridge), which guarded the south-east up to Suffolk and extended over half of southern England. Its commander was Air Vice-Marshal Keith Rodney Park, a tall, lean, energetic New Zealander who had fought courageously at Gallipoli and on the Western Front and distinguished himself later as a pilot with the RFC. Before being appointed to 11 Group he had served as Dowding's Senior Air Staff Officer at Fighter Command, and he had an excellent rapport with his Chief. He had kept up his flying by regularly piloting his Hurricane round the stations in his Group, and he had flown over Dunkirk to see things for himself. He was to prove himself in Malta later, as in Britain, one of the supreme fighter commanders of the war.

Being in the hottest spot and with the strongest *Luftflotte* (2) confronting it, 11 Group in early July held more squadrons than any other Group – twenty-two, or approximately 350 aircraft. Thirteen of these squadrons had Hurricanes, six Spitfires and three Blenheims. The Group's sector stations, which would control the squadrons by R/T once forces were airborne on orders from Group headquarters, were mostly disposed in a protective ring round London – from Northolt in Middlesex to North Weald and Hornchurch in Essex, Biggin Hill in Kent, and Kenley in Surrey. North of this ring was Debden in Essex, and to the south Tangmere, near the Sussex coast close to Chichester. Until the end of the first week in August, when 10 Group took them over, 11 Group also controlled the new stations at Middle Wallop in Hampshire and Warmwell in Dorset.

Flanking 11 Group on the west, and covering the south-west and half of southern England, was the newly formed 10 Group, with headquarters near Box, in Wiltshire. It became operational on 13 July. It was commanded by a popular South African, Air Vice-Marshal Sir Quintin Brand, who had earned a cluster of decorations in World War I – among other feats he shot down a Gotha in the last raid on London – and who had been knighted in 1920 after a pioneer long-distance flight to Cape Town. The installation of *Luftflotte* 3 in western France promised plenty of work for 10 Group, which was hastily built up to meet the situation: at the beginning of June the area held only one fighter squadron, but a month later there were seven – mostly disposed on Coastal Command airfields. For most of July the Group held four squadrons – about sixty aircraft – of Hurricanes and Spitfires, with Filton as its fully developed sector station, and sector outposts at St Eval and Pembrey. By early August it was much stronger with the addition of Middle Wallop, henceforth one of its sector stations.

North of 10 and 11 Groups, and covering the Midlands and beyond to some fifty miles north of York, was 12 Group (HQ Watnall, in Nottinghamshire). Its five sector stations ran from Duxford in Cambridgeshire to Church Fenton in Yorkshire, the intervening stations being Wittering, Digby and Kirton-in-Lindsey. Its 210-odd aircraft – six squadrons of Hurricanes, five of Spitfires, one of Blenheims and one of Defiants – were under the command of Air Vice-Marshal Trafford Leigh-Mallory, who had been in charge since the Group's inception in 1937. His experience in World War I and afterwards had been mainly in army co-operation. Energetic and strongly imbued with the spirit of the offensive, he exuded self-confidence and was popular with his pilots, whose views and experiences he regularly sought.

Finally, with headquarters at Newcastle-upon-Tyne, there was 13 Group, covering everything north of 12 Group, but running only up to the Forth as a continuous system. (Beyond that it had responsibility for the isolated defences guarding Scapa.) Its sector stations were at Catterick, Usworth, Acklington and Turnhouse (Edinburgh). Its 220-odd aircraft – six squadrons of Hurricanes, six of Spitfires, one of Blenheims and one of Defiants – were under the command of Air Vice-Marshal Richard Saul. A great sportsman who had represented the RAF at rugby and hockey and won its tennis championship, he had been an air observer in World War I. More to the immediate point, he had been Park's predecessor as Senior Air Staff Officer at Fighter Command Headquarters.

At the heart of this whole system were the ops room and the more recently instituted filter room at Bentley Priory. This acted as the filter for information before passing it to Groups, which took the initiative in passing orders to sectors, which in turn alerted the airfields. The underground filter room at Fighter Command, the first to receive reports from the radar stations, established firm tracks from the maze of plots and 'told' these tracks and their ensuing plots to the adjacent Command ops room, the beating heart of air defence.

This ops room was like a theatre, the stage a table depicting a vast map covering the territory of all the Groups. With the first reporting of enemy aircraft this stage reflected the reality of the outside world as a drama in miniature, the actors being the young men and women in headsets who stood about the stage manipulating the plots with magnetic wands – like so many Prosperos recording the tempest raging above.

The plots received from the radar stations and (by instant relay from the Groups) the observer posts were each given a numbered counter showing the approximate size of the attacking raid or defending fighters, and its approximate height. As these plots became old – or 'stale' – their colour was changed until they could be replaced by more recent – or 'fresh' – plots.

Above, in the royal box of this theatre, sitting in rows, were the officers with their telephones to conduct their urgent business, the duty controller, and for much of the time Dowding himself or his deputy. So this was no passive audience. There were to be days when the fate of the nation, and of the free world, seemed to rest on the shoulders of these senior officers of the junior Service.

Meanwhile, the filtered 'gen' at Bentley Priory was passed simultaneously down the line so that Groups and sectors, all with their own ops rooms, were as up-to-date with their picture as Dowding's headquarters. In this way, Groups took the executive decisions on which of their sectors should deal with raids as they developed and what forces they should 'scramble', while the sector stations communicated directly with the wings, squadrons or flights in the air, deploying them to the most favourable positions to intercept and destroy the enemy.

According to the system, but not always according to practice, only when the enemy was sighted – 'Tally Ho!' – did the pilots take over fighting responsibility.

Besides civil defence headquarters responsible for sounding air-raid alarms, the anti-aircraft guns and (when appropriate) the searchlights were tied in with the information system originating in Bentley Priory. Group ops rooms informed gun ops rooms, which in turn informed the gun sites.

The organisation was as complex as it was remarkable but seemed both simple and efficient in action. The whole machine was much more like the product of a Teutonic than an Anglo-Saxon people, and perhaps for this reason the Germans vastly underestimated its efficiency. They also knew about radar and had it themselves, but they also underestimated the refinement and efficiency of those towers which they were busily photographing from the air before the outbreak of war.

As the British and German forces confronted each other, confidence ran high on both sides – indeed, dangerously so on the German. The Luftwaffe had much the larger forces and more battle experience:

Spain, Poland, Norway, the Low Countries and France had convinced its leaders and pilots alike that they could brush aside all opposition. It also had the enormous advantage of the offensive, the ability to choose when and where it would strike. Leaving aside the quality of the aeroplanes and the aircrew, which was not too dissimilar, the RAF for its part possessed two advantages denied to the Germans. Its skilful and devoted pilots were mainly fighting over their own land; and in its early-warning radar and its fighter control system it had priceless assets whose value was initially far from fully understood by the enemy.

Such were the strengths and dispositions of the opposing forces at the outset of the Battle of Britain: the Battle which would halt Hitler's triumphs in the West, leave the British base unsubdued, and so make it possible, in the fullness of time, for Britain and her Allies to reduce his hideous Third Reich to the dust of history.

# PART TWO

# THE BATTLE

*War*

When the bloom is off the garden,
and I'm fighting in the sky,
when the lawns and flower beds harden,
and when weak birds starve and die,
the death-roll will grow longer,
eyes will be moist and red;
and the more I kill, the longer
shall I miss friends who are dead.

FLYING OFFICER A. N. C. WEIR DFC

# 8

*British Day One*

## 10 JULY 1940

T he official dates for the start and completion of the Battle of
Britain, 10 July and 31 October, can only make any sense with
the supporting argument that it had to begin and end formally at
some time for the sake of the history books and battle honours for the
aircrew who participated. But for all the efforts of historians, history
remains an untidy business. It was just bad luck that, say, a Spitfire
pilot who claimed a successful encounter on 9 July and was too badly
wounded to return to his squadron before 1 November did not qualify
for the Battle of Britain clasp or membership of the Battle of Britain
Fighter Association. And good fortune for a newly qualified Blenheim
air gunner who flew his first operational sortie on the night of 30/31
October.

In the event, there was some particularly tough fighting in November
and even December 1940, and some of the days leading up to 10 July
were quite as busy as the official first day. On 4 July, for example, the
Ju 87 Stuka dive-bomber confirmed its deadly accuracy, and the
vulnerability of coastal convoys to its 500 kg bomb. Events on that same
day proved how dangerous 'free chase' Me 109s could be, ranging at
medium altitude behind the coasts of Kent and Sussex in search of
sections of Hurricanes (preferably) and Spitfires. For instance, a *Staffel*
of 109s bounced a section of 65 Squadron Spitfires from Hornchurch on
7 July and killed all three pilots.

During these early days of July the weakness and inflexibility of Fighter Command's peacetime set-piece 'Fighting Area Attacks', which attempted to apply formality to what was essentially a dogfight mêlée, already revealed over France, became apparent to more of the British squadrons. But the tenacity with which some COs and flight commanders stuck to these numbered Attacks, and the close formation flying they called for, was to cost many lives.

The bombing of Manston airfield on 3 July was an omen of events to come. During these days, too, the undue pressure on the 11 Group sectors by contrast with 12 Group was first exposed. This was due to the main thrust of the Luftwaffe attack originating from captured French and Belgian airfields, rather than from bases in Germany as anticipated, when 11 and 12 Groups would have shared the responsibility more or less equally. Dowding, therefore, took steps to reinforce 11 Group, and as it became evident that Sperrle was now able to operate from the Cherbourg Peninsula, transferred 609 Squadron's Spitfires from Northolt to Middle Wallop in Brand's 10 Group, but still at this time operated by 11 Group.

First light on 10 July revealed a typical dirty English summer's day, with intermittent driving rain from the south-west: 'Harry clampers' to the fighter pilots of 11 Group, many of whom drank their early morning cup of tea and turned over in bed for a lie-in.

Reports were coming in to Fleet Street about the May bombing of Rotterdam by the Luftwaffe. Later in the morning *The Times* headline writer prepared the front-page story: 'Rotterdam a City of Ruins: 30,000 killed by German Bombs.' It was clearly only a matter of time before the Germans turned their attention to London. Already several provincial towns and cities had suffered bombing. There were many public air-raid shelters for the common citizens of the capital: the Savoy Hotel hoped to attract the elite to its own, and let it be known through the press that theirs was 'an exceedingly good shelter, below ground, the ceiling reinforced with a regular spider's-web of steel struts,' the whole patrolled by forty ex-servicemen.

Early in the day, in spite of the weather, RAF Blenheim light bomber squadrons were briefed for attacks on Luftwaffe airfields at Amiens and St Omer. The crews of 107 Squadron were confident that the ops would be scratched. They were not, and that afternoon only one out of six aircraft that took off returned.

Contemplating the events of the last weeks from Kelvedon Hall, the millionaire American-born Sir Henry 'Chips' Channon MP noted: 'The Third French Republic has ceased to exist and I don't care: it was graft-ridden, ugly, incompetent, Communistic and corrupt.'[1]

Churchill would have agreed with this judgment, but had no time to keep a diary. With the invasion of Britain becoming more likely day by day, among his priority preoccupations was, of all subjects, the design and production of landing-craft for the liberation of Europe from the Nazi yoke.

HRH Group Captain The Duke of Kent also had his eyes on the future. He was off to an Elementary Flying Training School for the day and night to check on the progress of some sixty Polish flying cadets.

The first enemy air attacks of 10 July developed not over England but far to the south in the Mediterranean. Here Italian bombers were sighted approaching Malta, and more were seen near Sidi Barrani on the coast just inside the Egyptian frontier. In both places the skies were clear blue, by contrast with northern Europe. Would the weather here improve? It was a question of critical importance to Kesselring and Sperrle – and for that matter to the whole of the Luftwaffe, which was anxious to get on with things.

At first light, almost every day, the Germans had been sending out weather and recce planes to photograph the previous day's targets, future targets and report on the weather. Do 17s or 215s (they were almost identical) or Ju 88s were usually used for this task, which included attacks on convoys if conditions were favourable, and they probed far out into the Atlantic as well as patrolling the Irish Sea and North Sea. They took advantage of cloud cover whenever possible and were often difficult to pick up on the radar sets. But in the past few days casualties among these lone recce planes had been high. No. 603 Squadron, with sections at three Scottish airfields, had acquitted itself particularly well on 3 July, catching and shooting down in turn three 88s from KG30 based in Denmark, while far to the south a Hurricane pilot of 56 Squadron had surprised a prowling 17 off Burnham and shot it down.

Up at Coltishall, in mid Norfolk, a flight of 66 Squadron (Spitfires) was on dawn readiness on this 10 July, the pilots still confident that there would be no trouble. In spite of 'Harry clampers', the phone rang soon after 7.30 a.m. ordering a section to scramble after a 'bandit' spotted off the coast by the CH station at West Beckham. No. 66, commanded by Squadron Leader Rupert Leigh, had been only the second squadron to convert to Spitfires and had scored their first success back in January.

Pilot Officer Charles Cooke led the section, climbing up through thick cloud in tight formation, breaking into summer sunshine as they were given a final vector on to the bandit. Cooke caught sight of the enemy at 8.15 a.m., the distant slim fuselage confirming its identity as a Do 17. Resorting to emergency boost, the three Spitfires caught up with their target, which was already jinking and sliding in an attempt to evade the fighters' gunfire.

Oberleutnant Bott, who had taken off from Antwerp on this recce flight at dawn, fought hard to survive, manoeuvring his big machine to give his three gunners repeated opportunities to knock out the two attacking Spitfires. A burst head-on at one of them caused the pilot to break off. But the eight guns of the second fighter during a number of deflection attacks soon overwhelmed the Dornier, killing Bott and his second-in-command, Leutnant Schroeder, and sent the other two crew members to their deaths, too, as the machine splashed into the sea off Yarmouth.

Charlie Cooke's windscreen had been damaged and was letting in a lot of cold air, so he rapidly lost altitude but continued to lead his section, keeping his eyes open for fields to land on if his engine failed. But the Merlin had survived the burst of 7.9 mm fire without damage, and before 9 a.m. the three pilots were on the ground celebrating their success.

The weather began to improve soon after the 66 Squadron pilots had landed, the scudding clouds thinning to reveal rapidly growing patches of blue. Farther south, off the Kent coast, Oberleutnant Sombern was completing his recce in another Dornier, and was off the North Foreland when his observer spotted a large convoy heading south-west for the Dover Straits. The wireless operator, on Sombern's instructions, immediately transmitted its position, course and size en clair in case he should meet trouble later. In fact, this seemed unlikely for, to meet the contingency of interference by the RAF, this privileged Dornier had been given an escort of a *Staffel* of Me 109s from Wissant.

This force had been picked up by both Foreness CHL and Dover CH stations at around 10 a.m., and 74 Squadron at Manston had been ordered to scramble a flight of their Spitfires. The heavily outnumbered Spitfires went straight for the Dornier and were immediately pounced on by the 109 'snappers', which scored hits on two of the attackers. But, weaving through the maelstrom of 1/JG51 Messerschmitts, two of 74's machines scored more damaging hits on the slim fuselage of the recce plane, killing Sombern and wounding other members of the crew. The Dornier was seen lumbering south across the water towards Boulogne, where it subsequently crash-landed behind the town.

But the news of the big British convoy set in train the midday events over the English Channel, which led to 10 July becoming the first official day of the Battle of Britain. Considering the privations for Britain to come, the code-name 'Bread' for this convoy has a certain ironical ring, but in fact the ships were in ballast en route to south-coast ports. The massive early afternoon fight over 'Bread' had a dramatic overture. In anticipation of a violent British reaction to the planned raid, Kesselring sent over a *Staffel* of 109s on a 'free chase', trailing its coat to get the RAF off the ground so that its pursuers might be out of fuel when the raid took place, and, secondly, as a bonus, might suffer casualties themselves.

This *Staffel* of 109s took off just before 10.30 a.m. and swept at low level across the Channel, over the white cliffs and, at very high speed, inland behind Dover. Nine Spitfires were scrambled from Biggin Hill, took up the pursuit and, by cutting corners, succeeded in getting among the Messerschmitts briefly although they failed to do any damage, while their leader, Squadron Leader Andrew 'Big Bill' Smith, was hit badly enough to make a forced landing at Hawkinge. First round to the Luftwaffe.

The main action began soon after 1.30 p.m. after radar plots at Dover CH were passed to Uxbridge, indicating an exceptionally heavy build-up behind Cap Gris Nez. No. 11 Group immediately scrambled five squadrons to deal with the threat, among them 111 Squadron (Hurricanes) from Croydon under Squadron Leader John Thompson, an enterprising and particularly daring leader. Thompson, in conjunction with his flight commanders, had devised the squadron's own individual method of attack: head-on with the entire squadron flying line abreast.

First on the scene was a flight of Hurricanes from 32 Squadron at Biggin Hill, which were soon reporting a force of twenty-four Dorniers flying in V formations (vics), closely escorted from the rear and above by about twenty Me 110s with the same number of 109s as top cover at 12,000 feet. The 110s were, in fact, from the 'Horst Wessel' ZG26 led by their famous one-legged commander, Oberstleutnant Joachim-Friedrich Huth. At this stage before the disillusionment with the 110 had set in, the morale of this *Geschwader* was second to none and there was every expectation, with their heavily armed, twin-engined machines, of bloodying the noses of the RAF.

The Hurricanes of 32 Squadron found difficulty in getting to the Dorniers, which were intermittently concealed by scattered cloud and defended more than one-for-one by the fighters. No. 74 Squadron's Spitfires, next on the scene, had better luck. Johnny Mungo-Park, who had already had some success over Dunkirk, got in a long burst on a Dornier which fell out of formation, and his number two damaged a 109 right over the centre of Dover.

The Dover guns, among the first to be radar assisted, now joined in, spotting the sky with black bursts and lines of tracer directed towards the lower flying Germans. Through this lethal barrage nine of John Thompson's Hurricanes came roaring in as if this were no more than a Hendon airshow display, their line abreast attack proving as fearful to the bomber crews as the British CO had predicted. The Dornier formation broke up before the Hurricanes had cut through the bombers, and then Thompson and his pilots turned, climbed sharply and began snapping like terriers at the rearmost sections of the demoralised Dorniers. A number of the Hurricanes latched on to one of them, giving it short deflection bursts until it broke up and fell away. Tom Higgs, an experienced peacetime regular, dealt with another Dornier on his own, becoming so enthused that he closed in too tightly and cut into it. The bomber immediately fell away out of control, taking its captain, Hauptmann Kreiger, and the rest of the crew with it. Higgs's Hurricane, lacking a wing, was photographed by another Dornier crew member spinning down after its victim. A launch sped to the area and found Kreiger and Willy Thalman still alive, but there was no sign of Higgs or the Dornier's other two crew members.

The fight over the convoy and Dover harbour deteriorated into a visual and aural mêlée, the cries of warning over the R/T mixed with unnecessary shouts of triumph. The only identifiable shapes were the circles into which the unwieldy 110s formed themselves defensively, making use of their rear guns. But these circles, too, were rapidly broken up, and the whole massive Luftwaffe force, to everyone's relief, re-crossed the Channel singly or in small sections. Except for one small ship, convoy 'Bread' was unscathed, and Higgs was the only RAF fatality, though three more of John Thompson's Hurricanes were damaged, one by an over-eager Spitfire pilot of 54 Squadron.

Sperrle's *Luftflotte* 3 bombers had better fortune over the West Country. He had wisely ordered a force of sixty-three Ju 88s to approach the Cornish coast from the west, which confused the radar controllers at Dry Tree, on Lizard Point. Too many minutes passed for 92 Squadron, scrambled hurriedly from Pembrey, to get among these fast bombers. The only pilot who got near the enemy was the much decorated, middle-aged Welshman, Ira Jones, Wing Commander (Flying) at a training station. 'Grandpa Tiger' Jones had shot down forty enemy planes in eight months in World War I and was hell-bent on adding to his score. He took off in an unarmed Henley target-tug and intercepted one of the 88s which had just bombed his native land.

'When I got near enough to see the black crosses on the Hun's wings and rudder [wrote Jones], I felt the old joy of action coursing through my body, though my only armament was a Very pistol which fired a cartridge of varicoloured lights.

'A bare 100 yards in front of the bomber, I pressed the trigger of the pistol. Then I turned gently to the left. The lights went floating down prettily in front of the Junker, and the pilot made a sharp flick towards the open sea. . . . I screamed along the top of the cloud, just to have the fun of seeing him run away.'[2]

This 88, and all the others, returned unscathed to France, leaving dead and injured, and a good deal of damage, at Swansea and Falmouth.

The day was marked by other incidents, some tragic, some ridiculous. The New Zealand All-Blacks star, Donald Cobden, of 74 Squadron, felt as if he had been heavily tackled on the rugby field when he landed his crippled Spitfire, wheels up, at Manston; while, late in the afternoon, Pilot Officer Basil Fisher found himself the target for another over-zealous Spitfire pilot. His fuel tank and tailplane were riddled with .303 bullets, but he, too, made it back slowly.

Far up north, intelligence picked up a German voice reporting another convoy – there were at least eight coastal convoys at sea this day. But, due to continuing bad weather here, the convoy was undiscovered by the Luftwaffe and the recce plane escaped from its searchers.

It had been a very high-scoring day. In fact, the claimed figures in *The Times* for Italian losses over Malta and Sidi Barrani were actually as great as the confirmed number of Luftwaffe aircraft lost around Britain: about a dozen in each case, though a further ten Germans were more or less damaged by fighters and anti-aircraft fire. Only one British fighter pilot was lost, indicating graphically the advantage enjoyed by the RAF in fighting over its own territory and coastal waters.

But the German raids were the lead story in the newspapers the next day, and the Americans especially were made aware that a new scale of ferocity in the attacks had been reached by the Luftwaffe. Frank Kelley of the *New York Herald Tribune* reported under the headline 'England Fights Off Biggest Air Attack':

Day-long sallies by waves of German bombers against coastal objectives in England, Wales and Scotland reached a grand climax yesterday in the greatest and fiercest air battle in ten and a half months of war when seventy-five Nazi bombers, escorted by forty-five or more fighters, roared across the English Channel in two formations and showered bombs on a strongly defended convoy bringing vital food and other supplies to these besieged islands.

# 9

*Channel Fight*

## 11 JULY–11 AUGUST

By contrast with the great battles of 10 July, and to a lesser degree 11 July, the following days saw only simmering activity, although all the defence forces were increasingly conscious that, when the time suited the enemy, the onslaught would be renewed on a much greater scale, no doubt as a preliminary to the invasion of Britain.

There were three reasons for this relative quiet. First, the weather was unfavourable for mass bombing attacks, with much fog, low cloud and intermittent summer rain. Second, *Luftflotten* 2 and 3 still needed time for preparation. These reasons were comprehensible to the defenders. The third reason was not, nor did it become clear for a number of years. The fact, as already indicated, was that Hitler, Goering and the German High Command had not yet worked out any strategic policy to deal with the recalcitrant British, who were, in their eyes, clearly 'dead but would not lie down'.

Meanwhile, both sides noted various lessons which would be valuable when the serious fighting began. For example, two Ju 87 Stuka raids in the west on 11 July showed what could be achieved with a well-timed and well-co-ordinated defence, and the price of being caught at a disadvantage.

First, a Flight of six Spitfires of 609 Squadron, vectored on to a Stuka raid, was overwhelmed by three *Staffeln* of Me 109s which had already dealt roughly with patrolling Hurricanes. No. 609, without scoring, lost a flight commander and another pilot killed. On the other hand, a late Stuka raid on Portland escorted by Me 110s at too great a height to interfere with the first swooping attack by 601 Squadron's Hurricanes resulted in the destruction of two of the bombers, and, later, two of the 110s, without loss to themselves. Moreover, the remaining bombers were forced to jettison their loads harmlessly.

Of the fighting the *New York Times* reported the next day:

From a balcony spattered with machine-gun fire and jarred by deafening bombardment, correspondents saw a new chapter in the Battle of Britain written today in a Sabbath sky thick with airplanes and spotted with mushroom puffs from anti-aircraft shells. The gunfire rolled like thunder. One flight of raiders was split into two parts by anti-aircraft fire which kept the group performing aerial aerobatics while British pilots engaged the other. Sometimes the planes were so high they looked like tiny specks of wind-blown paper. The battle raged so furiously that it was impossible to keep accurate track of the planes that fell. . . . Little files of townsfolk on their way to church looked back toward the coast for glimpses of the air fight and heard Messerschmitt cannon fire directed at the barrage balloons.

In this confused fighting over Portland one of the bomber formations had the opportunity to demonstrate the effectiveness of well-co-ordinated defence fire. But on the following day, 12 July, in a sustained attack on Kesselring's Dorniers and Heinkels over an east-coast convoy, two 12 Group Hurricanes were shot down fatally and 151 Squadron suffered serious damage to a number of machines as a result of accurate bombers' cross-fire.*

If these few days in mid-July showed the first hints of vulnerability of the Ju 87 Stuka, they also tragically proved the unsuitability of the Defiant for front-line fighter duties. These turret fighters of 141 Squadron were unblooded until 19 July, when they were moved down to Hawkinge from West Malling. The day had dawned clear, vulnerable convoys were numerous and trouble was expected.

All nine serviceable Defiants were ordered off soon after midday to patrol south of Folkestone. They were carrying out this duty in a model manner when, without warning from the controller, a *Staffel* of Me 109s fell upon them. Unmanoeuvrable and at a hopeless disadvantage, the gunners valiantly attempted to spin their turrets to get a bead on the swooping 'snappers'. Another *Staffel*, eager to join the massacre, added to the one-sidedness of the dogfight. One after the other the

*See page 156 for a note on the accuracy of German bombers' gunnery.

Defiants fell from the sky, some in flames, the gunners at a hopeless disadvantage in struggling to get out.

Only the belated arrival of John Thompson's Hurricanes of 111 Squadron saved the last of 141 Squadron. Three pilots got back to Hawkinge, one of them without his gunner and in an aircraft that could never fly again.

That evening, Hitler gave his 'last appeal to reason' speech to the Reichstag. If the outcome of this combat had been typical of the air fighting, Britain might have had to take some note of the German leader's 'thorny olive branch'. It was not, but this was a bad day all round for Fighter Command.

The outcome of the battles on the following day – 20 July – was very different. The heaviest fighting occurred over an eastbound convoy in the early evening, when Park ordered off two dozen Spitfires and Hurricanes to meet a likely Stuka attack. This duly arrived, heavily escorted, but the defenders were in the eye of the low sun and took the Me 109s by surprise. At a cost of two British fighters, four 109s fell to their guns, and in all nine of Kesselring's machines failed to return.

On the following day, the three *Luftflotten* commanders were summoned to Goering's presence for detailed discussion on the policy to follow preparatory to invasion. This turned out, in fact, to be very much 'the mixture as before'. The main concern was how to dispose of the RAF – the commanders were instructed to submit their detailed plans within a few days – but attention was also focused on the maritime war. In accordance with the wishes of the German Navy, minelaying off British ports was to be intensified, and every effort was to be made to close not only the ports but the passage of convoys up and down the Channel.

The attacks on convoys, in addition to damaging British trade and weakening the RAF, would help, it was thought, to train the German bomber and fighter crews in close co-operation. Special stress was placed on the need for a good air-sea rescue service.[1]

Kesselring did his utmost to comply, on 25 July sending over wave after wave of Stukas with heavy Me 109 escort in an attempt to destroy completely a large convoy off Dover. The German guns on Cap Gris Nez, and strong elements of E-boats, joined in, and between them they sank eight merchantmen and damaged several more, including two destroyers which attempted to come to the rescue.

In the prolonged air fighting, with the odds loaded at least four to one against 11 Group fighters, a number of Junkers – both 87s and 88s –

were destroyed. Squadron Leader James Leathart's Spitfires of 54 Squadron at one time took on a veritable armada of Me 109s, and even the skills of this crack squadron were inadequate to cope with such odds.

Douglas Turley-George remembered being led on this day by his flight commander, 'Wonkey' Way – 'tall, lean, though, a natural leader'. He recalled, too: 'The 109s coming at us from above as we still struggled for height – Way being hit and falling away out of sight [he was dead]. I remember the 109 attacking me from the port side, my trying to turn in towards him, the loud bangs of his cannon-shells striking my Spitfire as he hit me from an almost full deflection angle; and even through the pounding fear that I felt, admiring his marks-manship. A few seconds later, with my aeroplane miraculously still answering apparently normally to the controls, finding myself behind two Me 109s, aligning my sight on one, pressing the gun button – and the guns failing to fire; then diving out of the fight to return to base.'*

But Turley-George never made it. His oil pressure soared, the engine stopped and he searched for somewhere to land. 'I remember the swathe my Spitfire cut through the cornfield; the furious farmer who wanted to know "Why the bloody hell couldn't you have landed in the next field?" '2

The death of Flight Lieutenant Way serves to illustrate the attrition rate of fighter pilots during the French campaign and the early days of the Battle itself, which was to result in the loss of more than one-third of the number of those on operational squadrons at the outset.** Moreover, it was the most experienced who were most missed. Men like Flight Lieutenant Wynford Smith of 263 Squadron, Flying Officer James Allen of 151 Squadron, Flight Lieutenant Philip Barran and Flying Officer Peter Drummond-Hay of 609 Squadron, and Squadron Leader Cooke, CO of 65 Squadron, were all sorely missed in the weeks that lay ahead.

Squadron Leader John Joslin, CO of 79 Squadron, an exceptional pilot loved by his men, died in the first fighter combat over British soil on 7 July. His end, ironically, was reported by a newspaper as that of a German:

*More than 220 members of the Battle of Britain Fighter Association generously replied to the authors' appeal for details and reminiscences of the Battle. Hundreds of members of the public were equally generous with anecdotes of that summer. This is one of many quoted in the narrative and in chapter 23, 'Scrambles'.
**It in no way reduces the depth of the sacrifice to note that a great many more Bomber Command aircrew were lost during the same period.

They were quite low, and we realised unpleasantly, this was the Kill. There was a burst of machine-gun fire and an augur-like glow appeared in the body of the Messerschmitt. The glow spread to a flame and the machine rocketed to earth in a shroud of smoke and flame. The whole terrible drama lasted less than a minute.[3]

Flight Lieutenant Philip Cox of 501 Squadron was another who was expected to go far in the Service, which he had entered seven years before. He had already served in France and had taught fighter tactics to the Poles at St Athan when he joined 501 Squadron in July. He shot down his first Me 109 on 20 July, his victim being Major Kurt Riegel, the *Gruppekommandeur* of 1/JG27. The letter to Cox's mother, typical of so many written late at night by weary COs (in this case Henry Hogan), tells of the tragedy that followed a few days later:

Dear Mrs Cox,
 It is with great regret and very deep sympathy that I write.
 Your son, who was known to most of us as 'PAN' from his initials, was lost on July 27th. At the time that he was killed he was leading the Squadron in my absence. The Squadron fought an engagement in the late afternoon off the S.E. coast. No one actually saw him go but it was confirmed that he crashed into the sea. . . . PAN was such a splendid fellow and most popular with everyone he met. He was always cheerful and possessed a charming manner. He was a first-class pilot and leader. He had done so well at Cranwell and since. . . .
 Yours sincerely,
 (signed) H. A. V. Hogan.[4]

Cox's successful antagonist was Feldwebel Fernsebner of 111/JG52, flying a 109 just south of Dover.

Dover was in the eye of the storm at this early stage of the Battle, its harbour and shipping, presided over by a mass of barrage balloons, soon to be an irresistible target for the long-range guns on Cap Gris Nez and Kesselring's fighters and bombers.

The clear morning of 29 July was especially favourable for an attack on the harbour and two convoys nearby by fifty Ju 87 Stukas, protected up-sun by some eighty Me 109s. The sky above the town became the scene of a mighty combat, with the 109s bouncing the Hurricanes and Spitfires that had hurried to the town's rescue, and the considerable anti-aircraft gun defences firing off at friend and foe alike adding to the din and destruction. To onlookers, including an American bunch of correspondents who seemed to live above the white cliffs, it appeared at the time impossible that any aircraft could survive of the nearly 200 whirling about in a giant mêlée.

In fact only four dive-bombers splashed into the water and only one Spitfire was shot down, although there was much damage on both sides.

But this was only the overture. Ju 88s were soon making a low-level attack on one of the convoys. They, too, had little success and lost one of their number to the naval guns and another in a collision with a balloon cable.

For the first recorded time, an elite force of fighters and fighter-bombers, equipped with Me 109s and 110s, made its existence known when it attacked a sixty-ship convoy off the Thames Estuary. *Erprobungsgruppe* 210, which specialised in attacking difficult pinpoint targets, was to appear many times, and suffer many casualties, in the Battle.

With typical German thoroughness and far-sightedness, the Luftwaffe early formed an air-sea rescue service. Long before a coherent strategy was employed, it was clear that German aircrew would, by the nature of the fighting, come down in the water. This air-sea rescue command, equipped with He 59 seaplanes and Do 18 flying-boats, operated off the coasts of all the recently conquered countries, from Norway to western France. Controversially, they were often armed and always flew under the protection of the Red Cross. Their planes also tended to be discovered close to British convoys as if shadowing and reporting.

The RAF, which at first had nothing to compare with this service, took a brisk view of these planes, and issued this communiqué:

Enemy aircraft bearing civil markings and marked with the Red Cross have recently flown over British ships at sea and in the vicinity of the British coast, and they are being employed for purposes which His Majesty's Government cannot regard as being consistent with the privileges generally accorded to the Red Cross.

His Majesty's Government desire to accord to ambulance aircraft reasonable facilities for the transportation of the sick and wounded, in accordance with the Red Cross Convention, and aircraft engaged in the direct evacuation of the sick and wounded will be respected, provided that they comply with the relevant provisions of the Convention.

His Majesty's Government are unable, however, to grant immunity to such aircraft flying over areas in which operations are in progress on land or at sea, or approaching British or Allied territory, or territory in British occupation, or British or Allied ships.

Ambulance aircraft which do not comply with the above requirements will do so at their own risk and peril.

The Luftwaffe was predictably outraged when RAF fighters began shooting down these He 59s, two of them on 20 July. The word 'murderers' was frequently used by Dr Joseph Goebbels, chief of German propaganda, in accusations against the RAF, though it should be added that some of the Luftwaffe's most accurate gunners were employed as crew members, and several Spitfires and Hurricanes were shot down while attempting to deal with these 'Red Cross' seaplanes.

Nevertheless, a large number of Luftwaffe aircrew were picked up, often close to the British coast, to fight again. British fighter pilots had a much lower expectation of rescue than their German foes until long after the Battle, although some steps were taken to improve their chances:

It was not until fighting over the Channel became a daily feature of operation that the problems involved in building a rescue service were seriously tackled. On 15 July Air Ministry informed Fighter Command that arrangements were being made with the Admiralty for motor-boat patrols to be carried out close inshore when fighting was taking place, and that, in the meantime, the many small craft round our coasts which the Admiralty controlled had been signalled to keep a general watch while the air battle was in progress. The Air Force itself assisted by moving five high speed launches to the No. 11 Group area. . . .[5]

The Royal National Lifeboat Institution also contributed its unsurpassed services, but it remained a tragic fact throughout the Battle that many a fighter pilot, who had survived combat and escape by parachute, died of hypothermia, his body washed ashore sometimes weeks later.

Another consequence for Fighter Command of the German concentration on shipping and ports was the increasing importance of the coastal satellite airfields, which allowed the defending aircraft to reach the enemy with the least possible loss of time. Some of these satellites were no more than farmers' fields with a hedge or two removed. Others, like Warmwell in 10 Group, were only being completed when the Battle started. Sometimes pilots moved in at dawn and returned at dusk, grabbing bully-beef sandwiches and mugs of hot tea when they could, like the ground staff.

Accommodation was primitive, sometimes only in tents. At Warmwell, ten miles from the Dorset coast, 10 Group squadrons took it in turns to operate from this forward station, the pilots piling pyjamas and a change of shirt and underwear into the cockpit. Often sleep was snatched stretched out on a couple of chairs in the ready room, itself no more than a camouflaged wooden hut.

The servicing party, which was relieved only from time to time,

worked extremely hard under hazardous circumstances and in conditions that were even more austere than the pilots', with the most
elementary plumbing arrangements and camp-beds with the standard
issue, always filthy, blankets.

'July was a bit of a dog's dinner for the Hun,' one pilot summed up the
fighting. Individually, the enemy had shown skill and courage, and as
far as the *matériel* was concerned the twin-engined bombers, and
especially the Ju 88, had shown their excellent qualities. The Me 109,
with its cannon armament and two-stage, supercharged, Daimler-Benz
engine, had proved itself as formidable as feared, quite the equal of the
Spitfire, although the Spitfire and the Hurricane (with its much inferior
performance) had shown themselves to be more manoeuvrable in a tight
contest.
    But there were already signs that the much-vaunted '*zerstoerer*', the
twin-engined Me 110 and the Ju 87, were easy game for a skilled
Hurricane or Spitfire pilot. The RAF lost sixty-nine fighters between
10 and 31 July and shot down some 155 Luftwaffe aircraft. The Germans,
in the course of numerous pressed-home attacks on shipping, had sunk
eighteen small coastal vessels and one or two larger vessels, and four
naval destroyers.

During the latter half of July, while the Luftwaffe was completing its
deployment and attacking its interim targets, the German Army and
Navy were with great difficulty concocting plans for invasion. The
discussions were far from smooth. In the hope of splitting the defending
forces, the Army wanted three separate landings on a broad front
stretching from Ramsgate to Lyme Bay. But the Navy, conscious of its
great inferiority to Britain's, felt unable to safeguard the widely spread
crossings involved, or muster anything like the number of invasion craft
needed, and insisted on landings on a much narrower front – preferably
between Dover and Eastbourne. Not until 27 August was this dispute
finally resolved – largely in the Navy's favour, but even then with all the
marks of a smudgy compromise. The assaults would take place over a
front between Hythe and Worthing, with an airborne descent behind
Folkestone; but if things went well a further landing might then be
attempted at Lyme.[6]
    While this wrangling continued, the Luftwaffe's orders became
clearer. On 30 July Hitler told Goering to have his forces in readiness to
begin 'the great battle of the Luftwaffe against England' at twelve

hours' notice. The following day, during a conference at Hitler's mountain retreat, the Berghof, Raeder made it plain that the earliest possible date for launching an invasion would be 15 September 1940, but that he personally favoured May 1941. Displeased, Hitler said that the situation would not improve with time and ruled that preparations must be completed by 15 September.[7] But the die was not finally cast. In the words of the directive that then ensued from the OKW on 1 August: 'Eight or fourteen days after the launching of the air offensive against Britain scheduled to begin on approximately 5 August, the Fuehrer will decide whether the invasion will take place this year or not: his decision will depend largely on the outcome of the air offensive.' In fact, Hitler's mind was already pondering the merits of attacking Russia while the going was good. If Britain could be disposed of first, so much the better. If not, she could await her turn after the quick German victory in the East.[8]

On 1 August, too, Hitler issued his own directive (No. 17): 'In order to establish the necessary conditions for the final conquest of England', he instructed the Luftwaffe 'to overpower the English air force with all the forces at its command, in the shortest possible time'. The attacks were to be directed 'primarily against flying units, their ground installations and their supply organisations, also against the aircraft industry, including that manufacturing anti-aircraft equipment'. After achieving temporary or local air superiority the Luftwaffe was then to attack the ports, but only lightly those on the south coast 'in view of our own forthcoming operations'. Air attacks on shipping could meanwhile be reduced, but at any time the Luftwaffe must be ready to support naval operations and 'take part in full force in Operation Sealion'. 'I reserve to myself', Hitler added ominously, 'the right to decide on terror attacks as measures of reprisal.' His directive concluded: 'The intensification of the air war may begin on or after 5 August. The exact time is to be decided by the air force after the completion of preparations and in the light of the weather.'[9]

Meanwhile, Goering had been giving the forthcoming operations some – for him – serious thought. Following his conference on 21 July, suggestions from the *Luftflotten* had been arriving at the German High Command. The broad outline of a strategy – though none of its vital details – was by now taking shape in Goering's mind. The British fighter force would be destroyed, in the air and on the ground, in the course of a series of attacks moving progressively inland: for five days the assault would aim at targets within 150–100 kilometres radius south of London, then for three days within a similar radius of 100–50 kilometres, then for a final five days within a 50 kilometre radius extending right round the British capital. This fortnight's work, dubbed *Adlerangriff* ('Eagle Attack'), would make 'Sealion' unnecessary or a mere walk-over. The opening day – *Adlertag* – would be decided upon as soon as plans were complete and weather permitted.[10]

On 1 August Goering, resplendent in a new white suit, again met his commanders, this time at The Hague. The official record of the meeting has not survived, but one of those present, Oberst Theo Osterkamp, commander of JG51, the Me 109 *Geschwader* most involved in the recent Channel fighting, later wrote a vivid account. From this it is clear that, in regard to planning, the Luftwaffe was far from fully prepared for its next venture. Its intelligence reports, too, left something to be desired. The number of British fighters thought to be available to defend the vital southern half of the country was said to be at most 400–500, which was not far from the mark as far as Hurricanes and Spitfires were concerned; but this ignored the fact that Dowding could very rapidly move reinforcements or replacements down from the Midland and northern sectors. Brushing aside higher estimates as well as praise of the Spitfire from Osterkamp, Goering insisted on the simplicity of the task ahead. There was, however, a jolt to his confidence, as well as to that of others in the room, when he heard Kesselring and Sperrle declare that between them, for the start of an offensive beginning at that time, they would be unable to muster even 700 serviceable bombers. 'Is this my Luftwaffe?' its corpulent Chief enquired sadly.[11]*

The following day Goering issued his personal *Adlerangriff* directive to the three *Luftflotten*, but this was largely concerned with repeating broad objectives – the establishment of air supremacy and the destruction of British naval strength. Until the grand assault, harassing attacks should continue as usual against the usual objectives such as airfields, ports and factories. On 3 August further instructions emanated from Luftwaffe headquarters, including orders to attack British radar stations at the outset of the offensive. By 6 August, when Goering held another conference at Karinhall, plans were apparently complete for the opening phase, though not for any of the subsequent stages. But the great blow must fall as soon as there was a prospect of three days of fine weather.

*Nevertheless, by 10 August they had 875 bombers serviceable, as well as 365 dive-bombers (which they cannot have been counting).

Like much of July, some of the early days of August were unfavourable for bombing convoys, or anything else for that matter, and statistics show far more aircraft lost in accidents than in action. It was not until the second week of the month that the fighting intensified. Ironically, in view of what was to come when roles were reversed, it was a Bomber Command daylight raid on the German base at Haamstede that was the most effective operation of this quiet period. Twenty-nine Blenheims took part, though not all bombed the target. The bombs fell just as some Me 109s were taking off, killing or wounding six pilots and destroying or damaging seven aircraft.

It was not until 8 August that really heavy air fighting again took place. It lasted off and on for much of the day, its location governed by the movements of the large convoy 'Peewit', which *Luftflotte* 3 was determined to destroy. It nearly did so, too, but at a very considerable price in Stukas – eight lost in all, while many more dragged themselves home with dead or wounded gunners. The cost in 109s was even heavier. In all, in this day of intense fighting, the Luftwaffe lost thirty-one aircraft, the RAF twenty.

As a precursor to *Adlerangriff* and the critical fighting of the middle of the month, 11 August – a clear day at first with only high cirrus clouds – saw the hardest fighting so far. It took place mainly in the Isle of Wight area, where strong elements of *Luftflotte* 3 set their sights on the naval installations at Weymouth and Portland. Many of the great figures of the Battle, like Peter Townsend, 'Sailor' Malan, Denis David and Alan Deere figured in the records for this day, contributing to the total of thirty-eight Luftwaffe planes shot down, by far the highest figure so far.

By last light on this day, the preliminaries and the dress rehearsals were over. Goering had committed the Luftwaffe to a new strategy that was to endure for almost a month and bring Fighter Command almost to its knees. The weather seemed set; and, as already noted, like some revelation it had belatedly occurred to the German High Command, Goering and his staff (the name of the first officer to propose it will never be known) that the way to knock out swiftly RAF Fighter Command was to start by destroying its eyes – its radar stations. Another thirty-six hours and *Adlertag*!

# 10

## Clearing the Way

### 12 AUGUST

If the meteorological boffins had been over-optimistic earlier, on 11 August they were quite confident that a long, fine spell was on the way. The Luftwaffe, which daily flew weather flights far out into the Atlantic, was equally confident that barometric pressure was building up around the Azores. This meant the likelihood of a number of fine hot days and, in the context of the Battle, it also meant heavy fighting.

The German High Command was at this time by no means dismayed by the results of the first five weeks of air fighting. The optimistic claims of the pilots were matched by the favourable conclusions of the intelligence officers on the ground, and they all aspired to being angels with tidings of great joy. Their figures of RAF fighter losses set against their calculated output of new machines led Kesselring and Sperrle to believe that Fighter Command could muster no more than about 450 Spitfires and Hurricanes when the real figure was more like 750. Fourteen days was Goering's estimate for knocking out the last strength of the RAF in order to clear the way for the invasion: first *Adlerangriff*, to start the following day, with the weather clearly on their side as it had been during the *blitzkrieg* in France, then *Seeloewe*: 'Eagle Attack' followed by 'Sealion'. By November, Britain would be on her knees.

At the same time, German commanders and aircrew alike did not underrate the task ahead. The month of July had been a period of reappraisal. Both the skill of the British pilots and the quality of the machines had come as a surprise. After Poland and France, where they had fought the closely co-ordinated land–air battles for which the Luftwaffe had been prepared, this sustained attrition against an enemy who was often elusive, early-warned and co-ordinated, and always beyond a strip of water varying in width from twenty-three to 100 miles, was stretching their skill and resources beyond expectation.

But their cause would prevail, of that every commander, pilot, gunner, navigator and wireless operator had no doubt. At the German High Command Sperrle, Kesselring and their staff – all high-peaked caps, glinting leather, decorations and brass – awaited the arrival of Reichsmarschall Goering. He stepped out of a massive, open, camouflaged Mercedes, baton tucked under his arm, the personification of arrogant authority. Then came much clicking of heels, flicking of wrists to signify 'Heil Hitler!' and shuffling for position before entering the building. Today the supreme commander would follow the preliminaries. Already, at 7 a.m., the Me 109s were out on 'free chases', challenging and provoking, sweeping at 'nought feet' over the undulating fields behind the Kent coast, where the early harvesters were out and restraining their horses as the fighters streaked overhead.

And tomorrow's weather? Goering was informed that two weather squadrons had reported back from their Atlantic recces and all the indications were favourable. Meanwhile, the Reichsmarschall was not informed about the first loss of the day, which was serious and guaranteed to put him in an evil temper. Half-a-dozen He 111s of II/KG27 had been out during the night over the English West Country and South Wales to keep the people awake and drop their bombs on targets like Plymouth, Swansea and Bournemouth. B Flight of RAF 87 Squadron on detachment from Yorkshire to Filton, outside Bristol, had scrambled and Pilot Officer Peter Comely, new to the squadron, had intercepted one of these Heinkels after it had bombed Bristol docks. He damaged it so badly that the crew baled out into the dark soon after midnight. The German High Command knew no details; all that was known was that the *Gruppekommandeur*, Major F.-K. Schlichting, his second-in-command and two more senior officers had failed to return. There was nothing to be gained by passing this news on to the Reichsmarschall at the start of a day of such high hopes.

The 12th of August was to be the day for putting out the eyes and the airfields (or some of them) of the RAF. The tall radar towers, long since correctly identified, were clearly proving more effective than the

German High Command had reckoned. It was still not appreciated how efficient were not only the CH and CHL radar, but, equally important within the defence structure, the communications and co-ordination of the early-warning system. The last month's fighting had disquietingly revealed how, time after time, the weight and direction of Luftwaffe attacks had been anticipated so early by the RAF that the fighter squadrons were there, awaiting them like tipped-off gangland rivals. Only the previous day, the big raid on Portland and Weymouth had been met by Spitfires and Hurricanes from five squadrons, which were soon reinforced by twenty more Hurricanes and a dozen Spitfires.

For *Adlerangriff*, then, every radar station between Portland and the Thames Estuary was to be put out of action, mainly by low-level bombing attacks which, it was predicted, would topple the towers and destroy the buildings and communications. The first of these radar-breaking assaults, timed for around 9 a.m., was assigned to that superb pilot, leader and Me 110 specialist, Hauptmann Walter Rubensdoerffer of *Erpro* 210. He had already shown himself a pioneer in the exploitation of the single- and twin-engined Messerschmitt fighters in the bomber role, beginning with a single 250 kg bomb under the 109's belly and two 500 kg bombs for the 110.

All the previous day, Rubensdoerffer had been planning his operations against the easternmost radar stations, and his commanders and aircrew knew as exactly what they were to do as if they had rehearsed the raids for weeks. The locality of the targets posed no problems. From Gris Nez crews could see the obtrusive towers of Dover CHL, and in clear conditions others, too.

Rubensdoerffer led off his four sections of four fighter-bomber 110s from Marck, a few miles east of Calais, at 8.40 a.m. The Messerschmitts, taking a shade longer than usual to become airborne with their big loads, swung inland briefly through 360 degrees and then picked up a westerly course down-Channel. There was still a little haze about but not enough to obscure the white cliffs of Dover, and the sun was burning it off fast. Keeping at low level over the water and reckoning on confusing the radar 'eyes' by sustaining a 270 degrees course, south-east of Beachy Head the sixteen 110s suddenly broke north towards East-bourne and Pevensey Bay.

Now *Erpro* 210 broke up into its four sections, and Rubensdoerffer himself set course for a more inland CH station, Dunkirk, north-west of Dover. Hauptmann Martin Lutz had been assigned the first and easiest target, Pevensey CH, right at the start of their run and dead

Air Chief Marshal Sir Hugh Dowding, Lord Dowding of Bentley Priory GCB, GCVO, CMG, Air Officer Commanding-in-Chief RAF Fighter Command 1936–40 (portrait by Sir Walter Russell).

Bombing the Channel ports, September 1940 (painting by Eric Ravilious).

65 Squadron Spitfires at Sawbridgeworth, Herts., August 1940
(painting by Eric Ravilious).

A heavy anti-aircraft battery about to open fire (painting by C. W. Nevinson).

Air fight over Portland, September 1940 (painting by Richard Eurich).

The Battle of Britain (painting by Paul Nash).

Junkers 87 Stukas en route to England.

Messerschmitt 110 flying above the white cliffs of South-East England.

Messerschmitt 110
crews at an outdoor
briefing.

Messerschmitt 109s in
'finger four' formation
over St Margaret's Bay.

Group Captain Peter Townsend's decorations include (first four) Distinguished Service Order; Distinguished Flying Cross and Bar; 1939–45 star, with clasp for Battle of Britain; and Air Crew Europe Star.

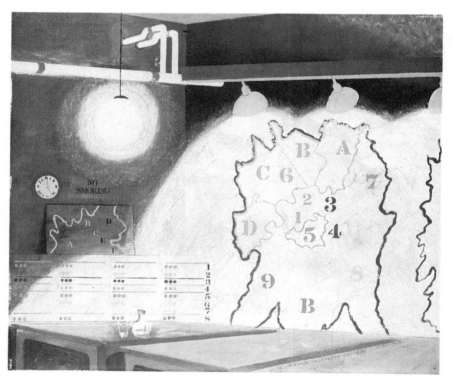

Civil Defence control room (painting by John Piper).

ahead as they raced towards land. Oberleutnant Wilhelm-Richard Roessiger had been ordered to follow the coast east to the towering masts just beyond Rye, while Oberleutnant Otto Hintze with his four fighter-bombers was deputed to knock down those provocative towers above Dover.

Lutz's fighter-bombers dropped their eight 500 kg bombs dead on their Pevensey target at the end of a 300+ mph glide. They could scarcely miss. There was no opposition on the ground or in the air. Concrete buildings collapsed and spread their fragments widely, as if made of paperboard. Telephone lines were torn apart, airmen and WAAFs were killed and injured, smoke and dust rose from the craters. The noise was stupefying, and the awful silence and darkness that followed seconds later told of severed power lines – in fact, the main supply cable had gone.

At Rye along the coast, Roessiger's foursome destroyed every hut, but as at Pevensey the reinforced transmitting and receiving blocks and the watch office survived though the personnel were severely shaken. The damage at Dunkirk, too, proved the success of Rubensdoerffer's training: every bomb bang on target.

At Dover, AC2 Clifford Vincent was on watch duty high up a radar mast, with views far to the north overland and across the Channel to enemy soil. 'Vincent just had time to marvel at the sight of the rapidly approaching fighter-bombers before the masts rocked from the explosions around their bases and shrapnel went clanging through the girderwork. As the dust and smoke cleared, he looked below to where Flight Lieutenant Peter Axon was shouting and gesticulating to him to climb down.'[1]

There was no need to hurry. None of the towers had more than superficial damage, and it was the same at the three other stations. Lattice-work radar towers, so visible and seemingly so vulnerable, were proving almost immune to high explosive.* Dunkirk continued to transmit and report without a break, and the other three stations, thanks to the cleverly contrived emergency measures – stand-by diesel power units, for example – were soon on the air again.

But at Dover the aftermath silence was broken by a different high explosive sound, 'a new bloody bang'. More a c-r-u-m-p. And in the town, houses collapsed and citizens died with not an aircraft in the sky.

---

*The same was to prove true with the lattice masts of American battleships at Pearl Harbor sixteen months later.

These were the first rounds of German long-range artillery fire from France to land on British soil, reducing by another degree Britain's island protection of past centuries.

While the shattered personnel, with outside help, strove to repair ruptured lines and implement emergency measures at the three most severely damaged radar stations, Kesselring received satisfying reports that Rubensdoerffer had been seventy-five per cent successful. These reports were issued by General Wolfgang Martini, head of signals at the German High Command, upon whom Kesselring utterly relied. The Feldmarschall concluded that he could now attack with impunity, confident that his *Geschwader* would have surprise on their side, and that *Adlerangriff* would open with the enemy all-but blind when the later raid to the west was also completed successfully.

To test his belief, Kesselring therefore mounted several attacks on convoys in the Thames Estuary and off the North Foreland, using the most precise, but most vulnerable, weapon he had: Ju 87s, which had already suffered such savage losses when caught with the promptitude radar-directed fighters could achieve. The Feldmarschall was partly justified in his confidence. The cogs of the elaborate reporting system had not been destroyed, but had been knocked temporarily out of synchronisation by Rubensdoerffer's accurate breakfast-time attacks. 'The next two hours [after 9.30 a.m.] saw one of those happily rare periods when the Fighter Command system worked inefficiently. Three squadrons were constantly in the air throughout the two hours, one over the Sussex coast and two over the Straits, but although German forces flew over the coast no interceptions were made.'[2]

It was the Foreness CHL station, untouched by the radar station attacks, that picked up the blips, first of 50+ over the North Foreland, on a northerly heading as if to cross the Thames Estuary. Then this force began flying to and fro east–west as if searching for the reported convoys. Another force of 12+ was picked up also moving north at no great speed, and the Biggin Hill and Hornchurch controllers surmised that the two groups were meeting before delivering their attack on the convoys 'Agent' and 'Arena' off the North Foreland in the Estuary.

To counter this threat, 65 and 501 Squadrons, already airborne near Dover, were ordered north to intercept, and the Spitfires of 54 Squadron at Hornchurch and the Hurricanes of 111, temporarily at Hawkinge, were ordered off. For once, they were all too late, and the German top cover of 109s came down and mixed it with the searching fighters.

But the second dive-bombing attack by Ju 87s on 'Agent', between Deal and Ramsgate, was driven off by a mixed force of Hurricanes, at a stiff price – four being shot down in the mêlée with the 'snappers', and none claimed. The Polish Pilot Officer Lukaszwickz, who had been with 501 for only five days, was killed. So was Pilot Officer Robert Beley, who had been with 151 for a month, and at about 11.40 a.m. was forced to bale out, badly wounded, over the sea. He was still alive when picked up by a launch, but died later. The other pilots survived.

Almost simultaneously with these convoy attacks off the Kent coast, Kesselring and Sperrle launched a ferocious attack on the centre of England's south coast, comprising – amongst much else – the naval bases at Portsmouth and Portland, the industries of Portsmouth and Southampton, including the vital Supermarine Spitfire works at Woolston, and the key radar station at Ventnor on the Isle of Wight.

The heart of this force comprised 100 Ju 88s of the *Eidelweissgeschwader*, KG51, based at Etampes, Orly and Melun-Villaroche. This force had taken off shortly before 11 a.m. and made a rendezvous with its fighter escort half an hour later. One hundred and twenty Me 110s of *Zerstoerergeschwader* 76 and 2, from other French airfields, accompanied the bombers north from the Normandy coast. Another twenty-five fighters, 109s of JG53, were then despatched direct, in order to save fuel, to the target area where they were ordered to give top cover. These pilots, especially, found the long sea crossing a taxing exercise, knowing that they would have little more than ten minutes combat time to spare at their extreme limit of range before having to return, or ditch in the Channel.

Meanwhile, the frantic British efforts being made to put back on the air the damaged radar stations were eventually successful. The back-up reserve stations were being activated too, but as with any unexpected and stunning blow time was needed to recover, and in the inevitable confusion the Ju 88s and their escort were missed by the CHs and CHLs including, less forgivably, the undamaged CH at Poling. Electronic magic gave way to the human eye, therefore, and the admirable, steady Observer Corps posts at Shoreham, Worthing and Middleton, west of Brighton, sent in long-range sightings of the 200+ hostiles proceeding like a distant cloud of locusts down-Channel.

The warning signal was flashed to the Observer Corps centre at

Horsham, and thence to 11 Group at Uxbridge and 10 Group at Box. Within minutes, more than fifty Spitfires and Hurricanes were airborne and heading for the obvious target of Portsmouth, anxious as always not to make contact with a height disadvantage. The squadron commander of 213's Hurricanes from Exeter, Hector McGregor, thought he might be best placed to make first contact. He had had a rough time the previous day when he had shot down a Ju 88, but had lost one of his flight commanders and four more of his pilots in a stiff fight over Portland. And now, as his Hurricane struggled for height, he was hell-bent on evening up the score.

KG51's *Kommodore*, Oberst Dr Fisser, led his *Geschwader* west, some fifteen miles off the flat west Sussex coast, the triangular configuration of the Isle of Wight dead ahead. Both he and his *Geschwader* had, in eleven months of war, been extremely lucky, their most recent loss being on 27 July. His map showed clearly the formation of the balloon barrage over Portsmouth and its vicinity, and he followed the plan of holding his westerly course down the Solent to deceive the defences that his force was going to repeat yesterday's raid on Portland. Then he ordered his armada sharply to starboard, just as a man o' war might do, in order to enter Portsmouth harbour through a gap in the balloons. Fisser and fourteen of his crack crews had other plans, though, and as he circled he watched his bombers going in like a huge serpent in line-astern.

The anti-aircraft fire, from every ship in the harbour, firing for once from a steady gun platform, and from the Army's guns ashore, was in its intensity like nothing Fisser, or any of his crews, had seen before – 4.7 and 4.5 inch, 3 inch, 2 pound pom-poms, Bofors and even 20 mm filled the sky with black puffs and criss-crossing tracer. Now Fisser himself turned south-west, losing height and gaining speed rapidly as he raced at 300 mph and at 5,000 feet over Foreland, the eastern tip of the Isle of Wight, heading for the little seaside resort of Ventnor. There, on a strip of high-level ground close to the town, were sited the tall towers of the CH station which covered the whole mid-Channel area, and whose screens were now scarred with the blips from Fisser's main force and, more ominously, the detachment coming directly for the station.

Fisser wasted no time. Like Rubensdoerffer, he wanted to get in and out as fast as possible, and he aimed the nose of his Ju 88 at the towers and the buildings, all connected by a criss-cross pattern of white concrete paths which would have given away the target in much less favourable visibility. Like most 88 commanders, he favoured the shallow dive approach which gave his bomb-aimer the best visibility and more time to make last split-second adjustments than in the 45 degree or steeper approach.

Fisser saw no anti-aircraft fire, and it was almost impossible to miss with the four 250 kg, delayed-action, high-explosives they all carried. Lighter by a ton, he pulled up steeply above the scattered boarding-houses and small hotels of the seaside resort, over the chalk cliffs and the breakers on the shore, and watched the bombs explode. Fisser was a veteran of the Polish and French campaigns, had dropped bombs across half of Europe (or so it sometimes seemed), but he could never have seen such concentrated devastation. The whole target was engulfed by white-and-black clouds, with more exuding from the inferno as he turned away and ordered his planes to close in, climbing at full throttle, to escape the avenging wrath of the British.

But already the first reports were coming in from behind that still distant Hurricanes were diving towards them. And, belatedly, the Bofors anti-aircraft fire had burst into action – or perhaps it had been firing when they were all too preoccupied with their run-in. It was accurate firing, too, and as Fisser continued his turn overland north of Ventnor, he suddenly realised that his whole detached force was in a dangerous position, with a height disadvantage and only a scattering of Me 110s to give them any support before they could clear the area.

McGregor's Hurricanes were first on the Ventnor scene, as he had predicted, but 152 Squadron's Spitfires came in seconds later, and a whirling fight ensued before Fisser could get his 88s away. McGregor himself got on the tail of a 110, ignoring the rear-gunner's fire, and despatched it with a single burst. Then two more of his squadron began harassing Fisser's 88 and were joined by two more of 152's Spitfires. The *Kommodore* was killed at the controls. The Junkers, trailing flames, dived towards the ground, was pulled up violently, presumably by one of the crew, and headed towards Godshill Park, yawing and only partly under control. It struck the ground heavily, sending up a cloud of pale earth, and slid to a halt, its back broken but the fire self-extinguished.

Leutnant Schad and Oberleutnant Luederitz, both wounded, staggered from the wreckage, and their captors succeeded in extricating the fourth crewman, badly burned, a few minutes later.

Most of Fisser's *Geschwader* were still attacking Portsmouth at

12.25 p.m. as he lay dead in this pleasant park on the Isle of Wight a few miles away. The anti-aircraft fire remained intense and accurate throughout the Portsmouth attack. Ten more 88s fell to the RAF fighters' guns, or the ground gunners (most likely both) besides McGregor's 110 victim, which went into the sea off Foreland. By a curious freak of the tides in these uncertain waters, the body of Fritz Budig was washed ashore near Gosport, while his pilot's body was found on the beach near Boulogne five weeks later.

In Portsmouth, by 1 p.m. the cacophony of battle had been succeeded by the mournful sounds of its aftermath, of the bells of ambulances and fire engines, the crackle of many fires and, intermittently, of falling masonry, and the cries of those needing help and those attempting to give succour. There were about 100 casualties, a small enough statistic compared with the massive raids later in the war, but a sharp and painful stab in the heart of this small city.

From the Luftwaffe's point of view, it had been an expensive business, less for the ten per cent losses of aircraft than the irreplaceable loss of two experienced leaders – one of them at the hands of Squadron Leader McGregor, whose squadron had suffered so seriously the previous day, and with two more pilots killed in this raid. On the other hand, Fisser's confidence – before he was killed – that he had knocked out Ventnor CH station was well founded. Of all the radar sites Kesselring and Sperrle had set their hearts on destroying, Ventnor came nearest to being completely crushed. Every building had been demolished, partly for lack of water to extinguish the fires, the lattice work of the masts had been damaged, and vital cables and power had been severed. But only three days and nights passed before this important radar station was on the air again, thanks to the rapid erection of a mobile station nearby.

By 2 p.m. on this day of softening-up, Kesselring and Sperrle could agree that the radar station attacks had fulfilled their purpose. Surely, it seemed to these two experienced commanders, the RAF's eyes had been put out. As for the enemy airfields on their target list for the day, there was every reason to believe that the *Kampfgeschwader* and *Zerstoerergeschwader* would prove themselves to be equally successful on these raids.

The RAF airfields scheduled for destruction were the three nearest the coast, Lympne, Hawkinge and Manston. By an odd and unfortunate stroke of fate the first two airfields were on the itinerary of the

RAF's Inspector-General, the admirable Air Chief Marshal Sir Edgar Ludlow-Hewitt. ('What a time for bullshit!' airmen exclaimed incredulously.) Lympne was first bombed before Rubensdoerffer's radar station attacks, Dungeness reporting a small raid building up soon after 7 a.m. No. 610 Squadron's Spitfires were at once scrambled from Biggin Hill and climbed to 10,000 feet, while the raid appeared to be heading for the Thames Estuary and the two convoys which were to be targets later in the morning.

The raid suddenly turned south-west and came in near Romney marshes at 16,000 feet, the bombers in three vics of three escorted by a dozen Me 109s. Squadron Leader Ellis found himself too low to get among the bombers before they dropped their bombs – more than 140 of them at 8.16 a.m. – on Lympne, and his pilots were soon in a one-to-one sustained dogfight with the Messerschmitts. Ellis was the undoubted winner. Four of his Spitfires were damaged, only one seriously, and one of his flight commanders had to bale out. But 610 put one of JG26's 109s into the sea, and a second had a more prolonged death over the village of Elham, watched by many of the villagers: 'The inhabitants came out of their houses to watch as the plane, chased by a frenzied group of Spitfires, flew wildly about the sky with its undercarriage lowered. After scything in low over the village, it flew into Running Hill, where it cartwheeled across a meadow and disintegrated in a cloud of dust without catching fire. The pilot, Oblt Friedrich Butterweck of JG26, was found dead in a field six miles away.'[3]

While this combat was still in progress, Lympne's station commander was issuing urgent orders to tidy the place up before Ludlow-Hewitt arrived with his entourage. War was important, but so was protocol. There was general relief when the word got round that the Inspector-General had rearranged his timetable to visit this airfield at 5.35 p.m. Cooks, clerks, kitchen staff, orderlies and batmen swarmed out on to the grass with shovels and barrows for a day of relentless digging in the sun.

The ubiquitous Inspector-General, with unfortunate timing, arrived simultaneously – to the very minute – with a second large force of bombers. Ludlow-Hewitt was hustled into a shelter while Ju 88s plastered the airfield from end to end, in many cases reopening the craters which had been filled in with such speed and diligence after the first raid. A second wave, intended to complete the work, was of Dorniers, dropping smaller bombs. The Inspector-General left as soon as it was suitable to do so. 'I'll return in a few days' time,' he told the station commander, Squadron Leader Montgomery. The crater-filling began again before he was out of sight.

After this pasting, even a Tiger Moth would have been hard put to land at Lympne. What was much more serious was that Hawkinge, a few miles to the north-east, was also being severely dealt with by a *Staffel* of Ju 88s. Hawkinge so far had had a mixed day. No. 501's Hurricanes, led by Squadron Leader Henry Hogan, had already scrambled several times before Mike Crossley arrived to give some support in the afternoon. The Inspector-General had additionally kept everyone on their toes, disregarding the hundreds of enemy contrails above.

Ludlow-Hewitt was on his way to Lympne when the Junkers came over Hawkinge just before 5 p.m. They had been picked up by the disrupted radar station at Rye and 32 Squadron was ready for them. No. 501 was scrambled yet again and 64's Spitfires were already in the air. No one has properly explained why the 88s at 5,000 feet were not dealt with more severely. An American, Pilot Officer A. G. Donahue, got amongst them, but the German rear gunners, unusually well-co-ordinated, coned him and set his Spitfire alight. 'Floating down by parachute in the evening breeze, he nursed his burns in the cool air.'[4] But no one made any claims. It seems likely that the high speed of this most modern German bomber once more got it out of trouble – that plus the relative invulnerability of its radial engine, by contrast with the glycol-cooled, in-line engine of the Dorniers and Heinkels.

The devastation was appalling. Two hangars, workshops and domestic buildings were all flattened and others were burning. The fire crew were for a while helpless as the water tower had become a surreal many-spouted fountain from bomb splinter holes.

Corporal Wireless Operator D. G. Lee, later a warrant officer, who was in charge of the Signals Sections of the Operations Block, had warning of what was to come from listening in to the R/T, which had become 'a confused babble of voices, with a few shouted "Behind you!'s". Almost immediately after this our building started shaking in a peculiarly regular manner but no bombs were heard falling and no explosions. While we were still puzzling over what had caused this rhythmic earthquake, the screamers started coming down out of the sky. We had no time to get out of the building to the air-raid shelters as all hell was let loose outside, so we scrambled underneath radio benches, teleprinter tables, etc., expecting every moment to be our last.'

The 'rhythmic earthquake' was caused by inaccurate, high-level 'carpet bombing', according to this Corporal, the bomb-aimers releasing at regular brief intervals while flying in close formation. The only damage from this high-level attack was to the next door golf course.

Over the station there lay a slowly drifting cloud of dust and smoke from the low-level attack, which gave the German pilots as they came in yet again enough evidence to presume that Hawkinge was out of commission. They would have been astonished to hear Mike Crossley, six feet six inches, with his squadron which would never make it back to Biggin Hill, call out on the R/T (at least *that* was working) that he had to come in – like it or not.

'OK,' replied the controller apologetically, 'but you see how we are.' He added, perhaps unnecessarily, 'Try and avoid the craters.'

All five Hurricanes made it, and moreover survived a second strafing and bombing attack a few minutes later. The tall Crossley led the way, looking as always when he had his hood open as if it could never be closed.

Corporal Lee also recalled the speed with which the recovery and repair services reacted. Although all electricity services had been severed, within minutes 'the civilian "Works and Bricks" engineers were already hard at work getting the [emergency] generators started up and very soon the Signals Section was back in business again. The Army then moved in and worked all night filling in the bomb craters on the landing field, blowing up a few unexploded bombs in the process and by next morning at first light, another squadron of fighter aircraft was able to land, refuel and get ready for the next attack.'

It was a swift sequence of recovery activity that was to be repeated time and again in the coming weeks at many airfields in southern England.

Earlier in the day Kesselring's other airfield target had been Manston, or 'Charlie 3' – a code-name quite well known by the Germans. Manston was – and is – the most forward of all airfields in south-east England. For this reason alone, it was one of the most heavily attacked during the Battle. It was also another all-grass airfield. In dry weather this gave it a distinct advantage over runways, which were much more difficult to repair; and it also allowed a squadron to take off together, if it so chose. No. 65 Squadron's CO always favoured this when conditions allowed. Just at a time when Hawkinge was being bombed, Flight Lieutenant 'Sam' Saunders was leading off the twelve Spitfires of

65 Squadron, in four vics of three, Jeffrey Quill leading the fourth section on the extreme right:

'We were just formed up [wrote Quill] on the ground and awaiting Sam's signal to start rolling. I was therefore looking out to my left towards the leading section when I became aware of, rather than actually hearing, a sort of reverberating "crump" behind and to my right. I looked quickly over my right shoulder to see one of the hangar roofs close behind us ascending heavenwards. . . . I caught a glimpse through smoke of what looked like a Me 110 pulling sharply out of a dive and immediately concluded that it was high time for Quill to be airborne.'[5]

Although 148 heavy bombs were dropped and Manston was raked by cannon and machine-gun fire, Quill succeeded in getting off the ground. More remarkable still, when he had got clear with flying speed and looked around, he saw one Spitfire after another emerge from the maelstrom intact. Only one had failed to get airborne and that was only because a bomb's blast had reversed his propeller and stalled his engine. The Spitfires survived their hopelessly vulnerable situation, at about 120 mph and with little height, because the 109s had never seen the enemy at this speed and overshot the lot with throttles wide open. So there were no casualties, and one 110 crashed in the centre of the devastation.

Although 54 Squadron were, not surprisingly, unable to catch any of the Manston attackers, these airfield attacks were strongly resisted. All day, 11 Group was despatching, directing and redirecting its fighter squadrons. There had never been a day like it.

Typical was one of 56 Squadron's attacks on a *Gruppe* of Dornier bombers at 18,000 feet protected above by a whole *Gruppe* of Me 109s, a formidable enough foe for twelve Hurricanes. This is how they set about their task in a fine piece of tactical extemporisation.

Attacks were carried out on the rear extreme left-hand and right-hand sections of the bombers from astern and from the quarter by the first three sections. . . . The rearmost section concentrated on protecting our fighters from an attack by the Me 109s. They did this by firing at long range in front of the Me 109s as they dived to attack our leading sections. . . . The Me 109s did not risk running into the tracer which they saw flashing in front of them.[6]

Only one of the German bombers was shot down, but this bold and aggressive attack apparently diverted them from their target.

But by early evening the German High Command were confident that all the radar stations, and the front-line airfields, they had attacked were permanently out of action. Disillusionment fast succeeded this comforting conclusion of the heaviest day's operations the Luftwaffe had indulged in so far. In order to confirm the blindness of the enemy, Kesselring laid on three raids of some twenty Dorniers each to coastal towns, each well escorted. They were picked up before they left the French coast, and from intercepted R/T transmissions it was clear to the Germans that the weight and likely target of each attack was correctly estimated so that the RAF put up the right defensive opposition in plenty of time. The disappointment was profound.

By working through the night, and with massive help from the Army, Manston, like Hawkinge, was operational by dawn on 13 August, as were all the radar stations except very severely damaged Ventnor. In the whole day thirty-one German aircraft had been shot down at a cost to the RAF of twenty-two fighters and eleven pilots killed.

Dowding and Park had reason for both satisfaction and anxiety. On the one hand, the resilience and powers of recovery of the main targets were encouraging. And once again both ground control (in spite of the damage to radar stations) and the pilots and machines had shown they were up to their jobs. On the other hand, thirteen out of 11 Group's eighteen squadrons had been in action, and most had been scrambled more than once. In all there had been some 500 sorties, and this sort of pressure on air and ground crews alike could not be tolerated for very long. With his usual impeccable timing, Dowding ordered down south Peter Townsend's crack 85 Squadron from the north.

Readers of the *New Statesman and Nation* were later informed by Vita Sackville-West in her gardening column: 'We are not allowed to buy bulbs this year. . . . Every bulb will go to the USA as gracious and lucrative envoys of a country which would rather say it with flowers than with bombs.'

# 11

## Eagle Day – and After

### 13 – 14 AUGUST

'FROM REICHSMARSCHALL GOERING TO ALL UNITS OF AIR FLEETS 2, 3 AND 5. OPERATION EAGLE. WITHIN A SHORT PERIOD YOU WILL WIPE THE BRITISH AIR FORCE FROM THE SKY. HEIL HITLER.'

So this was *Adlertag*, the day when Goering – whose signal was promptly deciphered at Bletchley Park – was to open the great *Adlerangriff* intended to crush all RAF opposition and clear the way for 'Sealion'. It was, instead, to be a day of anti-climax and gaunt tragicomedy.

The first black joke was the weather. As dawn broke, the clear skies of the prolonged anti-cyclone so confidently predicted by the weathermen on both sides of the Channel revealed only solid banks of cloud as far as the eye could see, with the density that an experienced airman knew would mean great depth.

The morning's operations for *Luftflotten* 1 and 2 were not contingent upon favourable weather. They were also immensely complex, with engine-starting and take-off times, climbing speeds, rendezvous between bomber, twin-engined and single-engined fighter cover, all dovetailed with the precision and accuracy at which German staff officers have always been masters.

The first armada, composed of seventy-four Dorniers of KG2, started engines at their three airfields before dawn, causing the usual consternation among the French peasantry and their livestock. By 5 a.m. Oberst Johannes Fink was leading out his *Gruppe* of bombers for take-off. The 'Horst Wessels' of ZG26, who had been busy the previous day and were at Barley, Crécy and Yvrench, were awoken at the same time, and their big Me 110s, provocatively painted (the jaws of a shark were popular) and packed with fuel and ammunition, rolled out for take-off. They were led by their hero, Joachim-Friedrich Huth. Huth knew that his machines had recently been equipped with new-issue radio crystals; he did not know that (surely not a staff failure?) his charges, the bombers, had not been so equipped.

They had scarcely formed up above cloud at 12,000 feet over Amiens for the rendezvous and the crossing (and, incidentally, been clearly identified by British radar), when a cancelled-operation code call came over the R/T. It was 6.15 a.m. Goering personally had made the decision to postpone *Adlerangriff* until later in the day and recalled all his aircraft. He had learned from a recce report that the cloud was as thick and unbroken over England, which meant that the bombers' targets – Eastchurch and Sheerness in KG2's case – would be obscured or only bombable from below cloud, a very tricky business, especially with the Thames Estuary littered with defensive balloons.

As Huth was about to reverse his 'Horst Wessels', he spotted the distant dots in the sky to the south, which could only be the Dorniers, gaining height on their north-west-by-north course. Why hadn't they turned back, as ordered? Handing over command, Huth made off to investigate. When he was near there was still no sign of any deviation by the bombers. He tried repeatedly to call up Fink but could get no reply. Finally, he was reduced to carrying out an unorthodox manoeuvre, zooming up in front of the perspex nose of Fink's leading machine, turning steeply and flying past extremely closely, at the same time frantically gesticulating.

Fink clearly regarded this as dangerous and rather bad form. KG2 continued on its journey, its sixty-odd, twin-engined bombers presenting a fine picture of aerial might in the early morning sun.

The gods of war were, for the present, on the side of KG2. For a while, the Observer Corps missed the formation entirely as they came in west up the Thames Estuary, due to poor weather, and the radar stations most closely concerned – Dover, Foreness and Whitstable – had somehow lost them. No one will ever know why. But the raid followed its scheduled course, Fink dividing his force ten miles north-west of

Margate, one *Gruppe* making for the naval base at Sheerness while he led his thirty Dorniers towards Eastchurch on the Isle of Sheppey. The sky had suddenly cleared and the Thames Estuary was laid out like a map below. Fink remained puzzled by the absence of his promised escort, but felt no need for them – not until 'Sailor' Malan's 74 Squadron came swarming on their tails.

The South African's shooting was always deadly. His fellow ace, Alan Deere, no bad shot himself, reckoned that Malan was the finest shot he had ever seen. Now he took out one of the Dorniers with deceptive speed and ease. The Spitfires were rapidly joined by John Thompson's 111 Squadron and John Gordon's 151 Squadron (Hurricanes).

The second of these Hurricane squadrons boasted a machine fitted experimentally with two 20 mm cannon and another with four cannon. Only one of the pilots showed keenness for these heavily armed Hurricanes, and chose one or other of them on every operation when they were serviceable. He was Flight Lieutenant Roddick Lee Smith, B Flight commander, with the added distinction of having over 1,000 hours on Hurricanes and Spitfires in his log book. Smith did not find the cannon altogether reliable, and the pods beneath the wings* impeded speed and manoeuvrability. 'The cannon equipped aircraft were slower and less manoeuvrable, but they packed a much greater punch and at a longer range,' he wrote later.

On this occasion, Smith attacked a tight formation of Dorniers from a range of about 300 yards and one of them burst into flames. Few pilots could have achieved such instant results from this range with eight machine-guns.

But the Dornier gunners, conscious that only they afforded any protection from the enemy, kept up a steady, accurate and well-co-ordinated fire.** Sergeant George Atkinson of 151 Squadron was one of the first victims. Then, a senior Polish Spitfire pilot of 74 Squadron, Flight Lieutenant Brezezina, was forced to bale out. He survived, to be killed in combat later. As proof of the fever of these critical days, on that

---

*Later enclosed within the wings.

**Of some 100 surviving Battle pilots who gave an opinion in 1988 on the quality of German bomber gunnery, forty pronounced it good or excellent ('they shot me down twice'), thirty-two thought it average and thirty poor. Donald Stones DFC, then a pilot officer, recalled that the gunnery 'varied greatly, and probably depended on the training and esprit de corps of the individual squadron or wing. Also on the efficiency and planning of our attacks. A badly thought-out and executed attack as we did on nine He 111s of a specialist unit over the Irish Sea on 29 September resulted in the loss of three Hurricanes out of the first six to attack. These enemy rear-gunners were highly trained and disciplined and the pilots kept perfect formation for the gunners to bring accurate and concentrated cross-fire to bear.'

very morning Hendon Borough Council sacked all Polish ARP (Air-Raid Precautions) and other foreign workers. The Hendon *Times* welcomed 'the removal of aliens from key positions in services of national importance'.

But, despite the stout defence put up by the gunners, both *Gruppen* began to pay heavily before they even reached their targets, five in all being shot down and six more badly damaged with wounded crews. One of the Dorniers managed to get back across most of Kent. The village of Elham, which had seen so much of the fighting on the previous day, was just overflown by this mortally wounded Dornier, which crashed on a railway line nearby, slewing into some woodland and spewing out four live crew members, who had good reason to be thankful for their escape.

Eastchurch, one of Martini's misidentified 'fighter' stations (in fact Coastal Command), was the temporary home of 266 Squadron (Spitfires), who expected to leave any day, so Fink's raid was not a complete waste. Flight Lieutenant Dennis 'Tage' Armitage was still in bed at 7.05 a.m.: 'I awoke to find my bed waltzing about my room which seemed most unpleasant but was caused by what was in reality a blessing in disguise, the bogginess of the land. The whole place shook as if it were in the middle of an earthquake but the bombs . . . buried themselves deeply before exploding, leaving nothing but a little pile of earth.'

It was not as innocent as all that, however. A number of airmen were killed, a hangar was set on fire, all the airfield's ammunition had gone up and, on a lighter note, six officers who had sheltered within the solid chimney of the mess lounge fire came out black as night. 'And six little nigger boys they remained, for the water supplies had been cut off,' Armitage recalled.

Fink claimed ten Spitfires were destroyed on the ground, a ten-times overestimate, which was a great deal higher than their average three-times overclaim in the air.

But 266 remained sting-less without rounds of .303 ammo, or the equally vital boxes to contain them. Armitage was deputed to get them, quickly. It was not as simple as he had expected. The trouble was that 266 had been detached from Wittering for 'special' work and the squadron fitted into no Command, Group or sector. He was greeted with deep suspicion by telephonists and supply officers alike, until after several hours he telephoned their old base.

'All right, Tage, leave it to me,' came a deep voice from the other end.

It was Harry Broadhurst, station commander, a notable 'strong' man with a razor-sharp knife for cutting corners. At midnight two Humber brakes arrived at Eastchurch, each loaded with ammunition and boxes. 'Someone realised the war had started.'

For a while the east of England was left in peace, while Goering, furious at the futility of the muddled operations so far, ordered *Adlerangriff* to start in the middle of the afternoon, concentrating the raids, mainly from *Luftflotte* 3, on the west and central south of the country, and some of the inland airfields.

Sperrle tried the old trick of first sending in 'free chase' Me 109s in the hope of getting the RAF airborne in defence, and in need of refuelling by the arrival time of the main force. Wing Commander David Roberts, Middle Wallop's controller, was not to be taken in, scrambling only 152's Spitfires, which quickly sent the 109s packing but without loss on either side.

With this tease out of the way, the radar operators awaited the real thing, and they did not have to wait for long. An enormous armada was building up over the Cherbourg Peninsula and the recently occupied Channel Islands. Not far short of 300 Luftwaffe aircraft, ranging from Ju 88s to Me 109s, from Ju 87s to Me 110s, were on their way by 3.30 p.m.: their orders, to smash 10 Group, its aircraft, its airfields and operations control. The great seaport of Southampton was also on the programme, in accordance with the German High Command's policy of spreading wide the targets in order to confuse and exhaust the defences.

Two Hurricane squadrons, 257 and 43, were despatched to deal with the bombers' mighty advance up the Solent. Outnumbered by at least ten to one, the pilots could do no more than distract the attention of the bombers' gunners of LG1, mostly Ju 88s. A few minutes later, the centre of Southampton was swept by high explosive and incendiary. The docks were also badly hit and many people killed. By any rational judgment, however, an air-raid on Southampton which failed to smash the vulnerable Woolston Spitfire factory was of minor importance. The only damage there was trivial, and the works had clearly not been a target.

By 4 p.m. every fighter in 10 Group was airborne, directed hither and thither by Middle Wallop as the armada which had arrived en masse broke up to deal with its wide range of targets. Scattered cloud and indifferent visibility made these targets difficult to locate. One force of

Stukas searched fruitlessly for Warmwell, and scattered their bombs about the countryside before beating as hasty a retreat as they could.

By this time the people of Sussex and Kent were becoming blasé about the fighting overhead. But for many of those living in Hampshire, Wiltshire and Dorset the raids of mid-August were their first introduction to the sound and fury of bombing and air combat. For children particularly, who seemed not to recognise the danger, it was an exciting time. Sybil Eccles, whose husband David was working in the embassy in Madrid, wrote to him of the children's introduction to the air war on this day:

I was struggling with the young ones to get them ready for a walk – John sauntered in and said, 'They're having a practice, I suppose, I've just heard an air-raid warning.' But I always underestimate the astonishing accuracy of my eldest and just pooh-poohed the poor boy and off we went up the hill – and a good thing we did for we had a fine sight of it all from the pub. Half-way up the boys ran off – a stream of aeroplanes came over at great speed and presently the crumps began and columns of smoke rose from Ludgershall. . . . One could see the salvoes hit the ground in rapid succession and the puffs go up. Presently the Spitfires were overhead and we watched a chase. . . . Our trio thoroughly enjoyed themselves and made a striking example of the insensibility to danger of the young.[1]

Two *Staffeln* of Ju 88s, which could have done appalling damage to the sector station, failed to find Middle Wallop, or mistook a reserve strip outside Andover for their target and tore up the grass with their 500 kg bombs. Another force of Ju 87s had a worse experience while trying to find Middle Wallop, because their Me 109 escort had allowed themselves to become too far separated from their charge. These unfortunate dive-bombers were found and pounced upon by 609's Spitfires.

That brilliant pilot, George Darley, ordered two sections above to keep an eye on the 109s and to disentangle themselves from them as soon as they could 'and come down and join us in dealing with the bombers'.

'I managed to get in below the fighters,' 609's CO continued, '– I don't think they even saw me. I throttled back a little – not too much: otherwise I would have thrown the whole formation out of position – and went through the whole lot of Ju 87s, letting fly with everything I had. The chaps coming in behind me were able to pick their targets.'[2]

Several of 609's pilots, however, were too preoccupied with the 109s to have much time to spare for the easier game. Pilot Officer David

Crook's combat was brief but sweet, typical of so many at this time: 'I saw about five Messerschmitt 109s pass just underneath us. I immediately broke away from the formation, dived on to the last 109 and gave him a terrific burst of fire at very close range. He burst into flames and spun down for many thousands of feet into the clouds below, leaving behind him a long trail of black smoke. . . . He crashed just outside a small village, and I could see everybody streaming out of their houses and rushing to the spot.

'The German force was flying at 15,000 feet on a northerly course, with fighters some distance behind, but the failure of the escort to carry out its duties is reflected in our pilots' claim to have destroyed nine of the dive-bombers compared to four Me 109s.'[3]

The final figure was not quite so high, but for one *Staffel* to lose six out of nine aircraft was a savage enough blow. Another of 609's successful pilots was John Dundas, brother of Hugh 'Cocky' Dundas, two of the most famous brothers in the Battle. He was already credited with a score of six, three in the last three days.*

A surprising eyewitness to all this air activity in Hampshire was the privileged, pacifist, literary figure of Frances Partridge, who deplored the war but suffered few of its discomforts. She wrote in her diary:

Suddenly we heard terrific air activity, and planes seemed to be dashing about in all directions. Then a great grey mushroom of smoke rose from the direction of Newbury . . . four large bombers swooped over the Down, making a deafening noise. They flew over our heads fairly low, and on over Ham Spray . . . how easily they could have machine-gunned our two little figures, I so conspicuous in my red shirt. . . . It was not until Nannie came back from her day out in Newbury that I knew what a good view we had had of German bombers.[4]

Not far away, a more purposeful figure was another eyewitness to the massive air battles over Dorset and Hampshire: C-in-C Home Forces, General Sir Alan Brooke, who was daily expecting a German invasion. 'We found a German plane', he wrote in his diary, 'which had just come down. Pilot was all burned up, but, as 500 lb bomb was in the debris which was burning, we didn't stop long.'[5]

The action returned east again later in the afternoon. Kesselring had his eyes on two more airfields, Rochester and Detling near Maidstone. He still believed with his pilots that the airfields they had struck the

---

*Later John shot down the German ace Helmut Wieck, but was shot down and killed seconds later by Wieck's number two.

previous day were knocked out indefinitely and that the Luftwaffe was well on its way to depriving the enemy of fighter airfields. In view of the heavy scattered cloud still over south-east England, he decided on a gamble and sent in his dive-bombers, with a heavy escort. There was nothing to compare with the accuracy of the Stuka when conditions were ideal.

The first force was no more successful than Sperrle's efforts on 10 Group. The Ju 87s never found Rochester, were intercepted by 56 Squadron and scattered all over the Kent countryside. They were lucky to get back more or less intact.

Under the overall command of Hauptmann von Brauchitsch, LG1's Stukas – some forty in all, and escorted by Major Gotthardt Handrick's JG26 109s – set off undeviatingly for Detling. It was a dive-bomber's dream target: hangars, stores, administration and domestic blocks, motor transport, offices, fuel supplies, easy to find near the Thames Estuary but high above sea level, the three main hangars visible for many miles. It was also highly vulnerable, the airmen's mess and sleeping quarters being of wood and concentrated in a small area, and many of the personnel under canvas.

One surviving flight mechanic and his brother remembered that they were (like everyone else) making their way to tea when they heard the air-raid sirens sounding in Maidstone and Chatham. J. R. Hearn wrote: 'We were unperturbed because the station commander had decreed that the airfield siren would not be sounded unless an attack was imminent. Suddenly we heard the roar of aircraft and looking up we saw about fifty Me 109s breaking formation and without warning bullets began ricocheting all around us. Ju 87bs then broke cloud and dived to the attack. We had been caught stone cold, airfield defences were antique and minimal.

'We managed to reach a shelter unscathed and fell down the steps into it just as the first bombs began to fall. The shelter was designed for about fifty but throughout the entire raid there was only one other occupant. . . . The enemy carried out the entire attack undisturbed and the bombing was lethally accurate. Two hangars and numerous [twenty-two] aircraft were destroyed, two shelters received direct hits, as did the airmen's mess. . . . The station commander was killed instantly at the entrance to SHQ, including several of his subordinates, and as the noise of the raid diminished it was broken suddenly by Blenheims [intended to raid invasion barge concentrations] blowing up with entire petrol and bomb-loads. We emerged from the shelter to a scene of utter devastation and carnage. The final death toll was put at sixty-eight and many more severely injured.'

As the smoke and dust rose higher and higher above the airfield on this warm Kent evening, survivors could – and did – reflect on the instant and epochal consequences should RAF Fighter Command lose control of the air completely, as they had, temporarily, over this airfield. Constrained only by hopelessly inadequate ground defences, the German bombers could have picked out any target in the United Kingdom – from armament factories to government buildings, port facilities to railway termini and junctions. Less than half of the Luftwaffe's bomber strength had so far been deployed against the island enemy, and the thin blue line of Fighter Command was already stretched almost to the limit.

The fact that Detling was a Coastal Command station, and unconnected with Dowding's command, was a blessing but did not diminish the seriousness of the lesson.

As for Kesselring, he wrote off with a piece of chalk one more RAF fighter station: *Kaput!*

The Luftwaffe lost no aircraft on the Detling raid, but elsewhere on *Adlertag* they lost forty-five aircraft in action, three in accidents and thirty-nine more seriously damaged. Fighter Command lost thirteen machines and three pilots killed.

Readers of *The Times* on 14 August were given not only a detailed account of the previous day's air fighting (no names, no place names, no targets beyond 'south-east England'), but also an assessment of the pilots' attitude to the fighting.

The RAF flying man's outlook [wrote the aeronautical correspondent] has run the whole gamut from the detached impersonal to the deadly personal. It is difficult to say exactly when it started, but it is there all the same, writ clearly for all who know the RAF men as they were then and as they are now. What has caused this radical swing round? It is not just the intensification of the air war. . . . It goes much deeper than that. From being daring young adventurers of the air they have become Men with a Mission, men who feel a personal responsibility for helping to destroy that threatening machine that is the Luftwaffe.

No one claimed that the German aircrews' attitude had been modified by the fighting so far. The spirit was as self-confident and determined as ever. But Luftwaffe pilots like Hauptmann Friedrich Aschenbrenner, *Gruppekommandeur* in KG100, von Brauchitsch, Walter Rubensdoerffer, Adolf Galland of the crack JG26 'Schlageter', Werner Moelders and Otto Bertram, *Gruppekommandeur* of III/JG2, and many more who had been uplifted by Goering's ringing call of the previous day, this morning felt let down. Bad news travels as fast among flying men as through any community, and the agony of II/StG2 Stukas over Hampshire and the Channel had spread to every French and Belgian airfield.

Nor was the dull overcast weather of the early morning of this day calculated to raise German spirits. As for the RAF fighter squadrons, undisturbed at dawn and for another six and more hours, there was great relief and much catching up on sleep, while cups of tea provided by batmen grew cold on bedside tables.

The night of 13/14 August had been less eventful, on both sides of the Channel. Bomber Command had been anxious for many weeks to mount a raid on Italian industry. It would give great confidence to aircrews, provide useful experience and give immense satisfaction to the public, who despised the opportunistic Benito Mussolini and his flashy forces who had waited until Germany had conquered much of Europe before crying 'Me too'!

So thirty-six Whitley heavy bombers staggered into the air at dusk, loaded with a greater weight of fuel than high-explosive, and set off across France for the Alps, Milan and Turin. Their bombing caused great outrage.

Meanwhile, the Luftwaffe sent nine He 111s of KG100 to the Spitfire factory in Birmingham. Four of them found it successfully, but caused relatively little damage. Others had more success in Belfast, where the new Stirling four-engined bombers were being completed. Five were destroyed.

But in daylight hours, nothing much happened before midday, when plots building up over the Pas de Calais led Park to scramble some forty fighters. The enemy force took some time to form up and then, as had happened so often before, appeared to pass up and down the Straits of Dover indecisively before, this time, turning towards Dover itself. Observer Corps reports, assisted by improving weather, told of several *Staffeln* of Ju 87s strongly supported by Me 109s.

This led to 'a hell of a donny' over Dover, with some 200 aircraft milling about in numerous dogfights. In this area, the Luftwaffe were little more distant from their bases than the RAF squadrons, and for once were prepared to mix it instead of making the one pass and then diving for home, waiting for the red-light blink warning of fuel shortage. No. 615 Squadron lost two pilots, and three of 32 Squadron's pilots, unhurt themselves, made forced landings, while JG26 and JG52 each lost a 109 in the mêlée.

More serious was another low-level attack, completely undetected again, on Manston, the handiwork once again of Rubensdoerffer. His Me 110s blasted four hangars and made a ruin of several of the dispersals. But for once the ground fire was effective. A single Bofors pumped several 40 mm shells into one of the fighter-bombers, and some enterprising ground crew who had rigged a 20 mm cannon had the immense satisfaction of seeing a second 110 hit the ground and explode.

Not far away, at Lympne, our conscientious Inspector-General turned up as promised, examined the bomb damage and promptly put in his report. It praised the courage of AC2 Anderson and his party, who had promptly extinguished a burning petrol fire above a tank dynamited for demolition, and it recommended the supply of more men and machines to fill up the 380 bomb craters. Some strengthening of the anti-aircraft defences – four Hispano guns – was also strongly urged.[6]

An even more august figure was also engaged on inspection work this day. Lieutenant-General Sir Frederick Pile later wrote:

I was escorting HM the King round the gun-sites at Dartford and Welling. Everyone enjoyed it very much, and the King was in great form, ticking me off for being improperly dressed, as I was wearing a cloth belt. He took a great fancy to the bakelite models of German aircraft and asked if he could have some, saying, 'Even if I don't play with them, the children will.'[7]

Both Sperrle and Kesselring had been ordered to prepare themselves for their greatest effort the next day, while keeping the RAF on its toes. Sperrle's answer was to mount a great number of small raids on the south and south-west, which he reckoned would serve the purpose of getting the enemy airborne without himself risking the severe losses he had suffered the previous day.

It was well-nigh impossible to intercept every one of these raids, mostly of three aircraft only. One of these trios pushed their luck far north into Cheshire, where they bombed the airfield at Sealand. There were no fighter squadrons within miles, but anti-aircraft fire had accompanied the He 111s on most of their journey, and the wing commander (flying) himself at a busy Spitfire Operational Training Unit (OTU) – well-named John Hallings-Pott DSO – took off and shot down one of the Heinkels near Chester.

Far to the south, Sperrle had at last succeeded in getting some of his bombers through to Middle Wallop. Hearing the approaching enemy, three gallant airmen turned from the nearest shelter and ran to close 609 Squadron's hangar door in the hope of providing some protection for the Spitfires inside. Alas, a 500 kg bomb struck the centre of the hangar, instantly forcing the huge steel door off its runners and on the unfortunate airmen.

But two of 609's finest pilots, John Dundas and David Crook, succeeded in taking off in the midst of the raid and pursued the leading plane relentlessly at low level, taking turns to make attacks and finally causing the Heinkel to crash and explode in the middle of a naval munitions dump at Dean Hill, near East Dean. It was not until later that the two pilots learned that they had killed KG55's navigation specialist, the Chief of Staff to *Luftgau* VIII and the *Geschwaderkommodore* Alois Storckl.

The pressure on the Middle Wallop sector had led Brand, that very morning, to move 234 'Madras' Squadron (Spitfires) up from St Eval. An armourer, C. R. Blachford, remembered their departure from the tranquillity of Cornwall to the hurly-burly of Hampshire: 'An advance party of mixed trades, armourers, fitters, mechanics and electricians were hurriedly bundled into two old Bombay troop carriers and off we went. After about an hour's flying we were overtaken by our Spits, and after another half an hour we found ourselves over Middle Wallop looking down on an airfield being bombed, and being involved in a dogfight with Spitfires and German fighters and bombers mixing it all around us.

'We viewed the scene with excitement and fear, rushing from one side of the plane to the other to get a better view, until the pilot cursed us in a mixture of Polish and English, told us to settle down as we were causing the plane to rock from side to side. He then made two remarkable attempts to land the plane, despite the bombing. Even more remarkable was the very courageous airman who ran out of the control tower, firing red Very light signals at us, which meant of course not to attempt a landing. The pilot of our plane then decided on an exit and flew away as quickly as possible, and to our great relief landed us safely at Boscombe Down a few miles away. The people at Boscombe Down could see our plane trying to land at Middle Wallop and each time thought we had been shot down or had crashed. After about half an hour or so, we got back on the transport plane and headed once again for Middle Wallop, which by now had had the all clear.

'We landed without any further trouble and managed to miss the

165

many bomb craters that were on the airfield. The Spitfires that had been engaged in the dogfight of course needed instant rearming and refuelling, so we didn't have any time to reflect on our fright.'

There was very little night activity by the Luftwaffe, confirming Dowding's hunch that the biggest daylight ordeal for his Command was imminent. He had already, during the last daylight hours of 14 August, reshuffled his Command's pack, taking out from the front line three of the most hard-pressed, 145 Squadron, 'Sailor' Malan's 'Tiger' 74 and 238, and reinforcing 11 Group's front line with experienced but less weary pilots. The weather forecast for the next day, Dowding learned, was for clear skies and continuous sun: the anti-cyclone had, it seemed, at last set in.

# 12

## *Enter – and Exit –* Luftflotte 5

### 15 AUGUST

All during the Battle, the lulls, usually caused by bad weather, provided blessed relief for the ground crews – not for purposes of rest and relief but to allow them the time to catch up on repairs and modifications.

An instrument repairer on 257 Squadron (Hurricanes), J. T. Ryder, recalled: 'It was quite hair-raising trying to keep twelve Hurricanes fully operational – robbing Peter to pay Paul was rife in those days. As supplies were short one looked after the aircraft like a mother. Riggers and fitters kept the aircraft spotless, and woe betide any airman who Chiefy found neglecting his pride in his aircraft. Fortunately, very few ever let the side down. Seven days a week it was up at dawn for engine runs and daily inspections for readiness operations. This went on until dusk, and it was a case of trying to get as much sleep as possible during the night ready for a repeat of this tiring round the following day.'

When aircraft returned shot up they were at once assessed for damage and those that could rapidly be made airworthy were worked on then and there. Engine-damaged fighters were taken down to the hangars (assuming these had not been levelled by bombing) to be dealt with by civilian Rolls-Royce staff. In most cases, this entailed an engine change, which, with practice, could be carried out with amazing speed.

As for mainplane damage, this was dealt with by civilian fitters from Hawker's (for Hurricanes) and Supermarine. Modifications, especially to the Spitfire, were numerous throughout the Battle and added another burden to the ground crews' responsibilities. The original Mark 1 Spitfire, lacking self-sealing tanks, rear-view mirror, armour-plate behind the pilot, and with fixed-pitch, two-blade, wooden propeller, was a very different aircraft from the Mark 2. The Rotol constant speed, three-blade airscrew greatly improved climb and allowed the Spitfire to operate effectively some 7,000 feet higher, thus narrowing the gap in performance with the Me 109 above 25,000 feet.

No. 19 Squadron, the first to take delivery of the Spitfire, for a time had planes that were similar in some respects to the prototype. To offset the tail-heaviness of these early machines it was at one time proposed to fit a once-only device in the event of a spin, a tail parachute secured beneath a hatch just forward of the fin and operated by the pilot by means of a bowden cable from the cockpit. These parachutes were never resorted to as Jeffrey Quill found testing the prototype perfectly straightforward, if a bit rough and with longitudinal pitching in spins. But these very first production Spitfires still retained the hatch.

'As engine and propeller development took place so the forward weight of the Spitfire increased,' wrote Leading Aircraftman William Eslick of 19 Squadron. 'It eventually became necessary to take off the slabs of lead mounted to the front of the forward engine feet and replace with lead ballast weights in the tail. These were circular and mounted on a threaded bar for accurate positioning.'

The fitting of armour-plate to these Spitfires was a more hectic business altogether. Eslick recalled an eventful evening at Hornchurch early in the Battle: 'Officially no one was allowed off-camp but the pub "Good Intent" just down the road from the main gate was conveniently considered to be in bounds. Maintenance Flight made it their headquarters off duty. One evening by 10 p.m. there was little prospect of further flying. Suddenly the sergeant poked his head round the door. "All Maintenance Flight report back." "What's cooking, Sarge?" All aircraft were to be armour-plated by morning. There was no technical difficulty in fitting the slabs of boiler-plate to the frame immediately behind the pilot's seat. The difficulty was in seeing which of the double-image rivet heads had to be drilled out when slightly pissed, and the innumerable visits to relieve us of several pints of best bitter as the night cooled.'

Most ground crew did not even have Eslick's luck in being able to put down a few pints at the local every now and again. Aircraftman Jack Oldham, an electrician on 253 Squadron at Kenley, after one of its heavy raids, wrote: 'I remember vividly sleeping in the dispersal dugout pens and rigging up emergency lighting which was supplied by a trolley-ac. [mobile engine-starting accumulators]. We seemed to live in our uniforms for days at a time with gumboots on continuously. My tunic during the Battle of Britain was an old Royal Flying Corps one from 1918 which I had been issued with when I joined up at Padgate in September 1939, and it was very handy as I didn't need to wear a collar and tie, the tunic being called a "dog collar".

'The feeling of camaraderie between all flight mechanics, flight riggers, instrument repairers, armourers and electricians was terrific.'

It is sometimes forgotten that the same pressure was applied as relentlessly to the ground crews, and especially to those who serviced the front-line squadrons, as to the aircrews. When the Luftwaffe assault on the airfields was at its height these men, and the WAAFs who worked with them, on maintenance, as drivers, in the cook-houses and messes and in other trades, were heavily at risk, too, and many were killed.

Exhausted armourers, engine fitters and riggers were often to be found lying on the grass sound asleep as their squadron took off again. Many of them never saw the outside of their base for the duration of the Battle; many more went for days without seeing their bunks or the inside of their mess. C. R. Blachford wrote of 'being at readiness from about three-thirty in the morning to eleven-thirty at night day after day. Meals were taken "as and when", and the rare days when we made it to the airmen's mess for a meal were usually interrupted by an air-raid. On one occasion I remember about six of us were on our way to a meal when bombs started to fall on the 'drome. We all dived into what we thought was an air-raid shelter, but it turned out to be the station's bomb dump.'

Very few of those who fought the Battle on the ground received any recognition for courage and endurance, and unlike the aircrew were not entitled to wear a Battle of Britain star on their service ribbon. A number of those who later referred to this injustice did so philosophically: the 'erks' gave much; expected, and received, little. Certainly the corporal in this anecdote of Blachford's received nothing: 'A Spitfire came back from a dogfight and, having fired its guns, needed rearming. Having removed the gun panels, they found that one of the .303 machine-guns had jammed with one round, unfortunately an incendiary, split. It was alight and could have caused serious damage to the wing of the plane if a corporal armourer had not had the presence of mind to urinate on it, thus putting out the fire. Someone, it was said, wanted to report him for indecent exposure as WAAFs were in the area.'

No one admired the courage of the ground crews more than the pilots who depended so completely upon them. A retired squadron leader, then Sergeant Pilot Iain Hutchinson of 222 Squadron, recalled a hectic landing at Hornchurch to refuel and rearm: 'The airfield was under attack and chunks of shrapnel from the nearby 4.5-inch AA [anti-aircraft] guns were raining down on the airfield. When I taxied towards dispersal no one was to be seen; all were in the air-raid shelters taking cover. Before I rolled to a halt and cut the engine, B Flight ground crew under their flight sergeant were swarming around my Spitfire, the bowser racing out to refuel the aircraft while the armament men, laden with ammunition, were reloading the guns. The noise from the explosions going on around us was terrifying but not one of these magnificent men faltered for a moment in their tasks. I was frankly relieved to be taking off again, leaving behind the inferno.'

Many original and ingenious devices were extemporised in order to maintain serviceability at a time when the aircraft might be called on to scramble three times in a day. No. 19 Squadron devised a mobile service wagon in the shape of an old car chassis. In Eslick's words: 'It carried glycol, ammo. tanks, starter cartridges, oil bottle with hand-pump, oxygen bottles and anything useful for a quick turn-round. This cabless chassis would career around the perimeter track and home in on the latest arrivals.'

Aircraft replacements were sometimes cheered on arrival such was the desperate need for them. 'A brand spanking new aeroplane was ferry delivered to us one day,' Eslick also recalled. 'It did not even have squadron markings. But it landed on a dead engine, a conn. rod had "put a leg out of bed". This was almost like winning the pools and finding the ticket had not been posted.'

Many different and widely spaced sources of supply were utilised to manufacture, complete and fly in that Spitfire for 19 Squadron. One of those responsible for engine accessories, for example, was Frank 'Rod' Banks, an experienced engineer officer who was called in by Beaverbrook. Banks wrote:

He asked me to form a department to develop and produce engine accessories. These were in very critical supply, and aero engine production and delivery was being delayed. . . . We proceeded to organise the companies on a twenty-four-hour a day basis and also expand them as quickly as possible. In addition we searched all the RAF stores for equipment that was urgently needed. . . . It was like pulling teeth from an unwilling child, but the stores people finally accepted with good grace – they had to! Everyone at the Ministry of Aircraft Production worked through the days and the nights, and hardly had time to read the daily reports of the progress of the Battle or even appreciate the excitement attending the hostilities overhead, only realising them by the urgency of the demands from the squadrons. . . .[1]

On 15 August, lunch was well under way at 12.40 p.m. It had been a relaxed morning up north, typical duff Yorkshire weather outside. Like others in 616 Squadron (Spitfires), Hugh 'Cocky' Dundas had read the newspapers, finding the wide coverage of the air battles of the previous day faintly irritating. They all felt that their squadron had sufficiently recovered from the rigours and excesses of the French campaign, and it was time they were back in business. So, too, did Denys Gillam, Dundas's flight commander – 'Denys really held the squadron together.'

Dessert was being offered when, without any preliminary warning, the Tannoy called out, '616 Squadron, scramble, scramble, scramble!' 'We couldn't believe our ears,' Dundas recalled. 'We raced for the dispersal, where the ground crews had everything ready, engines started. We just jumped in and went off, there was no organisation, we never joined up with anyone, and were told to fly out to sea.'

They were at 12,000 feet above Flamborough Head, where the American John Paul Jones had severely trounced the British just over 160 years earlier, when they saw the sky ahead marked by a mass of dots. These rapidly grew larger and developed into the configuration of some sixty Ju 88 bombers, in loose formation and without escort. The Spitfires, supported by half-a-dozen Hurricanes of 73 Squadron, went in head-on to break up the formation and then turned to pick their target for deflection attacks.

'I hit and shot down one of the 88s,' Dundas reported, 'and saw another one damaged.' Seven of this force were shot down there and then by the Hurricanes and Spitfires, with three more crash-landing from combat damage when they had recrossed the North Sea. But the survivors of KG30, which had taken off from Aalborg, Denmark, pressed on to their target, the important 'fighter' station, Driffield. Here they met heavy, early-warned, anti-aircraft fire, which accounted for another of their number, although the bombers did manage to hit four of the bomber station's hangars, destroying ten aircraft.

Driffield was the only credit mark *Luftflotte* 5 could claim in its widespread first operation on north-east England, which was as great a

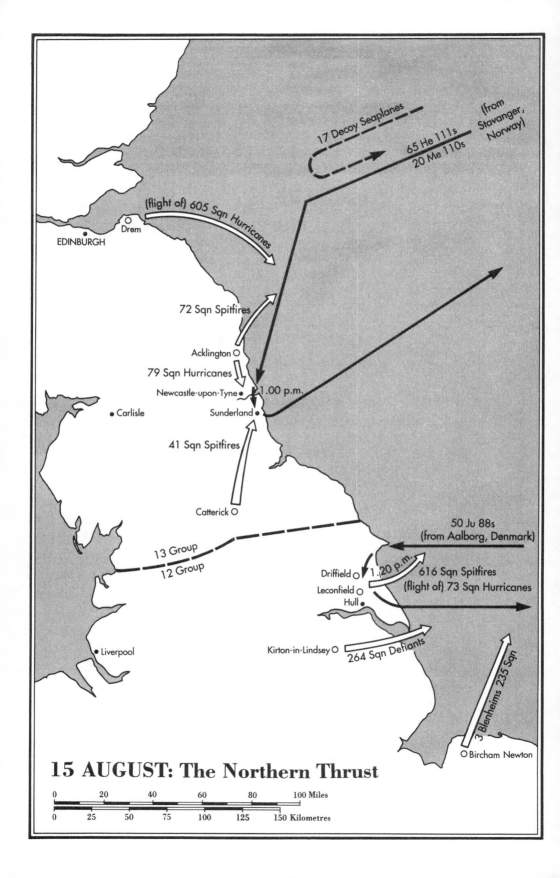

17 Decoy Seaplanes

65 He 111s
20 Me 110s

(from Stavanger, Norway)

(flight of) 605 Sqn Hurricanes

Drem O
• EDINBURGH

72 Sqn Spitfires

Acklington O

79 Sqn Hurricanes

Newcastle-upon-Tyne •  1.00 p.m.

• Carlisle

Sunderland •

41 Sqn Spitfires

Catterick O

13 Group
12 Group

50 Ju 88s
(from Aalborg, Denmark)

Driffield O  1.20 p.m.

616 Sqn Spitfires
(flight of) 73 Sqn Hurricanes

Leconfield O
Hull •

Kirton-in-Lindsey O  264 Sqn Defiants

• Liverpool

3 Blenheims 235 Sqn

O Bircham Newton

# 15 AUGUST: The Northern Thrust

| 0 | 20 | 40 | 60 | 80 | 100 Miles |

| 0 | 25 | 50 | 75 | 100 | 125 | 150 Kilometres |

surprise to the attackers as the defenders. To support the fierce, predictable raids in the south with surprise raids on airfields and industrial targets in the north-east appears to have been a sudden inspiration emanating from Goering's Chief of Intelligence, Oberst Josef 'Beppo' Schmidt. He was confident that all Fighter Command's resources had been concentrated in the southern Groups and that the north-east was wide open to attack. He knew nothing of Dowding's inflexibility, which had earlier combated the notion of sending more fighter squadrons into the bottomless pit of the French campaign. Now, in spite of the extreme pressure bearing on 11 and 10 Groups especially, he had insisted that the rotation of tired squadrons to the quiet north should continue.

In fact, besides 616 and 73 Squadrons, which were to maul so severely the Denmark-based Ju 88s, there were at least four more single-seat fighter squadrons available in 13 Group. Many of the pilots were highly experienced and all were yearning for action.

The commandant of *Luftflotte* 5, General Hans-Juergen Stumpff, had received his orders only the previous evening. We can be certain that they were as welcome to him and his staff as they were to his aircrews, who were as frustrated as the pilots of RAF Fighter Command, 13 Group.

For the Luftwaffe, this northern operation was stricken with grievous misfortunes. The plan was, in addition to the Danish force, for some seventy Norway-based He 111 bombers, escorted by a *Gruppe* of twenty-one Me 110s, led by the *Gruppekommandeur* Hauptmann Werner Restemeyer, to attack airfields in the Tyne–Tees area. Because of the range, the bomb-load was reduced to 3,000 pounds per aircraft, the range of the 110s was augmented by a belly-drop fuel tank, and, according to some RAF pilots who experienced no rearward fire, the gunners had been left behind to save weight. As a feint, a force of Heinkel seaplanes was to precede the operation by flying towards the Scottish coast north of Edinburgh to draw any unlikely fighters north and away from the main attack:

But the German bombers made a serious navigational error: they made landfall seventy-five miles too far north, thus almost coinciding with the point of the mock attack.

'Thanks to this error,' reported Captain Arno Kleyenstueber, 'the mock attack achieved the opposite of what we intended. The British fighter defence force was not only alerted in good time, but made contact with the genuine attacking force.'[2]

A ferocious running battle now developed between the Heinkels and their escort and the Spitfires and Hurricanes of 72, 605, 41 and 79 Squadrons. One of the first of the 110s to go down was that of Restemeyer himself. The enormous explosion which tore his Messerschmitt to shreds was thought by some of his fellow pilots to have originated in his empty drop tank which, perhaps, he had been unable to jettison. In all, one in three of the twin-engined fighters fell to the 13 Group fighters' guns, the survivors seeking cloud and escape.

The unprotected bombers began to pay their toll at the same time over the sea and over Sunderland and Newcastle, where they scattered their bombs haphazardly. Bob Deacon-Elliott reported: 'We'd never seen anything like it before. During our training, we'd learned to do "Number One Attack", "Number Two Attack". . . . You knew exactly what each of those meant. So someone called to our acting squadron commander, Ted Graham, "Have you seen them?" Ted, who stuttered, replied, "Of course I've seen the b-b-bastards. I'm trying to w-w-work out wh-wh-what to do." But we were already about to reach them. Graham hurtled in through the gap between the bombers and their escort and each of us picked a target. I saw two Huns literally disintegrate. The bombers quickly began jettisoning their loads. . . . We hacked them about so badly, the formation split apart and they made for home.'[3]

Stumpff's *Luftflotte* tried to cheer themselves up by claiming eleven Spitfires shot down in these northern raids, but the truth was that not one was damaged in the prolonged attacks. One Hurricane was obliged to return to base early, that was all.

By the time Dundas and the other 616 Squadron pilots returned to Leconfield lunch was over. But no one seemed to mind. Most of the afternoon was taken up with compiling reports for the intelligence officer, who had not been so busy for weeks.

Dowding in his *Despatch* made this comment on Stumpff's surprise assault on the north-east:

The sustained resistance which [the Luftwaffe] was meeting in south-east England probably led them to believe that fighter squadrons had been withdrawn, wholly or in part, from the north in order to meet the attack. The contrary was soon apparent, and the bombers received such a drubbing that the experiment was not repeated.[4]

The assault in the south to coincide with that in the north-east was once again delayed by the weather, and also by the uncertainties occasioned by the absence of so many senior officers of *Luftflotten* 2 and 3, including

Kesselring and Sperrle. They had all been called urgently to Karinhall by Goering, who wished his subordinates to account for the poor start made to *Adlerangriff.*

By noon, however, the skies over northern France were clearing and, like termites in warm weather, the Junkers, Messerschmitts and Heinkels emerged from their cover of trees or draped branches, engines turning over and whipping up dirt and leaves in their slipstream.

First away were two powerful forces of Ju 87s, one led by von Brauchitsch, the other by Hauptmann Anton Keil, based at Angers. The top cover of Me 109s was never accurately counted by the British but it was more than generous. This made good sense. What remained inexplicable was that the targets were two of the airfields which had already been marked twice (at least) as written off – Hawkinge and Lympne.

Park, well warned of the imminent arrival of these two powerful enemy forces, had three squadrons of Hurricanes on patrol and ten more squadrons more or less immediately available at Martlesham, North Weald, Hornchurch, Croydon, Kenley, Manston and Hawkinge. Nos 54 and 501 Squadrons were also scrambled by the Biggin Hill controller, Group Captain Richard Grice.

These Spitfires and Hurricanes were neatly placed to intercept von Brauchitsch's dive-bombers as they prepared to descend on Hawkinge, breaking them up, shooting down two and damaging others before the German 'snappers' descended and shot down four of the British fighters – all pilots safe.

Meanwhile, Lympne again suffered the ritual death rites, Keil's dive-bombers having a free run. Almost as ritualistic was the arrival, as the last dust settled, of Sir Edgar Ludlow-Hewitt, who inspected the fresh craters and ordered them to be filled in.

More serious in the long term was a surprise low-level raid by 110s on Manston, where the ground personnel were becoming very quick at getting to the shelters. Sixteen more were made casualties by cannon and machine-gun fire. Rubensdoerffer's low-level specialists followed this up with a superbly navigated and timed raid on Martlesham Heath, far north of the Thames Estuary. His sixteen Me 110s and nine Me 109s all carried 250 or 500 kg bombs, and not one of them missed the numerous targets available to them, and all returned safely. Two hangars were knocked out, stores were wrecked, water mains cut and a Fairey Battle bomber with 1,000 pounds of bombs (intended for the German invasion barge concentrations) was blown up, destroying the watch office and much else. But by some freak of chance there were only two serious injuries among the ground staff.

This raid took place at 3.00 p.m., and it could be said by then that the Luftwaffe's misfortunes up north had been redressed farther south. But the fighting day in 11 and 10 Groups had scarcely begun, as Park and Brand became increasingly aware. The first truly gigantic plots – bigger than ever recorded before – were building up over Normandy, the Cherbourg Peninsula and farther west in the early afternoon, and the hard-pressed pilots of 10 Group realised that they had more heavy fighting ahead.

These plots rapidly developed into individual raids, mainly of Ju 87s and 88s, heavily escorted by Messerschmitt fighters, both single- and twin-engined. Their targets appeared, as before, to be the Portsmouth–Southampton urban complex, Portland, Weymouth and inland airfields. It was thought that the Luftwaffe at one time had at least 300 aircraft involved, and to meet this threat 11 and 10 Groups scrambled the greatest ever number of fighters to meet a single enemy operation, some 150 Hurricanes and Spitfires from fourteen squadrons, ranging from Croydon to Exeter.

It was from Exeter that Ian Gleed led four more Hurricanes of 87 Squadron towards the likely scene of action soon after 4 p.m. His pilots were the Australian Johnnie Cock, the flight commander Derek Ward, Roland 'Bee' Beamont and Tom Mitchell. The controller told them to expect 90+ twenty miles south of Portland at 18–20,000 feet and heading north. A few minutes later this was corrected to 120+. It did not seem to matter. Gleed ordered them into search formation as they approached the coast. Soon they picked out a mass of dots dead ahead, mostly Ju 87s, heavily supported by fighters. The dive-bombers were in tight formation at 14–17,000 feet. Mitchell reported them first, and Gleed responded characteristically, 'OK I've got them – come on chaps, let's surround them.' According to Beamont, the CO 'made no attempt to climb above the oncoming formation or go round on a flank, but bored straight in to the thickest part with the rest of us ramming throttles open and pitch levers to fine pitch, checking gun sights and turning gun safety catches to FIRE. . . . Apart from the disparity in the numbers of the opposing forces this situation did not look too bad, and then there was no more time for meditation.

'Streams of smoke came back from the CO's Hurricane as he opened fire and I moved below and to port of him to obtain a clear line of fire on the next section of Stukas crossing my front from left to right. While

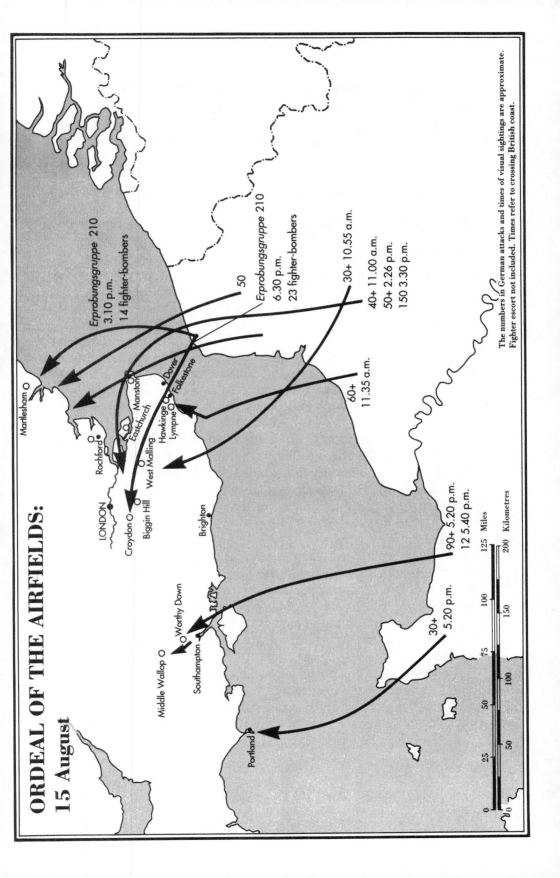

# ORDEAL OF THE AIRFIELDS:
## 15 August

*Erprobungsgruppe* 210
3.10 p.m.
14 fighter-bombers

*Erprobungsgruppe* 210
6.30 p.m.
23 fighter-bombers

50

30+ 10.55 a.m.

40+ 11.00 a.m.
50+ 2.26 p.m.
150 3.30 p.m.

60+
11.35 a.m.

90+ 5.20 p.m.
12 5.40 p.m.

30+
5.20 p.m.

Martlesham

Rochford

Manston
Eastchurch
Hawkinge
Lympne
Dover
Folkestone

West Malling

LONDON
Croydon
Biggin Hill

Brighton

Worthy Down
Middle Wallop
Southampton

Portland

The numbers in German attacks and times of visual sightings are approximate.
Fighter escort not included. Times refer to crossing British coast.

Miles
0    25    50    75    100    125
0    50    100    150    200
Kilometres

actually firing on them . . . trails of tracer flickered over and round my cockpit and a 110 appeared standing on his tail firing up at me from directly ahead and below. Using full port rudder and aileron and a lot of forward stick and still firing, I aimed directly at him and saw my own tracers entering the underside of his wing and fuselage before slicing past his nose at what seemed altogether too few feet. Rolling to the left and looking over my shoulder I saw this aircraft break into a number of pieces with much fire. . . .'[5]

In his turn, Beamont was almost immediately nearly shot down by another 110. It was typical of dozens of engagements all over the south of England that day, often at these ridiculous odds of twenty to one. On this occasion, Johnnie Cock was shot down and was seen by Beamont to splash into the sea, from which he was later rescued.

Inevitably in this fine weather, with the determination of the Luftwaffe crews to break through to their target equal to the RAF's solid resolve to resist them, the air battles fought mostly near Portsmouth and Portland were the fiercest so far that summer. There was abundant heroism and tragedy on both sides, with German rear gunners continuing to fire from doomed aircraft, and British and Allied pilots bringing back fighters so crippled it was a wonder that they could stay in the air.

Only two of the defending squadrons failed to intercept the enemy, and the losses on both sides were heavy, again the clumsy Me 110 and Ju 87 being the most numerous victims. Richard Hardy, severely hit and wounded by machine-gun fire in mid-Channel, disorientated and losing blood, managed to land his Spitfire, wheels-down, in a field. Unfortunately, the men who helped him from his cockpit wore the olive-drab uniform of the Wehrmacht.

On the other side of the Channel, and far to the north-east, the New Zealander Alan Deere was enjoying his busiest day. He had already shot down one enemy aircraft and probably two, had escaped the bombing of Manston by aborting his landing between unexploded bombs at the last second, and escaped a pursuing 110 as well as the airfield's defence fire. Finally, on his last mission of the day, he was shot down over Deal and baled out.

'I spent five agonising hours in the back of an RAF ambulance,' he recalled, 'which bounced and bumped its way through . . . the highways and byways of Kent in search of Kenley airfield, only to finish up at the Queen Victoria Hospital, East Grinstead.'[6] He did not allow himself to be delayed there for long.

In conclusion, of the Luftwaffe's unprecedentedly powerful assault on the central south of England:

It will be seen that most of the interceptions were successful in that they occurred before the coast was crossed, in the Portland and Portsmouth areas. Nevertheless it is apparent that if the enemy forces were indeed so large, very great numbers of aircraft must still have been able to shake off our fighters' attentions, and proceed on their mission. The bombing attacks which resulted were, however, as usual, insignificant. One [enemy] report speaks of Portsmouth being 'heavily bombed', but the Home Security Summary fails to mention a single bomb having fallen there. Indeed, once again the only significant damage was to an aerodrome, for Middle Wallop received about twenty-eight bombs. . . .[7]

But this long and exhausting day was not yet over, and once again the scene of most violent action shifted back to the south-east.

In the middle of that clear, warm afternoon, while the hop pickers were dealing with a fine harvest for the breweries, and the early hard fruit was also being gathered in Kent, some ninety Dorniers of KG3, led by the extravagantly titled Oberst Wolfgang von Chamier-Glisczinski and escorted by 130 Me 109s, headed across the Channel. The blips revealed by Dover radar were as big as anything seen by Poling or Worth Matravers a little earlier, swollen as they were by the presence of sixty more 109s from the crack JG26, which trailed their coat over Kent to distract any defending fighters.

For 11 Group the odds were stupefying. Nos 64, 111 and 151 Squadrons attempted to break through to the stately, massed Dorniers but only managed to get two of them, while 151 alone lost six Hurricanes, shot down or badly damaged. Over northern Kent, Chamier-Glisczinski split his force, sending off forty-five of his Dorniers to blast Eastchurch again, while he led his own *Gruppe* to Rochester. Intelligence had pinpointed the Short Brothers and Pobjoys aircraft works here, and the Dorniers devastated them. Production was indeed badly set back, but Short Brothers' aircraft were four-engined bombers, not fighters, which had been Schmidt's first concern.

It was still only just after 6 p.m., with hours of daylight ahead, when *Luftflotte* 2 carried out a final airfield assault. The targets were Biggin Hill and Kenley. A strong force of Dorniers was to attack the first, with 'free chase' 109s of JG26 sweeping ahead, behind and on both sides of the line of attack. Kenley was reserved for Rubensdoerffer's *Erpro* 210, bombed up, rearmed and still flushed from their successful raid on

Martlesham Heath earlier in the afternoon. Rubensdoerffer himself was again to lead his crack fighter-bombers, fifteen 110s and eight 109s.

Was even the tough, seasoned Hauptmann below his best by this relatively late hour after the earlier long double flight with all its inherent stresses and anxieties? Had a tiny margin of concentration, needed so acutely in these wave-brushing, daisy-cutting, ultra-low-level flights, been sacrificed? If anyone had so much as hinted that this might be the case, he would certainly have got short shrift from this authoritarian and utterly ruthless leader.

The first hint that Rubensdoerffer's luck might be slipping was his failure to rendezvous with his 109 escort. If he turned back – and this would have been quite out of character – he would have left the Dorniers alone to face the full might of the defences. He decided to go on, streaking across the Channel from the white cliffs of Calais to the flat beaches of Dungeness, boring inland over Walland Marsh, Rolvenden, Benenden, Cranbrook and other pretty villages, pulling back the stick to lift over the Downs and Sevenoaks.

Rubensdoerffer had glimpses of scuttling figures in the streets, of panic-stricken cattle, a farmer trying to steady his horses. It was a long flight at ultra-low level, only the railway lines providing sure confirmation of their position. He had decided to overshoot his target and come back on it from the north, in order to fool the defences and give his planes the advantage of leaving the target area on course for home. It was just one minute before 7 p.m. when he sighted hangars, watch office, numerous buildings and the broad splash of grass which confirmed that this was an airfield.

Having climbed at the last minute, Rubensdoerffer now led his fighter-bombers down on to the target, confident that this would be the second airfield *Erpro* 210 would write off on this day. No anti-aircraft fire. How could they miss?

Then suddenly, at the most critical moment as they were selecting targets, left thumb on bomb release, right thumb on gun button, they found unfamiliar aircraft, behind, at their side and above. . . .

John Thompson's 111 Squadron Hurricanes – just nine of them – had been scrambled from Croydon before *Erpro* 210 had crossed in at Dungeness, climbing to 10,000 feet and orbiting in the slightly hazy late afternoon sun. To the north lay the great urban sprawl of London, the dome of St Paul's, the tower of the Roman Catholic cathedral beyond the Palace of Westminster and the white splash of the Savoy Hotel between them, all identifiable beneath the silver-grey floating sea of barrage balloons.

The controller was feeding out the latest news of the two plots advancing swiftly across Kent and then Surrey: 'Wagon Leader, coming in from the north-east, losing height from angels six . . .'

The controller thought the likely target was Kenley, correctly anticipating Rubensdoerffer's instructions, Croydon being too close to the balloons. But the German planes overdid the turn and the Hurricanes caught the fighter-bombers in the very act of release over Croydon. Many of the bombs fell on the airfield's buildings, including a Hurricane repair plant, the armoury, hangars and the terminal building which, a year earlier, had been graced by the rich off to Paris or Cairo in the comfort of four-engined Hannibals.

One of 111 Squadron's armourers, Charles Cooper, was in the armoury with others when the alarm was sounded: 'I went to a gun position, with our Flight Sergeant Clements, which consisted of one Browning .303 machine-gun which we had mounted on a home-made steel tripod. On hearing the sound of the bombs coming down, we dived into a nearby shelter, fortunately in time to miss the bomb which hit the armoury. I think we lost four of our armourers off the squadron, including two friends of mine, Bernard Mills and Alf Couland. The same bomb killed Gangster, Flight Lieutenant Connors's* dog.'

Because of the Hurricanes' intervention, many of the bombs fell wide, outside the airfield's perimeter and on to the surrounding private houses which abounded in this area. Some seventy people were killed and many more injured.

Thompson himself gained his squadron's first success of the day, a 110 losing an engine and much of one wing before the pilot dextrously skidded down on to a field, wheels up, pilot and gunner unhurt. By this time several 32 Squadron Hurricanes from Biggin Hill had arrived to reinforce 111, and *Erpro* 210 was forced into defensive circles, from which, as opportunity and cloud cover allowed, individual aircraft would break free.

With the advantage of superior speed and the handicap of limited fuel, it was the 109s that were first to flee, throttles wide open and climbing for cloud or the more dangerous concealment of trees, valleys and railway cuttings. All but one got away. For the slower 110s, the price was higher, six of the fifteen failing to return.

*Stanley Connors DFC and Bar shot down one of the raiders and was also credited with a Ju 88 on this day. He was shot down and killed three days later.

John Thompson pursued one of these fleeing 110s across the undulating farmland of Surrey and Sussex, the pilot showing remarkable skill at taking advantage of the least cover. At one moment in this hectic one-against-one chase, the Squadron Leader saw his tracers removing tiles from a farmhouse roof. He then knew he was very low indeed. But the outcome was inevitable. Flames began to pour from one of the Messerschmitt's engines; then, close to the little village of Rothersfield, Thompson must have hit the pilot, for the 110 suddenly reared up vertically, turned over and was pulverised on impact. The pilot was Rubensdoerffer, and with him died his rear gunner Obergefreiter Kretzer.

As the last of the *Erpro* 210 fighter-bombers sped off back home over Dungeness, it was possible to reflect on the cost and relative futility of over 1,750 Luftwaffe sorties against England, from first light in the south to the catastrophic midday raids in the north-east, and finally the evening snap airfield raids, when that supreme low-level navigator and fighter-bomber pilot, Rubensdoerffer, had mistaken Croydon for Kenley. The Dorniers, too, had missed Biggin Hill and dropped their bombs from high altitude on the incomplete grass airfield of West Malling, damaging some wooden huts and killing one or two airmen.

When Sperrle and Kesselring returned from Karinhall late that evening, first reports of the activities during their absence were not encouraging, and Kesselring was especially anxious about the bombing of Croydon, which was well inside the Greater London area from which for the present Luftwaffe pilots were prohibited. Hitler, it must be added, was furious, but the perpetrator lay dead in the wreckage of his plane far away across the Channel. All the same the loss of Rubensdoerffer was a cruel blow for *Luftflotte* 2, and KG26 alone had lost three senior officers among eight He 111s which had failed to return. In all seventy-five fighters and bombers of the three *Luftflotten* involved had succumbed to the guns of the RAF and Anti-Aircraft Command, the biggest haul of the Battle.

Against this figure, Dowding had lost over thirty fighters and thirteen pilots, excluding the unfortunate Richard Hardy recovering in a French hospital, and two more made prisoner.

On this day, while the fighting raged far to the north, and to the south, the Cabinet met at 10 Downing Street. After the business had been dealt with, all left except Churchill himself and the Secretary of State for

# The Daily Telegraph

No. 26,583    LONDON, FRIDAY, AUGUST 16, 1940    and *Morning Post*    BROADCASTING—Page Two    ONE PENNY

**4 A.M.**

## 144 RAIDERS DOWN FOR LOSS OF ONLY 27 PLANES

### R.A.F. SMASH UP NAZIS' BIGGEST ONSLAUGHT

### 1,000 SENT OVER AND 14 PER CENT. LOST

### DIVE BOMBERS SWOOP ON CROYDON

The Royal Air Force, aided by Britain's ground defences, yesterday achieved the greatest air victory of any single day in the war, when out of more than 1,000 of Goering's raiders 144 were shot down, for the loss of only 27 British fighters.

The raids extended over a front of 500 miles, from Plymouth to the Tyne, and when dive bombers raided Croydon airport, brought to London its first warning since mass attacks began.

The total of 144 was the number confirmed by the Air Ministry to midnight and announced at 1.30 a.m. It is likely to be still further increased when late reports have been examined.

More than 14 per cent. of a great raiding force employed by the enemy was accounted for, and according to an Air Ministry statement issued at 1.45 a.m. little gain was achieved by the Germans at a huge cost.

The statement continued:
In the Croydon area a number of buildings were damaged, including a scent factory, and fires were caused which were soon brought under control. On the aerodrome itself no serious damage was done, but a number of people in the neighbourhood received injuries and one death is reported.

At Hastings bombs fell in a residential area. One person was killed and some were injured.

### NAZI LOSSES NOW 443

British official figures of the losses on both sides in fighting over the south coast area since mass air raids began on Britain a week ago are:

|  | German | British |
|---|---|---|
| Thursday | 18 | (3 R.A.F. pilots safe) |
| Friday | 61 | 5 |
| Saturday | 8 | (8 R.A.F. pilots safe) |
| Sunday | 36 | (2 R.A.F. pilots safe) |
| Monday | 67 | 13 |
| Tuesday | (1 R.A.F. pilot safe) | 13 |
| Wednesday | 31 | (10 R.A.F. pilots safe) |
| Yesterday | 7 | (2 R.A.F. pilots safe) |
|  | 144 | 27 |
|  | (5 R.A.F. pilots safe) | |
| **Total** | **443** | **165** |

### NAZIS ATTACK IN HUNDREDS

### DAY OF CHANNEL BATTLES

From RICHARD CAPELL, *Daily Telegraph War Correspondent*
DOVER, Thursday

To-day was again a day of tremendous air-fighting. One estimate of the number of enemy 'planes that passed over or approached this sector was 900. Battles were seen on and off during the morning, the afternoon and again this evening by onlookers on the southeastern coast.

What still strikes one as strange is the suddenness of the outbreak of these battles. At one moment the skies may be empty and land and sea seem to be at peace. Then, as if by a trick of a supernatural conjuror, aircraft swarm, batteries bark furiously, and 'desperate dramas are played on all sides.

At one moment this morning I could, by turning from one quarter to another, see great clouds of smoke and dust rising from explosions of bombs dropped by the Germans in a seaside town; then, looking inland, the descent by parachute of an airman whose machine had just gone crashing to earth; and then out at sea a number of small vessels which were searching for survivors from the aircraft brought down in the dog-fights

One of a party of raiders brought down yesterday crashed and damaged three houses. Part of the fuselage lies in a garden. No one in the houses was hurt.

### BUILDINGS HIT IN RAID ON CROYDON AIRPORT

### RESCUERS DIG IN DEBRIS: BUS WRECKED

*DAILY TELEGRAPH REPORTER*

Considerable damage was done to some buildings adjoining Croydon aerodrome and a number of casualties were caused in last night's raid. Conflicting statements were made to me concerning the number of German dive bombers engaged.

While one spectator said that he counted 11 machines, others put the figure at between 20 and 30. It seems fairly certain, however, that three were shot down. Large numbers of people were in the vicinity of the aerodrome when the attack was launched. Fires were started, but were quickly got under control by the fire brigades.

One building was demolished, and some hours after the raid rescue workers were still digging among the debris for the bodies

### RAID ALARM IN LONDON

### PEOPLE STAY IN STREETS

*DAILY TELEGRAPH REPORTER*

Last night London had its first

### TO DISARM—NOT TO FIGHT

### FRENCH SHIPS AT MARTINIQUE

### SUCCESS OF U.S. PERSUASION

FROM OUR OWN CORRESPONDENT
WASHINGTON, Thursday

Agreement has been reached for the disarmament of the French ships now in Western Hemisphere waters at Martinique and Guadaloupe, it was announced to-day.

The United States Administration has been extremely anxious to avoid any incident within the so-called safety zone similar to that at Oran, and has been seeking for some time to find a solution of the problem.

Discussions were held in Washington between the French Embassy and the Department of State and also at Martinique, where the United States Admiral Greenslade sent a special mission to act as intermediary and facilitate some reasonable arrangement. He reached Washington a few days ago to make his report.

The solution agreed upon is for demobilisation and the practical decommissioning of the French vessels.

Mr. Sumner Welles announced to-day that an American naval representative with the rank of Lieutenant-Commander would be attached to the Consulate office at Martinique to keep the United States Administration in touch with the situation.

### READY TO FIGHT

The French naval vessels which will now be immobilised for the remainder of the war are the aircraft carrier Bearn, the cruiser Emile Bertin and the training cruiser Jeanne d'Arc.

For a time the commander of the Emile Bertin took the line that he must obey orders and return to France, even if it meant fighting British and American warships. The French Ambassador at Washington in numerous discussions, including one with President Roosevelt at the White House, urged to make known to his Government the feelings of the American Administration that no hostilities should take place in the Western Hemisphere safety zone.

The French Naval Attaché then flew to Martinique to make the Washington views known, and finally the French naval commander was directed from making any attempt to break through the British squadron watching the port.

The problem of the ownership of the American 'dianes on the Bearn

### NAZIS DROPPED SPOOF OPERATION ORDERS

### PARACHUTES FAILED TO CAUSE INTENDED PANIC

After further intensive investigations into the dropping of between 70 and 80 German parachutes on the Midlands and the North, it was officially announced last night the authorities are satisfied that these "incidents" were faked by the Germans in an attempt to cause panic. They failed hopelessly in their purpose.

It was also disclosed that in some cases the parachutes contained what purported to be "operation orders." These were part of the Nazi spoof.

A statement by the Ministry of Information last night said: "The dropping of a number of parachutes by enemy aircraft during Tuesday night has been further investigated. A large number of the parachutes were dropped in widely separated areas.

"In many instances the harness had not been undone. In some places empty parachutes were seen falling and Home Guards were on the spot ready to pick them up on landing.

"In addition, bags containing instructions purporting to be operation orders, were found.

"At least one bag was dropped in a place and under circumstances which make it obvious that German intended the bag to fall into the hands of the military authorities. The documents contained in these bags have been examined and are clearly not genuine instructions.

### WAR OF NERVES

"It is evident that the whole incident was organised by the German party for the purpose of spreading alarm, which it noticeably failed to do, and partly as an aid to their defeatist propaganda which they have for a long time been attempting to carry out in this country by wireless and other means.

"If any further evidence of this were needed it is to be found in a German broadcast of a false account of the affair from a German broadcasting station masquerading as a British station which had recently been

### SIR ABE BAILEY'S WILL

### £250,000 EMPIRE TRUST CREATED

FROM OUR OWN CORRESPONDENT
CAPETOWN, Thursday

The will of Sir Abe Bailey, which was filed to-night, sets no figure on the value of the estate which is estimated to run into some millions sterling.

It provides for the establishment of an Abe Bailey trust of £250,000 for fostering the interests of the teaching of Afrikaans in English schools, for sending students from Afrikaans speaking universities on variation to visit England and other parts of the Empire, and for helping the Salvation Army when in need.

"At least one bag was dropped in a place and under circumstances which make it obvious that Germans intended the bag to fall into the hands of the military authorities. This trust is to be established to carry out Sir Abe Bailey's ideal that South Africans should progress in numbers and capacity, and in a spirit of national unity in their membership of the British Commonwealth of Nations so as to take their place among the peoples of the world befitting their past history and the resources with which our land has been endowed."

Among the trustees are Sir Patrick Duncan, Governor-General of South Africa, chairman; Gen. Smuts; Mr. J. H. Hofmeyr, Minister of Finance; Mr. John

The foresight of Air Marshal Dowding in his direction of Fighter Command deserves high praise, and even more remarkable had been the restraint and the exact measurement of formidable stresses which had reserved a fighter force in the North through all these long weeks of mortal conflict in the South. We must regard the generalship here shown as an example of genius in the art of war.[9]

When Churchill returned to Downing Street he ordered his private secretary to telephone his predecessor as prime minister, Neville Chamberlain, who had recently suffered a serious cancer operation. The man of Munich was in the middle of his dinner and was not best pleased at the interruption.

However he was overcome with joy when he heard the news and very touched at Winston thinking of him. It is typical of W. to do a small thing like this which could give such great pleasure. 'The Lord President was very grateful to you,' I said to Winston. 'So he ought to be,' replied W., 'this is one of the greatest days in history.'[10]

Readers of the *New York Times* were not encouraged to share Churchill's claim. It was the gravity of the situation that commanded the attention over there. Full eight-column headlines spread starkly across the front page as this newspaper told how '1,000 Nazi Planes Raid Britain', and the report on the Croydon raid recounted how the 'black-nosed Nazi bombers . . . sowed death and reaped ruin, barely skimming their targets, then roaring back to the clouds'.

On the same day, the American aviation authority, Major Alexander Seversky, published an article in the *New York Times*, which brought a new perspective to bear on the Battle and further intensified American interest, which was already being stirred in the city (and elsewhere throughout the United States) by black headlines:

The action now being reported is generally regarded as the 'prelude' to an invasion. . . . But it is nothing of the sort. What we are now watching is the authentic big push. If Great Britain loses the present battle, she will in effect have lost the war, at least as far as the mother country is concerned. Whether the victors then decide to 'invade' the island or prefer to lay it waste systematically from the air without anything more than a token occupation of a few spots will be a matter of detail, without essential military significance. . . . Air power makes possible the defeat of an enemy without occupation. But the sooner we in America learn this lesson from the tragic events of these crowded days and apply them in our own planning for national security the better.

The *New York Times* failed to pick up the story from its counterpart in London about the eighteen-year-old German airman who produced a photograph when he was captured. 'I was told if I showed a photograph of my mother I wouldn't be shot,' he claimed. Perhaps the *New York Times* editor no more believed this story than the British figures of German losses. It was true all the same, even if the losses were exaggerated.

Meanwhile, the American Ambassador in London, Joseph P. Kennedy, ensured that a more or less continuous flow of pessimism about Britain's hopes of survival still reached Washington. 'England will go down fighting,' ran one of his messages to the President. 'Unfortunately, I am one who does not believe that it is going to do the slightest bit of good.'

To Roosevelt's disgust, Kennedy ordered the Embassy and all its staff to flee London, the first to do so. Other Americans in London took a more robust view of the times. Besides the pilots helping to defend Britain, they formed their own Local Defence Volunteers unit. Kennedy did not approve, and told them they ought to go home before the inevitable invasion and defeat of Britain.

# 13

## The Assault Continues

### 16 AUGUST

One of the strengths of RAF Fighter Command in the summer of 1940, quite unappreciated by Schmidt, Goering and the *Luftflotten* staff, was its wide-ranging recruitment. The presence on almost all squadrons of pilots from the Empire and Commonwealth – Australia, New Zealand, South Africa, Canada, Southern Rhodesia – or from the European conquered countries, especially Poland, Czechoslovakia, Belgium and France, gave strength to the belief that they were engaged not just in a fight for survival but also a crusade of good against evil. In mess bars and dispersal huts the sight of shoulder flashes denoting Czechoslovakia, Canada, France or Belgium added a united nations spur to the enterprise before that name had been given authority.

None fought in the air with greater single-minded ferocity than the Poles and Czechs, many of whom had lost families as well as homes and had witnessed the depraved barbarism of the German invaders. Sergeant Josef Frantisek, for example, in a period of nineteen months from March 1939, fled his native Czechoslovakia for Poland, fought and gained his first victories in an absurdly obsolete Pulawksi fighter, escaped to Romania on Poland's collapse, broke out of his internment camp and reached France via Syria, where he fought with the Armée de l'Air in slightly less speculative aircraft, bringing his total of accredited successes to eleven before France, too, collapsed.

In England this remarkable Czech was happy to fly with the Poles of

303 Squadron (Hurricanes). His ardent spirit, his skill as a pilot, and his total dedication to the craft of killing Germans, impressed even his Polish fellow pilots. When he finally died on 8 October he was Fighter Command's highest scoring pilot with an accredited total of twenty-eight enemy planes.

Although none of them achieved numerical successes to match the little Czech sergeant, the handful of Americans made an impact far out of proportion to their numbers. As early as mid-July the RAF, anticipating severe pilot shortages, let American newspaper correspondents know 'the Royal Air Force is in the market for American flyers as well as American airplanes. Experienced airmen, preferably those with at least 250 flying hours to their credit, would be welcomed by the RAF,' ran a report in the *New York Herald Tribune* of 14 July. All they had to do was to cross into Canada, pass a physical examination and sign on: no swearing an oath to the British crown, it was emphasised.

Other Americans had anticipated events. Jimmy Davis, for example, was commissioned into the RAF before the outbreak of war and served in 79 Squadron (Hurricanes). The squadron was sent to France in an attempt to stem the advance of the *blitzkrieg*, and like all the others had a breathtaking time, fighting against grotesque odds and hustled from airfield to airfield.

Davis had a number of successes before the remnants of the squadron got back to England, and Biggin Hill. One afternoon in late June he and three other pilots of 79 were due to be decorated by the King. Davis never made the airfield investiture. When George VI enquired why he had a DFC left over, he was told that Flight Lieutenant James Davis* had just been shot down and killed. 'He was a first-class pilot and a great chap,' Pilot Officer Donald Stones commented.

No. 609 Squadron (Spitfires) was blessed with the greatest number of American pilots, a trio who could have formed a music-hall comedy team if the issues had been less serious. They were Pilot Officers E. Q. 'Red' Tobin, Andrew 'Andy' Mamedoff and V. C. 'Shorty' Keogh. Tobin was tall, loose-limbed, a Jimmy Stewart character with an engaging sense of humour who would cry out, when scrambled, 'Saddle her up, boys – I'm ridin'!'

Mamedoff was the second in height, a tubby fellow with a round face and a ready-grown RAF moustache, liked by all. As for 'Shorty' Keogh, he really was a midget, four feet ten only and requiring cushions to build up his cockpit seat, but once settled he proved to be a

---

*Because he was killed before 10 July Davis does not qualify statistically as a Battle pilot.

miracle-pilot, capable of making the Spitfire perform almost more than its full repertoire.

Before the war Keogh had been a barnstormer and professional parachutist, completely lacking in nerves. The three of them had come over to help the Finns fight the Russians in 1939, switched to France when the Finns surrendered and, like so many Poles and Czechs, made their way across the Channel to what they saw as the last island bastion of freedom in Europe.

In London it was not so easy to convince the authorities of the seriousness of their intentions, understandably enough in view of their joint appearance. One of 609's finest pilots, John Bisdee, later wrote of the trio:

These three were really down and out in England. They went to drown their sorrows in a pub in London, where they met an air commodore. They explained their sad predicament and he said, 'Get in touch with me tomorrow'. . . . By noon they had been commissioned in the Royal Air Force and sent off with some money to buy uniforms.[1]

By 8 August they had been posted to 609 at Middle Wallop. They served heroically and successfully through the busy weeks that followed, and then transferred to the first Eagle Squadron when it was formed in late September. All three were killed later in the war, and of the eight Americans originally in RAF Fighter Command up to August 1940, only one survived – J. K. Haviland DFC – whom no one has traced recently.

Perhaps the most memorable of all the American fighter pilots was Billy Fiske, young and immensely popular, from a privileged background,* which had helped him over the obstacles the American Ambassador placed in the way of American volunteers. His flight commander, Sir Archibald Hope Bt, wrote of him:

Unquestionably Billy Fiske was the best pilot I've ever known. It was unbelievable how good he was. He picked up so fast it wasn't true. He'd flown a bit before, but he was a natural as a fighter pilot. He was also terribly nice and extraordinarily modest, and fitted into the squadron very well.[2]

Billy Fiske was in the thick of the mid-August fighting when his squadron was operating from Tangmere. On 13 August he was in close combat with a great number of Me 110s, one of which succeeded in

---

*His 4½ litre open Bentley, in British racing green, complete with bonnet-strap and projecting supercharger, did his cause no harm at all.

hitting him. It was 12.15 p.m. over Portland. Fiske managed to get back home unhurt and his Hurricane was not much damaged. He was to be as deeply involved in the raids on the south coast on 16 August, too.

The contribution from the United States' northern neighbour was, of course, much more substantial. Many Canadians had signed on with the RAF before the war and most of these formed the revived 242 Fighter Squadron, with its moose head badge and '*Toujours prêt*' motto, at Coltishall in October 1939. The squadron became operational on Hurricanes under the command of Squadron Leader F. M. Gobeil in March 1940. After operating flights from Biggin Hill over France when the fighting became desperate in May, 242 Squadron became involved in the last days of Allied resistance from French airfields, suffering grave losses but also shooting down a lot of Luftwaffe aircraft. Pilot Officer Willie McKnight was the top scorer, and he went on to be credited with sixteen-and-a-half victories before the end of the Battle, earning a DFC and Bar.

By the time the remnants of 242 Squadron arrived back in England, the Canadian element had been much diluted. But meanwhile the first Royal Canadian Air Force (RCAF) fighter squadron was being formed under the command of that great fighter, Squadron Leader E. A. McNab. Even the aircraft of 1 (RCAF) Squadron were home produce, their Hurricanes being among the first to be shipped to Britain.

No. 1 (RCAF) Squadron worked up under the wing of 111 Squadron and finally went into action for the first time from Northolt on 26 August. It was a hectic baptism for the Canadians and there were many losses of aircraft, though pilot loss remained relatively low. The squadron claimed no fewer than seven enemy aircraft in the widespread fighting on 27 September and remained in the heat of the Battle until the end.

Of the critical day of 15 September, Squadron Leader McNab wrote: 'It was a terrific spectacle. There were so many aircraft in the sky that there was as much danger of colliding with another fellow as there was of being shot down. There were more than a thousand aircraft in the sky just south of London. I counted nine aircraft falling at one time, and there were parachutes everywhere.'

There were more Canadians scattered among other squadrons, the most successful and notable being Johnny Kent. After helping 303 (Polish) Squadron to become operational, Kent was promoted squadron leader and led 92 Squadron. He had already built up a sizeable score and was awarded the DFC and Bar, and later the AFC.

Twenty-one South Africans made a contribution out of all proportion to their numbers, and more than half that number were killed, among them Flying Officer Norman Barry of 3 and 501 Squadrons, and Flying Officer Chris Davis DFC of 601 Squadron, who succumbed to a ferocious attack by Me 109s on 6 September.

Three of the most notable South Africans were Flight Lieutenant G. D. L. Haysom DSO, DFC, of 79 Squadron, Flying Officer P. H. 'Dutch' Hugo DSO, DFC and Bar, of 615 Squadron, and certainly the most famous of all, Squadron Leader 'Sailor' Malan DSO and Bar, DFC and Bar (and numerous foreign decorations), whose inspiration was as pricelessly valuable as his sublime shooting.

There had been a particularly long and sustained recruiting drive for pilots in New Zealand in the years leading up to the war, which resulted in this relatively modest-sized country contributing a greater number of aircrew than any other Dominion. On a number of squadrons their fighting prowess was a significant inspiration, right from the beginning – from 3 July specifically, when Brian Carbury, a flying officer on 603 Squadron, shared with another 'Kiwi', Ken Lawrence, a Ju 88 off Land's End. Carbury went on to build up a fine score and was awarded a DFC and Bar.

Squadron Leader James Leathart's 54 Squadron was the most richly endowed with New Zealand talent. Among them was Pilot Officer Billy Williams, whose Spitfire was set on fire over the Isle of Wight just after he had sent a bomber down in flames. He managed to force-land successfully and ran clear as his plane blew up. No. 54 Squadron's two flight commanders, Colin Gray and Alan Deere, became New Zealand legends in their own time, and years later, heavy with decorations, retired as Group Captain and Air Vice-Marshal respectively.

Contemporary photographs show these two friends as strongly contrasting in appearance, Gray's face being as narrow as Deere's was square-jawed. Colin Gray had trouble being accepted at first for medical reasons, but succeeded in building up his strength and stamina with farming work, and arrived in England for his training in January 1939. His shooting was almost in the Malan class, and twice in mid-August he shot down two Me 109s in one day, no mean feat.

Al Deere, of Irish stock, made his mark six weeks before the official opening of the Battle. Accompanied by Pilot Officer Johnny Allen, he formed an escort for his flight commander, who had determined to attempt the rescue in a two-seat training plane of the CO of 74 Squadron, stranded between the lines at Calais-Marck airfield. The daring operation was a complete success, Deere shooting down two –

and probably a third – of the numerous Me 109s which attempted to interfere. Deere appeared to lead a charmed life but it was his peerless courage and instant reactions (he had been a champion RAF boxer) which brought him through.

As for the wide recruitment, these figures speak for themselves:

## Fighter Command aircrew not from the UK who took part in the Battle*

| Nationality | Flew operationally | Killed in the Battle |
|---|---|---|
| Australian | 21 | 14 |
| New Zealand | 129 | 14 |
| Canadian | 90 | 20 |
| South African | 22 | 9 |
| Rhodesian | 2 | - |
| Jamaican | 1 | - |
| Irish | 9 | - |
| American | 7 | 1 |
| Polish | 141 | 29 |
| Czech | 87 | 7 |
| Belgian | 24 | 6 |
| French | 13 | - |
| Palestinian | 1 | - |

'Black Thursday' was the name given by the Germans to the operations of the previous day, 15 August. The losses had indeed been heavy, but not on a scale to lead to any change of strategy. Goering, still adhering to the lessons of Poland, Norway and France, intended to persist with his policy of attrition against what he had been led to believe were vital RAF airfields. He could not bring himself to believe that they could not be put permanently out of action, thus forcing the enemy back farther and farther from the coast, at the same time reducing his numbers until Fighter Command deteriorated into a spent force.

The anti-cyclone continued its tight grip over northern Europe, but with each passing day conditions increasingly tended to bring early morning mist. This suited both combatants. The RAF pilots appreciated an hour or two longer in bed, and the ground crews treasured the bonus of time to service and repair their aircraft. As for the Luftwaffe, the loss of thirty-five bomber crews from KG3, KG26 and LG1 alone required the summoning of replacement aircraft and men, which could not be carried out instantly.

*Participating aircrew of Fighter Command from within the UK numbered 2,316, of whom 403 were killed (figures from RAF Battle of Britain Museum, Hendon).

The first bombs of the day fell on West Malling (uncompleted) airfield again soon after 11 a.m. Underestimating the size of the plots approaching the Kent coast, Park ordered only a nominal response. For this reason a force of Dorniers broke through unopposed and reopened a good many of the craters painstakingly filled in overnight. It was, as Park had suspected, no more than an overture, and sure enough at midday an indisputably big raid showed itself on the radar screens at Dover and Foreness. Estimating a total enemy force of around 300, he scrambled more than eighty fighters.

Soon the most identifiable threat appeared to be a strong force of Dorniers heading for the Thames Estuary and Hornchurch sector station. No. 54 Squadron Spitfires were in the most favourable position to deal with this heavily escorted raid. The CO, James Leathart, led his nine machines into the Dorniers, breaking them up, forcing them to jettison their bombs and scatter for home. All this took less than half a minute, which was as well for the Me 109s were now mixing it seriously, although they too had to head for home almost at once because they were at the limit of their range. Colin Gray, destined to be one of the big scorers – and to survive – picked off two 109s. One of these crashed on an enemy airfield, considered to be an excellent morale depressant for all eyewitnesses.

Combat on a larger scale was by now breaking out all over the southern and western home counties as a great wedge of Dorniers from KG2 advanced like a brigade of flying tanks and then split up, every one heading for an airfield. It was 12.15 p.m., and Park had the veteran 32 and 111 Squadrons (Hurricanes), and three Spitfire squadrons, including 266 led by the thirty-year-old Rodney Wilkinson. Wilkinson had fought hard to get on to ops, even turning down the Duke of Kent's offer to be his ADC.

His squadron and John Thompson's 111 went into the bomber formations the way they knew to be most effective and, as far as enemy return fire was concerned, safest: line abreast, head-on. Split-second timing was called for, and unfortunately, early in the proceedings, one of Thompson's flight commanders, the newly promoted and newly decorated Henry Ferris, held his line fractionally too long. Bomber and fighter exploded, breaking up the formation and scattering wreckage far and wide, along with the bodies of Ferris, Oberleutnant Brandenburg and his crew of three. A minute later Thompson's persistent attacks on another Dornier sent it crashing into hop fields north of Ashford.

At the same time, 266's Spitfires jumped a *Staffel* of 109s over the Kent coast, and shot down their leader, Hauptmann Ebbighausen. But as happens so often in fighter-to-fighter duels, the Spitfires were jumped in their turn, and no fewer than five of them, including *their* squadron commander, had been shot down, three of them killed.

Among the dead was Wilkinson. Of him one of his friends, 'Chips' Channon, wrote: 'I shan't forget his engaging charm, his curious shuffle and infectious gaiety. He had strange Egyptian eyes, long limbs and a natural elegance, but seemed fated to die. . . . He was typical of the type which is serving and saving England. . . .'[3]

Another who died in this intense battle was Sub-Lieutenant Henry la Fore Greenshields RN. Hard-pressed for experienced fighter pilots, the RAF had gladly accepted increasing numbers of volunteers from the senior Service. In all the Admiralty 'lent' fifty-eight Fleet Air Arm pilots to the RAF during the Battle, and the value of these seasoned men cannot be overestimated.

Less than one hour later an even greater massacre of a single unit was taking place eighty miles to the west. *Luftflotte* 3 had set up another big raid on southern airfields timed to coincide with the withdrawal of *Luftflotte* 2's raids and the expected refuelling and rearming of 11 Group's fighters. No. 10 Group's fighters had, however, not so far been disturbed; nor had 11 Group's Tangmere wing, although – mercifully – these were scrambled shortly before a mixed force of heavily escorted bombers turned up with exemplary promptitude off the Isle of Wight's eastern tip, the Nab.

Ventnor was still out of action, but Poling's CH aerials were not required by 1 p.m., when all with eyes could pick out the mass of dots assembling as if for some aerial display. A multi-coloured flare shot up from the leader's machine and, as it descended, the show was on.

The bulk of the dive-bombers made no effort to conceal their intentions, flying fast and straight for Tangmere, tumbling down from 12,000 feet, sirens screaming. This was the Stuka's most vulnerable moment, and one or two Hurricanes got in amongst them. But the great majority continued their near-vertical dives, picking out the hangars and other buildings, including stores and the officers' mess. Gunner J. J. Ingle, a QE layer of the 98th Heavy Anti-Aircraft Regiment, recently deployed to help defend the airfield, wrote: 'Neither us or the ground defences on the airfield could open fire as our fighters were taking off as fast as they could and were mixed up with the Germans.'

The timing of the attack was perfect, therefore, and two of Tangmere's hangars were totally destroyed and the other three damaged. Inside them six Blenheims and seven Hurricanes were demolished. The airfield was pockmarked with craters like the moon's surface and sinister earth bulges marked the position of delayed-action bombs.

Everyone who survived that Tangmere raid on the ground has vivid memories of the aftermath. An airframe fitter on 43 Squadron, Peter Jones, recalled: 'When the raid was over, the place looked a sorry mess. I remember looking at the broken aircraft and saying, "There's a hell of a lot of work to be done." Later on we heard a rumour that the group captain had floored a stroppy German prisoner with a good right hook. That cheered us up no end. Then the Women's Voluntary Service turned up, armed with churns of tea. I had a mug of tea thrust into my hand and a lighted Woodbine stuck into my mouth. That was my first cigarette, and I've been an addict ever since.'

It had been a routine, and characteristically accurate, attack by the experienced pilots of I/StG2 *Stukageschwader*. Equally effective was the Hurricane counter-attack, led by 43 Squadron, which shot down seven of the dive-bombers as they raced for home and damaged three more. The Tangmere anti-aircraft fire had put another into the ground, though quite gently, so that a crowd soon gathered to admire the near-intact plane; while at St Malo and Lannion there were many empty seats at dinner that evening.

In spite of the smoke and craters, the Tangmere aircraft all managed to land back safely – with one exception. Billy Fiske's flight commander, Archibald Hope, saw one of 601's Hurricanes lying on its belly, belching smoke, as he came in on his final approach. 'I taxied up to it and got out. There were two ambulancemen there. They had got Billy Fiske out of the cockpit. They didn't know how to take off his parachute so I showed them. Billy was burnt about the hands and ankles. I told him, "Don't worry. You'll be all right. . . ." Our adjutant went to see him in hospital at Chichester that night. Billy was sitting up in bed, perky as hell. The next thing we heard he was dead. Died of shock.'*

As the young American was being slipped into the ambulance, other tragedies and triumphs were occurring not far away. The naval stations at Gosport and Lee-on-Solent all suffered some damage, and repairs to Ventnor CH were put back another few days by some more pinpoint Ju 87 dive-bombing.

*On 4 July 1941, Independence Day, the American Ambassador, John Winant, unveiled a memorial tablet to Fiske in the crypt of St Paul's Cathedral.

Brand tried to cope with these widespread raids with a force which, even when complete, was manifestly inadequate. Many raiders got through unscathed, but three aircraft of red section, 249 Squadron, were in the right place at the right time. John Grandy had brought his squadron down from the north only two days earlier, and this section, led by Flight Lieutenant James Nicolson, was patrolling near Southampton when they sighted a strong force of Me 110s.

Nicolson led them straight in, but before they could open fire, like 266 Squadron earlier in the day, they were bounced by 109s. One of his pilots baled out of his burning Hurricane in the nick of time, while Squadron Leader (supernumerary) Eric King managed to escape and get back to Boscombe Down. As for Nicolson, he persisted in his attack on a 110 in spite of the flames licking round him, pressing it home before abandoning his machine, with severe burns to his hands and face.

The two pilots found themselves parachuting down close together. This was interpreted by a nerve-racked Royal Artillery officer as an enemy paratroop assault, and he ordered his men to open fire. It is believed that members of the Local Defence Volunteers joined in. The pilot officer was killed instantly when his shrouds were severed, and Nicolson was wounded as he landed, already in agony from his burns. He was awarded the Victoria Cross, the only fighter pilot of World War II to receive it.

Later in the afternoon both Sperrle and Kesselring launched further attacks south, east and west of London. But after about 4.30 the clear weather gave way to scattered and thickening cloud. This had the double effect of increasing the bomber groups' navigational problems and decreasing the defending fighters' ability to intercept. Overland, Park and Brand were almost entirely dependent on Observer Corps reports, and these were hard to come by when scattered raids of from two to fifty bombers were roaming the countryside at 10–15,000 feet, only intermittently visible from the ground.

The result was that for a few hours there were more undetected enemy aircraft over England than at almost any time during the Battle, and more misidentified airfields attacked (including grass landing-strips). One other record was broken, too: the number of aircraft on the ground destroyed in a single raid.

No one will ever know now whether it was luck or amazing navigation which led two Ju 88s to Brize Norton, west of Oxford, a busy training airfield with a maintenance unit attached. The bombers were said to have lowered their undercarriage as if coming in to land and in the hope of being identified as Blenheims, as they often were. They then proceeded to place their bomb-loads exactly where they wanted them to go.

The two Junkers each dropped sixteen bombs, mainly on the hangars, which were packed with Airspeed Oxford trainers, all with full fuel tanks for the next morning's flying. Forty-six were destroyed, more damaged, and eleven Hurricanes with the maintenance unit were also knocked about. Few people saw the Ju 88s come, none saw them go; in fact, the next people to see them were friendly and on the other side of the Channel.

In spite of this success, it had been another frustrating day for the Luftwaffe. 'Again the weather was in league with the British,' wrote Cajus Bekker bleakly. 'In *Luftflotte* 2's operations zone such salient bases as Debden, Duxford, North Weald and Hornchurch escaped the fate of Tangmere just because the attacking forces were unable to find them through the cloud.'

The German intelligence about the function of enemy airfields was further confounded by a grave slip, but a providential one, in British security. Sub-Lieutenant Greenshields of 266 Squadron had taken off with an unposted letter to his parents in his pocket. In it he described how his squadron had been bombed at Eastchurch. In fact, they had made only a brief landing at this Coastal Command station. But when this letter was discovered in the dead pilot's pocket when he was dragged from the Channel, it provided the confirmation German intelligence needed that it was, in fact, a front-line fighter station. Many more tons of bombs were dropped, and wasted, on this hapless airfield as a result.

While keeping a watching brief on the American press at the same time, that most excellent observer of life in Britain, Mollie Panter-Downes, wrote graphic accounts of the Battle and its effects on everyday life for the *New Yorker* magazine. Back in July, she had recorded how

it was hoped that the number of German planes destroyed would be duly noted by sections of the American press which appears to people here to act as though mesmerised by the achievements of the Luftwaffe. . . . Many astonished Britons taking time off from the war to read how American editors think it's going, have felt like protesting, like Mark Twain, that the reports of their death have been greatly exaggerated.

# 14

## Respite and Re-engagement

### 17–18 AUGUST

After six hectic and destructive days, the 17th of August surprisingly allowed both sides to 'stand in pause'. There was no apparent reason for this. The weather was as brilliant as it had been for days past, and by mid-morning the radar operators began to suspect the efficiency of their aerials or cathode-ray tubes. At Observer Corps posts all that could be heard was the occasional sound of a communications plane, or, briefly, a Hurricane or Spitfire on engine test. Later, convoy patrols off the coast could be heard but aroused no concern.

'Not a single sausage, scare, flap or diversion of any description today,' wrote the CO of 32 Squadron at Biggin Hill, Mike Crossley. 'Amazing. Heavenly day, too.'[1]

This unexpected hiatus allowed work to proceed unhindered on the repair of Ventnor CH station, on the clearance of hangar wreckage at Brize Norton and Tangmere especially, and the filling in of craters at several more airfields. GPO telephone technicians and RAF electricians worked to reconnect severed communications. Catering staff with damaged kitchens and messes to cope with sought to set up makeshift arrangements under canvas or commandeered buildings. In many cases, accommodation for bombed-out personnel, flying and non-flying, had to be sought in local houses – from which, by now, many residents had long since moved away. The dead were buried and the wounded moved from sick quarters to civilian hospitals.

At all levels of command, on both sides of the Channel, twenty-four hours for reflection came like a gift. No. 601 Squadron's intelligence officer was able to complete his reports on the previous day's activities, and the armourers of 19 Squadron were able to give time to their temperamental new cannons, which were jamming after a few rounds.

At Rosières-en-Santerre, Epinoy, Cambrai, St Trond and other French bomber airfields, Dorniers and Heinkels were serviced and battle-damage repaired. The same work was carried out at the *Stuka-geschwader* bases in Normandy and Brittany, but many new dive-bombers were flown in as replacements, and these, too, required checking over. The aircrew new arrivals were looked over, too, new names learned and wisecracks exchanged about the 'Tommy pilots'.

(It was generally agreed that it was better to bale out or crash-land over England than over the Channel; the cage would detain you for no more than a few weeks, the sea perhaps for ever.)

All German aircrew loathed the sea and coined the word *Kanalkrank*, Channel sickness, for their fear, which was compounded by the certainty that the cold would kill them within four hours, although a crash-landing in the sea might give a bomber crew the chance to launch a dinghy.

Perversely, they believed that the seafaring British did not share this fear. Paddy Barthrop of 602 Squadron was not the only British pilot who wondered why the Me 109s did not carry long-range drop tanks. 'They could have won the war,' he claimed lightly, 'and we would be rich and they poor.'

In fact, the *Dackelbauch* ('Dachshund belly'), which had enabled the Norwegian-based Me 110s to 'escort' the bombers to the north-east coast two days earlier, had been developed months ago, but no single-engined fighter on either side was equipped to carry drop tanks in August 1940. This was an astonishing German failure. Drop tanks for Me 109s and He 51s had been tried out successfully in the Spanish Civil War. 'Our range could have been extended by 125 to 200 miles,' wrote Galland. 'At that time this would have been just the decisive extension of our penetration.'[2]

Because of this intermission of 17 August, it is likely that more RAF fighter pilots read the newspapers in their messes than on busier mornings. It is also likely that they took 'a damn poor view' of a letter in

*The Times* from the naval writer, Bernard Acworth. This began by praising the 'incomparable' fighter pilots, but then continued:

This war will be won by the relentless and pervading influence of sea power, and until the Army is ready and the opportunity available, for the administration of a second Waterloo, every effort on land and in the air should be devoted to buttressing and strengthening our sea power.

The admiration for the RAF of Churchill, twice First Lord of the Admiralty, was unconditional, and three days later he was to utter the famous claim that 'Never in the field of human conflict was so much owed by so many to so few.'* But not for one moment did this lead him to relax his search for greater efficiency and the destruction of corrupt and ever-growing empires in this Service, as well as the Army and Royal Navy. On the contrary, the pause in the German assault from the air seemed to impel him to write the next day of 'local vested interests', especially at Hendon, where 'enormous numbers of aircraft' seemed to be kept out of the fight for inspections and other peacetime activities.

Churchill wrote to the Secretary of State for Air:

I should have thought that Hendon could provide at least two good squadrons of fighter or bomber aircraft of the reserve category. . . . Then they could be thrown in when an emergency came. Ought you not every day to call in question in your mind every non-military aspect of the Air Force? The tendency of every station commander is naturally to keep as much in his hands as possible.

Churchill had a great affection for 'Archie', his Secretary of State for Air, the Rt Hon. Sir Archibald Sinclair, a patrician Liberal. They had fought together in the trenches in the Great War, and there are few greater loyalties than those founded in old wars. A pilot of hard-pressed 64 Squadron (Spitfires) of 11 Group recalls at the height of the Battle a visit and an inspection by Archibald Sinclair. It was not, apparently, one of Sir Archibald's best days. 'His opening speech started by thanking the pilots of 12 Group for the work we were doing with our Hurricanes.'[3]

Churchill's minutes during this critical period of 1940 remind the reader of his concern to probe every aspect of the defence of the nation, from the development of photo-electric shell fuses to the double-

---

*Underpaid pilot officers especially were known to add '. . . and for so little', according to Pilot Officer Michael Appleby of 609 Squadron, whose savage deductions of tax from his pay were incorrectly attributed to his civilian earnings. Others suffered similarly.

checking of civilian gas masks, from anti-tank obstacles in St James's Park to training men to use the 'stickybomb' in the event of invasion.

On 28 August, Sinclair was the recipient of a minute (it could be called a 'rocket') from Churchill following his visit to the south-east to inspect the defences. The Prime Minister was displeased with the speed of repair to airfields, in particular Manston, where he was

much concerned to find that, although more than four clear days have passed since it was last raided, the greater part of the craters on the landing ground remain unfilled, and the aerodrome was barely serviceable. . . . I must protest emphatically at this feeble method of repairing damage. Altogether there were 150 people available to work. . . . These were doing their best. No effective appliances were available, and the whole process appeared disproportionate to the value of maintaining this fighting vantage ground.[4]

As was his custom, Churchill followed criticism with recommendations for a practical remedy. He called for 'crater-filling companies' of some 250 men each, 'with all helpful appliances and highly mobile, so that in a few hours they can be at work on any site which has been cratered'. He also recommended that, as a refinement, camouflage efforts should be made when craters were filled 'to pretend they had not been'.

Crater-filling of aerodromes, which generally was speedy, was important. The supply of replacement pilots was more important still and was rapidly becoming the most critical aspect of Fighter Command's continuing defence. Between 8 and 18 August no fewer than 154 pilots had been lost, killed, missing or so gravely wounded as to be out of the Battle. During that same period the OTUs produced few more than a third of this number. They had, it transpired later, made no effort to accelerate the final training course, to pack in more flying hours per day, or increase the facilities for firing practice. It was just as if peace still prevailed, except that the extent of the course was severely shortened. Keith Park later wrote:

I was worried daily from July to September by a chronic shortage of trained fighter pilots. . . . In December 1940 when I was posted to Flying Training Command, I found that the flying schools were working at only 2/3rds capacity and were following peacetime routines, being quite unaware of the grave shortage of pilots in Fighter Command.[5]

The crisis was compounded by the quality and experience of those lost, including a large number of squadron and flight commanders, and the dangerous inexperience of those replacing them. Taking a random sample in 1988 of the many survivors who reported on their OTU training after the Battle began, the average was eleven days, which could mean six to nine hours (several of them less) in the air. 'I fired my guns once into cloud,' was a typical comment; and few had any air-to-air gunnery practice, or experience with the reflector gunsight.

'I tried to take up my new pilots once or twice before taking them on ops,' one squadron commander, James Leathart, claimed. 'It was like sentencing them to death if I didn't, and not far short of it even if I did. They hadn't a clue about high-speed combat or deflection shooting or holding fire until 200 yards. . . .'

This added responsibility was a great burden, psychological and physical, on squadron and flight commanders who were already becoming tired and stale. Many survivors looking back nearly fifty years later recalled that this mid-August period was the hardest to get through, and some remembered feeling that the RAF might not finally prevail against these unremitting attacks.

Alan Deere, never one to over-dramatise, confided that, 'When we moved north we were really flaked out. I hardly knew what we were doing. We used to fly down to Manston [from Hornchurch], get bombed there, do two or three ops, get bombed again, then home again in the evening – when we could. Otherwise it was tents there. When we were sent up to Catterick [3 September], 54 Squadron was down to three experienced pilots, Colin Gray, a fellow New Zealander, George Gribble and me.'

The pilot crisis was eased by robbing Peter. Besides calling for volunteers from the Fleet Air Arm, Bomber and Coastal Command pilots, many just completing their training, were hastily converted to single-seat fighters. Desperate times called for desperate measures. But no one could bring back the skill and experience of Fighter Command pilots prevailing at the opening of the Battle in July. Although the structure of the Command, like nearly all the airfields, was operating effectively during the last half of August and the first days of September, this was the period of greater strain; a time when men like Alan Deere had to confess that they were 'really flaked out'.

C. Hector MacLean, who took over A Flight of 602 Squadron when Dunlop Urie was badly wounded on 18 August, told of his arrival at West Hampnett a few days earlier. 'I followed Pilot Officer [now Air Commodore] Paul Webb to the mess – a village type of farmhouse across the road. Through the door I could see two disconsolate young officers sitting at the foot of the staircase clutching their personal belongings. "Come on in," Paul Webb told me, "and meet 145 Squadron – great chaps, both of them." '

Even the toughest pilots like Bob Stanford Tuck and 'Ginger' Lacey began to feel the strain after many weeks of fighting, with two, three and sometimes four ops a day, and noting the absence of friends and fellow pilots from the mess – or seeing them go down in flames. 'My nerves were in ribbons and I was scared stiff that one day I would pull out and avoid combat,' Lacey recalled. 'That frightened me more than the Germans and I pleaded with my CO for a rest. He was sympathetic but quite adamant that until he got replacements I would have to carry on. I am glad now that he was unable to let me go. If I had been allowed to leave the squadron, feeling as I did, I am sure that I would never have flown again.'[6]

Harold Bird-Wilson, today a highly decorated retired air commodore, recalled the wretchedness of 'witnessing the execution in mortal combat of your friends. A fighter pilot was apt to place an invisible shield about himself, which may have given the air of callousness, but in reality it was a necessary protection against mental and physical strain.'[7]

On the British side, no day was to tax the resources and skills of those on the ground, and those in the air, more than 18 August. It was a day of sudden descents on airfields from heights ranging from fifty to 20,000 feet, of frantic refuelling and rearming of hot aircraft in the dust and heat of a cloudless summer Sunday, of snap decisions and actions taken against the background of exploding bombs and the unharmonious chatter of guns of many calibres firing from the air and from the ground, of blinding weariness broken by stabs of fear.

Never, since the outset of the Battle, had the Luftwaffe made such determined attempts to wipe out RAF airfields, and never had the defence been more indomitable. Scores of men died in the air, burnt or shot, died as they struck the ground, died by their aircraft on the ground, by their guns, in air-raid shelters, or simply going about their business, on airfields, or at home in the towns and villages of southern England.

No church bells tolled for the dead, nor even rang out on this Sabbath for Matins or Evensong. The sounds were all of war.

Following his most recent talk with Goering, Kesselring still believed that the only effective strategy was to send out very heavily escorted raids, supported distantly by 'free chase' *Geschwader* of Me 109s, the first to destroy the airfields and force the enemy to rise to the challenge, the second to meet this challenge and destroy Fighter Command in the air, too. But an important modification was introduced for the first time this Sunday: concentration on not more than two targets – Kenley and Biggin Hill – instead of more widely scattered raids, which both he and Sperrle had practised up to this time.

Briefings on both these attacks took place at numerous *Luftflotte* 2 airfields soon after dawn. For the Kenley attack, KG76 was fully involved and in three capacities. A precision dive-bombing attack on the station buildings was to be followed immediately by a high-level attack by Dorniers. The third act in this drama of destruction was to be performed by the 9th *Staffel* led by Hauptmann Joachim Roth, and promised a surprise ending.

Roth's briefing took place at Cormeilles-en-Vexin, fifteen miles inland from that 1920s' haunt of the leisured rich, Deauville, and what he had to say greatly intrigued and excited his pilots and crews. They were, for the first time, to fly all the way to the target, and attack, from ultra-low level. Roth showed them their route, which took them across the Channel on a north-westerly heading, using the great white promontory of Beachy Head as a landmark but edging to the low land of the River Ouse Estuary to the west and using 'the iron beam' – the railway lines from Lewes and Brighton north towards London – as their route guide. Kenley was conveniently located high up in the outer suburbs a few miles to the north after a long tunnel on the east–west railway line east of Reigate. Roth was confident they could not miss, forgetting how that veteran low-level navigator and attacker, the late Hauptmann Walter Rubensdoerffer, had failed to find Kenley on his last, fatal operation.

The nine Dorniers crossed the coast with no more opposition than a few bursts of machine-gun fire from a naval patrol boat offshore, and began to disturb many a family Sunday lunch as they raced north in wide line-abreast at 100 feet or lower, picking up the Southern Railway electric line without difficulty, amusing themselves machine-gunning the streets. They had been too low for even the CHL Beachy Head radar, but the Observer Corps post a few yards away had spotted them, counted them and reported them to Horsham. No. 11 Group ops had the news thirty seconds later.

Thanks to the visual sighting from Beachy Head, and subsequent Observer Corps reports as Roth led his bombers north towards the

North Downs, Kenley had plenty of warning of what was likely to come: 'Air attack imminent: all personnel not on defence duties to the shelters.' A lot of airmen and WAAFs were eating their midday dinner and resented the interruption, but only a few disregarded the warning. This sector station was well protected by anti-aircraft guns and by Parachute and Cable. PAC was a novel device by which a 500-foot length of steel cable was launched by a rocket. At the limit of its trajectory a parachute was opened, holding the vertical cable before slowly descending. If the cable was struck by any part of a raider, a second parachute at the base automatically opened, leaving the aircraft with the impossible burden of a heavy cable trailing two parachutes. At Kenley, the launchers were sited at sixty-foot intervals outside the northern perimeter track and were arranged to be fired in salvoes of nine.

All the gunners were at their posts, tense and ready. What they had not reckoned with was the extreme low level of the bombers, which appeared from over the trees and were on the airfield before a gun barrel could be swung in their direction. The nine Dorniers were dead on target, racing over the hangars, administration buildings, messes, domestic blocks, ops room and station headquarters, releasing their 110 pound bombs like broadcast corn from a farmer's pouch.

One of the German aircrew caught a glimpse of the bombs falling dead centre into the hangars. 'Other bombs were bouncing down the runway like rubber balls,' he recalled. 'Hell was let loose. Then the bombs began their work of destruction. Three hangars collapsed like matchwood. Explosion followed explosion, flames leapt into the sky.'[8]

Within seconds, the 9th *Staffel* had sown the wind; now they were to reap the whirlwind. As the Dorniers streaked across the airfield, every gun opened up. The leading pilot in the right-hand section was struck in the chest by a single Lewis gun bullet and fell dead on his controls. Wilhelm Raab, flying number two in the centre section, had just passed over a refuelling tanker when the PAC went into action. It was the first time ever, the circumstances were ideal and the timing was dead right.

'Suddenly red-glowing balls rose up from the ground in front of me,' Raab later wrote. 'Each one trailed a line of smoke about one metre thick behind it, with intervals of ten to fifteen metres between each. I had experienced machine-gun fire and *flak* fire often enough, but this was something entirely new. . . . I felt a hefty tug on my machine. "Now they've got us," I thought. "We are going to smash into the ground." '[9] But because the Dornier was in a steep bank when it struck the cable, Raab succeeded in clearing it and, although later damaged by anti-aircraft fire, he got back to base intact.

But the PACs succeeded in wrecking at least one, and possibly two more Dorniers, although it was impossible to distinguish between the effects of the intense ground fire and the cables. But one doomed pilot, Feldwebel Petersen, provided what amounted to a set-piece demonstration of the PAC's effectiveness. The cable caught the Dornier's wing and the drag of the two parachutes simply tipped the bomber straight into the ground. The explosion killed not only the crew of four but a high-ranking observer, Oberst Otto Sommer.

Although Roth had been confused to find the airfield untouched when he arrived, he later realised how fortunate it had been that the Junkers dive-bombers and the He 111 high-level bombers had mistimed their flights. The smoke and dust from the low-level raid offered perfect target identification, and at the same time obscured them from the anti-aircraft gunners who had the greatest difficulty in laying their guns with any accuracy.

There was probably no more than a three-minute interval between the departure of the surviving low-level Dorniers – hotly pursued by 111 and 615 Squadrons, with Roth himself in serious trouble – and the intense, high-level bombing, although for many of those on the ground, half-stunned by the noise and fury of the first attack, it was much longer. By a merciful chance of fate the vulnerable, brick ops room controlling the entire sector was not hit. But inside the silence that succeeded the explosions and the gunfire seemed even more intense in this enclosed space because all the power and almost all the telephone lines had gone dead. The airmen and WAAF plotters at the table, in their tin hats and with gas masks at the ready, looked up questioningly to the dais above where their officers were, for a few seconds, looking equally bemused.

Then one of the officers yelled at them angrily, as if they were responsible. 'Don't just stand there – take cover! There's nothing you can do now!'[10]

Not far distant from the ops room, an airman shouted down to some WAAFs in a shelter that there was an unexploded bomb outside. The corporal in charge led out her girls as if on parade: no panic please! They glanced at the blazing hangars in wonder before marching away in the best manner of coolness in the face of danger. But almost at once a clearly terrified RAF officer running towards them yelled, 'Get to a shelter you silly women. The bombing hasn't finished yet.'[11] He was right. As the WAAFs sought another shelter the high-level bombing began, heralding the further mutilation of Kenley.

Twelve thousand feet above, the most effective fighter attack was by Mike Crossley's 32 Squadron, which was in the right place at the right time. As he caught sight of a swarm of Dorniers with Me 110 close escort, he called out to the controller, 'Jacko leader, Jacko leader – Tally Ho!'

No. 32 Squadron had often practised the head-on, line-abreast attack. Now, after ordering B Flight to look after the escort, Crossley led A Flight straight in at a closing speed of well over 400 mph.

'The bombers were stepped up, in close formation,' Alan 'Shag' Eckford recalled. 'I remember thinking, as I was approaching the formation, that if I opened fire at the first one and then gradually lifted my nose and kept the button pressed, several would have to pass through my fire.'[12] But there was no time. Instead he was content to maul a Dornier, which lurched out of formation and fell away in a spin.

As for Eckford's CO, Crossley sent down a Ju 88, which crashed near Ashford, and also claimed a 110 as a probable, though he did not see it go in. But the most telling effect of this attack, by no more than half-a-dozen Hurricanes against some fifty escorted bombers, was to break up the formation as it was on its bombing run, causing many of the bombers to lose their target and drop their loads haphazardly elsewhere in most cases.

All this would have been impossible but for the desperate and expensive efforts of 615 Squadron's Hurricanes, who took on the bombers' top cover of uncounted 109s. Outnumbered at least five to one, it was not easy to score in a Hurricane against aggressive and skilfully handled 109s, which could choose their moment of attack and withdraw at leisure, as well as opening cannon fire far beyond the range of Browning .303s. Within a few minutes, 615 had lost four Hurricanes in the air, with one pilot killed, and with six more destroyed on the ground as a result of the raid 15,000 feet below them.

One of those shot down by the hardened veterans of JG26 was Petrus Hendrink Hugo – 'Dutch' Hugo for his thick Afrikaans accent – one of several brilliant South African pilots in the Battle. 'Dutch's' shooting was almost on a par with 'Sailor' Malan's, and he already had a number of victories to his credit, in France and on his return to England. (He ended the war as one of the most decorated fighter pilots with an accredited twenty-two victories.) But this was not his lucky day, and he

Lord Beaverbrook, Minister of Aircraft Production during the Battle; and Sir John Anderson, Home Secretary and Minister of Home Security. (This photo was taken in 1941 when they held different positions.)

Winston Churchill was persuaded to try out a shelter during one of his visits to Dover.

Hurricane assembly.

*Top:* Sir Cyril Newall, Chief of the Air Staff, and Keith Park, AOC 11 Group.
*Bottom:* Sir Quintin Brand, AOC 10 Group, and Trafford Leigh-Mallory, AOC 12 Group.

Werner Moelders, the Luftwaffe's greatest fighter pilot and tactician, devisor of the open 'finger four' formation in the Spanish Civil War, still used internationally today.

Reichsmarschall Hermann Goering on inspection duties with his protégé, Adolf Galland, whom he promoted during the Battle.

Sir Frederick Bowhill, AOC-in-C Coastal Command.

*Opposite*: R. A. B. Learoyd VC. His bombs blocked the Dortmund-Ems Canal and delayed the movement of German barges to the invasion ports (crayon by Eric Kennington).

*Above:* Sir Charles 'Peter' Portal, AOC-in-C Bomber Command (crayon by Eric Kennington).

*Above right:* H. A. V. 'Harry' Hogan, CO 501 Squadron throughout the Battle (drawing by Cuthbert Orde).

*Right:* John Hannah VC, Bomber Command wireless operator/air gunner decorated for heroism during an attack on the invasion ports (crayon by Eric Kennington).

*Commonwealth and Allied contributors to the British victory:*

*Top right:* Josef Frantisek from Czechoslovakia (drawing by Cuthbert Orde).

*Middle:* Alan Deere from

At the height of the Battle, Spitfire pilots of 610 Squadron at Biggin Hill recover from yet another operation, or discuss it; while across the Channel, the scene and the talk are not so different.

The Duke of Kent talking to pilots of A Flight 302 (Polish) Squadron. *Left to right:* Pilot Officer Kinel, Sergeant Beda, Sergeant Ritka, Pilot Officer Malinski and Sergeant Wedzik. Squadron Leader Laguna is with the Duke.

*Below left:* Three exceptionally gifted American pilots, 'Andy' Mamedoff, 'Red' Tobin and 'Shorty' Keogh, all 609 Squadron. They are with the adjutant.

*Below right:* A birthday party for the flight commander. E. N. Ryder cuts his cake for pilots of 41 Squadron, while the CO, D. O. Finlay, holds the plate. (Both officers survived the Battle.)

Goering and his staff study a troop-landing exercise – and the white cliffs of Kent.

Personnel of an Army Airfield Defence Unit, including (in tin helmets) Sergeant Davidson MC (*left*) and Sergeant Sharp VC (*right*).

was badly shot about when he managed to crash-land his Hurricane at Orpington – which, to his fury, put him out of the fighting for five weeks.

At Kenley, as soon as the smoke and dust had settled, it became clear that the airfield was temporarily non-operational, and ground stripes were put out to instruct aircraft to land at satellite airstrips, although R/T communication was re-established by 1.37 p.m. through the reserve transmitter. Without water supply, the fires raged unchecked for some time, until civil fire brigades answered the station's SOS – in the event rather too enthusiastically, leading to road congestion.

Three items in the station commander's report to 11 Group reflect well on the performance of his men and women:

27. The hospital and reserve hospital were destroyed. One of the medical officers was killed in a shelter trench near hospital. The remaining medical staff, however, worked splendidly and with assistance of civil doctors the situation was soon in hand.

28. The ground defences were seriously hampered by firstly the approach of raid being screened so that the low raid could not be engaged before it had released its bombs and the fact that smoke from low raid prevented the high raid being seen easily. Effective action was, however, taken by gun crews. . . .

29. All ground defence crews remained at their posts and engaged the enemy under heavy fire.

Two further items were covered with typical laconic economy: '24 unexploded bombs dealt with. . . . Aerodrome was made serviceable in about two hours.'

Corporal David Samson wrote about the loss of 'a very important officer, the MO, and I remember that for this reason our OR [other ranks] casualties were taken by private car to Purley Hospital as all medical facilities were out of action.'

As the first repair work began at Kenley, Kesselring's He 111s, Dorniers and Ju 88s were heading for Biggin Hill, the Heinkels in stepped-up waves between 12,000 and 15,000 feet, sixty of them in all with forty 109s keeping watchful guard above. The first squadron to get near them was 610, which had managed to put fifteen Spitfires into the air. But the odds of two-and-a-half to one made life very difficult for Squadron Leader John Ellis and his men. Ellis had already been credited with the singular distinction of shooting down three Me 109s in a day, and added to his score this lunchtime with an He 111.

No. 32 Squadron, 610's 'chummy' squadron from Biggin Hill, got in amongst the bomber stream, which seemed to grow minute by minute, and in variety of types. Pilot Officer John 'Polly' Flinders, whose Hurricane was unserviceable, belatedly grabbed the reserve training machine, which was not renowned for its performance. But at 12,000 feet – and, oh, how long it seemed to take to get there! – he chanced on a Me 110. The German pilot immediately dived for safety, hoping (quite reasonably) that he could outpace the Hurricane. But Flinders's veteran gained a new lease of life, and he found he was gaining on the big fighter. In desperation, the German dropped to 200 feet and began doing barrel rolls and half rolls at this height, which did not impress his pursuer and lost the Messerschmitt pilot speed as he raced unknowingly over the Kent countryside towards the well-defended inland radar station at Dunkirk near Canterbury. The Bofors gunners now took a vital part in the combat, hitting and further slowing down the 110.

Flinders was able to close in to 150 yards and open fire, with immediately fatal results, over the village of Harbledown. It was just after 1.30 p.m. and by this time the skies above Kent and Sussex had become the setting for countless mêlées. With Kenley out of action, sector controllers were fast losing control of events. At Biggin Hill Group Captain Richard Grice stood behind the controller watching the plots moving towards his station like hyenas on a tethered prey. When he calculated that they had less than five minutes to spare, he pressed the button which sounded the alarm over the Tannoy loud-speakers. As the howling died, he spoke, with his usual calmness: 'This is your station commander. At any moment we may be attacked. I want all personnel except those engaged on essential services to take cover immediately.'

The Luftwaffe's tactical plan was the same as for Kenley, but once again the low-level Dorniers were early, or the high-level bombers late, so it was a repeat performance, the nine Dorniers coming in at 100 feet, spreading flames and destruction:

> Pillars of flame in spiral volume rise,
> Like fiery snakes, and lick the infernal skies.

The noise was ear-splitting and prolonged, but these Dorniers paid an even higher price than those attacking Kenley a few minutes earlier. The PAC rockets soared, causing the same dismay to the pilots and wrenching two of the slim bombers from the sky. Moreover, Biggin

Hill's own squadrons, 610 and 32, were now thick in among the fleeing Dorniers.

Only two of the nine Dorniers returned safely and one of these was landed by the flight engineer, his pilot dead beside him.

There was an interval of no more than three minutes when, as at Kenley, the second attack fell on the airfield, this time from high altitude. Even if they had known, and believed it, it was no comfort to those huddled in the shelters and slit trenches, with arms over ears, that it would have been twice as bad, and twice as destructive, if their own fighters were not mobbing the bombers 12,000 to 15,000 feet above. Least of all could they appreciate the struggle these fighters were enduring to evade the 109s, which seemed to be everywhere and to be as tenacious as aroused wasps.

Thanks entirely to this intervention, the bombing was poor. The greatest weight of explosive fell to the east of Biggin Hill and on the airfield itself. Few buildings were touched. Then, with the last of the dust and smoke drifting away on the wind, the Salvation Army van appeared like a ghost from the holocaust, fulfilling the 'Sally Ally's' proverb of 'reaching a class of people that churches never do'. In less than a minute a queue had formed for its 'wads' and half-pint mugs of hot sweet tea.

Ignoring this swift return to routine, an almost middle-aged WAAF, Sergeant Joan Mortimer, emerged from her switchboard in the armoury where she had been relaying messages to the defence posts about the airfield, surrounded by high-explosive. She had a bundle of red flags in her hand as she walked purposefully on to the airfield to join the disposal team. Each sinister bulge indicating an unexploded bomb was marked, and when one exploded not very distantly, she carried on helping with the defusing as if nothing had happened. She received the Military Medal for this act, the first of three Biggin Hill WAAFs to be so decorated. She never understood why.

Few were caught out in the open during the Biggin Hill raid. But by ironical coincidence two of them were German aircrew, Joachim Roth, who had led the low-level raid on Kenley and been savagely mauled by Hurricanes, and his fellow surviving crew member, Rudolf Lamberty. Roth had crash-landed his burning Dornier in a field just outside the perimeter of Biggin Hill. The two shaken Germans, and their captors, lay flat on the grass close to the burning bomber and dead fellow crew members, wishing their comrades would desist.

After the loss of their CO, Rodney Wilkinson, two days earlier, and two more pilots lost and two badly wounded, the harsh treatment of 266 Squadron (Spitfires) continued. Dennis Armitage had temporarily taken over command and soon after noon had been ordered down from Hornchurch to patrol Manston. The Squadron mixed it briefly with some Dorniers, without success, and were then ordered to land to rearm and refuel at this battered base – so battered that the craters obliged them to park in one small area to await the attention of the servicing crews. 'Pilots stood around, the shimmering vapour distorting vision as the fuel was sent gushing into the fighters' tanks. Belts of ammunition were threaded into the guns, oxygen bottles changed, the whole operation moving swiftly. Overhead the sky was full of planes and the pilots and airmen hoped that someone knew what was going on.'[13]

Oberleutnant Wolfgang Ewald did. He was leading sixteen Me 109s of JG52, covering the withdrawal of the German bombers, flying high but not too high to see the little crosses of the massed Spitfires on the grass at Manston, and others on their final approach. He had completed his *Gruppe*'s duties and now decided to put in some overtime.

A 266 straggler, Sergeant Don Kingaby, was landing as the 109s came streaking down. 'They hit us soon after I taxied in. There was no warning, just the roar of their engines. I glanced round and found myself looking along the nose of a Messerschmitt coming straight for me.'[14]

Kingaby was later to be awarded no fewer than three DFMs, a DSO, an American DFC and a Belgian *Croix de Guerre* and survived the Battle and the war. But he had his closest brush not in the air, but while rolling over and over on mother earth, bullets and cannon shells tearing up the grass around him. He got away with one nicked finger. Pilot Officer Trousdale, also caught in the open and still wearing his parachute, simply knelt in the dust with his 'chute towards the enemy, 'just like a Mohammedan at prayer', Dennis Armitage ribbed him later.

But there was not much laughter for 266 that evening. They had lost most of their planes, destroyed or damaged, and there was not much left to command when Squadron Leader Desmond Spencer arrived to take over. Within days 266 was withdrawn to Wittering.

One of the most extraordinary incidents of the day was a massacre over Ashford, a town that probably witnessed more air fighting during the Battle than any other except Dover. Here, at about 1 p.m. 56 Squadron (Hurricanes) were patrolling defensively at their maximum efficient height of 22,000 feet when one of the pilots spotted five twin-engined aircraft flying in a tight defensive circle as if they had become lost and now scented danger. They were identified as Me 110s, which could probably have got home safely if they had at once put down their noses. Instead, they awaited the arrival of the Hurricanes with seemingly calm fatalism. The Hurricanes promptly tore into them, easily out-circling the big fighters and shooting them all out of the sky.

None of the unfortunate 110 aircrew baled out, but in all eight RAF fighter pilots used their parachutes in the orthodox way that early afternoon, and more later in the day. One of them was the ubiquitous Bob Stanford Tuck. He was on a visit to Northolt, far from his squadron in 10 Group, when every fighter there was suddenly scrambled. Although his radio lacked the correct frequency, and no permission was sought or given, he took off anyway, carrying out a one-man patrol at 15,000 feet over Beachy Head, which seemed a likely place for action. Two low-flying 110s, which he misidentified as Ju 88s, duly appeared below, heading home fast.

Tuck went down, made a head-on attack on one, which at once went into the sea, pushed his luck with another head-on and was hit by cannon shells, which should have told him this was no Junkers. He nearly made it back to an airfield, but fire drove him from his cockpit and he took to the silk.

Tuck was well received on the ground. As on 16 August, others had a hostile, some a downright dangerous, reception. Pilot Officer Kenneth Lee's was mixed: 'Having been shot down and lightly wounded I was taken to a local golf club, just inland from Whitstable, to await an ambulance. I was in shirtsleeves, slightly bloodstained, but couldn't help hearing members at the last hole complaining that the distraction of the Battle in the air was disturbing their putting, while once inside a voice demanded, "Who's that scruffy looking chap at the bar? I don't think he's a member."'

Peter Simpson of 111 Squadron, who was shot down by one of the low-flying Dorniers he was chasing home, crash-landed on to another golf course, Woodcote Park. His reception was even more hostile than Lee's. Enraged golfers brandished their clubs menacingly and threatened him. The Hurricane pilot hoped he had been mistaken for a German, as indeed he had, in spite of the prominent roundels on the machine in which he was sitting. Simpson was injured, and very angry, and shouted at his assailants, even producing a packet of Player's cigarettes to establish his identity.

The golfers cooled down, the pilot jumped off the wing on to the grass and let out a howl of pain. 'At that moment other people approached, one of whom said he was a doctor,' Simpson recalled later when he was a much-decorated wing commander. 'He sat me down, took my shoe and sock off, and pulled out one of the splinters. My foot was all numb, with blood pouring out; I thought the whole foot was going to have to come off! But he said it was nothing serious.'[15]

Unlike Kenneth Lee, Simpson was now given a sympathetic reception in the club house, with lunch and brandy, too much for his well-being. It was difficult to reconcile the desperate August air fighting with all its attendant dangers and destruction of human life and property with the habitual pursuits of walks, picnics, summer games or simply sitting out of doors enjoying the sun. But there was little that the vast majority of the citizens of Kent, Surrey and Sussex, many of whom were on holiday, could contribute to the epochal events taking place above them. And because the weather was mainly warm and cloudless, the fighting was witnessed by more non-participants than any other battle in history.

At Sissinghurst Castle in Kent the Harold Nicolsons spent most of the day in their incomparable garden, their son Ben coming over to luncheon. Harold Nicolson noted in his diary:

While we are sitting outside the air-raid siren sounds. We remain where we are. Then comes the sound of aeroplanes and, looking up, we see thin streamers from the exhausts of the German 'planes. Another wave follows, and we see it clearly – twenty little silver fish in arrow formation. There is no sound of firing, but while we are at luncheon we hear 'planes quite close and go out to see. There is a rattle of machine-gun fire and we see two Spitfires attacking a Heinkel. The latter sways off, obviously wounded. We then go on with our luncheon. Ben talks to us about Roger Fry and Virginia. . . .[16]

Lord Halifax, the Foreign Minister who had been tipped by many to take over the premiership in preference to Churchill only three months earlier, appears to have found the battles raging over the south-east something of a relaxation, for his biographer writes:

[Halifax] had little recreation that summer while the country waited for a German invasion. . . . He found the best restoratives of this time were the Saturday nights and weekends he was occasionally able to steal to visit friends within easy reach of London, watching from Victor Cazalet's garden in Kent one of the summer battles in the air and forgetting the war.[17]

The Secretary of State for War was also pleased with what he called his 'front seats with a view of the Battle of Britain' from his house, Park Gate, outside Elham. Anthony Eden wrote:

There were frequent air battles overhead, sometimes while we were playing tennis. There was great excitement one day while I was in my bath. One of our fighters and a Messerschmitt had a battle over the garden. It looked as though the German as he crashed must hit our house. Actually his plane fell in the wood a few hundred yards behind and he baled out in front, between us and the village.[18]

Fun though this might be, Eden decided that things were getting too lively for his wife and two small sons, and he moved them to a place near Oxford in relative safety.

Often planes were seen crashing and (as at Elham) people ran from all directions, eager to give a hostile reception as it was almost always assumed that the victim was German. Golf courses offered good open spaces for crash-landing, or baling out, but a pilot in distress could fare better elsewhere. It was at about this time in the Battle that Pilot Officer (later Wing Commander DFC) George Nelson Edwards 'crash-landed wheels up next door to a large country house near Oxted. I was knocked unconscious for a minute or so and on coming round the first thing I saw was a large, beautifully coloured parrot perched on the side of the cockpit, its beak wide open, eyes blinking at me as if in astonishment. Momentarily I wondered whether the "place up yonder" was all exotic birds. Then I realised I was still alive as a human head appeared and a hand stretched towards me proffering a large brandy.'

The brandy was a welcome pick-me-up. But as Pilot Officer Simpson learned, the hospitality could be too enthusiastic. Most aircrew, officers and non-commissioned officers drank beer and could put down half-a-dozen pints in an evening without regretting it. But many of them were very young and unaccustomed to spirits. David Cox DFC, *Croix de Guerre*, of 19 Squadron, was hit in the leg by six cannon shell splinters, but managed to bale out. He landed near a farmhouse and was carried to it by a farmer and one of his men, where he was simply given a bottle of whisky and a glass and told to get on with it.

'On arrival at the hospital and being taken to the operating theatre,' Cox recalled, 'the nursing sister in charge remarked that from the strong smell she wondered if an anaesthetic was required.'

The following is an assessment of the gains and losses to each side in these two midday raids of 18 August:

|  | RAF |  | Luftwaffe |  |
|---|---|---|---|---|
| Fighters lost in the air and on the ground |  | 23 | Fighters lost | 9 |
|  |  |  | Pilots killed | 9 |
| Pilots killed |  | 5 | Gunners killed | 6 |
|  |  |  | Bombers destroyed | 11 |
|  |  |  | Aircrew killed, inc. in damaged planes | 55 (approx) |
| Airfield damage: *Kenley*, very heavy: all hangars except one destroyed; out of action for approx. one hour operating two instead of three squadrons. Sector Ops Room out of action fifty hours. *Biggin Hill*, slight: not out of operation. Also slight damage at Croydon and West Malling. |  |  | Nil |  |

Once again the return of damaged German aircraft, many of which crash-landed with dead or injured aircrew, was not calculated to lift the enemy's morale.

This, then, was the position in the early afternoon of this eventful and bloody 18 August. For Kesselring and Sperrle, and many of the aircrew, the worst of the day still lay ahead.

By 18 August the Luftwaffe, having for some time recognised that photo-reconnaissance below 30,000 feet was far too expensive in men and machines, was using a specially developed, very high altitude machine. This was the Junkers 86P, a development of an unacceptably slow, twin-engined bomber tried out in the Spanish Civil War, and also used as an airliner carrying ten passengers. As a photo-reconnaissance machine, the Junkers was powered by advanced, double-supercharged, diesel engines, the crew enjoying a necessary pressurised cabin. These were the machines that were frequently plotted over England during the Battle, and being far beyond the range of any anti-aircraft gun and maximum altitude of any fighter, there was nothing that could be done about them.

On the other hand, at these altitudes, even superb German optical equipment was unable to reveal detail with any accuracy; and that was the reason why Sperrle's *Luftflotte* 3 had been informed by intelligence that the Coastal Command airfield at Thorney Island, and the naval air stations at Ford and Gosport, were important front-line Fighter Command airfields: the parked aircraft appeared to confirm it.

On this afternoon then, the Ju 87 Stukas from Normandy and Brittany were ordered to destroy these targets as decisively as Kesselring's bombers had apparently wiped out Kenley that day, or as comprehensively as they had 'destroyed' Tangmere two days earlier. As a bonus, Poling radar station was to be wiped out as they had wiped out Ventnor. From across the Channel, the tactical reasoning appeared as sound as, in the event, it was almost totally unsound.

One hundred and eleven dive-bombers were assigned to this early afternoon operation, with half as many Me 109s providing cover. They were plotted approaching the Isle of Wight soon after 2 p.m., and as they headed towards the mainland east of Portsmouth the massive formation shed units to left and right like infantry on parade-ground evolutions.

Fearful of another attack as destructive as the one on Tangmere, 10 and 11 Groups had scrambled every squadron within reasonable range, even from as far as Exeter, while controllers attempted to interpret from Observer Corps reports and radar plots the likely targets. There was a lot of luck as well as intuition involved in this decision-making. Of the four targets, Gosport was attacked without any interference, the twenty-two 87s causing mountainous damage and heading some distance towards home before seeing an enemy fighter.

The Thorney Island attackers, however, were caught by 43 and 601 Squadrons as they positioned themselves for the tip-over, and although distant 109s were on the look-out, the eighteen Hurricanes had a field day amongst the vulnerable 87s.

Thorney Island escaped the worst of the damage. Poling and Ford, bombed before the fighters could intercept, suffered badly. Damage to the three airfields was irrelevant to the effectiveness of Fighter Command.

The attack on Poling, in contrast, was a blow directly aimed at the Fighter Command system, and was the more dangerous since the station at Ventnor had already been wrecked. Approximately ninety bombs were dropped and the station was badly damaged. Emergency equipment was installed but it could no longer give comprehensive and reliable information on enemy movements.[19]

In fact, Poling remained effectively unserviceable until the end of

August. This was not as handicapping to Fighter Command's warning structure as it might have been, because back-up semi-mobile radar had been installed on the Isle of Wight and soon would be at Poling, and the CH stations were unaffected. But there is no question that the knocking out of Kenley sector control earlier, and now Poling CH,* were rather worse than inconveniences to Air Marshals Dowding and Park.

But *Luftflotte* 3 paid a price which Sperrle regarded as unacceptable. 'One Stuka *Gruppe*', Freiherr von Richthofen noted in his diary, 'was almost exterminated.' Mixing his metaphors, he added, 'It has had its feathers well and truly plucked.'[20] The *Luftwaffe War Diaries* noted:

The main victim was 1/StG77. Of its twenty-eight aircraft twelve failed to return, and six others were so shot up that they only just reached French soil. Amongst the missing was the *Gruppe*'s commander, Captain Meisel. Adding the casualties of the other *Gruppen*, thirty Ju 87s were either lost or severely damaged. The price was too high. The Stuka had to be withdrawn.[21]

This was an extremely serious blow to Goering. The Stuka with its bomb-load of one 550 pound and four 110 pound bombs was a pinpoint destroyer. Just as the US Navy dive-bombers turned the tide in the Pacific war less than two years later at Midway, so the Stuka could have done untold damage to the Royal Navy in the event of the defeat of Fighter Command and a German invasion, as it did later in the Mediterranean.

The chief beneficiaries of this last fling of the Stuka were the pilots of 43, 152 and 602 Squadrons, who cut the relatively helpless Junkers to shreds as they fled singly or in pairs out to sea. But many of the German gunner-radio operators fought back gamely with their single 7.9 mm gun. Flight Sergeant Bill Pond of 601 Squadron reported hitting repeatedly one Junkers, and waited for it to go down while exchanging bursts of fire with his eight Brownings with the gunner – 'a very brave man,' he commented: an accurate gunner, too, for before he was killed he hit the Hurricane's engine and forced Pond to break off and then, at the sight of 109s, to dive away for his life. The Stuka struggled home, the pilot wounded.

But it also took a special sort of courage to press home attacks against bombers knowing that Messerschmitts were falling on you from the heavens like avenging angels.

★   ★   ★

*The radar stations forming the chain enjoyed a degree of overlap which offered some cover, if restricted, when one station was not operating.

This was one of the greatest days of fighting on the 10 Group–11 Group border, and once again what the Luftwaffe regarded as England's soft underbelly demonstrated its muscular and destructive powers. Tens of thousands of people heard the bombing and the air battles, in this populous area of southern England; and thousands saw the smoke rising from the buildings of the bombed airfields. But they also witnessed fragments of the fighting, confirming clearly enough the superiority of the RAF, which the BBC and the newspapers proclaimed stridently every day.

A weekend guest of the Bessboroughs at Stansted Park, Rowland's Castle, took the daughter of the house on to the terrace in the hope of seeing 'one of these great air battles'.

It was after lunch and we were looking towards Thorney Island with the Portsmouth balloons just visible over the trees to our right. Suddenly we heard the sound of AA fire and saw puffs of white smoke as the shells burst over Portsmouth. Then to our left, from the direction of Chichester and Tangmere, came the roar of engines and the noise of machine-gun fire. 'There they are,' exclaimed Moyra, and shading our eyes to escape the glare of this August day we saw not far in front of us about twenty machines engaged in a fight. Soon a German bomber came hurtling down with smoke pouring from its tail . . . a parachute opened and sank gracefully down through the whirling fighters and bombers. Out of the mêlée came a dive-bomber, hovered like a bird of prey and then sped steeply down on Thorney Island.[22]

At 5 p.m. on this August day there were still more than three hours before sunset, and Park was confident that, as on so many previous evenings, *Luftflotte* 2 would be back for one last fling. He was right. Within half an hour big plots showed up off the Kent coast and off the Essex coast north of the Thames Estuary. Over 100 Dorniers and Heinkels in all were evidently bound for Hornchurch and North Weald.

Many of Park's pilots had flown two sorties already this day, but once again the Hurricanes and Spitfires were scrambled in maximum strength, the Hurricanes breaking up the formations while, in the main, the Spitfires dealt with the 109s. No. 501 was very hotly involved, and Flight Lieutenant George Stoney, with two Ju 87s to his credit, was seen attacking some fifty Dorniers head-on. Single-handed he broke them up and then was seized upon by the 109s. 'He fell like a rock,' commented one of the German pilots. 'A very brave man.' Then two wild 501 Polish pilots waded into the mêlée, burning with hatred and the lust for revenge. They quickly shot out of the sky a 109 each, including one of the highest scoring Luftwaffe fighter pilots, Hauptmann Horst Tietzen.

These fights that spread over the Kent and Essex countryside were like some Wagnerian climax to this 'the hardest day of the Battle', as it came to be known. Meanwhile, the reformed bombers struggled on, searching for their targets. But on this evening, the weather became Fighter Command's blessed ally, cutting visibility and spreading a merciful grey cloud over this corner of England. The sufferers were the civilians. Hundreds of bombs were jettisoned or dropped on half-seen secondary targets, which included built-up areas. Many men, women and children were killed in their homes, or their little domestic shelters. Their involuntary sacrifice was for the sake of Fighter Command, and this country, just as if they were fighting for it.

It was no more than a foretaste of what was to come as the nights grew longer and the days shorter, and the skies throbbed to the sound of unsynchronised Heinkel bomber engines from dusk until dawn.

# 15

## *Desperate Days*

### 19 AUGUST–6 SEPTEMBER

There was no greater conditioning factor in the air fighting of 1940 than the weather. Not only did it control the effectiveness of the bombers, but poor weather gave the commanders-in-chief on both sides pause for reflection and reconsideration, and to modify their order of battle. The relatively poor weather over the five days after 18 August allowed Goering time not only to tell his fighter pilots just what he thought of them, which was almost unprintable, but to replace some of the *Kommodoren*, those more cautious and elderly officers – in his judgment – with bright and daring fighter pilots, the 'young Turks', like Adolf Galland, who had proved their aggressive qualities.

They should personally lead their formations into battle and thus set 'a shining example'. . . . The young men soon proved themselves worthy of the responsibility suddenly thrust upon them. Their example became contagious, and the great competition began as to which *Geschwader* would become the top scorer. Major Moelders took over JG51 from Major General Osterkamp, Major Galland JG26 from Colonel Handrick. . . .[1]

Goering also ordered most of Sperrle's Me 109 *Geschwader* to relocate themselves in the Pas de Calais, under Kesselring's command. There they would be best placed to escort the bombers in their attacks on the airfields of south-east England.

The poor weather of these mid-August days led Goering and the

German High Command to go beyond offensive plans. The fact that after heavy fighting for over a month the RAF was still capable of putting several hundred fighters into the air, when it had once been predicted that fourteen days was long enough to bring about Fighter Command's destruction, forced the High Command to think defensively, too, distasteful though this was. At conferences which Goering held with his commanders at Karinhall on 15 and 19 August, important changes were decreed.

First, it was finally confirmed that the Ju 87 Stuka was to be withdrawn from first-line operations, at least for the present, except for two *Staffeln* which were to be held in readiness for any opportunity that might suddenly arise (an important convoy perhaps) for the sort of pinpoint bombing that only Stukas could carry out effectively – *if local air supremacy could be achieved* as a condition. They would, of course, remain in the vanguard in any invasion.

Second, no more than one commissioned officer was to be included in a bomber's crew. Over the past days no fewer than 136 officers, up to the rank of *Geschwaderkommodore*, had been killed and seriously wounded or were missing.

Third, in order to reduce the losses of Me 110s – seventy-nine in the last week and many more damaged – they were in future to be used only beyond Me 109 range, or else to be escorted by 109s – a sore humiliation for the proud '*zerstoerer*' crews and tactical lunacy: an escort for an escort indeed!

Fourth, and perhaps most surprising of all, attacks on the British radar stations were, after earlier optimism, judged to have been predominantly unsuccessful on account of the difficult nature of the target and were not to be repeated, save in exceptional circumstances.

On a more positive note, the German attacks were to be concentrated on a smaller range of targets. The destruction of the British fighter force was to take precedence over everything else, with the destruction of the British aircraft industry as the next most important aim.

In the RAF *Narrative* of the Battle, the authors take advantage of this break in the fighting to summarise and reappraise Fighter Command's record to date and expectations for the future, rather as the commanders at Bentley Priory and down to squadron level paused for a breath of fresh air and thought.

Referring to the superiority in numbers of the enemy,

the situation in which the country found itself on the eve of the battle, and throughout its course, was one that required much stronger air defences than were actually available. . . . On virtually every occasion that the Germans operated in force they grossly outnumbered the defending squadrons. There were not sufficient forces available for a reserve of fighters, a *masse de manoeuvre*, to be kept back and used only when the direction and strength of the enemy's attack were known. Instead the concentrated formations of German bombers and fighters were being met by squadrons containing no more than twelve, and frequently fewer aircraft. It was rarely, therefore, that the Germans failed to reach their targets, provided that the state of the weather was fair. Nor is the relative strength of the opposing forces employed in one operation an adequate gauge of the odds involved. For whereas as many as seventy or eighty British fighters might engage enemy formations totalling anything from one hundred to three hundred aircraft, the *individual* fighter squadrons, since they normally came into action independently of each other, were engaging up to ten times their number of the enemy.[2]

There appeared no hope at all of remedying this disparity. The Luftwaffe had reserves to draw upon, both of men and machines; the RAF was finding it harder and harder to replace losses of both. On 9 August there had been 289 Spitfires and Hurricanes ready for issue from the Aircraft Storage Units; on 16 August 235; on 23 August 161. There was still a reasonable margin in hand, but it was daily narrowing, and would narrow more swiftly if the aircraft factories were effectively attacked and/or the loss rate increased. (In the event both happened.)

On 8 August Fighter Command was 160 pilots short of establishment, even before taking into account that three or four pilots in every squadron were so inexperienced as to be non-operational. By 17 August, therefore, and even before the heavy fighting of the following day, the effective strength of Fighter Command was between 900 and 1,000 pilots compared to an establishment of between 1,300 and 1,400.

To counter this continuing dangerous situation, risks had to be taken. After authority had been given by the Air Staff, the course at OTU was ordered to be further intensified and shortened, and thirty-three volunteers were obtained from army co-operation squadrons. One of these, who rose to command 266 Squadron a few weeks later, in 1988 recalled that 'training on, and subsequent flying of slow, low-ceiling, World War I-type biplanes was a poor preparation for what the Battle really called for. Hundreds of hours of Army Co-operation so-called operational flying on the North-West Frontier [India] was of little help. It was quite a jolt . . . to come from Wapitis to Spitfires – 22½ hours crammed into a fortnight [later seven days] at OTU.'*

*Group Captain D. G. H. Spencer CBE. The Wapiti biplane dated back to 1927 and had a maximum speed of 140 mph.

Between 13 and 22 August six front-line fighter squadrons which had endured the worst casualties – forty-four killed and twenty wounded, amounting to a loss of fifty per cent over ten days – were moved to quieter areas for rest and refit, to be replaced by an equal number from the north and the Midlands. The squadrons relieved were 64 at Kenley, 74 and 266 at Hornchurch, 111 at Croydon (but only to Martlesham Heath in north 11 Group), 145 at Westhampnett and 601 at Tangmere. Nos 145 and 74 moved north on 13 and 14 August respectively, the remainder during the quieter spell on 19 and 22 August.

During this period, the disparity of activity between Fighter Command's four sectors, and the reason for the fearful casualties in 11 Group compared with 12 and 13 Groups, and, less so, with 10 Group, are all too plain.

Summarising the state of the Battle during the weather-induced break of 19 to 23 August, the *Narrative* concluded that no 'positive victory for either side' could be claimed so far.

We can say, however, that the Luftwaffe had suffered more severely than Fighter Command, and that it had not obtained a sufficient return in targets damaged or destroyed to compensate for its losses. On the other hand it had so far used barely one-third of its available strength in the west. Fighter Command, for its part, had lost pilots it could ill-afford; and the grim prospect of the fighter force slowly wasting away through lack of pilots was already apparent after little more than one week's intensive fighting.[3]

Sir Keith Park and his staff used this brief lull to reappraise squadron tactics, improve airfield defence, speed up airfield repairs and seek every means, beyond keeping his fighters on the ground, to cut any unnecessary losses. Recently many of these had been over the sea, and controllers had been instructed on 18 August not to pursue reconnaissance enemy aircraft out to sea, and to engage major formations 'over land or within gliding distance of the coast'. Controllers were also instructed always to despatch a minimum number of squadrons to engage enemy fighters. 'Our main object is to engage enemy bombers.'

The days between 19 and 23 August were by no means bereft of all activity by the Luftwaffe, and only a few weeks earlier would have been regarded as highly eventful. For example, on 19 August a massed formation of 100 Me 109s swept along the south-east coast in an attempt to provoke a fighter reaction, and were quite rightly ignored, while later in the day Ju 88s attacked the Southampton area and Pembroke docks.

A single aircraft from this group succeeded in setting fire to the oil storage depot at Llanreath. The fire burnt for a week, destroying two-thirds of the tanks and attracting further bomber attention by night and day.

One of the new Polish squadrons, 302 up in Yorkshire, which had been made operational only two days earlier, had its first taste of blood, when their British CO, Bill Satchell, led five of their Hurricanes on to a Ju 88 which was on its way to bomb the airfield at Thornaby. It was in the sea within seconds.

During this period there were also numerous airfield attacks, mainly in the south-east (Manston, of course, several times) and south-west, most of them by single aircraft flying low, and a good deal of damage was done, although none of it affecting the operating efficiency of 10 or 11 Groups.

No. 616 Squadron, which had been so intensely engaged in the north-eastern attack on 15 August, had been sent down to Kenley four days later, just too late for the 'blitz' of the 18th. After two relatively quiet days, these Spitfires were scrambled on the evening of the 22nd to deal with a number of 'free chase' 109s. The squadron bounced one lot of 'snappers' near Dover as it was heading for home, but was in turn bounced by another group. 'Cocky' Dundas was the worst hit: 'White smoke filled the cockpit and I couldn't see the sky or the Channel coast 12,000 feet below. Centrifugal force pressed me against the side of the cockpit and I knew I was spinning. I felt panic and terror and I thought "Christ, this is the end!" "Get out, you bloody fool; open the hood and get out." I tugged the handle with both hands where the hood locked into the top of the windscreen. It moved back an inch, then jammed again.'

His Spitfire remained in a spin, and for several thousand feet every effort to open the hood wide enough to get out failed. 'I pulled with all my might and at last it opened.' But there was more trouble in getting out, and 'Cocky' was very close to the ground when he at last broke free. 'Thank God my parachute opened immediately. I saw the Spitfire hit and explode in a field below. A flock of sheep scattered outwards from the cloud of dust and smoke and flame.' He had splinters in his left leg and had dislocated his shoulder, but was otherwise all right.

One feature of the Battle, the night bombing of cities, which had begun on a small and haphazard scale in June, now showed evidence of increasing, a significant precursor of things to come. In Goering's long

Karinhall résumé, or exhortation, of 19 August the Reichsmarschall said:

The cloudy conditions likely to prevail over England in the next few days must be exploited for [aircraft factories] attacks. We must succeed in seriously disrupting the material supplies of the enemy Air Force by the destruction of the relatively small number of aircraft engine and aluminium plants. These attacks on the enemy aircraft industry are of particular importance, and should also be carried out by night. . . . It would appear desirable for the purpose of night operations to allocate to units particular areas which they will come to know better during each successive raid. Within this area a list of target priorities should be drawn up, so that each sortie will produce some valuable result. . . . There can no longer be any restriction on the choice of targets. To myself I reserve only the right to order attacks on London and Liverpool.[4]

In the event, the ordeal of Liverpool, Britain's most important port with the virtual closing off of London, began at this time, many weeks before the 'night blitz' proper. Twelve He 111s were over the city on the night of 19/20 August, and many more over the Midlands. Over 200 night bombers raided the country on the night of 23/24 August, and 100 the following night. Several times Goering's orders were carried out. Some sixteen tons of bombs on the aircraft works at Filton on the night of 22/23 August seriously affected production, and on the big night of 23/24 August the pinpoint target of the Dunlop Fort rubber works near Birmingham was first illuminated by the pathfinders and then damaged by the bombers from *Kampfgruppe* 100.

There was very little the defences could do to oppose these night attacks at a time when almost all the guns were still without radar. As for the night fighters, the Blenheims, which were no faster than the bombers, had only the most primitive form of AI (radar air interception). One of the first Blenheim AI successes was that of Flying Officer Geoffrey Ashfield on the night of 22/23 July, shooting a Dornier into the Channel south of Brighton with a ten-second burst from his four .303s. In all about six German bombers were to be shot down at night by Blenheims in the course of the Battle, guided to their target by AI. But, as Dr E. G. Bowen, in charge of AI development, was once heard to remark, 'If a Blenheim was going to catch a German bomber, that bomber had to be dawdling.'

For the Hurricane it was a case of the old proverbial needle in the haystack. One Blenheim CO was so frustrated that he acquired a Hurricane and made over forty night sorties. He only twice spotted an enemy aircraft and immediately lost it.

The experience of a leading aircraftman shortly before the Battle typified the last-minute, makeshift arrangements made to deal with the night-bomber threat. Benjamin Bent found himself at Martlesham Heath 'being instructed in the use of Mk4 AI. I was promoted to sergeant, which I thought was a step in the right direction, but since AI was so very secret, there was no way I was entitled to a flying badge. . . . Without further ado, we started flying at night in the bomb well of the Blenheim with our AI, kneeling in front of the set for a couple of hours and freezing the while, sometimes being vectored on to "trade" but without success. So I think it true to say that apart from blood and icicles my real contribution to the Battle was nil.'

However, as with all Blenheim squadrons, it was a different story when re-equipped later with the much faster Beaufighter with new AI. Even the famed John 'Cat's Eyes' Cunningham had no success until he got his hands on a Beaufighter, which, in association with GCI (Ground Control Interception) stations, became a formidable night-fighting weapon the next spring.

Another night-fighter pilot, Ivor Cosby, who had a particularly busy summer switching from Army Co-op to Spitfires, and then to Blenheims, found the night-fighter role far more hazardous and taxing. At Gravesend 'we had only twelve Glim Lamps for a flare path and operated from a grass airfield surrounded by balloon barrages at Dartford, Rochester and Thameshaven, just across the Thames. No air-traffic control and no R/T link with the station. Indeed, we had no R/T contact with the fighter controllers below 3,000 feet and had to find our own way home at the end of a sortie – pretty grim in the dark, usually in cloud and poor visibility below with all the smoke etc. drifting down the Thames from London.'

Sergeant Sidney Holloway arrived at 25 Squadron (Blenheims) with just four night-flying hours in his log book, none of them on Blenheims. But he loved 'that kite, maybe because it was my first operational aircraft. I considered it strong, manoeuvrable, forgiving, with good pilot visibility, but slow for the job. It was also very draughty and cold with no heating. The AI was not reliable and was such a drain on the batteries that frequently power was lost after about ninety minutes so crews had to find their own way home. This was not too difficult at Martlesham Heath – fly east to the coast, turn left or right as appropriate, follow it to the River Deben, turn inland, take the left fork of the river, find the Glim Lamp flare path, and you were home.' Easy!

During the period 19–23 August, three German bombers were

claimed shot down at night by the anti-aircraft guns, but no confirmation was obtained, while out of 160 night-fighter sorties (almost all Blenheims), there was only one engagement and in this the crew could make no definite claim.

The period 24 August to 6 September was to mark the worst agony of 11 Group's airfields. Day after day the bombs rained down on Manston, Kenley, Biggin Hill and the other airfields of Essex, Kent, Surrey and Sussex. It may have been hard on the personnel at Eastchurch but it was a relief for Fighter Command that this Coastal Command station seemed to have an inexplicable appeal for the Luftwaffe. Time and again the Dorniers and Heinkels came back to this long-suffering airfield, used only in emergencies by fighters. Perhaps Kesselring's bomber crews mistook it for Gravesend, or considered it a useful, and highly vulnerable, secondary target.

Manston remained top of the league for frequency of attacks, however, both by bombers and strafing fighters. It has even been alleged by the novelist, Len Deighton, that the morale of the servicing crews broke, that 'the terrified men would not budge' from the shelters. Air Commodore James Leathart, and one of his flight commanders at the time, Air Vice-Marshal Alan Deere, have both stoutly denied this and expressed resentment at the slur on these brave men. 'I'm even supposed to have only just prevented another officer from threatening to shoot the first man who refused to come out,' commented Leathart. 'At the time I first read this I put it down to sensational exaggeration, like the rest of his book [*Fighter*], which does little to detract from the author's prowess as a writer of fiction.'

The Luftwaffe was also now prepared to attack more northerly airfield targets. This policy was presaged on the first clear dawn for days on 24 August and an 8 a.m. raid on the port of Great Yarmouth. A few minutes later, the old familiar build-up of massive forces over the Pas de Calais signalled the end of the five-day lull. Besides Manston, North Weald and Hornchurch became targets later in the day, stretching 11 Group's resources to the utmost. Park sent an urgent appeal for help to Leigh-Mallory, and 19 Squadron's cannon-armed Spitfires provided successful support. The three squadrons at Duxford attempted to form a 'big wing' but the *Kampfgeschwader* were already on their way home, leaving behind a trail of fires around the Thames Estuary, some caused by hastily jettisoned bombs which, themselves, were proof of the ferocity of the fighting.

Once again, Sperrle launched his own *Luftflotte* 3 raids as the last of Kesselring's bombers made their final approach back to their bases.

About 1545 hours, the first signs of an impending raid other than in the south-east were received. A force of fifty-plus was located just north of Cherbourg, and two others of twelve aircraft or more were somewhat to the south-west. The main force came straight across the Channel and at 1610 hours was about thirty-five miles south-east of St Catherine's Point.[5]

But Ventnor CH was still not working to full efficiency, the receivers requiring full calibration, and after 4.15 p.m. the accuracy of the plots seriously deteriorated.

What had previously been a single large formation supported by two or three smaller forces was reported as no less than seven medium-sized forces. It is clear, however, that there was in fact only one bombing formation, and that such other forces as were present were flanking and escorting formations of fighters. . . . The only British squadron to sight any bombers was No. 609 Squadron which, in its rueful words, 'found themselves 5,000 feet below a large formation of bombers and fighters, right in the middle of our own AA fire and down sun'.[6]

Overwhelmed by numbers and in a hopeless situation, the Spitfire pilots fought for their lives. Andy Mamedoff came nearest to losing his, but managed to put down in a field. The outcome for the city of Portsmouth was less fortunate. Over 200 250 kg bombs rained down on the buildings and streets and naval installations, causing the greatest number of casualties so far in the Battle, over 100 killed and nearly 300 seriously injured, including naval officers and ratings.

Even before darkness fell on 24 August the first night-raider plots showed up off the Cherbourg Peninsula and the Yorkshire and Lincolnshire coast, heralding an almost non-stop continuation of the day raids. This night activity was no more intense than on recent nights, but the citizens of London, who had so far escaped the Luftwaffe's attention in darkness, could be forgiven for believing that all-out warfare on the Wellsian scale had at last come to their homes. For the first time since the Gotha bombing raids of 1918, bombs fell on the City. Fires were started and burnt for long, as did an oil tank blaze at Portsmouth, and many more fires in the Midlands and the west signalled across the country that the *blitzkrieg* over Britain had already begun.

This first day of renewed day fighting also tragically signalled the imminent end of the Defiant as a day fighter and its transfer to night duties. In spite of the virtual annihilation of 141 Squadron (Defiants), similarly equipped 264 Squadron was now thrown into the Battle. On this, and the succeeding three days, 264 lost a dozen of this awkward machine, fourteen pilots and gunners killed including the CO, and more wounded.

One of the few survivors, Pilot Officer Desmond Hughes (now Air Vice-Marshal Hughes CB, CBE, DSO, DFC and Bar, AFC) recalled the compounded folly of 264 being despatched to the forward airfield of Manston. 'Our vulnerability was well illustrated by the occasion when B Flight commander had difficulty in starting his engine. It took him a couple of minutes to get it going and, as he took off, he saw his faithful Nos 1 and 2 waiting for him on the circuit. He flew in front of them and waggled his wings – only to be shot down because they were 109s!

'He managed to do a belly-landing back on the airfield but all the way down he was in severe trouble because the 109s' fire had hit his store of signal cartridges which resulted in various coloured flares buzzing round the turret and cockpit like nobody's business.'

It was not only that this turret fighter was a sitting duck for the 109 now that its characteristics were fully known to the enemy, but, even if the engine started promptly, it was slow to scramble in an emergency owing to the difficult entry for the gunner. On 29 August the remnants of a brave squadron were returned to Kirton-in-Lindsey.

It says much for the Defiant squadrons that pride in the aircraft and esprit de corps never seem to have faltered, in part perhaps because of the team spirit of the crews; and when it could position itself beneath the belly of a bomber, those four .303s were lethal.

On 25 August the absence of any serious activity before mid-afternoon, in spite of the good weather, deluded some controllers into the belief that it was the lull rather than the bombing that was being renewed. Brand was not a party to this hopeful interpretation and was not surprised when substantial plots were reported by Ventnor CH. In the subsequent heavy fighting over Portland and Weymouth George Darley's Spitfires of 609, Cedric Williams's Hurricanes of 17 and Wing Commander John Dewar's Hurricanes of 87 were most engaged. Of these squadrons, 17 suffered worst, Williams being shot down and killed by the pilot of a Me 110 and one of the flight commanders being forced to bale out. Although, as usual, heavily outnumbered, these 10 Group squadrons succeeded in blunting the *Luftflotte* 3 attacks. One of 17 Squadron's most determined and successful pilots, Flying Officer

Count Manfred Beckett Czernin, had a field day with the Me 110s of I/ZG2, being credited with destroying three within less than a minute by a neat combination of head-on and rear attacks. Inevitably, though, a few of the bombers got through and damaged hangars at Warmwell, and, by a lucky hit, cut all communication with the outside world. It was reported by several pilots that the proud 110 *Staffeln* were reduced to appealing for assistance from the high-flying 109s (themselves at the limit of their range) by firing red Very lights. In all the Luftwaffe lost twenty aircraft, but the relatively high figure of sixteen RAF fighters marked a new and menacing trend which was to continue.* Thus:

|             | Luftwaffe losses | RAF losses |
|-------------|------------------|------------|
| 26 August   | 41               | 31         |
| 27 August   | 9                | 1          |
| 28 August   | 30               | 20         |
| 29 August   | 17               | 9          |
| 30 August   | 36               | 26         |
| 31 August   | 41               | 39         |
| 1 September | 14               | 15         |
| 2 September | 35               | 31         |
| 3 September | 16               | 16         |
| 4 September | 25               | 17         |
| 5 September | 23               | 20         |
| 6 September | 35               | 23         |

These more depressing figures for Fighter Command were largely attributable to the great increase in the numbers of 109s in Kesselring's *Luftflotte* 2. For his part, Sperrle, after a massive start with daylight raiding, from 24 August was drawn more and more into night raids on the Midlands and the north. Since most of his 109s were being transferred to Kesselring in preparation for the invasion, his main task was becoming night bombing. This was another harbinger of future events.

Operations the following day, Monday 26 August, were marked by a Dornier raid on the important sector station of Debden, the deepest penetration by daylight on an airfield so far in the Battle. Only half-a-dozen bombers broke through the defending screen of

*For the subsequent reversal of this trend, see p. 365 ff.

Hurricanes, Spitfires and Defiants, but that was sufficient to do significant damage. Among the defenders was 310 Squadron from Duxford in 12 Group, up on its first operation, the Czechs being led by Squadron Leader George Blackwood. He had the greatest difficulty in restraining his ultra-aggressive and independent-minded young pilots, who were always trying to go off south on their own in search of prey. In a mêlée with Dorniers and their escort, the Czechs claimed three victims, three of their Hurricanes being shot down, including the CO's, but without pilot loss. No. 1 Canadian Squadron, also recently made operational, roared into the battle with equal zeal but without sufficient awareness of the dangers of well-co-ordinated, bomber, rear-return fire, and they, too, lost three of their Hurricanes, including the CO's, with one of the pilots killed.

But the worst sufferers on this heavy day were the pilots of 616 Squadron (Spitfires) from Kenley, belatedly scrambled and bounced by a swarm of Me 109s, which shot down no fewer than seven of their number, killing two and wounding four more.

In the afternoon, Sperrle laid on his usual tea-time party with a raid by some fifty Heinkels, escorted by twice that number of Messerschmitts, against Portsmouth. Nos 10 and 11 Group controllers managed to scramble eight squadrons, and while most of these failed to make contact (visibility in the south was indifferent all day), the three that succeeded were sufficient to break up the bomber formations and save the great naval base and city from serious damage.

Sperrle's failure seems to have confirmed the German High Command's doubts of the value of these daylight *Luftflotte* 3 efforts to knock out both naval and RAF bases in mid-southern England, and this was the last for several weeks.

The dawn of 27 August revealed drizzle and low cloud, and Park hoped for a respite after the three days of all-out fighting. His wish was granted, and Dowding took advantage of the day by relieving three of his most exhausted squadrons. But this time it was only a one-day lull, and Wednesday the 28th proved to be a suitably busy day for Churchill's visit to the south-east. Almost all the combat the Prime Minister witnessed from the ground was fighter-to-fighter, which was what Dowding was doing his best to avoid. However, both Spitfire and Hurricane squadrons (but not, alas, 264 [Defiants], on their last operational day) acquitted themselves well. Peter Townsend's 85 Squadron (Hurricanes) especially were very successful, the CO claiming one 109 and his pilots five more without loss.

The shooting of baled-out pilots as they fell was not something Churchill raised on his visits to squadrons, but it was a matter, like everything else connected with the Battle, which had received his attention, and he had expressed his revulsion and opposition. It was a highly emotional subject, especially among the pilots concerned. Some German pilots certainly took advantage of the utter vulnerability of an airman swinging slowly down. Denis David, for example, saw Johnnie Cock being shot at by a 109 pilot on the afternoon the Australian went into the sea: 'His parachute cords went ping! ping! ping! – beginning to separate him from his 'chute canopy as the bullets flew around him. I managed to get behind that murderous Hun and shot him down. I circled Johnnie till he hit the water, because I wasn't going to let another Hun shoot him down.'

Later, 87 Squadron lost their CO, Johnnie Dewar, after he parachuted out. When his body was found it was riddled with bullet wounds. Two days after Churchill's visit, a Kenley pilot was seen to be killed by two 109 pilots as he came down under his silk. On this occasion, ironically, the German pilots collided, and both crashed fatally.

'Wilkie' Wilkinson, CO of 266 Squadron, whose death on 18 August so affected 'Chips' Channon, in fact escaped from his Spitfire after the collision with a 109. He was seen to bale out apparently unhurt but, like Johnnie Dewar, his body 'was found as full of holes as a sieve', according to Dennis Armitage. 'Our "Wilkie" was much loved and the thought that he was shot-up while dangling helplessly from a parachute filled us with a vindictive hate which had not been there before.'

Goodness knows, this anger and revulsion against killing the defenceless is understandable. But it has to be said that the lines of ethical distinction are very fine when considering the acceptability between shooting a pilot who on landing will be made a prisoner anyway, and shooting a pilot who will very likely return to fight again. From the early days of this Battle, as we have seen, Fighter Command pilots were officially encouraged to shoot down, or shoot on the water, German rescue seaplanes which, in all probability, had just plucked from the water a pilot who had survived by baling out.

British and Commonwealth pilots refrained from shooting at parachuting pilots, which would have brought the wrath of their flight and squadron commanders about their head if seen to do so. The ferocity and hatred of the Poles and Czechs could not be held back when opportunity occurred, however, as it did on 31 August. 'The Poles of

303 Squadron could not be restrained from queuing up to fire bursts at Oblt von Perthes as he descended by parachute.'[7]

Much as this was officially deplored, other pilots understood the violence of the Poles and Czechs, who were loved and admired. 'Thank God they're on our side!' The CO of 238 Squadron (today Air Commodore H. A. Fenton CBE, DSO, DFC) writes: 'The Poles and Czechs (of blessed memory) were vital as it turned out. . . . It was amazing how quickly we became real friends. I flew with a Pole on one side and a Czech on the other and was delighted to be so well looked after.'

The last two days of August stretched Fighter Command, and 11 Group especially, to the limit. Kesselring had staked his military reputation on breaking the back of the defence before September, and he used every permutation in his tactical arsenal. To attack the airfields of south-east England and wear down the British fighter force, he sent over vast formations of Me 109s on provocative sweeps and, when Park refused to rise to the bait, he sent them again with a small force of fast Ju 88s. He varied the timing between mass raids in an effort to catch the British fighters rearming and refuelling. He sent over massive formations of around 200 bombers, and then split them up into groups of twenty or thirty to attack airfields from Duxford to Oxford and the usual targets south of London.

At one time on 30 August forty-eight Observer Corps posts reported raids overhead, the fighting was everywhere and unsurpassed in its fury. Eleven Hurricanes of 85 Squadron put to rout a massive bomber formation with a single head-on attack followed by individual combats. Geoffrey Allard, a red-headed sergeant from Yorkshire who had earlier been credited with shooting down ten Luftwaffe planes in seven days over France before it fell, was especially adept at the head-on attack technique pioneered by 111 Squadron, and was now adding to his score at a great rate – six in three days.

Dennis Armitage of 266 Squadron became a very experienced head-on exponent: 'It has several advantages if you can get into the right position. You avoid the concentration of fire from the bombers' rear gunners, they have no guns firing forward, in twin-engined aircraft the pilot and crew are more vulnerable from the front, and perhaps above all it makes it very difficult for the escorting fighters to carry out their protective role. The disadvantage is that there is so little time. The relative closing speed would be something approaching 600 mph and this is very nearly 300 yards per second. The optimum range of our guns was about 300 yards so if you could get your sights on at 600 yards you could press the button for one second and this left you one second to break away . . . but the effect on the enemy formation was devastating.'

Donald Stones of 79 Squadron recalled a head-on attack on 30 August which dramatically demonstrated to them all just how fine the timing had to be. Teddy Morris, a South African who had been carefully briefed on this form of warfare, was among those who bored into a huge formation of He 111s. He did not evade in time and bounced off the nose of a 111. The impact destroyed it, and his Hurricane.

'He found himself still strapped in his seat, surrounded by debris from both aircraft, and pulled his ripcord. He suffered only a broken leg, and loss of confidence in our advice. When we saw him in sick quarters he complained, "I thought you told me they would break formation if we pressed home a good frontal attack."

' "No, Teddy," we said. "They don't if the pilot is dead. You are supposed to allow for that."

' "How the hell are you to know if he's dead or not?"

' "The way you did," seemed to be the only answer.'

From time to time deliberate ramming of the enemy was reported. No doubt some of these incidents were accidental or involuntary, perhaps with the fighter pilot already dead. But there can be little doubt that several pilots made the supreme sacrifice, whether or not they judged that they were about to die anyway. When the great Victor Beamish was leading 249 Squadron in a combat with a large number of 110s, Pilot Officer Percy Burton was badly hit and was trailing smoke and flame. Charles Palliser DFC, of 43 and 249 Squadrons, recalled: 'I saw his contortions, then I saw him straighten and fly straight into the German aircraft; both crashed and Percy was killed. I was close enough to see his aircraft letters, as other pilots must have been and who also confirmed this incident, which in itself caused me to realise my young life and its future, if any, had jumped into another dimension.'

One of the best reasons for adopting head-on tactics against bomber formations was the increasing adoption of heavy armour-plate by the Luftwaffe, especially as protection for the crew and the engines. This was installed on the assumption of attacks from the rear, above or below. There was, in any case, no means of protection against frontal assault.

Dowding had disapproved of the head-on attack, though he knew it was increasingly resorted to. But on 25 August he urged its use whenever there was an opportunity as a means of counteracting the armour-plate which was being fitted to German fighters as well as to bombers. Nor is there much doubt that this was a type of attack that the German bomber crews most feared.

By this time – the end of August – all Hurricanes and Spitfires had been fitted with a slab of armour behind the pilot's head and shoulders, which saved many lives. It was often hastily fitted, overnight in some cases, to the dismay of other ground crews besides William Eslick and his friends in 19 Squadron.

Another modification to RAF fighters which had also been adopted by all squadrons was the rear-view mirror, with the benefit of hindsight an extraordinary omission in the original design. A regular, Sergeant Pilot George Johns (now a retired group captain DSO, DFC, AFC), recalled going to the nearest local garage and cleaning out the stock of car mirrors, which they fitted themselves to their Hurricanes. 'I don't think we were ever reimbursed.' On 19 Squadron pilots had 'rear-view mirrors made up in the chippy [carpenter's] shop, great blocks of streamlined wood housing a mirror bolted to each side of the fuselage forward of the cockpit. These were later removed with the belated arrival of the official top-of-the-windscreen version.'

On 30 August, the same day that Donald Stones (something of a veteran by now) carried out a head-on attack, Iain Hutchinson of 222 Squadron at Hornchurch encountered the enemy for the first time: 'The sky was blue from horizon to horizon and our squadron was climbing to our allocated altitude. Suddenly from the east, I became aware of masses of dots which resolved themselves into aircraft as the enemy formations approached. Our fighters were converging on them and, in an instant, the orderly enemy lines wavered as the first of our aircraft attacked. A great whirlpool of planes developed, spiralling downwards. Within seconds there were several plumes of smoke as stricken aircraft plunged earthwards leaving some tiny gossamer mushrooms seemingly suspended in the air as pilots took to their parachutes.

'Then our squadron, now in battle formation of line astern, swept in to engage the enemy. . . . I clearly remember the hammer blows as my aircraft was hit by cannon shell and the dense grey smoke that immediately poured from the engine cowling before me.

'I decided to try to land my Spitfire and, as I swept over the hedge of a field being ploughed, I caught a quick glimpse of the ploughman, some fifty yards to my left, reining in his horses, his face turned towards me in incredulity. Then the aircraft impacted in a flurry of earth and my face struck the reflector sight. I sat for a moment, feeling dazed, in the quiet that descended.'

Hutchinson could, perhaps, consider himself lucky. All too many pilots on their first op. experienced only the stab of a fatal bullet or the searing heat of fire – and oblivion.

In mid-August, to the outrage of the new young commanders, orders had been issued to all *Luftflotte* 2 Me 109 *Geschwader* to escort the bomber formations more closely. Park countered this move by instructing his controllers to despatch Spitfire *and* Hurricane squadrons against the bombers, which had previously been the more or less exclusive preserve of the slower Hurricanes. But as soon as sufficient numbers of 109s from Sperrle had been established in the Pas de Calais and the escort level could be doubled, high screens of fighters were reinstated at 20,000+ feet in addition to the close escort.

Park at once instructed controllers to revert to the old policy. But with 109s close to the bomber formations as well as above, ready to pounce, the division of responsibility became less tidy, Hurricanes often finding themselves engaged with the close escort 109s and Spitfires breaking through first to the bombers.

The dilemma of RAF squadron commanders, and the reason for the heavy casualties from 109s is made sharply clear:

For most of the phase [24 August–6 September] the defending squadrons were flying and fighting singly. Only too often the units of combat were a British squadron of twelve aircraft at most and a German formation of twenty to forty bombers and up to 100 fighters. Some British squadron commanders attempted to contain the enemy escort with one flight, and with the other attack the bombers; but time after time there were sufficient German fighters to engage both British flights.[8]

An additional anxiety that ever increasingly weighed down upon Dowding during these desperate days was the maintenance of the delicate organisation and communications that kept alive the whole structure of RAF fighter defence. The restoration of operational landlines and the repair or rebuilding of ops rooms and damaged radar stations were made possible by the priceless gift of time offered by the earlier five-day lull. The loss of hangars could be endured. The emergency erection of tents or commandeering of local houses solved accommodation problems caused by wrecked domestic blocks, and in this summer weather food could be cooked and eaten out of doors if need be. As had been shown time and again, even the most pockmarked landing grounds could be made usable again in a short time, especially since the formation of mobile repair squads.

During this intense late August–early September period, the battle on the ground was against the damage caused to the body corporate of Fighter Command. When ops rooms were destroyed, as at Kenley and Biggin Hill, existing emergency rooms were rushed into service. These, however, could not accommodate a full staff or provide all the landlines necessary for the control of the full quota of their squadrons. Improvisation was the order of the day, while at the same time the rushed construction of fully equipped alternative ops rooms within five miles of the sector station was put in hand.

Those who carried out this repair work were among the unsung heroes of the Battle, like the ground staff, anti-aircraft gunners, ARP workers and members of the Observer Corps. Operational landlines were the responsibility of the GPO (War Group) and these were among the hardest worked people on the ground, often working right through nights, doggedly tackling the repair to vital lines which they had reconnected perhaps only twenty-four hours earlier. Equally busy were the station signals men and members of the Royal Corps of Signals who dealt with internal station lines.

Sir Keith Park in mid-September made no bones about the extremity of the situation between 28 August and 5 September:

Contrary to general belief and official reports, the enemy's bombing attacks by day did extensive damage to five of our forward aerodromes and also to six of our seven sector stations.* There was a critical period when the damage to sector stations and our ground organisation was having a serious effect on the fighting efficiency of the squadrons, who could not be given the same good technical and administrative service as previously. . . . The absence of many essential telephone lines, the use of scratch equipment in emergency operations rooms, and the general dislocation of ground organisation, was seriously felt for about a week in the handling of squadrons by day to meet the enemy's massed attacks, which were continued without the former occasional break of a day.[9]

Very little intelligence was percolating through to the RAF from France and the Low Countries about German morale. The undercover network on the continent had not yet been established, wireless intercepts and the Enigma traffic shed no light, and only the interrogation of

*Only Northolt escaped. The forward airfields were Lympne, Hawkinge, Manston, Rochford and Martlesham.

236

prisoners provided any sort of clue to the effect that the high rate of casualties and failure to break Fighter Command was having on German aircrew. Air Ministry interrogation officers believed that they saw some signs of nervous strain and low morale among the prisoners passing through their hands during this period. They also discovered that virtually all bomber crew and fighter pilots had been trained in peacetime and had an average service of four years in the case of bomber pilots and three years in that of fighter pilots. This alone did not suggest that the Luftwaffe was experiencing the same replacement difficulties as Fighter Command, whether or not their morale was falling.

*The Luftwaffe War Diaries* confirm the conclusions of these interrogation officers. Hans von Hahn of I/JG3 stated: 'There were only a few of us who had not yet had to ditch in the Channel with a shot up aircraft or stationary airscrew.' And Hellmuth Osterman of III/JG54 recalled: 'Utter exhaustion from the English operations had set in. For the first time one heard pilots talk of the prospects of a posting to a quieter sector.'[10]

In the German High Command hierarchy this attitude did not prevail, and any pilot uttering such defeatist remarks would have had short shrift. 'The British fighter arm has been severely hit,' pronounced Major Freiherr von Falkenstein, ever optimistic, on 1 September. 'If, during September, we seize every opportunity of favourable weather to keep up the pressure, one can assume that the enemy's fighter defence will be so weakened that our air assault on his production centres and harbour installations can be greatly stepped up.'[11]

On that same day, Dowding was obliged to face the fact that on 31 August his Command had lost thirty-nine aircraft, the highest so far – and, as it turned out, the highest figure for the Battle.

The last day of August and the first days of September were again marked by exceptionally heavy blows to certain squadrons, which had already suffered severe losses, and to a wide spread of airfields.

No. 111 Squadron, which had been in the thick of the fighting for so long, moved at last to Drem in Scotland. John Thompson's pilots had suffered appalling casualties, and the survivors and the ground crew were utterly exhausted. Aircraftman Charles Cooper, the armourer who had narrowly escaped death on 15 August when Croydon was bombed, described two incidents which bear this out: 'On one of our busy days at Croydon we were watching the return of our Hurricanes, and ready to rearm quickly, when we noticed one aircraft landed and taxied a short distance only to stop some way off with the engine still turning over. Thinking the pilot had been wounded, we dashed over to the aircraft, only to find the pilot, Johnny Walker DFC, a Canadian, was leaning forward with his body held by the Sutton harness, head on his chest and asleep with exhaustion.'

More tragically, Cooper recalled the arrival on the squadron straight from OTU of two eager young pilots in a car with their baggage: 'They immediately went up with the rest of the squadron since we were so short of pilots, but only one returned, badly injured. I do not even remember their names. Their car stood outside the airport building still with their baggage in it.'

No. 257 Squadron (Hurricanes), which, until now, had not enjoyed the highest morale, lost a pilot on Saturday 31 August and another on 3 September, with two wounded. 'We were a very demoralised squadron until Bob Stanford Tuck arrived. He vitalised us and we soon went to the top,' Jack Ryder, an instrument repairer, recalled. No. 72 Squadron lost three Hurricanes in one engagement on this same day, the very day they arrived at Biggin Hill.

*Erpro* 210 raised its ugly head again on this last day of the month, coming in low and unannounced on the south-east radar stations as before. The fighter-bombers made a great deal of noise and did some damage, but all the stations were back on the air again by the end of the day.

After a single bombing the previous day, the mutilated remains of Biggin Hill were twice attacked, for the second time late in the afternoon by the ever-active *Erpro* crews, which in all lost eight Me 110s on this day, 31 August. No. 72 Squadron, possessions not yet unpacked, had to move out to Croydon. 'I'll never forget the courage of home-wrecked Londoners as they cheered our maintenance convoy from one station to another,' recalled Flight Lieutenant Ted Graham. No. 56 Squadron, lacking a CO and most of their aircraft, were moved from North Weald to Boscombe Down.

Two notable figures suffered lucky escapes at the cost of their aircraft on this last day of August: Peter Townsend was shot down by 109s north of North Weald, took to the silk and landed with a piece of shell in his left foot; and Alan Deere had an extraordinary escape while taking off from Hornchurch. Deere later wrote: 'I was not quite airborne when a bomb burst on the airfield, ahead of me and to my left. "Good, I've made it," I thought. To this day I am not clear exactly what happened next; all I can remember is that a tremendous blast of air, carrying showers of earth, struck me in the face and the next moment thinking vaguely that I was upside down. What I do remember is the impact with the ground and a terrifying period of ploughing along the airfield upside down.'[12]

With the help of a fellow pilot who raced to help prise Deere out of the wreck, which was likely to go up in flames any second, the New Zealander got clear. Bandaged, patched and plastered, he was in stern combat again the following day. On 3 September 54 Squadron was at last relieved and sent north.

Biggin Hill celebrated the first day of the new month by suffering three more severe bombing attacks. After the last of these, two WAAFs, Sergeant Helen Turner and Corporal Elspeth Henderson, were found in the debris of their telephone switchboard building, from which, in order to keep the lines open, they had refused to move. They were relatively unhurt; both later received the Military Medal. The officer in charge of these girls at the station, Assistant Section Officer Felicity Hanbury, who later rose to be Director of the WAAF, also received commendation for her courageous conduct and fine example.

While the WAAFs were dusting themselves down and the weary rescue and first-aid squads were searching for more victims at Biggin Hill, a mere fifteen miles away in the heart of Mayfair, Archibald Sinclair, the Secretary of State for Air, and Dr Hugh Dalton, the Minister for Economic Warfare, were taking luncheon at the Mirabelle in Curzon Street. Dalton confided to his diary:

It goes very well and we are very co-operatively conspiratorial. It seems that the idea of bringing Lloyd George into the War Cabinet has faded out a bit. Sinclair says that the excuse was that Lloyd George was a man of the Left so he would do something to balance Beaverbrook. I said that was all rubbish.[13]

In these first days of September there were renewed attacks on aircraft factories. The first to suffer again, on 2 September, was the Short Brothers plant at Rochester, where the drawing office was among the buildings destroyed. The old motor racing circuit of Brooklands, where Vickers had a factory producing Wellington bombers, was another target.

The 3rd of September was a quieter day, though not for the Czechs, who had a fierce encounter with I/ZG2's Me 110s. For the cost of one Hurricane (pilot safe) they shot down four of these big fighters above North Weald, all the crews being killed.

On the following day, the Short Brothers works and Brooklands were

'Eglantine Cottage? Go down the lane past the Messerschmitt, bear left and keep on past the two Dorniers, then turn sharp right and it's just past the first Junkers.'
*Punch*, 4 September 1940.

the object of more vigorous attacks. At Brooklands a heavy price was paid by both sides. A strong force of 110s was intercepted close to the target by nine Hurricanes of 253 Squadron, which shot down six in a few seconds (all confirmed by wreckage) and damaged another. A few survivors got through, either mistook the Vickers works for the Hawker factory (producing large numbers of Hurricanes some distance away and protected by balloons), were wrongly briefed, or did not care for the balloons, and put six 500 kg bombs into Vickers' machine shops. It was the worst single incident so far in the Battle, with over 700 casualties, eighty-six of whom were killed instantly. Fifteen 110s were destroyed and more damaged on the afternoon of this day.

On 5 September the morning started with two major attacks which crossed the coast at Dungeness almost simultaneously at 9.45 a.m. One of them, consisting of thirty Do 17s, escorted by seventy fighters, was intercepted by 501 Squadron, who were forced to deal with the Me 109s and failed to break through to the bombers and lost one of their number – but not the pilot, who baled out safely.

The second raid, of equal strength, was first dealt with by the Spitfires of 41 Squadron, which had the advantage of an altitude of 27,000 feet and completely surprised the 109 pilots of II/JG3. No. 234 Squadron, patrolling almost as high, then joined in when the fighting was over Maidstone. Oberleutnant von Werra, the adjutant of II/JG3, who was flying with his CO, Hauptmann Erich von Selle, later described how they were bounced by three Spitfires. Von Selle jerked his stick forward just in time, but von Werra's machine received a long burst from the Australian, Flight Lieutenant Paterson Hughes.*

Von Werra crash-landed on the east side of Winchet Hill, Curtisden Green, south of Maidstone, and was made prisoner by the excited 'hatless, collarless, shirt-sleeved and unarmed cook'[14] of a nearby searchlight battery. Von Werra was eventually taken to a prisoner-of-war camp in Canada, escaped to the USA and made his way home via Mexico, Panama, Peru, Brazil and Spain.

Also on 5 September, a small raid did succeed in penetrating the defences of the Hawker factory at Brooklands, but little damage was caused and production was unaffected. Meanwhile on this day, and the next, Fighter Command remained at full stretch, dealing with the usual massive bombing raids on airfields and (a significant new target) the oil storage tanks at Thameshaven.

No one at Bentley Priory, at Group or sector, or at the dispersals where in the late evening pilots put away their parachutes, 'Mae West' flotation jackets and helmets, could have predicted that the next day would bring about such relief and such a radical change in the nature of the Battle.

---

*Hughes had already accumulated a large score and was awarded the DFC. He scored against another 109 later the same day. He was shot down and killed by a 109 pilot two days later.

# 16

## Strategic Turning-point

From the moment on 14 May when the War Cabinet and the reluctant French gave permission, Bomber Command had been doing its best to wage a strategic air offensive against Germany. By August it had not, in fact, made much progress – for which there were many reasons. Among them were its involvement in other tasks, such as attacking the German Army's communications and the Luftwaffe's newly occupied airfields in France and the Low Countries; its very limited size; and the fact that, if its aircraft were not to be shot down over Germany in droves, they had to operate solely by night.

There was also another difficulty, of which the Command and the Air Staff were ignorant. They held the firm belief that the Command's navigational methods of the time – mainly dead reckoning and astro-navigation, with D/F fixes nearer home, without benefit of later radio and radar aids – were good enough to enable well-trained crews to find and bomb, particularly on clear or moonlit nights, precise targets such as oil plants, factories and rail centres. Not until after the Battle of Britain was it discovered, mainly from photographs, that though the British bombers had their occasional successes they were commonly missing their targets by as much as five miles.[1]

In these circumstances it was not surprising that attacks by forces of twenty or thirty Wellingtons, Whitleys or Hampdens against industrial targets in the Ruhr and elsewhere in West Germany, which had been going on intermittently since 15/16 May, did little damage to factories. They did, however, have an intentional nuisance value by putting areas under air-raid warning, which was bad for both production and morale. They also had another effect, which was at that time not intended. They destroyed, though not in large numbers, German homes and killed German civilians.

On the night of 25/26 August Bomber Command struck at objectives far beyond its normal reach. The previous night, as already noted, German bombs had fallen on the City of London – to be exact in Fore Street, near the Barbican – for the first time since 1918. There had been a scatter a little farther out, too – all through navigational error or by jettisoning, for which the German pilots were promptly reproved. The accidental nature of this episode was not manifest to Churchill, nor would he have troubled about it had he known. Bombs had fallen on the British capital, and to his mind there was only one appropriate response. He had already ascertained from the Air Staff, who deprecated attacking distant targets when there were good ones nearer at hand, that, if required, Bomber Command could put on a raid against Berlin within twenty-four hours. Almost precisely twenty-four hours after the German bombs fell on Finsbury, Islington and the East End, some eighty Wellingtons and Hampdens sought to attack the German capital.

They were directed mainly against industrial targets on the outskirts and failed to hit them. But on three of the four following nights British bombers were over Berlin again, in one incident killing ten civilians. Negligible though the damage was, the moral effect was considerable. W. L. Shirer, an American newspaper correspondent, recorded his impressions: 'The Berliners are stunned. They did not think it could ever happen. Goering assured them that it couldn't. Their disillusionment today is all the greater. You have to see their faces to measure it.'[2]

On few Germans did these raids produce a greater effect than on Adolf Hitler. Though he understandably dismissed with scorn their material effect, his pride was bitterly hurt and he was eager for revenge. His plans had for some time included bombing the British capital at the right moment in his invasion strategy. He could now do so wholeheartedly under the guise of reprisals.

So it came about that on 4 September Hitler took the occasion of a meeting in the Berlin Sportpalast, at which the Nazis were to open their Winter Relief campaign, to reveal something of his intentions. He did so in a way which evoked storms of clapping and cheering. 'He had to stop', wrote Shirer, 'because of the hysterical applause of the audience, which consisted mostly of German women nurses and social workers.'[3]

The words which evoked such enthusiasm were delivered in the speaker's characteristic tones of menace and heavy sarcasm: 'When people are very anxious in Britain and ask *yes, but why doesn't he come?* we reply, *Calm yourselves! Calm yourselves! He is coming! He is coming!*' This promise followed another which had gone down almost equally well:

The British drop their bombs indiscriminately and without plan on civilian residential quarters and on farms and villages. For three months I did not reply because I believed they would stop, but in this Mr Churchill saw only a sign of our weakness. The British will know that we are now giving our answer night after night. Since they attack our cities, we shall extirpate theirs.[4]

This public intimation of fresh work for the Luftwaffe followed a meeting between Hitler and Goering on 30 August. There the Fuehrer had withdrawn his ban on bombing London and expressed an ardent desire for attacks on the British capital in retaliation for Bomber Command's raids on Berlin. An appropriate directive from Goering followed.

On 3 September the Luftwaffe chief then met Kesselring and Sperrle at The Hague. It emerged that though Kesselring strongly supported switching the main attack from Fighter Command's airfields on to London, Sperrle did not.[5] He felt that the RAF fighter defences were not yet sufficiently worn down. Kesselring, on the other hand, still misled by his pilots' high claims of enemy aircraft destroyed and some reports that resistance was weakening, was all in favour of the new policy. He felt that even if the Luftwaffe destroyed all the fighter stations south of London, the squadrons there could move to airfields north of the capital from which they could still challenge the German raids. By contrast his Me 109s, with their short endurance, would be powerless to escort German bombers sent to attack such distant bases. What was needed, in his opinion, was to crush the last remnants of fighter opposition – Luftwaffe Intelligence estimated that it was now down to somewhere between 150 and 300 Hurricanes and Spitfires – and to do this by attacking an objective which the British fighters were bound to defend in force. Later, he was to write in his memoirs: 'Our difficulty was not to bring down enemy fighters, but to get the enemy to fight.'[6] The obvious answer was to attack London.

In this, Kesselring was echoing the feelings, at least in part, of his brilliant subordinate Adolf Galland. Galland's constant complaint was that the Hurricanes and Spitfires would not come up in sufficient numbers to be destroyed in quantity.[7] If London was attacked, they would have no option. Galland, however, was far more conscious than Kesselring of one weakness in the new plan. Over London, the 109s would be operating with a flying and fighting time of perhaps only ten minutes. Would they ever get back across the Channel?

Sperrle's views were disregarded. On 5 September a further directive, this time from Hitler's Supreme Headquarters, enjoined 'harassing attacks by day and night on the inhabitants and air defences of large British cities', especially London.

This switch in the main objective of attack – of which the British had no advance knowledge – thus came about for several reasons. There was the vengeance motive: the determination of Hitler to exact revenge for the RAF's bombing of targets in Berlin and other German towns. There was the tactical motive: the belief of Goering and Kesselring that attacking London would induce great air battles in which the remnants of Fighter Command would be destroyed. And there was the overall strategical motive: to bring about the conditions for invasion or British capitulation. A grand assault on London, it was hoped, would create administrative chaos and terrorise the British into submission.

In this context, Feldmarschall Wilhelm Keitel, the Chief of Staff of the Wehrmacht, had issued from Supreme Headquarters on 3 September a schedule to govern the preparations already in train for the launching of 'Operation Sealion'. The earliest date for the landings (D Day) was now fixed for 21 September instead of 15 September – a deferment at least partly caused by Bomber Command's raid on the Dortmund-Ems Canal on 12/13 August, which had temporarily blocked the movement of invasion barges from the Rhineland to the coast.* The definite order for the launching of the invasion was now to be given ten days, and final commands three days, before 21 September.

In all this, Hitler still fully understood, and indeed emphasised, that an invasion would not be possible until the Luftwaffe had established air superiority over the Channel and southern England. Moreover, he already had in mind, as indicated by remarks to Army leaders during July, that it might soon be desirable to 'take the initiative' against Soviet Russia.[8] This provisional element in Hitler's invasion thinking was reinforced by the continued lack of appetite with which Raeder and the German Naval Staff regarded 'Sealion'. Though Raeder had won his battle against the Army for landings on a narrow front, he remained

---

*For his outstanding part in the attack, carried out by five Hampdens of 49 and 83 Squadrons, Flight Lieutenant R. A. B. Learoyd was awarded the VC.

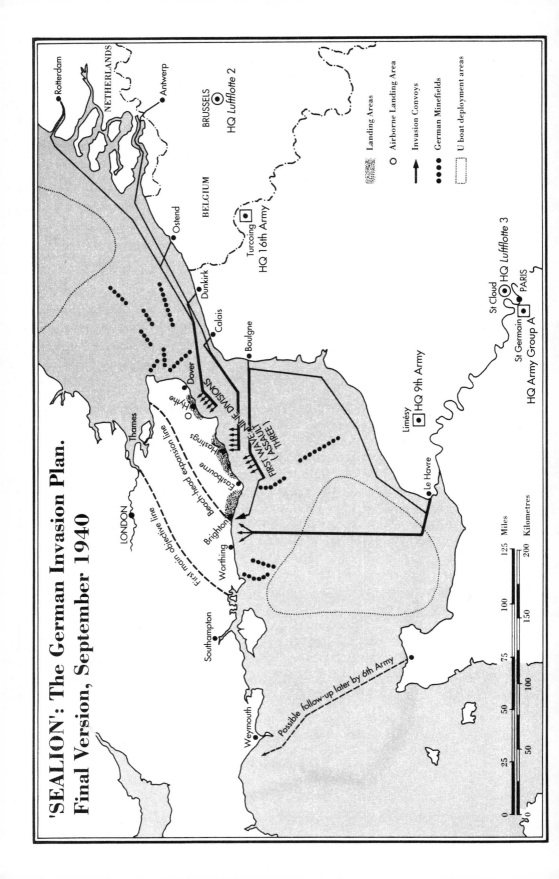

# 'SEALION': The German Invasion Plan.
# Final Version, September 1940

NETHERLANDS

Rotterdam

Antwerp

BRUSSELS ⊙ HQ *Luftflotte 2*

Landing Areas
Airborne Landing Area
Invasion Convoys
German Minefields
U boat deployment areas

BELGIUM

Ostend

Dunkirk

Turcoing ⊡ HQ 16th Army

Calais

Boulgne

Dover

Hythe

Thames

HYTHE DIVISIONS

FIRST ASSAULT (THREE)

Hastings

Eastbourne

Beach-head expansion line

LONDON

Brighton

First main objective line

Worthing

Southampton

Le Havre

Limésy ⊡ HQ 9th Army

St Cloud ⊙ HQ *Luftflotte 3*

PARIS

St Germain ⊡ HQ Army Group A

Weymouth

Possible follow-up later by 6th Army

Miles
0        25        50        75        100        125
Kilometres
0   50        100        150        200

throughout extremely unhappy at the thought of facing the Royal Navy and an unsubdued RAF. He obediently speeded up preparations, and even requisitioned enough craft to attempt an invasion, but never ceased to explain that the success of the operation would depend entirely on favourable weather and on winning supremacy in the air.

How accurate were Goering and Kesselring in their view that by now, in the opening days of September, Fighter Command was worn down and ripe for the knock-out? The Luftwaffe knew that since the beginning of its major attacks in mid-August it had lost 467 bombers, dive-bombers and fighters – just over one-sixth of its original operational strength. The British losses for the same period were reckoned by the Germans to

Front page of the *Daily Telegraph*, 7 September, showing the daily tally of the number of enemy aircraft shot down.

be 1,115, nearly all fighters. They thus imagined that they had destroyed at least the equivalent of Dowding's entire front line, leaving him to make good the losses from his reserves and from replacements. The full extent of this task they considered to be well beyond Britain's productive capacity, either of aircraft or pilots. Moreover, they knew that the Luftwaffe had hit several aircraft factories and had done serious damage to many Fighter Command stations – some of which Kesselring had even 'crossed off' his list. As he and Goering saw it, a final massive blow or two could finish off their enemy.

The truth of the matter was somewhat different. Fighter Command was certainly heavily stricken, but not so heavily as the Germans imagined. From 24 August, when the Luftwaffe shifted its main weight of attack to objectives well inland, the damage to Fighter Command's ground organisation had steadily increased. Twenty-four of the Luftwaffe's thirty-three heavy attacks between then and 6 September had fallen on airfields – all but one in 11 Group. The key targets had been 11 Group's sector stations. Of these, Kenley had already been badly hit on 18 August and could thenceforth operate only two squadrons instead of its normal three. Between 24 August and 6 September only one of these seven master stations – Northolt – had escaped attack. But only at Biggin Hill, bombed seven times within a week, had the damage been severe enough to restrict operations for more than a few hours and to reduce operating capacity to a single squadron. On the other sector stations craters, ruined buildings and severed communications had been handicaps quickly overcome: the controllers had continued to direct their normal forces.

In so far as Kesselring was crossing off airfields and overestimating Fighter Command's casualties, he was certainly deluding himself. Nevertheless, the damage to several airfields had been severe and the casualties grievous enough. Between 24 August and 6 September Fighter Command had lost 295 Hurricanes and Spitfires destroyed – including eighteen in flying accidents – and another 171 badly damaged. During this time the gross output of these fighters, including repairs of the badly damaged, had totalled 269. Reserves had enabled the front line to be fully replenished; but with production not fully counterbalancing losses, those reserves were sharply declining. Another three weeks at the same rate of attrition, and they would be exhausted – even sooner if there was serious damage to the aircraft factories (or, worst of all, to the Vickers works in Sheffield, where the only drop-hammer in Britain capable of forging crankshaft castings for

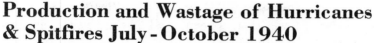

# Production and Wastage of Hurricanes & Spitfires July - October 1940

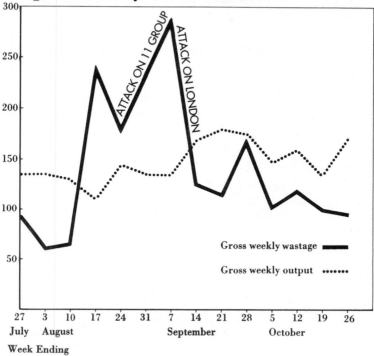

the Merlin engine was working round the clock, producing eighty-four stampings per shift).

Thanks to the titanic efforts in the aircraft factories and the repair depots, the front line on 6 September was still numerically intact. There were still enough machines to fight the enemy and dismay German pilots who each day expected to find diminishing opposition. All the same, the crisis was real enough: not so much because of the declining reserves but because of the loss of pilots – above all, of skilled pilots. This was Dowding's nightmare, which haunted him more and more as the Battle progressed. Between 24 August and 6 September 103 of his pilots had been killed or reported missing, and 128 wounded. This nearly equalled an entire month's output of new fighter pilots from the OTUs. By early September Dowding's squadrons were down to an average of nineteen pilots each in 11 Group, as opposed to the official

249

complement of twenty-six, while in the quieter Groups they were down to an average of fewer than sixteen. And all the newcomers from the OTUs, except pilots from other Commands or Allied air forces, lacked any experience of battle.

Such experience was, indeed, a vital factor. When fresh squadrons were posted into the hot spot, 11 Group, they usually suffered more casualties than the tired squadrons still there. Battle-hardened 501 Squadron, at Biggin Hill for the whole period of inland attack preceding 7 September, lost nine aircraft and four pilots during that fortnight; but 616 and 253 Squadrons, posted in from other Groups, lost respectively twelve aircraft and five pilots, and thirteen aircraft and nine pilots, within a week.

To the initial vulnerability of newcomers was added the inevitable loss, as the fighting went on, of fully experienced leaders. By 7 September roughly one in five of all Dowding's squadron commanders, and one in three of his flight commanders, had been killed or wounded. Many of those who survived were flying two, three, or even four combat sorties a day. Sooner or later, such intolerable nervous strain must lead to disaster.

Dowding's successive steps to maintain the battle strength of 11 Group were a clear indication of his troubles. In the early phases he had simply withdrawn squadrons which suffered heavy losses or became exhausted and replaced them with others from outside the Group. This, however, meant a cumbrous movement by road to shift all the squadron ground staff and equipment. So in the interests of speed he had soon begun to move in only the squadron's aircraft and pilots, together with sixty or seventy – later, as few as thirty or forty – of its key ground staff.*
With many of the normal services being supplied by ground staff of the departed squadron, this tended to weaken squadron organisation and esprit de corps. Park's own preferred solution was simply to bring in experienced pilots as individuals from other Groups, but at first Dowding had rejected this. Squadrons, with their strong corporate loyalty and keenness to excel, resented being 'milked' of their best pilots – who, in any case, were needed to 'bring on' their less experienced colleagues.

By 6 September every Hurricane or Spitfire squadron that could reasonably be used in 11 Group or the two 'hot' adjoining sectors

---

*There were twenty-one squadron movements between 24 August and 6 September. A transport flight and motor transport units were formed to help deal with this traffic, which could range from Kent to Scotland.

(Duxford in 12, Middle Wallop in 10) was either serving there, or had been serving there in the previous month. There were no further fresh squadrons fit to take the place of the battered ones. As Dowding later wrote: 'By the beginning of September the incidence of casualties became so serious that a fresh squadron would become depleted and exhausted before any resting or reformed squadron was ready to take its place.'[9] On 6 September, Fighter Command, though still very much in being, was a wasting asset.

So, as the losses mounted, Dowding was forced to introduce what he called his 'Stabilisation Scheme', promulgated on 8 September. By this, the squadrons were divided into three classes. Category A, the operationally fit, were all packed into 11 Group and the Duxford and Middle Wallop sectors. Category B, partially fit, with a number of experienced pilots in each squadron, were all located in 10 and 12 Groups and were to be brought up to strength so that they could relieve A squadrons. Category C, as yet deemed unfit to tackle enemy fighters, and with only half-a-dozen experienced pilots each, could serve in any Group except 11, but were to be placed in the areas most remote from the German bases – mainly in 13 Group. Cross-posting of experienced pilots from squadron to squadron, to maintain the strength of the As, was now to be the norm. Such a scheme, with its depressing effect on the traditional belief of each squadron that it was better than the next, would never have been contemplated by Dowding had he not been virtually at his wits' end how to sustain 11 Group in face of the intense attacks on its sector stations.

Fortunately, relief was soon to be forthcoming: not from Dowding's new arrangements, but from the enemy's change of objective.

# 17

## The New Target

### 7 SEPTEMBER

At Northolt, Tangmere and Gravesend especially, where the previous day's losses had fallen most heavily and the absent faces at breakfast in the officers' and sergeants' messes were most conspicuous, there was immense relief when the sunny early morning passed without a telephone call at the dispersals. The young WAAFs at Dover, Rye and Pevensey CH radar stations stared at tubes that remained blip-free for so long that, once or twice, an officer had to remind them not to relax their attention. Cigarette ends in old tobacco tins piled high and there were more calls than usual for tea. Only at Wittering – of all places – was there any excitement. No. 266 Squadron had recently been transferred to this Midlands sector station for a rest, much to their disgust. But early in the morning A Flight had been brought to immediate readiness. The CO warned that it was only the usual German recce to check the previous night's bombing, in this case of Liverpool, but the pilots felt particularly satisfied that the authorities' efforts to wrap them in cotton wool had been thwarted, especially as they had just received their new, more powerful Mark 2 Spitfires.

At 8.30 a.m., the New Zealanders Dick Trousdale, Wycliff Williams and Bob Roach – all pilot officers – were scrambled and took off in formation down the tarmacadam runway, which felt like a billiard table after grass. 'There's a single bandit angels twenty-eight approaching from the north-west,' the controller told them. Williams ordered

B Flight at dawn readiness: George Welford of 607 Squadron, early awake, sketched this characteristic scene at Tangmere, September 1940.

emergency boost and five minutes later they caught sight first of the German's contrail and then of the minute dot that was marking the sky. As if suddenly aware of the identifying trail the plane – it looked like a Do 215 – was leaving, the pilot gained or lost enough altitude to extinguish it.

As the Spitfires passed over the Norfolk coast, the enemy was still far distant and travelling faster than their climbing speed. The three Spitfire pilots glanced anxiously at their engine temperature gauges, for they had already far exceeded the period permitted for emergency boost. The Dutch–Belgian coast was a grey smudge ahead when they achieved the Dornier's altitude at last and began to overhaul the enemy, although Trousdale's engine was feeling the strain and he was obliged to pull back the throttle and then to turn for home.

The two remaining Spitfires closed in on the Dornier and opened fire at around 500 yards from port and starboard, using twenty to thirty degrees deflection, making no strikes on their first pass and receiving some highly accurate return fire. Williams and Roach reported later that this made them so angry that they both, in turn, closed in to much shorter range during their second attack. The Dornier pilot slewed and jinked for all he was worth, but the effect of fire from sixteen .303 Brownings ignited the big, twin-engined machine like a scraped match. The ball of flame dropped beneath them, and to the two pilots' astonishment, they saw that it was going to crash on enemy soil – in fact, as they identified later, on Walcheren at the mouth of the Scheldt Estuary. No one was seen to bale out.

Williams and Roach turned for home, nursing their fuel and keeping a sharp look-out for the enemy. But the sky was clear to every horizon. Fifteen thousand feet below an invisible boat trailed a wake as white as the demolished Dornier's earlier contrail. It might almost have been a pleasure boat out from Lowestoft on this peaceful summer morning. All the portents suggested another lull.

At the time when the two Spitfire pilots were recrossing the Norfolk coast, a heavily escorted pair of open Mercedes staff cars drove up the dusty straight road towards St Omer. In the first car, beaming contentment after a massive breakfast, sat Reichsmarschall Goering, resplendent in unbuttoned long leather coat which artfully failed to conceal his decorations and orders, the Iron Cross First Class and pilot's wings. Facing him were Bruno Loerzer, commander of II *Fliegerkorps*, who had travelled from his headquarters at Ghent, and Kesselring. Goering had arrived to witness personally from the nearest point on French soil the opening of the final stage of the Battle, and, as he announced over the radio, 'I have taken over personal command of the Luftwaffe in its war against England.'

Meanwhile, there was time to visit some of his aircrew before they took off, and he had chosen the Me 109 *Lehrgeschwader* based at Calais-Marck. There was nothing that Goering enjoyed more than 'mixing in with the boys' as he called it, recalling his own fighter pilot days back in 1917, joking about the relative performance of his 120 mph Fokker and these E-type 109s with their 370 mph top speed and cannon armament. How 'the boys' loved it when he attempted, with predictable non-success, to squeeze his massive frame into the slender Messerschmitt cockpit!

By 2 p.m. the two Marshals, surrounded by their staff, and on the outer fringes two dozen combination BMW motorcycles bristling with Mausers, had moved on to an elaborate picnic yards from the cliff edge at Cap Gris Nez. But for the absence of women in long summer dresses and wide hats, this repast might have been taking place in the enclosure behind the best stand at Longchamps. But instead of the thunder of hooves on turf, the sound that this party heard as they sipped their champagne was the distant rumble of aircraft engines. It grew, at first slowly and then more rapidly, to a deep roar. A sharp-eyed major was the first to spot the vanguard of the armada far to the south, and he pointed its direction to one of Goering's staff, who in turn indicated to the Reichsmarschall the multitude of crosses in the sky, in serried ranks like the World War I graves beside the road along which they had driven through Flanders.

Goering stood up from his collapsible seat, settling his binoculars on the first spearhead of the Heinkels and Dorniers which were now circling some ten miles away before forming up with the twin-engined fighter screen on each flank and, almost invisible above, the little 109s – some from the airfield they had recently inspected. As the bombers and their escort groaned deafeningly overhead, gaining altitude, to these senior officers it was as if the frustrating weeks of struggle in the air, with its distressing casualties, and the Phoenix-like reappearance of the Hurricanes and Spitfires when none should have survived, had been wiped clean. Now the real battle was about to begin – and surely nothing on earth, or in the air, could prevail against this massive destructive power. . . .

Oberleutnant Ferdy Goetz, 109 pilot of I/JG2, and hundreds more commissioned and non-commissioned officers of the Luftwaffe air-crew, shared none of this impression that the past was the past and the real battle was about to begin. For the 109 pilot Goetz, August, and July before that wicked month, had formed in his mind an indelible grey picture of tense waiting, the predictable scramble in loose formation from grass airfields, the crackle of orders on the R/T, becoming more urgent as the English coast was crossed, the everlasting search of the skies, the uneasy winking of the red light warning of low fuel, the impossibly swift arrival and the equally swift departure of enemy fighters – and crammed between the whirl of wings, the chatter of gunfire, the stench of cordite filling the cockpit, the sickening sight of oncoming tracer.

Back at Guines, it was possible to scrub oil from hands, wipe the tracing of goggles and mask from the face, and soak clean a sweat-caked body. But the notion of clearing all this from the fighting experience of weeks and weeks – sometimes three ops in a day – was as ridiculous as bringing back to the dispersal the faces of Hans Moeller or Heinz Blume and all the others who had failed to recross this damnable, untrustworthy, hateful Channel. . . .

The CHL station at Foreness, at the extreme tip of Kent, was the first with the news again. Only seconds later, a WAAF corporal in front of her tube at the Dover CH station confirmed that there was a big build-up over the Pas de Calais. At precisely 3.54 p.m. a track plotter at Bentley Priory reached forward and placed a plot on the big map table. It indicated 20+, but less than a minute later more reports came in from the coastal radar stations, and by 4.16 p.m. visuals from the Observer Corps were reaching the Maidstone centre. It was like the approach of a thunderstorm after a long, hot, summer day.

Park at 11 Group headquarters ordered eleven squadrons into the air. At Kenley, Hendon, North Weald and Northolt, the telephones rang at the dispersals and red Verys formed pretty parabolas, some of them over Hurricanes with engines already running. Trolly-ac. plugs were ripped out and raced to the next machine, blue smoke rose from the Merlin exhausts. A sergeant pilot of 43 Squadron at Tangmere taxied out standing in the cockpit, and others were still clipping their straps as they moved forward fast for take-off. Nos 253, 504, 249, 1 and 303 Squadrons were all airborne by 4.20 p.m.

A few minutes later four more 11 Group squadrons were off on patrol, the Hurricanes from 43 Squadron, John Thompson's 111 Squadron from Croydon, 79 Squadron's Hurricanes from Biggin Hill and 501 from Gravesend. Soon the Duxford Wing and other 12 Group squadrons were ordered to scramble.

Goering and his staff may have seen the greatest air armada ever launched as a single mass of aircraft, but within minutes the *Gruppen* were breaking up and reforming in an immensely complex pattern of separate strikes, each with its unprecedentedly numerous fighter escort, and embarking in stately drill formation over the Channel at different times and from different directions, crossing in anywhere from Beachy Head to Essex. All this elaboration was intended to confuse the 11 Group warning systems, both radar and visual, and the move worked as well as intended:

Throughout the operation enemy tracks were disappearing and reappearing with disconcerting frequency; and to the extent that this narrative is incoherent it only reflects the situation as it appeared to those who were controlling the defence at the time.[1]

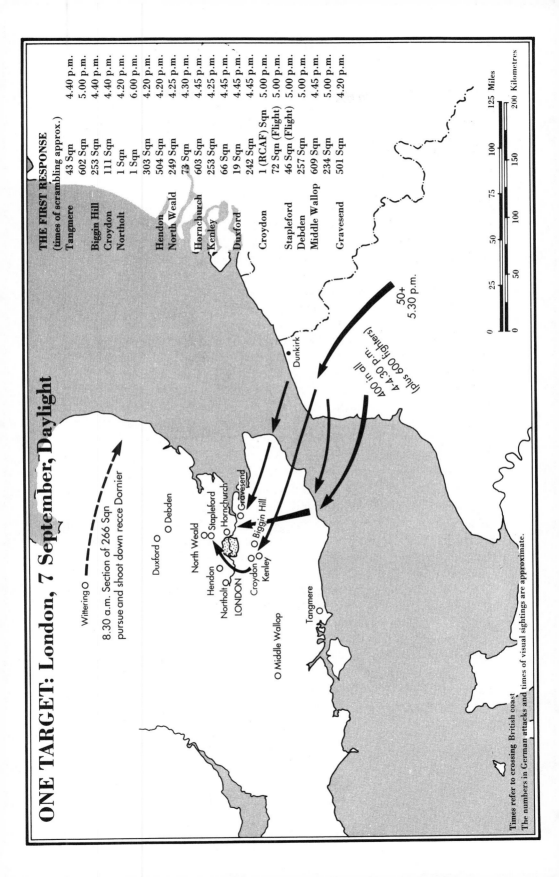

# ONE TARGET: London, 7 September, Daylight

**THE FIRST RESPONSE**
(times of scrambling approx.)

| | | |
|---|---|---|
| **Tangmere** | 43 Sqn | 4.40 p.m. |
| | 602 Sqn | 5.00 p.m. |
| **Biggin Hill** | 253 Sqn | 4.40 p.m. |
| **Croydon** | 111 Sqn | 4.40 p.m. |
| **Northolt** | 1 Sqn | 4.20 p.m. |
| | 1 Sqn | 6.00 p.m. |
| | 303 Sqn | 4.20 p.m. |
| **Hendon** | 504 Sqn | 4.20 p.m. |
| **North Weald** | 249 Sqn | 4.25 p.m. |
| | 73 Sqn | 4.30 p.m. |
| **Hornchurch** | 603 Sqn | 4.45 p.m. |
| **Kenley** | 253 Sqn | 4.25 p.m. |
| | 66 Sqn | 4.45 p.m. |
| **Duxford** | 19 Sqn | 4.45 p.m. |
| | 242 Sqn | 4.45 p.m. |
| **Croydon** | 1 (RCAF) Sqn | 5.00 p.m. |
| | 72 Sqn (Flight) | 5.00 p.m. |
| **Stapleford** | 46 Sqn (Flight) | 5.00 p.m. |
| **Debden** | 257 Sqn | 5.00 p.m. |
| **Middle Wallop** | 609 Sqn | 4.45 p.m. |
| | 234 Sqn | 5.00 p.m. |
| **Gravesend** | 501 Sqn | 4.20 p.m. |

Witering O - - -

8.30 a.m. Section of 266 Sqn
pursue and shoot down recce Dornier

Duxford O          O Debden

North Weald

Stapleford

Hendon          Hornchurch

Northolt O      O Gravesend

LONDON      Biggin Hill

Croydon O  O

Kenley

O Middle Wallop

Tangmere O

Dunkirk ●

400 in all
4.4.30 p.m.
(plus 600 fighters)

50+
5.30 p.m.

Times refer to crossing British coast
The numbers in German attacks and times of visual sightings are approximate.

| 0 | 25 | 50 | 75 | 100 | 125 Miles |
|---|---|---|---|---|---|
| 0 | 50 | 100 | 150 | 200 Kilometres | |

Although 11 Group pilots were puzzled that so much time elapsed before they even sighted any enemy aircraft, this did allow some scrambled squadrons to gain the required height – and, after finding themselves so often below the enemy when contact was made, this altitude was nearly always more than the controller had ordered.

But as the hands of the ops-room clocks moved on minute by minute, the controllers themselves, observing the ever increasing number of plots on the table, and the numerous variations in their direction, like typhoon wind arrows on a weather map, knew that they were facing their most testing hour. As the first contacts were made, the squadron commanders and their pilots were feeling the same way. 'I'd never seen so many aircraft,' wrote Squadron Leader Sandy Johnstone★ of 602 Squadron. 'It was a hazy sort of day to about 16,000 feet. As we broke through the haze, you could hardly believe it. As far as you could see, there was nothing but German aircraft coming in, wave after wave.'[2]

Flight Lieutenant James McArthur of 609 Squadron reported that, 'Whilst on patrol at 10,000 feet between Brooklands and Windsor, we saw about 200 enemy aircraft surrounded by AA fire. We climbed towards them and I led the squadron into a quarter attack. . . .'[3] Another pilot, commenting on the sight of a bomber formation which he estimated as twenty miles long, with an escort of fighters above, said simply, 'It was a breathtaking sight. You couldn't help feeling you'd never again see anything as remarkable as that.'[4]

Many of the defending squadrons had been ordered to patrol above the airfields. Day after day these had been the primary target for high-level, low-level, glide- and dive-bombing attacks, and no one airborne that afternoon made any other target assumption. The sector controllers, too, felt no reason to believe that the Luftwaffe's strategy had made a sudden and dramatic departure from the pattern prevailing for a full month.

The precise moment of truth can only be estimated, but it was probably a few minutes after 5 p.m. on this Saturday afternoon when some of the pilots most closely in touch, the sector commanders and Park himself realised that this was no ordinary series of raids. It was not just in size that the assault was unique, but in objective. It became suddenly evident that the bombing had come to London, and London was the sole target.

As the Medway guns opened fire, the Hurricanes of 501 and 249 Squadrons, outnumbered as usual by more than ten to one, hurled

★Later Air Vice-Marshal A. V. R. Johnstone CB, DFC, AE.

258

themselves at the bombers, and, as usual, within seconds were in combat with the escort as well.

The formations of Heinkels and Dorniers shuddered at the impact, like the three-deckers of the Dutch wars receiving a full broadside. But the bombing run was scarcely disturbed, and the 250 and 500 kg bombs fell with great accuracy on the Woolwich arsenal, and Harland and Wolff's works. It was only the first of many waves.

By chance – or mischance – Park had chosen this afternoon to visit Dowding at Bentley Priory. There is little likelihood that the redeployment of squadrons would have been any swifter if he had been at the Uxbridge ops room, for his subordinates were skilful and experienced. But it was galling for the Air Marshal to be in the Fighter Command ops room with his superior at this critical time, without the executive power to which he was accustomed.

But Park, with Dowding at his side, saw in miniature replica from the raised dais above the plotting table this first wave turning north over east London, and then assuming an easterly course out towards the North Sea.

This was the danger time for the bombers, the difficult withdrawal, with all 11 and 12 Groups alerted and the 109s gone home for lack of fuel. The rearguard was already being attacked by 603 Squadron and the Hendon squadrons, 1 and 303 (Polish), being in the ideal position to open hostilities, with superior height and the sun behind them. The formations had already been partly broken up by anti-aircraft fire, according to pilots' reports, and 303 tore into them with all their fearlessness and ferocity. Within a few minutes they had claimed eleven destroyed.

The three squadrons – 19, 66 and 242 – which became known under Douglas Bader's leadership as the Duxford Wing, and 73 Squadron from North Weald, picked up the bombers after this mauling, as the enemy turned south for home. In the fierce fighting that followed, much of it with the 110 escort, eighteen more of the enemy were claimed. Last to join in, before the survivors of this first wave streaked across the Kent countryside, was 73 Squadron.

Combats as satisfactory in outcome as these [though the figures were greatly exaggerated] cannot be ignored. But the fact remains not only that they were with enemy formations which had dropped their bombs, but that bomb-carrying formations were bombing London or approaching to bomb it while one-third of the fighter forces were thus engaged.[5]

Now, with the implacability of storm rollers breaking on a beach, successive following waves of between twenty and sixty bombers were boring north at around 20,000 feet, swarms of 109s above each. And there could no longer be any doubt of their destination.

Flying Officer George Barclay (of the banking family), aged twenty, took off in his Hurricane with the rest of B Flight 249 Squadron from North Weald. They had been ordered to patrol Maidstone at 15,000 feet, and they were there at the right time at the right place. The squadron had just been equipped with new VHF radios, and to Barclay's fury his had not worked. It was OK now though, and he heard the controller calling, 'Hullo, Ganer leader. Hullo Ganer leader, bandits on your right – over.'

'We turned towards them. I turned the gun-button to "fire" and looked to see that the reflector sight was working OK. I opened the hood, and immediately I could see fifty per cent better, though it was fifty per cent colder. I saw that the rapidly closing bombers were surrounded by black dots, which I knew to be Me 109s. So we were in for it this time!'[6]

In the fight that followed the Dornier bombers suffered casualties, but Barclay became separated from the rest of his squadron. 'As I broke off I turned and two yellow Me 109s shot past beneath me. I turned back and fired at the nearest – no result. Had a burst at the farthest and immediately there was a puff of black smoke, a brilliant flame and down he went, slowly turning over on his back. The whole hood and perspex flew off and the fuselage began to disintegrate. . . .'

Seconds later Barclay was hit and his engine went 'dead as a gatepost'. He crash-landed in a field only four miles from North Weald and got back in an army lorry just after the last of his squadron – what was left of it – landed. Only seven out of twelve made it back.

Of the German commanders in that Saturday afternoon battle Oberst Johannes Fink was by far the oldest at forty-eight years. He was quite fearless, uniquely experienced, deeply religious and loved by his men, even if his stock injunction before every operation was, 'You must make your wills.'[7] He led *Kampfgeschwader* 2 over the English coast at 5.30 p.m. at 12,000 feet. The leader of II *Gruppe*, Paul Weitkus, reported that, 'Right from the French coast, on the way in, we could see the vast columns of smoke from the burning oil tanks.' These were the Thameshaven tanks, bombed the previous day, burning more fiercely than ever now after further bombing.

The first fighter attacks, scattered and perfunctory, occurred soon after they crossed the English coast, and continued north towards the North Downs and the silver-grey smudge of the balloon barrages ahead. The escort had no trouble in dealing with these fighters, and the Dornier crews claimed they saw several of the enemy go down. Then, over Sevenoaks, the 109s, which had been extravagant with their fuel in combat, turned back for the Pas de Calais and Fink's *Kampfgeschwader* continued alone towards London's docklands.

Weitkus took his *Gruppe* over the India Docks, which they bombed in unison on his bomb-aimer's signal. With his own Leica, fitted with telephoto lens, the leader took some photographs to prove his claim. *Kampfgeschwader* 2 then

turned away *Gruppe* by *Gruppe*, not much bothered by the AA fire. When occasionally, a stray shell splinter thumped against the belly of a bomber, the crew yelled, 'Come in!' Weitkus could make out the gun positions around London – the battery positions, that is, not the individual guns. Then, with bombs gone and streaking for home, they met the first furious attacks by full fighter squadrons – the defenders had reacted in strength at last.[8]

The wills of only four of Fink's men – the crew of a single Dornier – were resorted to that evening. Another of his Dorniers was damaged and two of the crew wounded. But that was all. It had been a successful day. Only thirteen bombers in all in that giant armada, which Goering waved off after lunch, had failed to return or crashed fatally on French soil. The Reichsmarschall was, for once, thoroughly satisfied when he heard of the devastation and immense fires raging in London. Later he telegraphed his wife to tell her a great victory was imminent. 'The English have had enough!'

The 109s had done their work valiantly, and Goering had reason to be pleased with them, too. But they had paid a heavy price. Among the dead was Ferdy Goetz. His 109 was seen losing height in a long glide, trailing smoke, over the Weald of Kent. He may already have been dead when a group of soldiers near Elham got the fighter within range and hastened its end with their .303 Lee-Enfields. It crashed in the grounds of St Radegund's Abbey.

At Tunbridge Wells station at about the same time Harold Nicolson was changing trains when he saw two captured airmen

handcuffed together and guarded by three soldiers with fixed bayonets. They shuffle along sadly, one being without his boots, shuffling in thick grey socks. One of them just looks broken down and saturnine; the other has a superior half-smile on his face, as if thinking 'My Fuehrer will pay them out for this.' The people on the platform are extraordinarily decent. They just glance at them and then turn their heads away, not wishing to stare. . . .'[9]

The effect of the bombing on London's East End and dockland was devastating. Street after street of slumland property collapsed with scarcely a house escaping in some terraces. There were bombs elsewhere too, but (as it was to be over the next months) it was the poor who took by far the worst beating. Nearly 450 people were blown up or killed in the wreckage, and many more were injured. Smoke from burning warehouses and ships filled the sky, blotting out the sun.

London, the first city to be subjected to all-out air attack yet remain unsubdued, paid the first instalment of a terrible toll on that hot September afternoon. Fate struck with cruel inconsistency. Some citizens had remarkable escapes when their houses collapsed about their ears; others fell dead in the street from a piece of falling shrapnel. It was the same in the air above. How else could that brilliant and seasoned campaigner, Caesar Hull, have been struck out of the sky by 109s over the Thames Estuary? Or Dick Reynell, who as Hawker's test pilot knew more about the Hurricane even than Caesar? James McArthur's 609 Squadron flew all the way from Middle Wallop to catch the German bomber stream, knocking down two Dorniers and (much more difficult) two 110s and a 109, without injury or damage to themselves. One squadron claimed ten 'kills' over Essex at the cost of four Hurricanes, all the pilots surviving.

The people of London now, as well as the people of Sussex and Surrey, Essex and Kent, who had looked up into the clear late afternoon sky on that day, had watched the careless tracing of fine lines that broke unpredictably into circles – the one marking pursuit, the second tight and desperate combat. The sound of the machine-gun fire had been like the continuous distant ripping of calico, broken by the more deliberate and deadlier thud-thud of German cannon fire.

Much of the fighting had been above 15,000 feet and with the naked eye the fighters were scarcely visible; it was only when a Hurricane or Messerschmitt came spiralling or plunging down, sometimes in a funeral pyre of smoke and flame, that the material evidence of battle presented itself.

George Barclay's squadron had lost yet another Hurricane on a second op., and at the end of the day he recorded, 'The odds today have been unbelievable and we are all really shaken!'[10]

★ ★ ★

Less than two hours elapsed between the landing of the survivors of Barclay's squadron, and others in 11 and 12 Groups, and the approach from the south of the first night raiders. It was certainly not a long enough interval to allow the fire services, striving to get under control the gigantic fires among the warehouses and ships of dockland, to complete their work. In fact, darkness had not yet set in when the Heinkels with their characteristic unsynchronised throb crossed the coast just west of Beachy Head at 8.22 p.m. at 15,000 feet. Unescorted as they were, they would have been ripe game for fighter attack, but for some inexplicable reason the only single-engined fighters that were scrambled were two Hurricanes from 213 Squadron at Tangmere, which simply patrolled their sector station and did not attempt to intercept.

As the stream of bombers, almost entirely from Sperrle's *Luftflotte* 3, became more numerous, two Blenheims took off from Martlesham, and a Blenheim and Beaufighter from the Fighter Interception Unit also patrolled. 'Numerous AI contacts were obtained,' they reported, 'but constant interference from undirected AA fire and searchlights prevented success.' Meanwhile, at Hornchurch, ironically, the drifting smoke from the docks, which the night fighters were supposed to prevent spreading, was so thick that 600 Squadron's Blenheims could not get off the ground.

As for the guns, many of these had been redeployed for airfield and aircraft factory defence, and the 120 guns in the Thames and Medway area could not engage because the bulk of the bombers operated too far to the west. However, the relatively few guns available, all within the Inner Artillery Zone, fired away between 9.05 p.m. and 3 a.m. It was not much comfort for the people of London to learn the next day that one bomber had been brought down, when they recalled that what seemed to be many hundreds had made their life hell until the early hours. This night's work, then, for the German aircrews was what their enemy called 'a piece of cake'. More than ninety per cent of their bombs – about 333 tons of high explosive and 13,000 incendiaries – had landed in the built-up London area.

London was to suffer worse nights than this, but for a population poised for so long in expectation of catastrophe of Wellsian proportions, it came as a savage shock. The night bombing had not been so limited to the docks and East End as the day attacks, and all over the centre of London fires raged, roads were blocked, three main line railway stations put out of action entirely while sixteen more stations were hit

# The Daily Telegraph
### and Morning Post

No. 26,803    LONDON, MONDAY, SEPTEMBER 9, 1940    LONDON LATE EDTN.    BROADCASTING—Page Two    ONE PENNY

## AIR ATTACK ON LONDON RENEWED LAST NIGHT

**1,374 NAZIS DOWN IN FIRST MONTH**

### PERSONAL DIRECTION BY GOERING

### DOCK TARGETS MISSED IN FIRST BIG RAID

#### HOUSES HIT : MANY FIRES : 1,700 KILLED AND INJURED

*IN THE TRAIL OF THE NAZI BOMBERS*

A scene of desolation in a London area on which German airmen rained explosive and incendiary bombs during Saturday's raid.

### "BRITISH PEOPLE CAN HOLD OUT TO THE END"

*FROM OUR OWN CORRESPONDENT*
NEW YORK, Sunday.

## R.A.F. COUNTER THREAT OF INVASION

### BOMBS RAINED ON CHANNEL PORTS FOR HOURS

**LOSS OF FOOD STOCKS SMALL**

**RATIONING WILL NOT BE AFFECTED**

---

and damaged. The Rotherhithe tunnel had been blocked, like countless streets in the West End as well as the City and the East, where the entire surviving population of Silvertown, surrounded by raging infernos, had to be evacuated by water.

Ivan Maisky, the ambassador representing the Soviet Union, for the present Germany's inactive ally, had as alarming a night as everyone else. 'Exactly at 9 p.m.', he noted, 'there began high in the darkened sky a kind of strange and unaccustomed roar. It seemed as though a multitude of enormous birds was circling in the sky, each of them giving out a protracted howling and piercing sound. At once it was frightening and revolting. Then dull blows could be heard. We went up to the top floor of the Embassy building, and saw from there how there were, shooting up in various places, high tongues of flame.'[11] In a few months' time, the cities of his own country would be experiencing worse ordeals than this.

At the time there were very few who believed that the ordeal of the airfields had ended, that the day and night bombing of London when the defences were so gravely worn down marked a radical and permanent change of strategy by the Luftwaffe. For the Luftwaffe, and the citizens of London (especially the working people in the East End), 7 September appeared to be a day and night of German success. For Dowding and Park it was a day of immense relief and growing conviction that Fighter Command would prevail.

Meanwhile, events connected with the threatened invasion now appeared to be approaching their expected climax. At the end of August the barges, steamers, tugs, trawlers and motor-boats which the Germans had been requisitioning since 19 July had begun to move along inland and coastal waters towards the invasion ports. Until then the British Combined Intelligence Committee had seen no sign that the German preparations were well advanced and had thought an attack on the east coast more likely than one across the Channel. But from 31 August Hudsons and the high-flying Spitfires of Coastal Command's Photographic Reconnaissance Unit had picked up a sudden increase in activity along the Dutch canals and coast. Daily the RAF cameras had recorded the growing concentrations: no barges in Ostend on 28 August, 18 on 31 August, 70 on 2 September, 115 on 5 September, 205 on 6 September. At Flushing, Dunkirk and Calais it had been much the same story. Its implications were reinforced by photographs of new gun emplacements and dive-bomber concentrations in the Pas de Calais and by Enigma intercepts indicating reinforcements of Kesselring's bombers. The threat from across the Channel, for weeks feared but uncertain, was suddenly all too real.

On 5 September Bomber Command made its first major attack on the invasion ports. The following day all RAF units were placed under Alert No. 2 – 'Attack probable within the next three days'. Twenty-four hours later, on that fateful Saturday afternoon of 7 September, the Chiefs of Staff met in Downing Street. General Brooke, keeping a diary for the benefit of his wife – a practice which, if known, would have horrified his colleagues – wrote at the end of the day: 'All reports look like invasion getting nearer. Ships collecting, dive-bombers being concentrated, parachutists captured. . . .'[12]

In the light of all the indications, the Chiefs of Staff, meeting just as the first German bombs crashed down on Woolwich, decided that the possibility of invasion had become imminent and that the defences should stand by at immediate notice. The Navy and the RAF were already at sufficient readiness, but the Army movements needed eight hours' notice. That evening, at 8.07 p.m. Home Forces headquarters issued to Southern Command, Eastern Command, the London region and two corps in GHQ reserve the code-word 'Cromwell' – all troops to battle stations.

It was a night to remember in the countryside, as well as in bomb-torn London. There was uncertainty as to the full implications of the code-word, and whether it should be acted upon forthwith. In the prevailing tension a few bridges were blown, and the Home Guard, not meant to be generally involved, was in some places called out by the ringing of church bells – the signal reserved for invasion or at least a large parachute landing. Confusion abounded. But, according to Churchill later, the night's work 'served as a useful tonic and rehearsal for all concerned'.[13]

# 18

'*Ominous Quiet!*'*

## 8–14 SEPTEMBER

Even after the news spread among Fighter Command squadrons
of the fearful bombing of London on the night after the first great
day battles over the capital, most pilots registered in their minds
only an intensification of the Battle as a preliminary to invasion. At a
higher level of command the switch in German tactics was seen as the
possible salvation of 11 Group. It also caused a certain amount of
bewilderment. There had been plenty of evidence over past weeks that
enemy intelligence was weak and ill-informed, so the failure to recognise how close to breakdown the command and communications
structures of 11 Group had become might account for the folly of not
giving it the coup de grâce.

Clearly, the invasion threat remained real. But why bomb London as
a preliminary? There was little military advantage in setting fire to a lot
of warehouses and killing a few thousand civilians. On the other hand,
the invasion of Poland and of Holland had been accompanied by
intimidating attacks on Warsaw and Rotterdam, presumably to cow
the population. Did Goering really believe that a few thousand tons of
bombs on the capital would lead the British to succumb to the threat of
invasion? Yet early morning recce flights on 8 September showed no
sign of an invasion fleet sailing. It was all very puzzling.

*General Sir Alan Brooke, C-in-C Home Forces.

Meanwhile, the relative quiet over the south-east after the tumult of the past twenty-four hours led Dowding to relieve two of his hardest pressed squadrons. No. 43, which had lost its exceptional and much loved CO, Caesar Hull, and a flight commander the previous day, was pulled out and sent north – what was left of its pilots and aircraft. And John Thompson's 111, already extracted from the heat of Croydon to Martlesham, was now sent far north to Drem with its remaining seven Hurricanes, when they were fit to fly.

In their place, Dowding brought in 92 Squadron's Spitfires from South Wales, where life had not been as quiet as it might seem.

There was little daylight activity, but as night fell the people of London, whose lives had been greatly disrupted and sleep disturbed the previous night, heard again the ominous murmur of bombers as an accompaniment to the chorus of howling air-raid sirens. For the next week, the average number of bombers attacking London at night was 200, with supplementary raids on provincial cities. On this second night of the London 'blitz' (as the victims called it), with fifty-seven more consecutive nights to come, over 400 citizens were killed and some 750 injured, not a great number relative to later bombing on both sides, but worth noting by the anti-Bomber Command historians of today who perhaps have not heard of Macaulay's dictum that 'the essence of war is violence'.

Besides destroying civil property, the bombing did unexpectedly heavy damage to railway lines and stations. The Combined Intelligence Committee commented on this:

The selection of targets for attack was evidence of a thorough and carefully thought-out plan. There is insufficient evidence, however, to show whether it was designed for its nuisance value by the disruption of passenger traffic and of the transit of goods for industrial purposes, or whether it was definitely intended as a prelude to invasion.[1]

There was never any difficulty for the German bomber crews in finding London even on the darkest of nights, unless the cloud was 10/10ths: its proximity and the estuary of the Thames, pointing to its heart, were quite sufficient. It was a different problem with the provincial cities and towns and specific isolated industrial targets. For these targets, the Luftwaffe relied heavily on *Knickebein*, the intersecting-beam navigational aid first found on that shot-down He 111 the previous year. Knowledge of this dangerous navigational aid had since been enhanced by a combination of Enigma intercepts, 'bugged' conversations of German prisoners and information from more German bombers which had crashed on British soil.

British counter-measures, devised by Dr R. V. Jones and others, were installed rapidly after June 1940 in the form of listening posts and jamming apparatus which distorted or blotted out the *Knickebein* signal. By these means the accuracy of *Knickebein*-aided bombing, which had been roughly within a square mile of the target, was more or less destroyed.

In addition, within two or three days, the gun strength of the Inner Artillery Zone round London was more than doubled, partly at the expense of the airfields to which the guns had only recently been despatched.

Although no official orders had been given, there was much informal and competitive talk among *Kampfgeschwader* air crews about destroying Buckingham Palace, and at least three attacks were made in daylight. Of the second of these, on 11 September, the King wrote in his diary:

We went to London & found an Air Raid in progress. . . . The day was very cloudy & it was raining hard. We were both upstairs with Alec Hardinge talking in my little sitting room overlooking the quadrangle; (I cannot use my ordinary one owing to the broken windows). All of a sudden we heard an aircraft making a zooming noise above us, saw 2 bombs falling past the opposite side of the Palace, & then heard 2 resounding crashes as the bombs fell in the quadrangle about 30 yards away. We looked at each other, & then we were out into the passage as fast as we could get there. The whole thing happened in a matter of seconds. We all wondered why we weren't dead . . . 6 bombs had been dropped. The aircraft was seen coming straight down the Mall below the clouds having dived through the clouds. . . . There is no doubt it was a direct attack on Buckingham Palace. . . .[2]

These individual bombing attacks, which hurt no one and did less damage than the numerous photographs suggested, were a blessing to the King and Queen, and provided a great lift to the morale of Londoners – 'a bond forged between the King and his people', as George VI's biographer wrote. 'Now', remarked the Queen, in relief, 'we can look the people of the East End in the face.'

But generally the cloudy weather, which did not trouble the night bombers, was the cause of a reduction in the number and strength of daylight raids during this period. On the other hand, when they did cross the coast, it was very much more difficult to keep track of them by contrast with those blue days of August and early September. The Observer Corps did their best, but it was hardly possible for them to follow the flight path of, say, 100+ Me 109s flying at well above 20,000 feet and separated from the earth by several cloud layers.

One of the most successful daylight bombing raids of this week was carried out on 10 September not by any of Kesselring's *Kampfgeschwader* but by Bomber Command Blenheims on the Luftwaffe base at Eindhoven in Holland when nine He 111s were destroyed, more than were shot down by AA Command in a week at this time.

After 9 September, when 200 German bombers attempted unsuccessfully to attack London and the enemy lost twenty-eight aircraft, the busiest, and bloodiest, day during this period was 11 September. After a series of feint attacks designed to draw up 11 Group's fighter squadrons, two formations of 50+ and 100+ respectively were picked up by Dover CH at around 3.20 p.m. Seven squadrons were at first scrambled and then nine more, including the Duxford Wing, at around 3.45 p.m.

As on 7 September, the German fighter escort was extremely heavy, and none of the defending squadrons could make much impact on the usual tight vic formations of Heinkels and Dorniers which thundered north across Kent at the unusual height of up to 24,000 feet. There was very heavy fighting between the single-engined fighters, with many casualties, until the Me 109s had to duck away back home, red lights flickering on the instrument panel like urgent Morse code signals.

Once the 109s were out of the way it was a different story. About half the bombers had dropped their loads over the City and dock areas of London when they became vulnerable. KG26 fared worst. This *Geschwader* had been involved in the raid on the north-east on 15 August, flying from Stavanger in Norway, and had suffered heavily then. Now they were operating under Kesselring, and several of their senior officers died this afternoon, among them Hauptmann Kuenstler, leader of 1 *Staffel*, and his crew, who were shot down over Horsham by Sergeant Pilot Brzozowski of 303 (Polish) Squadron. (He got another He 111 later.) Sergeant Pilot Ted Scott of 222 Squadron was responsible for the destruction of another KG26 Heinkel over Hornchurch, killing Oberleutnant Abenhausen and all his crew. Four more of this *Geschwader* crashed near London or into the sea, and many more aircrew were killed or wounded in eleven more seriously damaged 111s.

To set against these and many more Fighter Command successes were some savage losses, including five Spitfires of 92 Squadron alone.

The filter room, RAF Fighter Command, Bentley Priory.

Defences, active and passive: Bofors light anti-aircraft gun and crew; and balloons over London, with Buckingham Palace and the Victoria Monument in the foreground.

Observer Corps post.

Precursor to radar: sound locators for the guns, inspected here by King George VI on 14 August 1940.

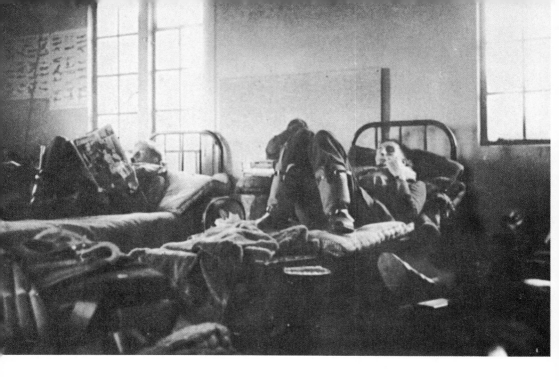

Pilots relax; *from left:* Will E. Gore and Mike Irving of A Flight
607 Squadron at Tangmere; and (*below*) 610 Squadron pilots at
Biggin Hill.

Ground crews: bombing-up in France (*left*) and refuelling in England (*below*). The bomber is an He 111, the fighter a Hurricane (recently in action judging from the punctured gun patches, which led to an involuntary warning whistle for the armourers when the plane was on its final approach).

Sergeant Elizabeth Mortimer, Corporal Elspeth Henderson and Sergeant Emily Turner, switchboard operators who remained at their post even when their building received a direct hit, and were each awarded a Military Medal. The switchboard building behind them is still in ruins months later, and Corporal Henderson has been commissioned.

'Near miss' between attacking Spitfire and He 111.

Me 110 under attack.

Bombs away!' – from a Heinkel.

Crew away – from a ditched Me 110.

Village 'square-bashing'.
Home Guard prepare
for the invasion, as
viewed in a painting by
Edward Ardizzone.

Home Guard on
duty over a
wrecked Dornier.

Aircraft salvage dump (painting by Frances Macdonald).

Wednesday 11 September was one of the very few days in the Battle when Fighter Command's losses were greater than the Luftwaffe's.

At 4.20 p.m. Pilot Officer Carver of 229 Squadron, Northolt, was shot down by a 109. His Hurricane caught fire and he baled out, badly burned about the face and wrists. Ken Carver, who was awarded the DFC, was only one of dozens of pilots who suffered burns injuries, the most dreaded of all. Many of these sufferers were treated at the Maxillo-Facial Unit of the Queen Victoria Hospital, East Grinstead. Here Archibald McIndoe treated Richard Hillary, the surgeon and patient who between them made this work known to the world. Another notable patient was Tom Gleave, CO of 253 Squadron and later a pillar of the Battle of Britain Fighter Association.

After dealing successfully with four 109s on one sortie, Gleave himself had been shot down on 31 August: 'I heard a metallic click above the roar of my engine . . . a sudden burst of heat struck my face, and I looked down into the cockpit. A long spout of flame was issuing from the hollow starboard wing root. . . . I had some crazy notion that if I rocked the aircraft and skidded, losing speed, the fire might go out. Not a bit of it; the flames increased until the cockpit was like the centre of a blow-lamp nozzle. There was nothing to do but bale out.'[3]

Stunned by the shock, Gleave was not conscious of the agonising pain until, after his landing, he was in an open car being driven rapidly to hospital. Later there was an injection of morphia, his burns were covered with damp gauze, and then he was on another journey, this time, the first of so many, to the operating theatre on a trolley. He later wrote: 'From that moment I started to accumulate a debt that mounted daily, and still mounts; a debt I can never repay, against which human thanks seem utterly inadequate. Every time I see a nurse or a doctor now I feel a hidden sense of humility, prompted not only by the ceaseless care and attention I received and still receive from them, but also what I saw them do for others far worse than myself, all but dead casualties who have become living miracles.'[4]

A WAAF stenographer, Olive Noble, also recalled the tender care and patience that was needed to help aircrew to recover in these Burns Units. At her hospital, ' "the first of the few" aircrew were put together again after being injured and burnt escaping from their burning aircraft. I typed up the case reports and worked with the doctors and nursing sisters. These reports sometimes made gruesome reading. In my spare time off duty I used to read to the airmen who had been blinded and whose morale was pretty low. All of them were encased in plaster, from head to toe in some cases. The surgeons did remarkable work in skin-grafting, and I was very privileged to be able to work alongside them. . . .'

Further tactical developments of some significance occurred on both sides during this period. Once the Luftwaffe's main attention had turned to targets well inland and there was more time to intercept, Park had decreed that squadrons should as far as possible work in pairs. His order to this effect went out on 5 September. This was a sensible decision, giving a greater impact to every attack.

For his part, Kesselring offered the first intimation not only that this tactic was working, but that Fighter Command remained rather stronger than the tattered remnants of a defeated defence as had earlier been imagined: 'In the event of formation leaders meeting heavy opposition they are now permitted to disengage,' ran the German High Command instruction.

A marked deterioration in the weather on 12 and 13 September gave the defences a respite from large-scale attacks, but on both days the Germans took advantage of the cloudy conditions to send single aircraft deeper into the country than was usual in daytime. Air Ministry buildings at Harrogate, an aluminium works at Banbury and the railway junction at Reading were attacked by single aircraft on the 12th, and at the last two places railway traffic was affected. On the 13th there was rather more of the same sort of activity, commencing with the first incidents to be reported from Ulster.[5]

The weather was not much better on 14 September, but Kesselring sent over some Ju 88s from KG1 and some twenty Heinkels, which hovered about the southern suburbs of London and dropped their bombs haphazardly over the flimsy semis, killing fifty people. Others flew over the coastal resorts of Eastbourne and Brighton, killing or seriously injuring sixty more civilians, belying any further ridiculous claims by Joseph Goebbels, Hitler's propaganda machine, that the Luftwaffe attacked only military targets.

And so this week of mixed fortunes for both sides drew to an uncertain conclusion; and at his usual late hour, General Sir Alan Brooke wrote in his diary: 'Ominous quiet. . . . Have Germans completed their preparations for invasion? Are they giving their air force a last brush and wash up? Will he start tomorrow, or is it all a bluff . . . ?'[6]

He could not know, despite all the information derived from

'Sigint',* reconnaissance and agents, that on 3 September the Germans had moved back their earliest possible invasion date from 15 to 21 September, with a firm decision to be taken ten days beforehand.[7] Nor could he know that when 11 September came, Hitler had deferred the decision for three days, and that on 14 September he had postponed it for a further three.[8] The Luftwaffe, it seemed to the German Service chiefs, was near its goal but still not near enough. Fighter Command was weakening, but the British bombers and minelayers were proving increasingly disruptive. Everything would now depend on the success of the final hammer blows about to be delivered.

*Signals intelligence, including the 'Ultra'-secret information derived from breaking the top-grade German codes.

# 19

'The odds were great; our margins
small; the stakes infinite'*

## 15 SEPTEMBER

I t was his sense of history, and genius for timing, that led the Prime
Minister to visit 11 Group headquarters on this day. Waterloo had
been fought on a Sunday, and much of the heaviest fighting in this
battle had been waged on Sundays. Besides, 'the weather on this day
seemed suitable to the enemy,' he wrote.[1] So the car was called early to
the front door of Chequers, and Churchill and his wife stepped into the
back.

By the middle of September, the confidence and combat power of
Fighter Command, which had been under such stress during the last
days of August and first days of September, had been re-established.
Pilots and ground crew were like a patient who has fought his way
through a near-mortal illness, and to his immense relief and delight has
survived, partly because, when there was time to think about it, he was
convinced he would do so.

The ruins that were 11 Group's airfields told of the desperate nature
of the fight, and the halt in the bombing of their bases reinforced their
sense of satisfaction. Their equipment was on the top line, there was
now no longer any threat of shortage of planes, or of De Wilde

*Winston Churchill on this day.

ammunition, and many of the new pilots had had time to prepare themselves for combat. All were ready and eager for the continuation of the fight.

Across the Channel a different spirit reigned. For well over two months the aircrews of *Luftflotten* 2 and 3 had been told that victory was just around the corner – just one last great effort! *Adlerangriff* seemed as distant in time as the French campaign of May, but what a different outcome! Galland himself later wrote:

Failure to achieve any notable success, constantly changing orders betraying lack of purpose and obvious misjudgment of the situation by the Command, and unjustified accusation had a most demoralising effect on us fighter pilots, who were already overtaxed by physical and mental strain.[2]

The weather was so brilliant and clear, the barometer so high, that a child could predict a fine day, but the Luftwaffe dutifully sent out its pre-dawn Heinkels on weather reconnaissance. One of these was picked up by Denis David (in his pyjamas) and Trevor Jay of 87 Squadron, who shot the machine into the sea before even having a cup of tea, killing one senior and two junior officers and an airman.

In spite of the weeks of combat, Kesselring still did not understand the efficiency of the RAF's warning system, and especially the clear, early picture of events as they developed provided by the CH and CHL stations. Once again Uxbridge was given pricelessly valuable warning of events over the Pas de Calais, and by 11.00 a.m. it was obvious that a massive attack was threatening.

It was a further half hour, however, before the first enemy forces crossed the coast of Kent; and the success that our squadrons later enjoyed was not least due to the unusually long interval between the first warning of attack and the enemy's advance. The controller at No. 11 Group not only had sufficient time to couple ten squadrons into wings, he was able to bring in reinforcements from the adjacent Groups before the first German force crossed the coast: in particular the Duxford Wing was airborne at 11.25 a.m. whereas the enemy did not cross until 11.35.[3]

In turn during this tense late morning, the airfields in all three southern Groups thundered to the sound of Merlins, and more fighters were airborne before noon than at any time in the Battle: the Biggin Hill squadrons at 11.05, Northolt ten minutes later, Kenley, Hendon, Hornchurch and Middle Wallop at 11.20 and the Duxford boys five minutes after that. Five more squadrons joined them before 11.45 a.m. Their patrol altitudes varied from 15,000 to 25,000 feet, and, confirmed in this impression by the cool voice of the controllers, the pilots of all these twenty-one squadrons knew that this was going to be a big day.

Most of this first big *Luftflotte* 2 formation was from III/KG76 at Beauvais and Cormeilles led by Oberstleutnant Stefan Froelich, with the usual screen of JG3 109s above and on each beam, yellow noses glinting in the sun. Among the pilots was a rarity indeed, a survivor of the Fokker war of 1917–18, who had been appointed official historian to the Luftwaffe and thought he had better see the action himself. He was Professor Hassel von Wedel.

The Herr Professor witnessed early combat from the cockpit of his Me 109 (which was just three times faster than his Fokker straight and level), for twenty Spitfires from Biggin Hill greeted the raid as it crossed the coast and continued to harass the fighters until the first wave of 253 and 504 Squadrons' Hurricanes came in to deal with the bombers. They did this in an unusual way, head-on in a shallow climb, claiming three of them, and later two 109s.

Others joined in, and in such numbers and with such aggression that it was like gulls mobbing an albatross. Seven more Dorniers were claimed as destroyed before the Duxford Wing, in all its multiple glory, hurled itself into the whirling mêlée. The raid had now entirely broken up over south London, and any idea of the bomb-aimers identifying let alone attacking their assigned target had disappeared, like so many of their own kind.

Bader's Duxford squadrons claimed no fewer than nineteen more bombers and seven fighters – a greatly exaggerated figure, like most of the others on this day, when so often a gravely damaged machine, already and reasonably claimed by one pilot, was attacked once and perhaps twice more before plunging into the ground or the sea.

George Barclay of 249 Squadron was among the hundred or more pilots who got in among the Dorniers after they had been broken up. 'We turned and crossed beneath them but the squadron got split up. I followed three of our Hurricanes climbing up on the left of the bombers for a head-on attack, lost patience and turned to do a beam attack on the leader. . . . I opened fire with more than full deflection and let the Do fly into the bullets like a partridge. . . . I came back and did a short quarter attack. The Do 215 then broke away from the formation and I saw that the engines were just idling as it glided down. Then about eight of our fighters set on the lame duck about 3,000 feet below me. On landing I claimed this as a "probably destroyed".'[4]

And how many more, one wonders, made a similar claim? Never

mind, it was all very different from eight days earlier when the squadron had been torn apart.

For the citizens of London, many intending to take lunch out of doors on this beautiful day, the progress of the battle high above could not be discerned. All they knew was that the sirens had wailed at around 11.30 a.m. and the bombs were raining down, as they had done on almost every night, and sometimes by day, for weeks. Intermittently between the explosions came the distant ripping sound of machine-gun fire. To a woman in an Anderson shelter in the back garden, clutching her two children to her, a bomb was a bomb, whether or not it had been jettisoned by a hastily retreating German bomber, and no matter that the enemy was shortly to crash somewhere in Kent.

The worst hit suburbs were Battersea, Camberwell, Lewisham and Lambeth. 'Up west', Sybil Eccles 'watched a Hun sail over Hyde Park – the guns boom, booming in his wake. A few seconds later he dived and got Buckingham Palace with a loud noise. Poor King and Queen. . . .'[5] In fact, in this third attack one bomb landed on the immaculate lawn to the rear of the Palace and failed to explode, and a second destroyed the Queen's private apartments. But Their Majesties were, thankfully, not in residence.

Nos 504 and 609 Squadrons were getting in among these intruders with some success. Sergeant Holmes blew one up with such violence that his Hurricane was thrown into an uncontrollable spin and he baled out, landing on the sloping roof of a Chelsea house and then into its open dustbin. The Dornier crew did better, coming down on to the Oval cricket ground, while the major part of their bomber (fortunately with an empty bomb bay) crashed on Victoria Station.

Most of the 109 escort had turned for home, as usual leaving the bombers when they were most vulnerable. But even the 'snappers' did not have a clear run. Among those who fell victim to some unidentified Hurricanes was Professor von Wedel, who never even saw his assailant. The veteran managed to keep some sort of control and tried to crash-land on Romney Marsh. He failed to make it and could not entirely miss a farm right ahead: 'The small farm was occupied by William Daw, who was about to take his family out for a Sunday jaunt in his car. Alice Daw and her four-year-old daughter were waiting in the car that was garaged in a shed when the Messerschmitt came sailing down fast and smashed the building into matchwood, giving the little car a terrific blow that mortally injured Alice Daw and her daughter.'[6]

The Professor, after climbing from his smashed Messerschmitt's cockpit, was found wandering about in a daze with tears in his eyes, trying to apologise for what he had done. The policeman who apprehended him gave the German a strong cup of tea.

No one, not the sweating pilots also drinking mugs of strong tea and eating bully beef sandwiches, nor the armourers feeding in long belts of ammunition, nor the controllers and their staff, the Observer Corps personnel and the anti-aircraft gun crews – no one doubted that the enemy would be back, and almost certainly in greater strength this time.

And so he was. With awful inevitability, the plots began to grow in the sky above France like germs under a microscope. The raids developed into three waves of Dorniers and Heinkels of KG53, KG2 and KG56, 150–200 in all, escorted by twice as many 109s and 110s. This assault formed up much more rapidly than the morning one and was over the coast at around 2 p.m. before the scrambled squadrons had gained sufficient height to deal with it.

Then, mysteriously, the bombers began circling and reforming high above Maidstone and Sevenoaks, almost as if they had lost their nerve and might turn for home. In fact, there was probably some mix-up with the rendezvous with the 109s of Galland's JG26 and Trautloft's JG54 – and not for the first time. While this armada wallowed about the sky, almost invisible from the ground, 11 and 10 Group fighters strained for altitude, and Bader's Duxford Wing moved south at full speed.

These bomber formations took thirty minutes to cover the sixty miles from the coast to their targets in south and east London. Well over 150 Hurricanes and Spitfires fell on the formations over the southern suburbs of the city. At first, while the 109s still had fuel enough in their tanks to fight, the defenders had great difficulty in penetrating to the bombers.

Bader and his men came on the scene again, along with six more 11 Group and two 10 Group squadrons, just as the 109s were withdrawing and the bombers, still in tight formation, were approaching their targets. The impact was like that of artillery against a cavalry charge. But this was no 'six hundred' and these sorely tried Luftwaffe pilots, brave men as they were, showed no interest in 'the jaws of Death'. A few put their bombs roughly as intended before retreating, but mostly the 100 and 250 kg bombs were again jettisoned on the unfortunate population of the southern London suburbs.

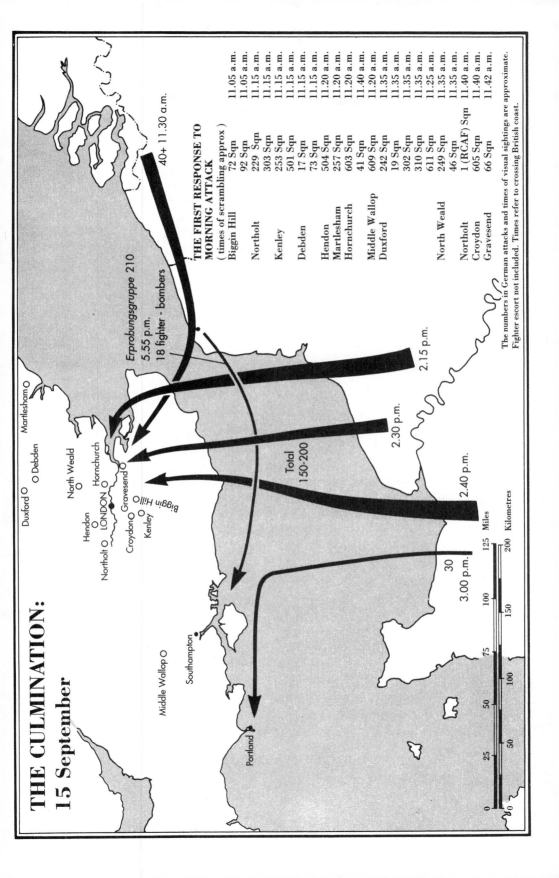

# THE CULMINATION:
# 15 September

**THE FIRST RESPONSE TO MORNING ATTACK**
(times of scrambling approx)

| | | |
|---|---|---|
| Biggin Hill | 72 Sqn | 11.05 a.m. |
| | 92 Sqn | 11.05 a.m. |
| Northolt | 229 Sqn | 11.15 a.m. |
| | 303 Sqn | 11.15 a.m. |
| Kenley | 253 Sqn | 11.15 a.m. |
| | 501 Sqn | 11.15 a.m. |
| Debden | 17 Sqn | 11.15 a.m. |
| | 73 Sqn | 11.15 a.m. |
| Hendon | 504 Sqn | 11.20 a.m. |
| Martlesham | 257 Sqn | 11.20 a.m. |
| Hornchurch | 603 Sqn | 11.20 a.m. |
| | 41 Sqn | 11.40 a.m. |
| Middle Wallop | 609 Sqn | 11.20 a.m. |
| Duxford | 242 Sqn | 11.35 a.m. |
| | 19 Sqn | 11.35 a.m. |
| | 302 Sqn | 11.35 a.m. |
| | 310 Sqn | 11.35 a.m. |
| | 611 Sqn | 11.25 a.m. |
| North Weald | 249 Sqn | 11.35 a.m. |
| | 46 Sqn | 11.35 a.m. |
| Northolt | 1 (RCAF) Sqn | 11.40 a.m. |
| Croydon | 605 Sqn | 11.40 a.m. |
| Gravesend | 66 Sqn | 11.42 a.m. |

The numbers in German attacks and times of visual sightings are approximate.
Fighter escort not included. Times refer to crossing British coast.

40+ 11.30 a.m.

*Erprobungsgruppe 210*
5.55 p.m.
18 fighter - bombers

2.15 p.m.

2.30 p.m.

2.40 p.m.

Total 150-200

3.00 p.m.

Marltesham O

Duxford O    O Debden

North Weald O

Hornchurch O

Hendon O    Gravesend O

Northolt O  LONDON  O  Biggin Hill

Croydon O

Kenley O

Middle Wallop O

Southampton

Portland

Miles

0    25    50    75    100    125

0    50    100    150    200

Kilometres

30

No one was more decisively aware of the turn of the tide in the progress of the Battle than Group Captain Stanley Vincent, Northolt's station commander, who seized a spare Hurricane and got into the combat zone before it was all over. He reported making a head-on attack on eight Dorniers which had managed to cling together, and then to his amazement added that they had broken up and zoomed away south, flat out for France.

Bobby Oxspring of 66 Squadron recalled: 'Every squadron in 11 Group had intercepted, and at that moment I saw Douglas Bader's wing of five squadrons coming in from Duxford. That was the day Goering had said to his fighters the RAF was down to its last fifty Spitfires.* But they'd run up against twenty-three squadrons for a start, when they were on their way in, and then, when they got over London, with the Messerschmitt 109s running out of fuel, in comes Douglas Bader with sixty more fighters. . . .'[7]

Oxspring, among many other pilots, claimed a Dornier that day. Another was C. A. W. 'Boggle' Bodie, also of 66, who was credited with four. One of them had a long and tragic end: both engines done for, rear gunner baled out and, on close examination of the cockpit, the pilot dead at the controls. The other gunner tried to bale out through the belly hatch, got stuck half-way and, as the glide steepened towards the ground, struggled more and more frantically, losing his shoes and then his socks. At 1,000 feet with the imminent prospect of seeing this gunner 'cut in half like cheese on a grater', Bodie put his sights on where the body would be and gave a burst. The white feet were still. 'I didn't feel particularly jubilant,' he confessed.[8]

In the afternoon of this historic day, forever commemorated as Battle of Britain day, Sperrle sent in another small raid to Portland, as if showing he was doing his bit. A few of the remaining Spitfires left in 10 Group knocked down one bomber and damaged another. Anti-Aircraft Command had its finest victory later this day, too. Recognising once more the vital importance of the Woolston Supermarine works at Southampton, *Erpro* 210 made a low-level attack just before 6 p.m. There was not an RAF fighter in sight, and the gunners knew it was up to them. Though they did not shoot one of the fighter-bombers down, the fire was so hostile and accurate that not a bomb hit the factory.

Like front-line soldiers in a great land attack, it was the Fighter Command pilots who were first to learn of their own victory. You could

*A slight exaggeration!

Group Capt.Vincent,     FORM F

J3075

# COMBAT REPORT.

Sector Serial No. ......................................................... (A) .................................................

Serial No. of Order detailing Flight or Squadron to
Patrol ............................................ (B) .................................................

Date ................................................................... (C)     30/9/40.

Flight, Squadron .......................................... (D) Flight : ............ Sqdn. : ............

Number of Enemy Aircraft .......................... (E)   18 Bombers & escorting Fighters

Type of Enemy Aircraft .............................. (F)   He.111's & Me.109's.

Time Attack was delivered ......................... (G)   1645 hrs.

Place Attack was delivered ......................... (H) UXBRIDGE To Farnborough

Height of Enemy ....................................... (J)   17,000 ft.

Enemy Casualties ..................................... (K)   1 ME.109 Destroyed.
                                                          1 Me 109 destroyed by another

Our Casualties ............ Aircraft ................ (L)   Nil              Me.109.

                Personnel .................. (M)   Nil

GENERAL REPORT ................................... (R)

I was climbing over Northolt to watch the Northolt wing in action, and saw
approximately 5 miles S.W. and West of base, streamers from very high enemy
fighters. When at 20,000 ft. I saw approaching from the South a formation
of about 18 He.111's at approx.17,000 ft, with a very large number of Me.109's
on each side, above and behind, mostly about 2000 ft. above the bombers.
    I was therefore able to carry out a head on attack on the Bombers, breaking
away below, and then one from vertically below and stalling away. I was unable
to see any possible result of either attack owing to the Me 109's. The Bombers
then turned back to the South.
    I climbed up towards the sun and tried to attack a Me 109 but had to leave
it owing to others coming down onto me from above, but I saw three Me 109's
chasing a Hurricane at right angles to me from left to right, and when the
Hurricane dived away (straightening out 5000 ft below) and the Me's turned back
onto their course, I was able to get in a good position on the tail of the third
one. Before I opened fire I saw No.1 burst into flames and the pilot jump
out in a parachute; he had obviously been shot down by No.2 who was close in
astern of him.
    I then gave one very short burst of about one second at No.3. at about 200 yds
and immediately pieces came off from the Port side of his fuselage, and he burst
into flames, half rolled and the pilot jumped - He would come down, I estimate,
to the South of Farnborough. I could not then see No 2 as my attention was
diverted by the two parachutes.
    All Me 109's had light blue undersurfaces and dull blue grey mottled top
surfaces with black crosses on fuselages.

                                    Signature     Vincent.
                                                  Group Capt.Vincent.
                        O.C. { Section
                             { Flight
                             { Squadron     Squadron No.

One of Group Captain Vincent's combat reports.

not, like Bodie, destroy four twin-engined bombers, or, like Vincent, witness the frantic break up and retreat of a whole *Staffel* of Dorniers in the face of a single Hurricane, without recognising that this day was different, that something had cracked in the fighting eagerness of the bomber crews who had pressed on so manfully against heavy opposition for so many weeks.

Every one of Bader's sixty pilots had witnessed the stunning impact of their two attacks; every pilot who had looked down over the Weald of Sussex and the hop fields and orchards of Kent and counted the fires of crashed planes, like warning beacons addressed to the German High Command; and every Hurricane and Spitfire pilot who had earlier witnessed those orderly mass armadas of bombers and fighters heading north for the capital, and then seen the consequence of their own mass attacks – all knew by late afternoon that they had participated in a great victory.

For those on the ground – the WAAFs in the ops rooms and the ground crews down at the dispersals awaiting the return of their planes – the news was delayed. In sector and Group ops rooms, and at Bentley Priory itself, much anxiety was experienced before it became clear that the day had gone well.

Churchill, who had been standing beside Park observing every move of the battle, watching the colour of the lights change as squadrons were brought to readiness, were scrambled and changed to red 'in action', watching the raid counters, 'twenty plus', 'sixty plus', moving across the big map board, at length 'became conscious of the anxiety of the commander, who now stood still behind his subordinate's chair. Hitherto,' Churchill recalled, 'I had watched in silence. I now asked, "What other reserves have we?" "There are none," said Air Vice-Marshal Park.* In an account which he wrote about it afterwards he said that at this I "looked grave". Well I might.'[9]

By the time the Prime Minister left to return to Chequers still no overall picture of the outcome of the contest had emerged. It was not until well into the evening that his Principal Private Secretary was able to give him the news: 'We have shot down one hundred and eighty-three for a loss of under forty.'

It did not matter that the true figure of German losses was one-third of this claim; the Germans usually multiplied by four. It did not matter that London had still to suffer more daylight bombing. And in the strict

*If this was true, Park might have been dramatising the situation for the Prime Minister. Other squadrons from 12 Group could have been drawn into the battle.

GREEN PARK HOTEL
Half Moon St. Piccadilly
Mayfair 7533

7/6

# The Daily Telegraph

LONDON
LATE
EDTN.

No. 26,609  LONDON, MONDAY, SEPTEMBER 16, 1940  and Morning Post  BROADCASTING—Page Two  ONE PENNY

'PLANE CRASHES OUTSIDE VICTORIA STATION

# 175 RAIDERS DOWN

## ONE IN TWO DESTROYED

### 1,726 IN 5 WEEKS

Since mass air raids began on Britain on Aug. 11, just over five weeks ago, the Germans have now lost 1,726 machines. The R.A.F. losses in the same period were 486 'planes, the pilots of 247 being safe. These totals include yesterday's figures.

Following are the weekly losses on both sides up till last Saturday:

| Week Ended | German | British |
|---|---|---|
| Aug. 17 | 492 | 115 (46 safe) |
| Aug. 24 | 243 | 51 (30 safe) |
| Aug. 31 | 296 | 113 (70 safe) |
| Sept. 7 | 343 | 128 (71 safe) |
| Saturday | 177 | 69 (30 safe) |
| Total | 1,551 | 456 (227 safe) |

### QUEEN'S ROOM STRUCK

#### INCENDIARIES IN PALACE GROUNDS

DAILY TELEGRAPH REPORTER

A thrilling air fight in which a Dornier 17 'plane which had just bombed Buckingham Palace was shot to pieces in mid-air by Spitfires was witnessed by Londoners during the first of yesterday's 'air raids. It was the third attack on the Palace in a week.

The King and Queen were not in residence at the Palace when the raid was made. Only a skeleton staff of servants and others was in the building. They were all in the basement shelter and there were no casualties.

Two bombs fell, one on the building and the other on the lawns. Neither exploded. The one which hit the Palace crashed through the Tapestry Room, which is used by the Queen as a private sitting room...

## R.A.F. LOSE 30

### MASSED DAY ATTACK ON LONDON SMASHED

### THE PALACE BOMBED FOR THIRD TIME

R.A.F. fighter 'planes and anti-aircraft guns yesterday delivered a smashing blow at the German air offensive against London.

Of 350 to 400 enemy 'planes launched in two waves against the capital and south-east England 175, or nearly 50 per cent., were shot down, according to returns up to early this morning.' We lost 30 fighters, but 10 of their pilots are safe.

The Germans' loss yesterday was their highest since Aug. 15, when 180 of their 'planes were shot down. On Aug. 18 they lost 153. In personnel, their loss yesterday was over 500 airmen against 20 R.A.F. pilots.

During the first raid, for which the warning period lasted from 11.51 a.m. to 12.56, Buckingham Palace was bombed for the third time. Crowds watched the attacking 'plane shot to pieces in the air by Spitfires.

The King and Queen were not in residence at the Palace, and there were no casualties. Her Majesty's apartments were damaged by a bomb, which, however, did not explode, and another "dud" fell on the lawns.

#### NIGHT RAIDERS SCATTERED

Last night, after the sirens had sounded at 8.11, London's A.A. barrage, for the fifth time in succession, scattered raiders who flew over the inner area. Some bombs were dropped indiscriminately over a wide area.

Part of a Dornier bomber which crashed on shops outside Victoria Station after being shot down by a British fighter. The tail and part of the fuselage (seen in the inset picture) fell on a roof near the station.

### ST. PAUL'S SAVED: TON BOMB DUG UP

#### EXPLODED AFTER PERILOUS DRIVE THROUGH LONDON

St. Paul's Cathedral has been saved by the magnificent courage of a handful of men. The high explosive bomb which had menaced it since Wednesday was safely removed last evening by a bomb disposal section under Lt. R. Davies, after three days' unremitting struggle.

The missile proved to be a ton in weight and looked like a vast hog, about 8 ft long. It was fitted with fuses which made it extremely dangerous to touch or move.

The bomb fell in Dean's-yard, close to the west end of the cathedral. It entered the roadway at the end of the pavement.

## HEAVY ITALIAN LOSSES ON LIBYAN BORDER

### BRITISH ARMOURED UNITS AND 'PLANES IN ACTION

From ARTHUR MERTON, Our Special Correspondent
CAIRO, Sunday.

Heavy losses have already been inflicted by British mechanised units and armoured cars on the Italian forces which yesterday crossed the frontier from Libya into Egypt. Troop concentrations are being continually bombed by the R.A.F.

The enemy occupied Sollum, the escarpment to the south-west, and the frontier customs post of Musaid.

This morning's communiqué showed that the Italians had managed to descend the gorge of Halfaya on the edge of the escarpment. A second column is approaching the coastal road south of Sollum.

### NORWAY COAST CLOSED

### SECRET GERMAN PREPARATIONS

FROM OUR OWN CORRESPONDENT
STOCKHOLM, Sunday

Every effort is being made by the Germans in Norway to keep secret preparations of a military character for the invasion of Britain. Nearly the whole of the south and west coastal area has also been constituted a prohibited zone.

All persons over 15 years of age living inside the zone or wishing to enter it must obtain special permits from the Nazi police. Inside the prohibited zone big areas have been fenced off and only German soldiers or officials are allowed in.

The control of civilian activities has everywhere been tightened up. It is now almost impossible for residents in the coastal zone to communicate with those outside it, either by letter or by telephone.

### U.S. CONFIDENCE IN BRITAIN

### GROWING BELIEF IN VICTORY

FROM OUR OWN CORRESPONDENT
WASHINGTON, Sunday.

American confidence in Britain's ability to repel the most formidable attempt at invasion in history has increased perceptibly over the week-end.

That Hitler will make the...

#### COLUMN SUFFERS HEAVILY

The British communiqué stated that the enemy has already exposed himself to severe bombing by aircraft and armoured fighting vehicles. One enemy column descending to the coastal road across the escarpment south-eastwards. One defended camp at Bir Nuh on the approaches seven miles south of Sollum has been severely handled by the British.

A submarine is operating in co-operation with the land forces, helping them to locate their positions in this difficult country and giving a severe warning of any danger from the sea.

### VICHY ARRESTS M. BLUM

# 20

## The Scent of Victory

### 16–30 SEPTEMBER

Air Vice-Marshal Park, not an unreasonably hard taskmaster, expressed himself less than satisfied with the performance of 11 Group on the previous day, in spite of what his pilots considered to have been a stunning victory. First, in less than twenty-four hours, it became suspected from a crash-count that the German losses were nothing like as many as had been claimed – possibly less than half. Second, his controllers had scrambled, and had operated into a favourable position, some 300 fighters, which had been opposed by half that number of German fighters, protecting some 150 bombers. With the added advantage of fighting in their own air space, the results, Park reckoned, were just not good enough.

If Park was justified in his criticism, then the quality of the pilots, and – especially – of the leadership, needed examining. The overall professionalism and skill of the average pilot had certainly declined since mid-July for the reason that experience had been replaced by inexperience, with some exceptions, like the Fleet Air Arm pilots and the Czech, Polish and Free French, a number of whom had been flying professionally for years.

There is little doubt that the quality of leadership had overall similarly declined. Many of the peacetime veterans had been killed and others had been rested or posted elsewhere. One of the most successful, and most missed, James 'the Prof' Leathart of 54 Squadron, for example, had been despatched to special work at the Air Ministry. Others were found wanting and left quietly, some to training command. Their replacements usually brought about improvements of fighting quality and morale. But the replacement of others, promoted from outside or from within the squadron, did not always enhance the quality of the squadron.

To lead a fighter squadron, or *Staffel*, during the demanding days of August and September 1940 was a taxing business for young men, many of whom had not been alive in World War I when the RAF and the Luftwaffe were created. They were full of zeal, a determination to show their superiors and their own men that they were fully qualified to lead in the air and on the ground. But the pressures were sometimes almost too many and too heavy to withstand.

Leathart recalled how the circumstances of the Battle obliged him to work from three bases, his assigned, regular base at Hornchurch, the satellite at Rochford and the forward base at Manston: 'At Hornchurch I had an office, at Rochford a corner of the mess table, at Manston nothing. There was a great deal of admin. work, writing to the bereaved, fixing problems about, say, the maintenance of aircraft, trouble with the Merlins and so on.

'I was immensely helped at Hornchurch by the station CO "Daddy" Bouchier [Group Captain Cecil Arthur Bouchier OBE, DFC] – a marvellous man. Pat Shallard, our IO [intelligence officer] was a great help, too. I had to compile squadron reports with Pat at least twice a week. Then all claims of victories had to be dealt with with Pat, and then Group took about a week to confirm or otherwise.

'The adjutant was a great support through all this, too. But the heaviest duty of all was dealing with new pilots. These varied widely. Some showed immediate promise, others couldn't even fly properly. Most had done no more than five hours on Spits and never fired their guns. I never saw them at first. Al Deere or Colin Gray [flight commanders], or John Allen before he was killed, would report to me.

'If they didn't take them up to see if they were any good, I did. I'd get on their tail to see if they could throw me off – all that. I knew that it was murder to send them off without any squadron training. I said to "Daddy" Bouchier one day, "I can't train them all!" So between us we fixed for the squadron to go for a few days to Catterick and not return until the new boys were trained. We swapped places with 41 Squadron. Of course, some of these youngsters sacked themselves – pranged their aircraft and so on. Then they just disappeared.'

Another, and very sensitive, responsibility was making judgments on which pilots needed a rest. There were familiar tell-tale signs, like too much drinking, heavy smoking, shaky hands, etc. They were sent off to 12 or 13 Group as a rule.

Squadron loyalty was not something that usually had to be cultivated, though to a degree it depended on the quality of the CO. Leathart recalled: 'We all lived in our tight little squadron worlds and hardly ever saw anyone outside, not even our chums. We were totally dedicated to what we were doing, and at the time it is true to say that we were more loyal to the reputation of the squadron than we felt loyalty to our country. Of course that narrow view changed later, but it was how we felt at the time.'

There were always supplementary tasks for the CO. Before the advent of VHF radio sets, for example, the pilots of 54 Squadron could hear Hornchurch but Hornchurch could not hear them. 'This was ridiculous, so I went to the nearest Radio Rentals shop and for 2s 6d a week rented a set with a high-frequency channel that could pick us up. We kept it at the dispersal beside a telephone, and the duty airman simply passed on our messages by landline.'

Leathart also recollected how he persuaded 'Daddy' Bouchier of the advantages of De Wilde ammunition, of which this squadron was suffering a particularly severe shortage. 'I set up a range at Hornchurch with full petrol cans as targets. Then I used rifles, first with ball or tracer – no effect except a leak. Then with De Wilde, and these immediately caught fire. That did the trick, and "Daddy" went hunting for us.'

While Leathart had commanded 54 Squadron for some time, including during the French campaign, Dennis Armitage had leadership thrust upon him soon after 'Wilkie' Wilkinson had been killed beneath his parachute and the senior flight commander had been burned a week later. He did not relish the job of leading 266 at the time: 'It was the evenings that got me down. We would return to our home base at dusk, tell our crews what repairs our aircraft needed and get a bite of grub. Then the lads would let themselves go. Some would go pub-crawling; some would seek out the local female attractions; some would stay in the mess playing darts and snooker and shove-halfpenny; nearly all would get a belly-full of beer before they went to bed. But as temporary acting squadron commander I would retire to my office by the hangar where I would find the squadron adjutant, the engineer officer who was responsible for the aircraft maintenance, and a male typist waiting for me. I would deal with the wants and worries of the engineer officer first and then with the aid of the adjutant and the typist I would get down to the awful job of writing to the parents or wives – not often wives, I'm glad to say – of the lads who had not come back. For several days there was at least one to do every night. . . . I tried hard at first, often tearing up two or three letters before I was satisfied, but I'm afraid before the end I had developed a more or less stereotyped letter which needed little more than the name and address adding.

'This part of the job was indeed a harrowing one but once you were in the air it was all right. . . .'

Some 200 of the surviving fighter pilots commented on the quality of leadership almost fifty years later. The answers varied widely, the great majority being satisfied and in most cases greatly admiring of their COs. Others experienced a bewildering succession of COs and there were undoubtedly exceptions to the general excellence. One Australian, with an exceptionally fine record, lost his first CO at Dunkirk, and there were five more before the end. One he described simply as 'mad'; another who was posted away was not missed – 'the best thing that ever happened to us'. Another was 'a disaster' and lasted two days. The final one 'was completely without experience and took us to 15,000 feet on 15 September of all days when we had been ordered to 25,000. We had no real leaders from the time the squadron was formed until the end.'

Another Australian commented unfavourably on the hierarchy. 'Leigh-Mallory was a leader with no understanding of flying fast fighters and he was quite hopeless in his selection of squadron commanders.' As for his own CO, 'he should never have been given command of a fighter squadron. He had flown into a tree landing on his first and only night flight in a Spitfire.'

Nor did he have much respect for Fighter Command's C-in-C: 'I met "Stuffy" Dowding at Wittering when I was acting CO of 266 Squadron and was shaken by his aged appearance and complete lack of understanding of the problems faced by a squadron formed with pilots straight from an Anson [elderly, twin-engined, general-reconnaissance machine] Flying Training School.

'I thought that "Stuffy" failed to appreciate the fact that when the Low Countries and France fell Fighter Command was outflanked. The Group boundaries had been drawn on the assumption that attacks would come direct from Germany. If he had redrawn the Group boundaries to meet the new threat he could have had the attack spread between two Groups and taken the strain off 11 Group.'

Perhaps Pilot Officer Richard Jones of 64 Squadron was luckier.

'Squadron Leader A. R. D. Macdonald', he writes, 'was an exceptional leader and gentleman inspiring confidence and complete loyalty, and always commanding maximum respect. He was always concerned and personally interested in everyone who served under him.'

Sergeant Pilot Cyril Bamberger DFC of 610 and 41 Squadrons found it difficult to evaluate leadership 'because we were nearly always climbing at low speeds. In these circumstances the enemy aircraft leader nearly always initiated the attack and we were on the defensive. . . . One had confidence in and trusted certain flight commanders and squadron leaders – others gave you the jitters from take-off.'

Flying Officer Edward Morris was one more of those who suffered frequent changes of CO if not of station commander: 'The leadership of the station commander, Group Captain Grice, whose calm presence always seemed to be in the thick of things, stands out. In the background was the Group commander, Sir Keith Park, who one knew by sight from visits and in whom my superiors had confidence, which was good enough for me. One knew of the C-in-C by repute but he was a shadowy figure at my level. The squadron commander was the most important leader to the ordinary pilot. In 79 Squadron we had experience of a range of COs from outstanding to inadequate. . . .'

Norman Norfolk DFC of 72 Squadron recalled that 'the only time during the Battle I received any sort of spur and encouragement' was after he had been the target between two *Staffeln* of Dorniers, one firing rear and the other front guns, which had left him badly shaken.

As so often, in peace and war, it was leadership's failure to communicate that could be cited as the worst fault. Norfolk continued: 'We never saw or heard from the hierarchy and were never told the general strategy or day-to-day tactical principles, and as far as I know the squadron commander was in the same position. As far as leadership at squadron level was concerned, it was difficult because changes due to casualties and postings resulted in lack of continuity. Only once do I recall a general discussion on tactics which occurred after mostly finding ourselves thousands of feet below the bombers on interception. The CO was persuaded to ignore ground controllers' initial vector south and fly north until some height had been gained. This resulted in a much better attacking position but made the squadron unpopular with the ground controllers.'

An Australian survivor, Charles Palliser, retained a high regard for the leadership he witnessed. Like many others, he singled out Victor Beamish as an exceptional leader, 'a most remarkable personality'.

Beamish's first words to this pilot were, 'Palliser, do you feel frightened in combat?' When the Australian replied that, 'Leading up to the fight, I'm scared stiff,' Beamish said promptly, 'Right me lad, so remember that the German pilot you're approaching is just as frightened as you, so if you hit him first and hit hard, you have the ascendency, so get in there!' Palliser never forgot those words.

' "Butch" Barton, a diminutive Canadian, was a wonderful example of dedication and tenacity when he assumed command of 249 [Palliser continued]. This was after John Grandy's* move to Air Ministry. I and the rest of 249 would have followed "Butch" anywhere. Leadership generally was excellent. Douglas Bader was extremely headstrong and brash in some of his ideas; however, he was a "fighter pilot". Bob Tuck, then OC 257, was "one of the boys" who commanded much respect.'

It is as difficult to make a general judgment on the German as the British leadership. There were the exceptional leaders like Galland, Walter Oeusau, Hans von Hahn, Hannes Trautloft, the one-legged Huth, Luetzow and Schellmann. And *Erpro* 210 was led in turn by several of the boldest and most admired pilots after Rubensdoerffer was killed on 15 August. There were exceptional *Kampfgeschwader* leaders, too. But as the Battle continued, more and more of the best leaders were lost, as in Fighter Command, and not all the replacements were of the same high quality.

But the real advantage enjoyed by Kesselring and Sperrle was that the majority of their pilots were peacetime trained, some had fought in Spain and nearly all of them in Poland, Norway or the French campaign. No German leader had to cope with young men of nineteen and twenty straight from wholly inadequate OTU training, without even any air-to-air gunnery experience behind them.

Because of the relatively larger reserve of *experienced* pilots the Luftwaffe possessed to plug the gaps as the fighting intensified, the overall standard of leadership of the German fighter squadrons, towards the end of the Battle, may possibly have been higher than that of Fighter Command.

Those tumultuous fine days, 18 August and 7 September, had been followed by breaks in the weather, followed again by a resurgence of the fighting. When 16 September dawned rainy and overcast with little or no daylight action, many were considering the likelihood that the same

---

*Another immensely popular and highly praised CO.

pattern in the fighting would be re-enacted. Meanwhile, on this day and the next, Kesselring and Sperrle despatched individual bombers, which relied upon cloud cover for protection, to specific targets, without much benefit or damage. Phil Leckrone, an American of 616 Squadron who later helped to form the first Eagle Squadron, and Colin Macfie pursued a Ju 88 lurking over an east-coast convoy and shot it into the sea. It proved to be a useful 'kill', too, as the all-officer crew included a hauptmann, an oberleutnant and, for some inexplicable reason, a senior officer in the Luftwaffe's medical corps.

There were several provocative fighter sweeps from the Pas de Calais on the 17th, when the losses were about even, but Sub-Lieutenant Anthony Blake added to his score with two 109s in rapid succession. He was the highest scoring Navy pilot, but he and eight more naval pilots did not survive the Battle.

The following day dawned brighter, and 11 Group prepared itself for a renewal of heavy fighting. Tony Bartley of 92 Squadron started the day promisingly when he intercepted a recce Dornier and shot it down into the sea near Gravesend. Kesselring then started sending over very heavily escorted Ju 88s in small numbers, and 92 Squadron quickly added to its first score with three of these fast bombers in the mid-afternoon period.

A combination of good interceptions by the Duxford Wing and the relative inexperience of the aircrew of 8/KG77, who had only recently been brought into *Luftflotte* 2, led to unusually heavy bomber losses. Nine in all were shot down, including the *Gruppekommandeur*'s plane, with almost all the other crews killed, too.

The civilian population's concern now was almost entirely with the night bombing, the daylight raids a minor sideshow for those who witnessed them. This night bombing, which had been rumbling on for weeks before the great assault of 7 September, now reached a new pitch in the third week of September. For pilots coming in to London for a night out, the bombing was an alarming experience, even for those whose airfields had been frequently bombed earlier in the Battle. Sergeant Ian Hutchinson of 222 Squadron remembered: 'When we went into London from the airfield, we'd see houses on fire and others that had been destroyed. I must confess that I was more terrified being in London during a bombing raid than ever I was when flying. . . . It was a very frightening experience. . . . I was very relieved to get back to Hornchurch.'[1]

As distant from being a fighter pilot as was conceivable, the fashionable photographer, Cecil Beaton, was at a typical Bloomsbury party in Fitzroy Square at this time – 'eight of us, the majority socialistic young women with lank hair.

'When the guns were heard some of us went on to the roof to see if there was anything to be seen – and, my heavens, there was! The Germans were dropping chandelier flares all the way from the docks along the river to Chelsea. . . . An enormous red glow lit up the sky, against which domes and steeples, and the bobbles of near-by plane trees, were silhouetted.

'It was cold on the roof, and so much shrapnel was falling around us that it was foolhardy to remain. But a raid is more exciting and stimulating, and somehow less unnerving, when one is out of doors.

'However, we came below . . . the bombs were not confined to the docks. A terrible swishing noise, like the tearing of a giant linen sheet, ended in a vast explosion preciously near the house . . . the entire solid building rocked. Then followed the sickening noise of air-raid wardens running to the scene of the crime. . . .'[2]

Hundreds were dying nightly in the London and Liverpool blitzes in particular, and the wardens, heavy rescue workers, firemen, ambulance men and nurses were as much in the front line of the Battle as Sergeant Hutchinson of 222 and the hundreds of others who made up 'the few' in the sky. The injured had to be cared for, the mutilated dead dealt with.

Nurse Frances Faviell reported: 'After a heavy raid with many casualties there was a task for which we were sometimes detailed. . . . This was to help piece the bodies together in preparation for burial. The bodies – or rather the pieces – were in temporary mortuaries. . . . It was pretty grim, although it was all made as business-like and rapid as possible. We had somehow to form a body for burial so that the relatives, without seeing it, could imagine that their loved one was more or less intact. But it was a very difficult task – there were so many pieces missing, and, as one of the mortuary attendants said, "Proper jigsaw puzzle, ain't it, Miss?" '[3]

In the fighter-to-fighter duels that took place during this quiet daylight spell, the fighting qualities of the Me 109 and the (generally) greater experience of the pilots of *Luftflotte* 2 led to occasions when RAF fighter losses were heavier than the Luftwaffe's losses in 109s, although – as always – many RAF pilots escaped to fight again, whereas every 109 shot down over Britain meant a lost pilot, too. For example, on 20

September, 11 Group lost six Spitfires, including three from 222 Squadron, while only one 109 fell over this country or the Channel. (A second crash-landed on the French side.) Among those who were shot down and lived was that great survivor George Bennions DFC of 41 Squadron. He had already crash-landed three times, and his aircraft been damaged by shells two days earlier, when the ventral gunner of a Ju 88 he was pursuing put 200 bullets into his Spitfire, forcing him to land at Lympne. (After being credited with twelve enemy aircraft, Bennions was forced to bale out, seriously injured, on 1 October.)

The continuing absence of any really large-scale raids following the débâcle of 15 September seemed to support Dowding's belief that his Command had so much gained the upper hand that the worst was over. But it was not in his nature to celebrate even a confirmed victory, and the prolonged lull did not deceive him into believing that there would be no more 100+ raids. Instead, he ensured that the required equipment and supply of aircraft remained satisfactory, and on 21 September ordered the formation of very high-flying spotting flights to patrol the coast with Spitfires to give early warning in the kind of detail neither the Observer Corps nor the CH stations could hope to provide. This was dangerous work indeed, for the 109 operated at a higher ceiling than the Spitfire and was also faster at the 35,000 feet level these new patrols flew.

It was not only in the air assault against England that the enemy had by now run into serious trouble. In Holland, Belgium and France, and even in Germany and Norway, his airfields, ever since the fall of France, had come under intermittent attack from Bomber and Coastal Commands. In July the two Commands had flown 383 sorties against these objectives, in August 714. By night they had found the targets difficult, and by day almost suicidal: on 9 July seven of twelve Hudsons had been lost attacking Stavanger, on 13 August eleven of twelve Blenheims attacking Aalborg. Without fighter escort – because none could be spared – the daylight bombers had finally been instructed to abandon their missions if there were less than seven-tenths cloud cover. Yet despite all difficulties the two Commands had maintained an offensive, and the German-held airfields, though only minimally disrupted, had been at least made less comfortably secure for their occupants.

Very much more productive had been the attacks which followed against the German barge concentrations. The major effort had begun on 5 September, after Coastal Command had photographed invasion craft moving in large numbers towards the Channel ports. On the night of 7 September, when Invasion Alert No. 1 came into force in Britain, Bomber Command's Blenheims, aided by eleven Battles and twenty-six Hampdens, struck at the shipping and docks at Calais and Ostend. Then, progressively, almost the whole British bomber force began to join in the work: on the night of 13/14 September 91 sorties, on 14/15 176, on 18/19 180, on 19/20 171. The targets now were easy to find: just across the Channel, on or near water, and well illuminated once the first bombs had gone down. 'Blackpool Front' the crews dubbed it; and the effect of these attacks was even more spectacular than that resort's peacetime illuminations. 'It was an amazing sight,' one pilot reported, 'Calais docks were on fire, so was the water front at Boulogne. The whole French coast seemed to be a barrier of flame broken only by intense white flashes of exploding bombs and varicoloured incendiary tracers soaring upwards.'

By 13 September, according to the German figures, 994 German invasion craft had reached the ports of Le Havre, Boulogne, Calais, Gravelines, Dunkirk, Ostend and Nieuport, and another 1,497 were on their way. That night, RAF bombers sank eighty barges at Ostend, to give striking confirmation to the German naval staff's report to Hitler three days earlier:

The English bombers and the mine-laying forces of the British air force, as the experiences of the last few days show, are still at full operational strength, and it must be confirmed that the activity of the British forces has undoubtedly been successful, even if no decisive hindrance has yet been caused to German transport movements.[4]

Two nights later, on 15 September, one of the bomber crews, like Learoyd a month earlier, performed an act of extreme heroism which earned him the Victoria Cross. Sergeant John Hannah, a youthful wireless-operator/air gunner with 83 Squadron, was over Antwerp when his Hampden was hit and set on fire. The navigator and rear-gunner were compelled to bale out, but Hannah stayed, fought the flames with extinguishers despite bursting ammunition and a melting aluminium floor, and finally, badly burned, crawled forward to hand the navigator's maps and log to the pilot, who made a successful return.

On 19 September the German High Command ordered the invasion shipping to be thinned out in order to avoid further losses from the British attacks, and by 23 September the decrease was obvious to Coastal Command's reconnaissance. From then on Bomber Command could turn its main attention once more to Germany. During September over 1,600 bomber sorties were, in fact, directed against the invasion ports, and over 1,000 tons of bombs cast down upon them.

In the fortnight of intensive attack only 21 out of 168 transports, and 214 out of 1,697 barges, had actually been put out of action – just over twelve per cent in both cases. But the disruptive effect of smashed jetties, docks, roads and railway lines had been considerable – as was that of the lucky hit which blew up an ammunition train on the night of 17 September. At all events it was too much for the Germans, who found that in addition to failing to subdue Fighter Command, they could not keep an invasion fleet safely waiting in the Channel ports.

No hint of relaxation of alertness against the threat of invasion was allowed to percolate through to the armed forces, nor the civilian population. It was premature for that. But the view of the War Cabinet and of the most senior officers in all the Services was that with the days shortening, the weather deteriorating and the equinox approaching, it would now be most foolhardy of Hitler to attempt a crossing in 1940. On 21 September 'Cromwell' was cancelled and Alert No. 2 reinstated.

Anthony Eden, while relaxing one morning at Elham, was therefore all the more surprised to hear from Churchill by telephone on 22 September that he had just received a call from the American President that, *for sure*, the Germans would invade that very day. Eden took a walk to the Dover cliffs. He peered down through the fog and noted an exceedingly choppy sea. He then returned home and telephoned Churchill. An invasion, he said, seemed highly unlikely, and in any case they would all be sea-sick by the time they arrived by barge.

The next day Roosevelt telephoned again, this time to apologise. 'I'm so sorry,' he said. 'The codes got mixed. It was Indo-China, not England, and Japan, not Germany.' And that, indeed, was the case.

If any shape could be made of Luftwaffe strategy by day at this time, it tended to reveal a renewal of interest in the aircraft factories. On 24 September the current leader of *Erpro* 210, Martin Lutz, made a carefully prepared glide bombing attack on the Spitfire works at Woolston. The material damage was less important than the loss of skilled personnel when a 250 kg bomb struck an air-raid shelter killing almost 100 of the senior staff and wounding fifty more.

Much more serious damage was done the following day to the Bristol factory at Filton, Bristol. The Middle Wallop controller had good notice of the build-up of a moderate to large raid heading for the West Country, and early deductions suggested it was heading for the West-land aircraft factory at Yeovil. A sudden change of course by the sixty escorted bombers of *Luftflotte* 3 took everyone by surprise, and it was suddenly clear that the entire force was heading for Bristol. There was no interference except by anti-aircraft fire with the high-level precision bombing, which did great damage to the works and to its rail communications. Five of the bombers were shot down on the way back to the coast, but that was poor consolation for the 170 injured and the relatives of the eighty-two dead.

On the following day, Thursday 26 September, the target was again Woolston, and again cleverly concealed approaches by strong forces of Heinkels, and uncharacteristically poor control work, led to another failure to intercept before the bombing, although ample numbers of fighters were in the vicinity. The consequences were baleful:

The Germans had struck almost as severe a blow at the British aircraft industry as on the previous day at Filton. The northern part of the Supermarine works was extensively damaged; two workshops received direct hits and production was completely stopped; and over thirty people were killed.[5]

Earlier in the Battle the consequences of these raids would have been more serious. But there were other centres by now producing Spitfires, and overall output was only briefly affected.

Although there were no serious long-term consequences to these two days of successful Luftwaffe attack on aircraft factories, the pride of the controllers had been heavily dented. The last days of the month, however, fully restored everyone's spirits and confirmed once again the superiority of the defences.

It was both tidy and appropriate that the last day of September provided the undeniable confirmation that the Battle of Britain had been won. By no means was it the last day of fighting. Unlike at Waterloo or Blenheim, the enemy was not put to rout. No battle standards were taken, no article of surrender signed, no laying down of arms took place. More fighting lay ahead, some of it ferocious and costly. But from 1 October 1940 control of the daylight strikes over Britain was firmly in British hands, and the enemy invasion threat had been reduced to the status of suicide.

On 30 September Park, Brand and Leigh-Mallory at their headquarters all looked up at the dawn sky, consulted meteorological reports and made provision for a busy day. It started with the usual individual weather and recce flights. One of these, a Ju 88, was intercepted over North Devon by Pilot Officer Eric Marrs DFC of 152 Squadron and shot down – his fifth victory.

An hour earlier, at 8 a.m., the first signs of a big build-up over the Pas de Calais were noted at Rye and Dover. By 8.30, in spite of quite a lot of cloud, Kent and Sussex Observer Corps stations were reporting numerous formations of 'bandits' crossing the coast. Park had suspected that these raids might be a blind to get his squadrons airborne and low in fuel when the bombers began to arrive, and he did not fall into the trap. Some of the Corps posts reported certain identification of fighters and none of bombers, so Uxbridge was once again proved right.

About one hour later two *Gruppen* of 88s, later identified as from KG77, crossed in at Dungeness, entirely without escort. There had, it seems, been another misunderstanding over the fighters' rendezvous. It says much for the determination of the crews of the KG77, which had recently suffered so many casualties, that they continued alone. Inevitably, they soon paid the price. Park had over 150 Spitfires and Hurricanes ready to intercept them, and they went in at around 10 o'clock.

For a few minutes the fighters had things all their own way, before hastily summoned Me 109s and 110s came to the Junkers' help. No. 92 Squadron did the greatest damage, claiming nine of the bombers but paying the price of four pilots killed, including one of the flight commanders, and five Spitfires destroyed. In all a dozen 88s fell over Kent and Sussex, and the rest jettisoned their bombs or dropped them on random targets, and fled home.

In the west at midday, Sperrle made his contribution by attempting a further extremely heavy, mixed raid on Bristol and the Westland works at Yeovil. The hard-flying ubiquitous *Erpro* 210, led by Lutz, was once again involved. Brand was as efficiently ready for the Heinkels, Me 110 fighter-bombers and 109s as Park had been earlier.

Five squadrons of Hurricanes and Spitfires literally barred the way to the He 111s over Yeovil. There was a tremendous fight, involving inevitably the escorting 110s – the 109s had returned by then – and the bombers' gunners doing what they could. But it was all too much for KG55, which, scattered and distraught, and dropping their loads around Sherborne, turned and made for the Dorset coast. Here they were met by more 110s, disposed for this protective purpose, and headed at full power for the Cherbourg Peninsula.

Lutz with his fighter-bombers meanwhile streaked for an aircraft factory north of Bristol and, as usual, succeeded in reaching it. But once again *Erpro* 210 paid a dreadful price. Of nineteen 110s that set out four were shot down, including Lutz himself and one of his *Staffel* leaders – both killed.

For the Luftwaffe the day's fighting had been a disaster. The total losses of around fifty aircraft in the course of raids which almost entirely failed to reach their targets, and the failure to return of numerous officers, some of senior rank, were the deciding factor in the decision to withdraw not just the Stuka but all bombers from daylight attack. Never again were those vast and dreaded arrow-head formations to be seen in the sky.

For RAF Fighter Command, 30 September was, indeed, a day to remember.

# 21

## *The Battle Fades*

### OCTOBER

The last month of the Battle was marked by the variable autumn weather, the closing in of the daylight hours, new Luftwaffe tactics and the appearance of a new variant of that most deadly German air weapon, the Me 109.

Like previous periods of high endeavour and maximum German effort, the fighting of 30 September was followed by days of rain and low cloud which restricted flying to individual attacks by darting Ju 88s. One of the most successful of these was on the de Havilland works at Hatfield, where final preparations were being made to put into production the remarkable 'wooden wonder', the multi-purpose, twin-engined Mosquito. From ultra-low level this Junkers tossed four 250 kg bombs into one of the buildings, which unfortunately contained most of the material intended for the production of this aircraft, also killing or gravely injuring almost 100 of the staff.

In spite of the unfavourable weather, a new form of German mass attack quickly became evident. This was carried out, in part, by the new 109E7 and E4/N, both powered by an uprated engine, the first having attachment points for a long-range tank (at last!) while both new variants could carry a single 250 kg bomb. On most days during this month these 109s came over from the Pas de Calais very fast and very high, sometimes in a more or less continuous stream. The single bomb was dropped flying straight and level on a hit or miss basis. In the greater London area, which at first most of these 'snappers' reached without serious trouble, there was more hit than miss about this arbitrary bombardment, which killed or maimed many civilians: at Piccadilly Circus on 12 October, or Waterloo Station on the 15th, for example.

Park's new problem was to intercept these raids before they reached the capital, for even an immediate response to the first CH warnings scarcely allowed the defending fighters time to reach the average 25,000–33,000 feet at which the bomb-carrying and straight fighter 109s came over.* Only his Spitfires could reach this altitude, and they numbered only about one-third of his force.

The pressure on 11 Group's Spitfire squadrons again intensified as a result of these new tactics, and pilots began to feel something of the same strain as in late August and early September. In some respects the stress was even greater because of the very high altitudes at which they were patrolling, where they were constantly on oxygen and suffering very low temperatures. 'The mud on my flying boots froze them to the rudder bar,' complained one pilot. The CO of 602 Squadron later recalled: 'We were still going up every day, several times a day. We were still on high alert. We were doing two, three, sometimes four sorties a day. People were coming back and falling asleep, sometimes on the floor at dispersal, or sitting upright in a chair. We were that tired.'[1]

And 501's CO, Harry Hogan, said, 'In fair weather they still came over two or three times a day. A formation of fifty 109s could draw up practically the whole of our available force.'[2]

On several days the number of 109 sorties well exceeded 1,000, more than during those earlier deadly days of maximum effort. But at least Fighter Command had had time to build up its numbers and squadron-train the new pilots, so that it was markedly stronger than at the crisis of the Battle and better equipped to take the strain.

On 4 October, Park issued new observations and instructions to sector controllers and to squadron commanders, whose pilots were becoming fretful at the frequency with which they were still at an unfavourable height when they met the enemy. Park assured them:

I wish the squadron commanders and sector controllers to know everything humanly possible is being done by group to increase the warning received of incoming raids. . . . With the prevailing cloudy skies and inaccurate heights

---

*Performance and ceiling of the Me 109 while carrying a 250 kg bomb was markedly inferior to that of the pure fighter – which it became again on relief of the weight and resistance.

given by the RDF the group controllers' most difficult problem is to know the height of the incoming enemy raids.

Park then detailed what steps were being taken to correct this situation, including the formation of the special reconnaissance flight at Gravesend. He exhorted his controllers:

Whenever time permits I wish [you] to get the readiness squadrons in company over sector aerodromes, Spitfires 25,000 feet, Hurricanes 20,000 feet, and wait until they report they are in good position before sending them to patrol lines or to intercept raids having a good track in fairly clear weather.

Four days later, Park was forced to institute standing patrols, at first of one squadron, later of two, in his effort to deal with the high-flying raiders. By the end of the month these patrols were virtually continuous in daylight hours, covering Biggin Hill–Maidstone–Gravesend. Though in some ways a reversion to older, costlier methods, they improved the rate of interception; in fact, as the month wore on few of the British squadrons were able to intercept unless they were already on patrol, or at least at 'stand-by'.

To add to the difficulties at Uxbridge, and by contrast with the very high-level, fighter-bomber raids, *Erpro* 210 made its inevitable re-entry on 5 October in weather that was still poor. Its target was the newly completed airfield at West Malling, and the Polish pilots of 303 Squadron were offered the opportunity of dealing with the bomb-carrying Me 110s. They seized it eagerly and got in among the enemy during and after the bombing. It was almost a repeat of 111 Squadron's attack on this same specialist unit after the Croydon bombing. Four of the 110 crews, including yet another new commander, were shot down and killed and two more of the fighter-bombers crash-landed with wounded crews in the Pas de Calais.

To set against this Polish success, 607 Squadron from Tangmere were bounced by 109s over Swanage and four of their Spitfires were shot down, all the pilots escaping unhurt. Six 109s in all were shot down on a day of drizzle and low cloud, but this figure was achieved at the price of 1,175 Fighter Command sorties – a record.

Two days later, 7 October, an Ulsterman, Pilot Officer Kenneth Mackenzie, demonstrated that not all new pilots needed careful working up to operational standard. On one of his first ops, he shared in the destruction of a 109, exhausting his ammunition in doing so. Then, in full view of the people of Folkestone, he chased another 109 out to sea, battering away at its tailplate with his wingtip until it spun in.

Mackenzie, who was later credited with a score of fourteen and a half, managed to get back to the coast where he crash-landed his sorely damaged Hurricane. 'He was found on the cliff tops above Folkestone bleeding from a nasty gash under his bottom lip and with some of his teeth knocked out.'³ A doctor put some stitches in the mouth of this pilot, who was then invited to take tea with a local retired admiral.

Earlier in the Battle, tea was also offered to Dickie Turley-George of 54 Squadron after he had crash-landed in a cornfield, which had so upset the farmer. 'I gratefully accepted and was taken to a delightful Kentish farmhouse and given lashings of strawberries and cream and scones and butter. . . . I arrived back at Manston to be severely castigated by James Leathart. . . . "Christ, the war doesn't stop so that T-G can have a cream tea just because he happens to have been idiot enough to get himself shot down." '

But, instead of a rocket, Mackenzie received an immediate DFC after his tea party.

In the hectic if comparatively small-scale fighting of the following day, 8 October, the Czech pilot serving with 303, Sergeant Josef Frantisek DFM, *Virtuti Militari*, went missing somewhere over Sussex. With seventeen credited victories, all obtained in the month of September, he was one of the top-scorers of all pilots.

The sum total of the debt owed to Josef Frantisek, and to the hundreds more RAF aircrew who gave their lives in the Battle, was being drawn up in Berlin as this brave and skilful pilot fell from the sky, although no one on this side of the Channel had any knowledge of it. Four days later, on 12 October, Hitler ordered Keitel to circulate this directive:

The Fuehrer has decided that from now until the spring, preparations for 'Sealion' shall be continued solely for the purpose of maintaining political and military pressure on England.

Should the invasion be reconsidered in the spring or early summer of 1941, orders for a renewal of operational readiness will be issued later. In the meantime military conditions for a later invasion are to be improved.⁴

The interpretation of these words was plain to all who read them. The Luftwaffe had been rebuffed in its sustained and massive attempt to destroy RAF Fighter Command. Where the air forces of Poland and France, and the less powerful victims of Nazi aggression, had been knocked out within days, the RAF, substantially reinforced by men like Frantisek, remained undefeated after three months of fighting. The Battle of Britain had, indeed, been won.

★   ★   ★

No orders had been issued at the same time by the German High Command for the fighting to cease after this directive of Hitler's, and in the event Kesselring and Sperrle continued to send over variable numbers of raids until the end of the month (the official British date for the end of the Battle) and well into November, as if the habit could not be broken. For example, 14 and 15 October were, on a diminished scale, comparable with 14 and 15 August, with 11 Group hard at work all day dealing with the high-flying Me 109s, both fighters and fighter-bombers, while single Ju 88s and occasionally Dorniers took advantage of low cloud to navigate to, and bomb, airfields, killing a number of personnel and inflicting some damage.

But nothing serious was achieved and these raids could only be likened to the calls of defiance and ineffectual thrusts of a one-time champion defeated in the ring. Moreover, the changing season and light were more and more limiting flying, thick fog on a number of days prohibiting all operations on both sides of the Channel, or catching out those who attempted to do so. Four pilots of 302 (Polish) Squadron were killed on 18 October while attempting a forced landing on Sandown Park racecourse, and the casualty lists for both the Luftwaffe and Fighter Command included many more who lost their lives in the bad weather or crashed their machines while taxiing. On the same day that the Poles were tragically killed, no fewer than nineteen Luftwaffe aircraft were damaged or written off in crashes.

There remained one last day of the Battle for the RAF to demonstrate that they were still masters of the air over Britain and had overcome even the new German tactics, the pin-pricking, high-flying, German fighter-bombers.

The 29th of October was a typically misty and cool autumn day, the sun breaking through only hazily. The Battle had spanned the farming season, from ripening crops in early July, when crash-landing aircraft cut swathes through the corn. Now the fields below were dark from ploughing or ochre with stubble, the fruit orchards still dark green.

But on this morning, at around 10.45 when the first Spitfire squadrons scrambled, the patchwork below soon lost its definition. At 20,000 feet horizontal visibility was excellent, offering early sight of a *Gruppe* of Me 109s crossing the coast at Deal. A single *Staffel* of fighter-bombers streaked for London, while two more *Staffeln* fought it out with the Spitfires. Two of the bombers got through and apparently chose Charing Cross railway bridge as their target, though their two 250 kg bombs landed instead close to the station. Five out of thirty of this *Gruppe* were shot down, while a sixth crash-landed on the other side of the Channel.

The next waves of 'snappers' fared even worse. After so many contacts which opened with Merlins striving for altitude, Park had his Hurricanes at 22,000 feet and his Spitfires at 28,000 (and up-sun at that) when they sighted what looked like a plague of locusts crossing the coast. The four Hurricane squadrons tore into the flanks of the bomb-carriers, while no fewer than five Spitfire squadrons fell out of the sun on to the 100+ 109s of JG51.

Both fighters and fighter-bombers were bounced at a hopeless disadvantage, the bombers jettisoning their loads and racing away to the Channel and safety, leaving several of their number as smoking pyres among the fields far below. The fighters suffered a worse fate, eleven of their number falling to the Spitfires' eight Brownings, five of them to 602 Squadron.

Two more 109 pilots of JG51 and 52 were rescued from the sea by the extremely efficient air-sea rescue service, but most of the others, including the adjutant of I/JG51, were killed.

On this day, too, *Erpro* 210's finale was as spectacular as all the other acts this remarkable body of airmen had played throughout the Battle. Led now by Otto Hintze, the 110s, accompanied this time by some bomb-carrying 109s, headed for North Weald. They arrived safely just as the Hurricanes of 249 and 257 Squadrons were taking off, and destroyed two of their number before they could get clear. A good deal of damage was done in this low-level attack and some twenty personnel were killed, but once again the *Erpro* paid the price. Hintze was shot down, although he baled out successfully and was made prisoner.

Because 29 October was effectively the last day within the official limits of the Battle, activity on 30 and 31 October being almost nil because of the weather, the final raid of the day had about it a touch of *opéra bouffe*. Stung by Bomber Command's raids on northern Italian cities, Mussolini had persuaded a reluctant Goering to allow a contingent of bombers and CR42 fighters to operate against Britain. Just as the Italian armies had invaded France when she was already beaten, so now the Regia Aeronautica belatedly participated in the last raid of the Battle of Britain.

A group of fifteen bombers of unfamiliar configuration but faintly similar to He 111s was sighted crossing the Kent coast at a relatively low level as if performing for the Italian equivalent of the Hendon airshow, in formation wing tip to wing tip. Accompanying them in equally immaculate order were some seventy biplanes apparently left over from the last war – open cockpit, single-seat machines with fixed undercarriage. All the aircraft were gaily painted pale green and bright blue, camouflage for a more exotic climate than Britain's in late October.

The anti-aircraft gunners were as puzzled as everyone else by this strange sight in the sky, and it was a few minutes before fire was opened. The Italian armada then turned right in one formation, content to have over-flown enemy soil in order to provide the Milan newspapers with appropriate propaganda, and departed over Ramsgate – upon which a few bombs were scattered.

Two weeks later, on 11 November (the same day half the Italian battle fleet was knocked out at Taranto by British naval aircraft) the Regia Aeronautica attempted another raid in similar force, this time against Harwich. Some thirteen bombers and CR42 biplane fighters were shot down. Evidence from bomber wreckage revealed an extraordinarily large crew of six, all wearing tin hats and armed with rifles *and* bayonets. As for the fighters, Churchill wrote, 'They might have found better employment defending their fleet at Taranto.'[5]

For Hitler now it was simply a question of keeping up the pressure on Britain until 1941, when invasion would again become possible – perhaps before the defeat of Russia but probably after. The fighter-bomber raids meanwhile could do no more than keep Fighter Command at stretch, and with worsening weather and shorter hours of daylight they were becoming barely profitable. More and more the Luftwaffe turned to the night bombing which it had practised in a minor way since June, and intensively since 7 September. London overwhelmingly – more than 7,000 tons of bombs during October – but also Liverpool, Manchester, Birmingham and other places suffered in these October weeks from bombing which normally had specific aiming points, but was in practice indiscriminate. By the end of the month, over 13,000 British civilians had been killed and nearly 20,000 seriously injured in these attacks, which were to continue without respite until May 1941, when most of the Luftwaffe moved east in preparation for the onslaught against Russia.

The ordeal was grievous, but in the context of the strategic progress of the war, almost immaterial. Thanks to the victory in the daylight Battle during July–October, the island base remained unconquered, and soon Hitler would have created for himself situations beyond redemption even by the might and courage of the German Army and the Luftwaffe.

# PART THREE

# AFTER THE BATTLE

Into the vortex of synthetic hate we flung
our eager bodies . . . we were so very young
and thus we reasoned: 'Out of chaos came
once, long ago, a world of flowers and corn;
the dignity of cities and church spires
and love and laughter, grew from hideous flame.
All that endures
of these our fading dreams was borne
out of the pain and tumult, out of the storm . . .
surely from out the loins of *this* fire
will grow the shining world of our desire . . .'

But why do you grin, O Death, as at the gate
of every golden dawn you stand in wait?

WARRANT OFFICER RONALD WILCOX

# 22

*Retrospect*

Fifty years on, the pattern of the Battle of Britain appears very much as it did at the time: appears, that is, to the interested British. The Germans, less well pleased with the outcome, for long affected to regard the campaign as of minor importance and swept it under their historical carpet.

At the time, it was agreed by Dowding, Park and everybody else in a position to know, that the Battle had moved through a number of phases.[1] During the preliminary, warming-up or redeployment period in July and early August, the Luftwaffe had attacked mostly shipping and coastal targets. Then, during the second week of August, the full assault (*Adlerangriff*) had opened, at first mainly against radar stations and airfields near the south and south-east coasts. During this period, on 15 August, the Luftwaffe had made an attempt to outflank the southern defences by attacking the north-east with forces from Norway and Denmark – an attempt so costly as never to be repeated. After that, while not neglecting coastal targets, the German offensive had moved progressively inland. By the end of August it was falling with such severity on the southern airfields, and especially on the vital sector stations guarding London, that Fighter Command was coming under a strain which, if prolonged, might have proved fatal. The supply of Hurricanes and Spitfires never failed, but losses were now overtaking production. Most serious of all, the output of new pilots, who must in any case be less experienced than those they replaced, was failing to keep pace with casualties.

And then, at the critical point, the Germans had switched their attack on to the irresistible target of London – 'a tremendous fat cow tied up to attract the beasts of prey', in Churchill's pre-war phrase.[2] At once the strain on Fighter Command's ground organisation had eased; production of Hurricanes and Spitfires, if not of fully operational pilots, had begun again to outstrip losses; and the defeat of the great attack on London on 15 September had presaged the final victory. By October the Luftwaffe had been reduced to fighter-bomber forays by day and the pounding of British cities by night – tragic for the many who suffered but, with the scale of attack possible at the time, strategically insignificant.

Equally clear at the time, and since, is that the Germans had been trying to destroy the RAF, and particularly Fighter Command, as the necessary preliminary to invasion. What was not so clear, until post-war access to German records, was the relationship between the air attacks and the timetable of invasion. After the war it was possible to see, for instance, that the vital switch to London, while also satisfying Hitler's desire for revenge for the raids by Bomber Command, occurred as a step in the invasion programme. Fighter Command, the Germans thought, *must* come up in strength to defend the capital, and so might in strength be shot down. And massive blows on London, beginning on 7 September, might produce the chaos and collapse of morale which would make invasion possible, if all went well, by the then projected date of 21 September.[3]

Though there was ample evidence from every kind of source of the German preparations to invade, and later of the dispersal of invasion shipping from the Channel ports, even the Enigma decrypts did not directly point to Hitler's decision, taken on 12 October, to postpone 'Sealion' until the following spring. On that day the Fuehrer had also decreed that preparations should be actively continued, in order to keep Britain under pressure. It was these continued preparations that the Enigma intercepts mostly reported,[4] not the strategy behind them – a matter discussed in closed rooms or by landline, not over the ether. But because the threat to Britain seemed to continue, yet nothing happened, the British public began to wonder whether there had ever been any serious intention to invade at all. So began the first, mildest and shortest-lived of the controversies associated with the Battle of Britain. Did the RAF really save Britain from invasion – or was Hitler only bluffing all the time? Post-war investigation amply confirmed that Hitler was far from bluffing, but that he knew he had to beat the RAF first.[5] He tried to do precisely that, and failed.

The reasons for that failure were, of course, manifold. The switch to London was certainly one. The superiority of Dowding as a commander-in-chief to the increasingly self-indulgent and remote-from-reality Goering was another. So too was the extraordinary weakness of German intelligence – a surprising feature in view of its excellence before and during the Battle of France. While Fighter Command knew precisely what faced it, the Luftwaffe was ill-informed not only about the complexity and methods of the British defensive system, but also about Fighter Command's locations and strength. At the lower levels, too, there was a singular lack of information. Fighter pilots in a *Staffel* never saw an intelligence officer; these, to be found in every British squadron, existed only at *Geschwader* level for the Germans. The result was that throughout the swiftly moving battle vital experience and information about the British spread among the German crews only casually and informally, sometimes through adjutants or commanding officers, but usually by word of mouth from pilot to pilot.

There were reasons for the German defeat more fundamental than any of these. The British fighters were part of a scientific system of air defence evolved over many years, operating in exactly the role for which they were designed. The German bombers and fighters, in contrast, were attempting an unfamiliar task by a series of improvisations. The Luftwaffe had not been equipped or trained for a campaign of attrition against long-distance, fixed targets, as Luftwaffe doctrine had not for many years envisaged such a campaign. In the 1930s the Luftwaffe, for all its organisational independence, had developed as a closely related partner of the German Army, trained for quick response to calls for support in swiftly moving campaigns.[6] In Poland, Norway and France it had played that part with ruthless efficiency, eliminating the opposing air forces as a preliminary to unleashing its full might against enemy troops, communications and strong points. But those opposing air forces had all been weak. In the Battle of Britain it had to face powerful and determined opposition – and there was no German Army at hand to follow up such successes as it achieved.

For the Battle of Britain, there were also fatal flaws in the German equipment. Against German expectations, the bombers proved too vulnerable to operate by themselves and had to be escorted. But the long-range Me 110 could not live with the Hurricane or Spitfire skilfully handled, and the excellent Me 109 had only short endurance. Over London, having wasted fuel while escorting slower bombers there, it had only some ten minutes' combat time remaining. If it flew beyond the capital more than a few miles, it simply could not fight. To fighter commanders like Adolf Galland, this was the decisive factor in the German failure.[7]

There were also other factors which told against the Luftwaffe. There was the dreaded Channel, waiting to swallow up damaged aircraft on the return flight; and there was the certainty of the prison camp for any German pilot who baled out over England. By contrast, British pilots who 'took to the silk' were usually quickly reunited with their squadron. Such factors, together with their rising losses and the prolonged British resistance, had their inevitable effect on even such consistently brave and determined men as the Luftwaffe aircrews. Flushed with their success over France, they began with an abundance of confidence, which they progressively lost. The RAF pilots, with for most of them the spur of fighting in direct defence of their homeland, maintained with few exceptions a magnificently high morale throughout.

But for its task in hand, perhaps the Luftwaffe's greatest weakness was one not commonly appreciated. Though it had a big general numerical advantage over Fighter Command, its advantages in the vital single-engined fighters was by no means overwhelming (see page 43 ff). Against skilful and determined opponents operating as part of a scientific system of air defence, the Luftwaffe proved to be simply not strong enough. Quite apart from the collapse of the invasion project, its losses alone were sufficient to force the diversion into the safety, at that time, of night bombing.

The second controversy to bemuse the British public concerned the numbers of aircraft shot down. Throughout the Battle both sides had announced totals which proved, when all was over, to be greatly exaggerated. Between the official beginning and end of the Battle, the RAF reckoned to have destroyed 2,698 German aircraft. It actually destroyed, according to the German records, 1,733. This overstatement was much closer to the mark than that of the enemy, who reckoned to have destroyed 3,058 RAF planes and actually destroyed 915. Fighter Command had overstated by less than twice, the Luftwaffe by more than three times.[8]

All this was completely understandable. On days of minor fighting the British assessments in fact proved to be extremely accurate, but as soon as two or three dozen aircraft were involved, accuracy disappeared; in the confused fighting more than one pilot, to say nothing of the gunners on the ground, often claimed what must have been the same aircraft. When the actual German losses, based on the replacements called for each day by the Luftwaffe units from the quartermaster general, were revealed in 1947, they of course came as a shock to the public. 'Battle of Britain Day', for instance, was celebrated on 15 September not so much for its strategic significance as because it was supposed to have been the day of the Luftwaffe's greatest losses – 185 aircraft. The actual loss on that day turned out to be sixty, fifteen fewer than on 15 August.

Some of this shock could, and should, have been avoided. During the Battle Park and others began to suspect that the assessments were exaggerated, not least because on no day were more than fifty or so German aircraft found on the ground. Churchill was quickly on to this and quizzed Dowding about it. He asked Dowding, if ninety enemy aircraft were found on the ground, what was the additional number likely to have come down in the sea or been destroyed in landing? Dowding replied, 'Another ninety,' thereby perpetuating the illusion.[9] More realistic was his answer to Sinclair's questioning during the Battle when the Americans began to doubt the British claims – because of the completely contradictory claims made by the Germans. Dowding replied, 'If the Germans' figures are correct, they will be in London in a week. Otherwise, they won't.'[10]

The 'true figures' were a nine-day wonder for the general public, who quickly appreciated that it was the result, not the details, which mattered. For more interested parties, however, the debate lingered on. It raised, inevitably, the pertinent but rather embarrassing question of the pilots' own individual successes. If only something over a half of the German aircraft accepted by Fighter Command as having been shot down had, in fact, been shot down, what should happen to the 'personal' scores? Clearly they could not all be correct, yet there was now no means of reassessing them all. It is a subject which, understandably, few chroniclers of the Battle have chosen to explore in depth.

A controversy which became known only gradually outside the Service concerned the tactics of the British fighters during the Battle. There were two aspects of this. The first was about the standard flying and attacking groups within the squadrons, and the standard forms of attack. The second was about the merits of operating squadrons singly, or in pairs, or in three or more squadrons as a 'wing'.

The first issue took shape within an increasing number of squadrons as the Battle wore on. Pre-war fighter training had placed extreme emphasis on formation-flying as a necessary discipline, as an aid to navigation, particularly through cloud, and as the basis for successful attack and self-defence. With the increasing speed of aircraft in the late 1930s it was not visualised that more than one squadron could maintain formation and manoeuvre quickly enough for interception.[11] The single squadron, then, was the main formation, but within this were the basic tactical units – the sections, each of three aircraft, flying in the tight arrowhead or inverted V formations known as vics. In a full squadron patrol there would be four of these vics, all closely grouped together, usually in line astern. The leader of the first section, usually the squadron commander, on sighting the enemy and giving the 'Tally Ho!', was then supposed to order one of the standard prescribed forms of attack such as 'Attack No. 6' ('by a squadron from astern against a large formation'), and the squadron then, in theory, went in section by section, swiftly reforming for further action. All the prescribed forms of attack, known as 'Fighting Area Attacks' from the days before the formation of Fighter Command, enjoined attack from astern.[12]

In practice, over France and in the Battle, things had not normally worked out that way. Flying so close behind their leader, Nos 2 and 3 in the section often found themselves unsighted at the very moment of attack; and while concentrating on maintaining tight formation pilots sometimes found themselves 'bounced' by an unobserved enemy fighter. Also, once the initial attack had taken place, parade-ground symmetry in the air instantly disappeared, the encounter usually degenerating into a series of unrelated individual combats or dogfights. For these many, if not most, of the British pilots at the outset of the Battle were virtually untrained.

The difference between theory and practice is evident in the recollections of many pilots. One pilot remembered how 'in air training sessions our CO, Squadron Leader Heyworth, had been very hot on "keeping a cool head and working as a team". He was leading the squadron on a first sortie when he sighted an enemy formation which, unusually, was below us. He at once shouted, "Tally Ho! There go the bastards," and rolled over on his back to make a vertical attack.'[13]

Another pilot, later Air Chief Marshal Sir Frederick Rosier, recalled: 'My squadron commander in 43 Squadron before the Battle would not agree to dogfighting practice because: 1) It was not needed because enemy fighters would not operate over the UK, and 2) it resulted in dirty aircraft (oil spills).'[14] The standard prescribed attacks had, in fact, been evolved to deal with unescorted and largely unarmoured bombers. In the Battle they proved far from ideal against increasingly well-armoured bombers escorted by plenty of Me 109s.

To decrease their vulnerability in the standard tight formation, some squadrons during the Battle detailed a 'tail-end Charlie' to maintain a rear-guard watch. If this unfortunate pilot, 'weaving' back and forth behind the rest, did not himself get 'jumped' and shot down, he tended to run out of fuel. So that was no solution. A better one was to hand, but it was the one practised by the Germans.

As far back as the Spanish Civil War Werner Moelders, most famous of all the Luftwaffe World War II fighter pilots, had employed a tactical formation of four aircraft, the *Schwarm*, in which the pilots flew in a pattern corresponding to the fingertips of an open human hand. In this analogy the longest finger represents the leader, the index finger his No. 2. The other fingers, Nos 3 and 4, are to the right and somewhat above. In both pairs the wingman flies lower than his leader in order not to risk placing himself against the sun, the area of most danger.

This open position with the fighters some 200 metres apart allowed total flexibility and the greatest possible opportunity for spotting the enemy early. In combat the *Schwarm* broke into its component pairs, each No. 1 being the prime attacker, and No. 2 covering his tail. 'The finger four,' 'Johnny' Johnson* later wrote, 'if properly flown in varying height intervals, is the best means of covering blind spots below individual aircraft. The formation is loose and manoeuvrable. The three pilots following their leader can search their respective areas of sky and keep him in sight without a great deal of uncomfortable neck-twisting. . . . [It] is easy to fly and much less tiring than the line astern formation.'[15]

Towards the end of the Battle, only a few of the British squadrons, notably 501 and 605 on their own initiative, had begun to fly 'finger four'. Almost all, however, had given up the 'Fighting Area Attacks' – the drills coded by numbers as if life over southern England in 1940 were a prolonged Hendon airshow. Sheer survival had demanded swift and radical rethinking and new practices, such as head-on attacks, attack from directly above and wide-angle deflection shooting. Recommended by Air Tactics at the Air Ministry and by the Air Fighting Development Unit as early as July, these were discouraged by Dowding but formally approved in August by Park. However, the *Schwarm*

---

*Later Air Vice-Marshal J. E. Johnson CB, CBE, DFC.

pattern, the excellence of which is proved by its continuation into the 1990s, though it received warm commendation from Park early in November, was not generally adopted in Fighter Command until after Dowding's departure. Had Fighter Command headquarters or the Air Tactics branch of the Air Staff been quicker to perceive a lesson which might have been learnt from the fighting earlier over France, British casualties in the Battle would surely have been fewer.

As to the relative effectiveness of large or small units of fighters against a mass bomber formation, the Flying Training Manual stated a truism rather than a shibboleth when the authors wrote, 'The larger a formation is, the more restricted will be its power of manoeuvre.'

In exhaustive exercises shortly before the war, which provided the last opportunity to rehearse for the real Battle twelve months later, it was shown that 'the school of thought which is in favour of large fighter formations' had lost its case.

'It is considered that a fighter tactical unit consisting of more than one squadron', reported the Wing Commander Operations to Senior Air Staff Officer Fighter Command, 'would not be able to carry out the role of interception and attack as efficiently as a squadron formation. . . . Time is the important factor in interception and attack. The aim should be to attack the enemy as soon as possible, and not to wait until we have concentrated in strength before attacking.'[16]

On the following day, 19 August 1939, Dowding delivered a memorandum to the Under-Secretary of State at the Air Ministry on 'Tactics v. Massed Bomber Formations'. The pace of tactical development since the introduction of the Hurricane and Spitfire is hinted at in the second paragraph:

It is only a year ago since there existed a considerable body of opinion to the effect that high-speed monoplane fighters would not be able to deploy and deliver a simultaneous attack against an enemy formation owing to the danger of collision and of shooting one another. These fears, though not groundless, are proving to be exaggerated, and sections and flights are now habitually deployed for attack and we are working towards the habitual deployment of complete squadrons. . . .

My own opinion (which I do not wish to over-stress at the moment) is that the squadron will always be the largest tactical unit which it will be practically expedient to employ.

This is as uncompromising a statement of the Commander-in-Chief's beliefs on deployment as could be, and there is no record that Dowding acquired any evidence that could cause him to change his policy.

This made the more sense in that the attacks were frequent, widespread, and not usually in great strength. Later, as the German bombers penetrated farther inland and became more and more heavily escorted, Park tried to operate his squadrons in pairs, often with a Hurricane squadron assigned to the bombers at around 16,000 feet, and a Spitfire squadron, with its superior performance at high altitude, taking on the protective Me 109s above.[17] On the whole this worked well, though there were many occasions when the squadrons failed to make rendezvous before one or other encountered the enemy. At all times Park was determined to meet the enemy as far forward as possible, to prevent him reaching and destroying his targets, such as the vital airfields and aircraft factories. In this his views were completely in accord with those of Dowding.

Up at 12 Group in the Midlands, however, a different school of thought developed. It was clearly asking much of pilots to send them repeatedly into engagements in which they were outnumbered by ten or even twenty to one. Did it matter if the enemy dropped a few more bombs while three or four of the British squadrons became grouped together, as long as he was then met in force and suffered heavy losses? After a few such engagements, he might never come again.

Such was the thinking of the legless Douglas Bader, CO of 242 Squadron at Coltishall, in Norfolk, and in it he was strongly supported by the 12 Group AOC, Leigh-Mallory. On Leigh-Mallory's instructions, the Duxford Wing had come into being: not a recognised formation, but three or more of the squadrons at Duxford, Coltishall and Fowlmere operating on occasion as a single unit under Bader's leadership. Bader's ardent spirit longed to lead this Wing of up to sixty aircraft down into the southern counties, there to hit the raiders with devastating force after they had first run the gauntlet of 11 Group's initial attacks. Instead, his normally appointed role, in response to Park's requests to Leigh-Mallory, had been to patrol over 11 Group's northern airfields, in case they were subjected to attack.

Not surprisingly, Bader thought that his Wing (which he maintained could be assembled in five minutes,[18] though critics asserted it took twenty) should be more aggressively used. When set to patrol North Weald–Hornchurch, he not only sped towards the enemy if they came within sight, but also on occasion went looking for them. More than once 11 Group controllers were perplexed by the sudden appearance of what might have been a large hostile formation, but turned out to be Bader's Wing.[19] As the Battle developed, so did friction between Park and Leigh-Mallory.

A clear sign of this, which nevertheless evoked no action from Dowding, was Park's Instruction (No. 7) to his Group controllers dated 27 August. It told them that whereas they could go on making requests for reinforcements directly to 10 Group, they would have to put their requests to 12 Group through Fighter Command headquarters, in order to ensure that the requests were properly complied with. With remarkable and ill-advised candour in a document likely to be seen by many eyes, Park's order included the following sentences:

Thanks to the friendly co-operation offered by No. 10 Group, they are always prepared to detail two to foûr squadrons to engage from the west mass attacks . . . approaching the Portsmouth area. . . . Up to date No. 12 Group, on the other hand, have not shown the same desire to co-operate by despatching their squadrons to the places requested. The result of this attitude has been that on two occasions recently when 12 Group . . . were requested to patrol our aerodromes, their squadrons did not in fact patrol over our aerodromes. On both these occasions our aerodromes were heavily bombed.[20]

During September, as the Germans struck farther inland against London, 12 Group's forces became more regularly involved. On at least three occasions Bader's Wing came strongly into the action and claimed big successes. In the single week 7–15 September the Duxford Wing was, in fact, credited with the destruction of 105 German aircraft, and forty probables, for the loss of only fourteen of its own.[21] It was Bader's confidence in his Wing's ability to inflict such losses repeatedly, and his exasperation at not being given more chances of doing so, that at length brought this trouble to a head.

It happened that the adjutant in Bader's 242 Squadron, the well-liked Flight Lieutenant Peter Macdonald, was a Member of Parliament. Knowing of Bader's frustration, and that Leigh-Mallory was completely behind Bader, he took it upon himself to bring Bader's views to the notice of two fellow MPs, the Under-Secretary of State for Air (Harold Balfour) and the Prime Minister – no less.[22] Wheels turned; and very soon the Chief of the Air Staff was calling a meeting to discuss 'Major Day Tactics in the Fighter Force'.

This meeting, much written of since, took place on 17 October. Newall being indisposed, the Deputy Chief of the Air Staff, Air Vice-Marshal W. Sholto Douglas, took the chair. Also present were Dowding, his Group commanders Park, Brand and Leigh-Mallory, the

Chief of the Air Staff designate (Air Marshal Sir Charles Portal), a signals representative, four members of the Air Staff – and Bader.

The calling of this meeting, and in particular Bader's presence, have been taken gravely amiss by many of those who fought in the Battle. With loyalties for the most part firmly in the Dowding–Park camp, and convinced that Park's policy was correct, they have felt strong resentment at the indignity to which they feel their two heroes were subjected. An investigation, as they regard it (and as Dowding and Park came to regard it too), was bad enough. But an investigation in some way prompted by politicians, at which Dowding had to defend his tactics in front of one of his own squadron leaders – intolerable!

It is not necessary to go all the way in sharing this indignation. Macdonald doubtless acted as he thought best in the interests of the country, and there are worse crimes than cutting Service corners. The presence of Bader in such elevated company certainly needs explanation: he was taken along by Leigh-Mallory in the hope that he would be admitted, but apparently without prior arrangement with Sholto Douglas. No one else present at the meeting had actually been involved in the air fighting. If there is a criticism to be made of Bader's presence, it is that Leigh-Mallory should have consulted Dowding beforehand, and that other active squadron commanders should have been there as well.

The minutes of this famous meeting record no sensational disagreements. Leigh-Mallory spoke of the need to meet the increasingly large German formations with forces as strong as possible, and pointed to the outstanding results achieved by the Duxford Wing. Park, while not disagreeing with the general principle, stressed the importance of the time factor in 11 Group. The raids, he emphasised, must be intercepted before they reached important targets, and a pair of squadrons – sometimes only one – was the most that could be brought to bear in time. The summing-up, by Sholto Douglas, recognised the different circumstances of the two Groups, but suggested that in 11 Group both methods could have a place, with, on occasion, 'forces from the two Groups co-operating'. Dowding promised that he would arrange for 12 Group wings to participate freely in suitable operations over the 11 Group area, and added, optimistically, that he would be able to resolve any complications of control.[23]

The minutes suggest a serious discussion on the best policy for the future, with an indication that wing formations could thenceforth play a greater part. They do not at all read like the minutes of an 'investigation' into Dowding's, and Park's, conduct of the Battle – 'like putting them on a charge', as the complaint goes. The minutes, however, do not tell the whole story. When he received them, Park promptly sent in two pages of closely typed foolscap, repeating what he had said and urgently requesting that his remarks should be embodied in the minutes. Apart from stressing the time factor and the need to intercept before the fall of bombs, his statement included sharp comments on the Duxford Wing. It had operated, he asserted, under favourable conditions, arriving in time only to intercept outgoing raids, 'fairly easy to deal with'. His own squadrons had produced results fully comparable, though under more difficult conditions. And the Duxford Wing had caused great confusion: 'It had proceeded, unknown to No. 11 Group, to the Kentish coast . . . thus causing new raids to be originated by the Observer Corps and AA units.' Air-raid warnings had been prolonged, and 11 Group squadrons 'had been sent to intercept friendly formations which had been reported as fresh raids'.

In addition, Park wished his view to be put on record that it would be bad for squadron morale if the impression spread 'that it was not safe to enter the south-eastern area except with four or five squadrons'. He also asked for a note to be included that his views on forward interception were supported by DCAS (Sholto Douglas), AOC-in-C Fighter Command, and Sir Charles Portal.[24]

As diplomatically as possible, the Air Staff secretariat declined to incorporate Park's amendments. His statement was held to be too long and 'out of keeping with the rest of the minutes, which are intended more as an *aide memoire* than as a detailed report of the discussion'.[25]

Clearly there were strong currents at this time, not only in 12 Group and the Air Ministry but also among some of the pilots in 11 Group itself, in favour of trying to meet the enemy with bigger formations. On 1 October Park had felt obliged to write to his sector commanders explaining why he did not use three-squadron formations more often, and emphasising the time factor.[26]*

In considering this issue, historians of the Battle have almost unanimously concluded that in the circumstances of August and September 1940 Park's use of single and paired squadrons was inevitable and completely sound. The proximity of the enemy, and the desirability of intercepting before the bombs fell, dominated all. And even in the technical aspects of control when a wing was airborne, there was still

---

*After the Battle, wing formations soon became standard in the very different conditions of the offensive, when there was ample time for the squadrons to form up before sweeping across the Channel.

great difficulty in the summer of 1940. As late as 1 October, only sixteen of the fighter squadrons had been re-equipped with VHF radio:[27] HF was patchy and extremely difficult to hear if more than three squadrons were operating together.

Although posterity has largely agreed that Park's use of single and paired squadrons was right, and brilliantly right, in the circumstances of the Battle, Sholto Douglas and the Air Tactics directorate were more impressed with Leigh-Mallory's concepts as a recipe for the future. There was a certain irony in this. One great proof of the value of Leigh-Mallory's ideas was thought to be the big 'scores' achieved by the Duxford Wing – 105 in its first five operations. But post-war research has revealed these 'scores' to be among the most exaggerated in the Battle, as might be expected from the number of aircraft engaged. The fifty-two German aircraft claimed by the Wing on 15 September, for instance, is not far short of the entire number actually shot down by the whole of Fighter Command on that memorable day.

A further thought about the Duxford Wing is suggested by P. B. 'Laddie' Lucas's absorbing and perceptive biography of his brother-in-law, Douglas Bader. Referring to the movement of squadrons into 11 Group to replace the battered squadrons there, Lucas states that Leigh-Mallory would not allow the Duxford squadrons to be called upon in this way. 'Around 242, 310 and 19 he threw an iron cordon. . . . This was L-M's corps d'élite. Nothing and no one was going to be allowed to disturb it.'[28]

If this was remotely so, it raises some very curious questions. If Dowding decided to order any of these squadrons south, who was Leigh-Mallory to stop him? So either Dowding partly approved of Leigh-Mallory's concept – we know that his Senior Air Staff Officer, Air Vice-Marshal Evill, did[29] – or else he hesitated to go against Leigh-Mallory's wishes, or else he did not concern himself personally with the choice of squadrons to move. None of these explanations completely satisfies. What seems a pity is that Dowding, who clearly had to keep a strong force in so vital a sector as Duxford, did not, in fact, order at least 242 Squadron south. Bader was yearning for more action, and in the daily hurly-burly of 11 Group, he would surely have found plenty. In that case this controversy, assuming it arose at all, might never have taken the unfortunate form it did.

The 'big wing' issue played a part, though only a part, in the next great matter of controversy – the 'dismissal' (i.e. replacement) of Dowding and Park. Towards the end of November, Dowding was relieved at Fighter Command, and Park the following month at 11 Group. To believers in the conspiracy theory of history, and indeed to many who have no theory of history but sympathise with Dowding and Park, it has always appeared that these changes were not unconnected with ambition: for Sholto Douglas moved upwards into Dowding's place and Leigh-Mallory moved sideways, but also upwards, into Park's.

It does not need the conspiracy theory, however, to explain or understand these moves. Both commanders had been under enormous strain, and Park was visibly tired. Sholto Douglas and the Air Tactics directorate were keen to experiment with the 'big wings', and if these were to be tried there was much to be said for having an enthusiast, Leigh-Mallory, directing the Group which would put most of them into the air. As the senior Group commander, in charge of 12 Group since its inception, Leigh-Mallory had excellent qualifications for the post. His later appointments – as the head of Fighter Command, the Allied Expeditionary Air Force and the Allied Air Forces in South-East Asia – show that he was considered fit for much higher command than that of a Group.

For his part, Park resented leaving 11 Group, which he had commanded only since April. He was offered an Air Staff post, but demurred. He went instead to command a Flying Training Group (No. 23), where his intelligence, energy and recent experience were well applied and where his success set him again on the upward path – to high command in Malta, the Middle East and South-East Asia. Well rewarded in his later career, he received only moderate recognition for his great achievement in 1940 – the CB, often bestowed on upwardly mobile civil servants as their second slice of the honours cake.

Despite all that he had contributed to the victory, there were good reasons for replacing Dowding at Fighter Command. He had held his post for the exceptionally long period of four years and had been scheduled for retirement since before the war. To avoid a change during the Battle and the months leading up to it, his period of command had been three times extended by short periods – so short as to make Churchill complain to Sinclair that it was 'entirely wrong to keep an officer in the position of Commander-in-Chief, conducting hazardous operations from day to day when he is dangling on the end of an expiring appointment'.[30] Now that the daylight battle was dying down the urgent demand was for success in countering the night bombing and then, looking further ahead, for offensive operations over the continent.

Dowding seemed to the Air Staff, at this juncture, the wrong man for either task. He was having no obvious success against the 'night blitz', and he would certainly resist the use of his fighters offensively over France.

Moreover, by ignoring the Park/Leigh-Mallory dispute until it had become widely known, Dowding had given the Air Staff the impression that he was losing his grip. On 3 November Sholto Douglas felt obliged to tell him to resolve the differences, which seemed to be leading 'to a good deal of bitterness not only between the two AOCs but between the squadrons in the two Groups'. 'This obviously cannot go on,' concluded Douglas, 'and it is for you to put the matter right.'[31]

Other matters of dispute had also arisen during October. In view of the ineffectiveness of the defences against the night bomber, the Air Council had recently set up a high-powered Night Air Defence Committee under the greatly respected Marshal of the Royal Air Force Sir John Salmond, a former Chief of the Air Staff.[32] Salmond and Dowding were already no great friends; and to two of the Committee's recommendations, backed by Sholto Douglas, Dowding strongly objected. One was that three of his Hurricane squadrons should be specially trained and given over to night fighting. The other was that, to eliminate congestion of plots from the radar stations and to speed reaction, separate filter rooms should be opened at each Group headquarters to replace the central filtering room at Stanmore. Pungent in expression as always, Dowding on 24 October wrote to the Prime Minister explaining his opposition to the filter-room proposals. His summing up was characteristic: 'I think we shall pay £100,000 in material and labour in order to secure a slight reduction in efficiency.' But he clearly regarded the proposal as one more piece of interference from the Air Ministry:

My main grievance . . . is in the matter of the expenditure of my time in arguing with the Air Staff every intimate detail of my organisation. . . . I agreed to decentralisation under strong pressure because it is not a matter that is going to lose the war for us, and I have to fight the Air Staff on so many important issues.[33]

With such divergences between them, it is not surprising that the Air Staff now favoured a swift termination to Dowding's period of command. Their view was shared by Sinclair and Balfour, who had both paid recent visits to Duxford and learnt something of the 'big wing' dispute at first hand. It was also reluctantly accepted by Churchill;

apparently he later said the decision was right, but 'nearly broke his heart'. So on 25 November Dowding had to depart and the cleverer, and much more worldly, Sholto Douglas took his place.

In at least one of the final matters of dispute Dowding proved more perceptive than his successor. In their desperation to beat the night bomber Douglas and others on the Air Staff had urged Dowding to try 'fighter nights' – using a fairly large force of day fighters on moonlit nights in the hope of catching the enemy. Dowding would agree to only a limited effort in this direction. The answer to the night bomber, he insisted, could come only from radar and better night fighters – Beaufighters equipped with better AI and operating in conjunction with radar control from the ground (GCI), not yet perfected. It would, he explained, take some months to secure a significant improvement in the number of enemy night bombers destroyed. He was quite right, as Douglas was to find.*

Dowding's later career tended to justify the view that by the end of 1940 his best days were over. To save him from the retirement intended by the Air Ministry, Beaverbrook, with Churchill's agreement, found other work for him: they sent him to the USA to head the British Air Mission already there, with the task of 'selecting, modifying and purchasing aircraft and air armament'. But he soon caused embarrassment to his colleagues by voicing his own personal views – such as that there was no need for the increased production of heavy bombers that the Mission was encouraging the Americans to undertake. Day bombing, he told some of Roosevelt's chief advisers, was too expensive, and within a few months night bombing would lose its sting, so the Americans had better make tanks. This and other idiosyncratic utterings (for an air marshal sent out to help get the best aircraft and more of them) caused Lord Halifax, the British Ambassador, to forward complaints about him to the Foreign Office, and Air Commodore Slessor, in Washington for staff discussions, to write to the new Chief of the Air Staff, Portal, suggesting his recall. 'I hate writing like this about a very senior officer,' wrote Slessor, 'but in the national interest I must express the fervent hope that you will contrive to get him out of this country before he does much more harm.'[35]

So Dowding returned, and in June 1941 was asked to write his *Despatch* on the Battle of Britain, which he did admirably. Gazetted

---

*Flight mechanic William Eslick, modifying a Spitfire for night operations, described the process as 'like trying to make a sow's ear out of a silk purse'.[34]

then for retirement on 1 October, he had scarcely been off the active list for a month when at Churchill's insistence his Service career reopened. The Prime Minister pressed him, much against his will, to undertake a review of RAF establishments, in the hope of achieving economies. It was a task which inevitably aroused opposition. Neither enjoying the job nor considering that he had made much of a success of it, in July 1942 Dowding then retired again, this time at his own request.

Though there were ample reasons for making a change at Stanmore in November 1940, it is more than understandable that Dowding departed feeling aggrieved. After the three very short extensions of his tenure, the latest time-limit, fixed for 31 October, had on 21 August been completely withdrawn. Then, quite unexpectedly to him, he was required to relinquish his Command at a few days' notice. In later years he even told his biographer, Robert Wright, that in the second week of November he received 'a sudden phone-call' from Sinclair telling him he was to relinquish his Command 'immediately'.[36] But here memory played Dowding false. Sinclair, a devoted minister and the soul of courtesy, was not a man to sack a respected commander over the telephone. In fact, he saw Dowding at the Air Ministry on 13 November to tell him that Sholto Douglas was shortly to take his place, and to extend to him the invitation to lead the British Mission in America.[37] The telephone call, saying the change at Stanmore was to take place immediately, must have come a day or two later.

Be this as it may, Dowding felt that he had been treated inconsiderately and with scant acknowledgment of his services. He told Wright later: 'They just got rid of me. . . . But I want it to be quite clear that I had no grievance on that score. It was the way it was done that hurt, when I was sent away as if I had been rather an indifferent sort of commander.'[38]

If Dowding's replacement on the morrow of his great victory has generated controversy, still more so has the question of adequate recognition of his achievement. During the Battle, on 1 October, he was appointed GCB, but on relinquishing Fighter Command and on his two retirements he got nothing. At the time of his second retirement King George VI raised the question whether he should not be made a Marshal of the RAF,[39] but official opinion in the Air Ministry demurred. To do so would set a precedent – only the heads of the Service, the Chiefs of the Air Staff, had ever been accorded that exalted rank. Also, Dowding had been quite 'difficult'; and he had already retired previously. It was left until 1946 for the precedent to be broken, when Sir Arthur Harris, who had never been Chief of the Air Staff, was made a Marshal of the RAF, in compensation for the barony which the Attlee Government denied him.

Six months after his retirement, Dowding received much fuller recognition. On 1 January 1943 he became Lord Dowding of Bentley Priory, the first RAF officer to be ennobled apart from the great Trenchard. By that time the magnitude and decisive nature of his victory was clear to all. It was not quite so obvious in November 1940 when the invasion threat was still a reality and German bombs were raining down night after night on Britain's cities.

Among the many charges brought against the Air Ministry in its treatment of Dowding is that it put out, in the spring of 1941, a pamphlet describing the Battle in which no mention was made of the Air Officer Commanding-in-Chief.[40] This curious omission quickly evoked the ire of the Prime Minister who, like Dowding, thought the pamphlet otherwise 'admirable'. On 12 April 1941 Churchill wrote in characteristic vein to Sinclair:

The jealousies and cliquism which have led to the committing of this offence are a discredit to the Air Ministry, and I do not think any other Service Department would have been guilty of such a piece of work. What would have been said if . . . the Admiralty had told the tale of Trafalgar and left Lord Nelson out of it?[41]

Difficult as this may be for some to believe, it was probably not 'jealousies and cliquism' which caused the omission of Dowding's name. The pamphlet, which cost the Air Ministry £50 in fees to the author and sold six million copies, mentioned no names at all on the British side except that of Churchill, and only two on the German – Goering and Goebbels. The Air Ministry's Department of Public Relations at that time was trying to avoid the personality cult, and in particular it was trying to discourage the press from building up fighter 'aces'. This was because adulatory reports about certain individual pilots or squadrons in the early days of the war had tended to create ill-feeling among others equally valorous but less well publicised. In applying a policy of anonymity in *The Battle of Britain* pamphlet to the extent of not even mentioning Dowding, the Department had clearly taken leave of its senses.

Despite a campaign which has more or less continued to this day, Dowding was never elevated, either in retirement or posthumously – that *would* have been a precedent – to the rank of Marshal of the RAF.

He was, however, buried in Westminster Abbey and then, in the fullness of time, accorded the supreme tribute – a public statue in London, splendidly sited outside the beautiful 'RAF church', St Clement Dane's. He would have thought it entirely appropriate, and it would have pleased him very much to know that the initiative for this came from his own surviving aircrew, in the Battle of Britain Fighter Association, and not in the least from the Ministry of Defence.

From the controversies surrounding the Battle it is a relief to turn to the myths, which have flourished freely. There is the popular myth that the Spitfire alone won the Battle – when there were many more Hurricanes,* which certainly shot down more of the bombers. There are the myths that Dowding's intervention alone stopped the flow of fighters to France in May and June 1940, and that throughout his time at Stanmore he met with nothing but delay and obstruction from the Air Ministry. There is the myth that Lord Beaverbrook waved a magic wand and lo! there were aircraft where none had existed before. There is the myth that at one time Fighter Command was down to its last few aircraft. If a group of the more persistent of these myths were to be embodied in a pantechnicon sentence it might conceivably run something like this: 'The Battle of Britain, despite Fighter Command's being down to its last few aircraft, was won by unfailingly cheerful young officers flying Spitfires magically produced by Lord Beaverbrook and directed by "Stuffy" Dowding, who first had to beat the Air Ministry, Winston Churchill and the French before he could beat the Germans.'

Most of these myths have received some attention in the foregoing pages. Of one which has not, about the unfailingly cheerful young officers, it is perhaps sufficient to point out that very often the officers were non-commissioned ones, in the rank of sergeant; and that though these young men, mostly in their early twenties, were indeed incredibly cheerful, they were not invariably so. Particularly not when, as was always happening to someone, they were dog-tired from flying and long hours at readiness, or tense with nervous strain from repeated danger, or badly wounded, or burnt.

The most recent and sophisticated of the myths seems to have been started by Group Captain F. W. Winterbotham, the RAF Intelligence Officer responsible for liaison with the Secret Intelligence Service and

*See Appendix VII.

the Government Code and Cypher School at Bletchley Park. The first revelation to the public that Britain had consistently read the high-grade cypher messages produced by the Germans on their Enigma machine, and transmitted by W/T, came in Winterbotham's *The Ultra Secret* (1974), which was soon followed by Ronald Lewin's *Ultra Goes to War* (1978). Both painted an affecting picture of Dowding at the famous Air Staff 'investigation' of 17 October 1940 unable to defend his tactics properly because he could not honourably mention his most secret sources of information, the Enigma decrypts from Bletchley, since their existence could not be divulged to the others present. The implication was that Dowding, often aware in advance of the enemy's extensive plans, had to hold back squadrons to deal with later raids he knew were coming, rather than quickly throw in the big formations advocated by Leigh-Mallory.

There is a double myth in this. Dowding himself, according to Martin Gilbert, was not placed on the very restricted list of those who received the actual Enigma decrypts until late October, when the Battle was nearly over.[42] But long before that his headquarters, like others, was being kept informed of anything important, or of immediate operational value, which was emerging from the Enigma traffic, without being told its exact provenance. In the same way if he had wished to defend his tactics by reference to secret information, Dowding had no need to divulge the precise source.

Beyond this, the picture of a muzzled Dowding is misleading in another way. Dowding did sometimes have information in advance about German operations, but usually it came too late for any immediate use, or else the operations were cancelled or postponed. He learnt, for instance, from Enigma that a mass attack on London was arranged for 13 September and was then postponed to 14 September. He did not learn that it was then rearranged for 15 September, when it actually happened. Similarly, he knew that widespread raids were planned for 15 August; but the first indication that Stumpff's forces from Denmark and Norway were approaching the north-east came from radar, not Enigma.

And so it was in general throughout the Battle. Ultra made extremely valuable additions to the many other sources of intelligence, such as the interception of the bombers' wireless messages in low-grade code or cypher or the monitoring of the German fighter pilots' chatter over the R/T, but it was not at this stage nearly as important or decisive as it became later in the war. Its myriad gleanings were particularly useful in constructing an exact picture of the Luftwaffe's organisation, order of battle and equipment, but as yet they rarely produced enough to permit an instant and profitable operational reaction. Information in general had to be built up over a long period and conclusions inferred; very rarely did Ultra speak plain in a single message about a major matter – such as the date projected for the invasion, or where the German troops were to land. The official history, *British Intelligence in the Second World War*, thus sums up the subject: 'For all his major decisions C-in-C Fighter Command depended on his own strategic judgment, with no direct assistance from Enigma.'[43]

It would be too much to describe as a myth the popular impression that the Battle was won by Dowding and a thousand or so dashing young fighter pilots. There is a world of truth in that, but it is an incomplete truth. For the more one studies the Battle, the more one becomes aware of all the complex forces and factors which had to cohere perfectly to get those young men into the air in the right place and at the right time and with the right weapons to deal with the enemy.

Moreover, there were vast organisations right outside the RAF which helped to shape and win the Battle. Quite apart from bombarding the invasion ports, maintaining watch round the British coasts with 200 or more craft on daily patrol, and keeping the sea lanes open, the Royal Navy by its sheer existence constituted the prime obstacle to Germany's hopes. Since the German Navy could not expect to master the Royal Navy, the Luftwaffe had to do so instead, and for that it had first to master the RAF. It was this single fact alone which determined the enemy's strategy for the Battle.

Whether the Navy, in actual fact, would have intervened in the Channel in the full strength feared by the Germans, is an interesting question. At a meeting to discuss the anti-invasion plans at the end of July Admiral of the Fleet Sir Charles Forbes, Commander-in-Chief of the Home Fleet, stated firmly that in no circumstances would his heavy ships operate south of the Wash. Churchill, expected to explode by the others present, merely met this 'with an indulgent smile'. The Royal Navy, he asserted, invariably undertook the impossible when the situation demanded: 'If two or three nurses were wrecked on a desert island, the Navy would rush to their rescue, through typhoons and uncharted seas: and he had not a shadow of doubt that if the Germans invaded the south coast of Britain we would see every available battleship storming through the Straits of Dover.'[44] And while Churchill was in charge, no doubt they would have done. In any case the

Admiralty soon went half-way towards justifying the Prime Minister's belief. During August it agreed that if the German heavy units appeared in the southern North Sea, the British capital ships would follow suit.[45]

The Army, too, contributed much to the victory, not only by its preparations to meet the invader, in which it would have had stout support from the Home Guard, but by its expertise in the highly dangerous work of dealing with the hundreds of unexploded bombs – including the famous one which threatened St Paul's Cathedral on 15 September – and by providing most of the vital ground defences. The anti-aircraft gunners, especially those at Dover and the airfields, played an important part from the beginning, the searchlight crews an increasingly useful one as the German night offensive developed. Without these ground defences, far more low-level attacks would have been made, and far more damage done to aircraft factories and Fighter Command installations. Anti-aircraft fire also disturbed the concentration of bombers at higher level on the vital run up to the target. And though the guns hurled a vast quantity of steel and explosive into the sky for every aircraft they shot down, the mere sight and sound of them was a valuable boost to civilian morale.

It should also be recalled that the civil defence services were already highly active during the Battle well before they performed so long and magnificently during the 'blitz'. The air-raid wardens, full-time and part-time, of both sexes; the heavy rescue services, recruited mainly from the building trades; the firemen, professional and auxiliary; the ambulance teams; the police, whose work was so vastly extended when raids occurred; the Women's Voluntary Service, who in their green suits and purple blouses (bought at their own expense) seemed to be everywhere, and to undertake anything from supervising evacuation and distributing clothing to tending disconsolate children and serving cups of tea – all these organisations and many more made their essential contribution. And so, of course, did the workers in the aircraft and other factories and in the fields, who well knew how vital their output was to the struggle being waged in the sky.

Some of these groups were more closely associated with the RAF than others. The Post Office War Group, for instance, did magnificent work in restoring shattered landlines and keeping each part of the whole complex defence system in touch with the next. And the 30,000 or so members of the Observer Corps, women as well as men, and mostly part-time, were as essential to the Battle as the RAF's own radar stations.

There were many more such bodies. The Civilian Repair Organisation, involving scores of garages and workshops, performed an invaluable service in rebuilding damaged aircraft, as many as 150–200 a week. Hurricanes leaving a factory or a maintenance unit on Saturday would often be in action by the Tuesday, suffer damage, be called away for repair and be back again at the squadron by the weekend. No. 1 Civilian Repair Unit, at Oxford, had a working week of nearly 100 hours. Civilians in the RAF's No. 50 Maintenance Unit helped servicemen to build vast dumps of badly crashed aircraft which could be raided for parts useful in the process of 'cannibalisation'.[46] And when the aircraft were repaired, or were coming new from the factories, the admirable civilian pilots of the Air Transport Auxiliary, women as well as men, were at hand to deliver them to the maintenance units or the squadrons.

Most closely associated of all with the RAF, since they worked alongside, were the members of the WAAF. At the time of the Battle they were still admitted to only half-a-dozen trades, but whether 'admin.', or cooks, or clerks or 'drivers (petrol)' or telephonists or balloon fabric repairers, they played an essential part. The MT girls, officially limited to driving a car or a 30 cwt truck, cheerfully took on much heavier vehicles and risked the chance of breaking a delicate wrist by cranking up 2½ tonners in cold weather. Most publicised later – not at the time, for security reasons – were the 'clerks (special duty)', the plotters, tellers and others who worked in the ops rooms or the radar stations. They maintained their quiet efficiency even when the bombs were falling nearby or when, emotionally involved with a pilot, they overheard his voice on the R/T to the Controller in the ops room, crying out in triumph or in agony.

Perhaps those most often affected by the cries that came over the air were the girls of the Y (Interception) Service, who monitored R/T over the Channel and southern England. They heard the shouts and screams of the German pilots as well as the British. One WAAF sergeant at Hawkinge, after reporting the regular appearance of a certain cheery-sounding German pilot on his Channel reconnaissance run, then overheard the resulting interception by Spitfires, who shot him down in flames. 'He was unable to get out and we listened to him as he screamed and screamed for his mother and cursed the Fuehrer. I found myself praying: "Get out, bale out, oh please dear God, get him out." But it was no use. We heard him the whole way down until he fell below reception range. I went out and was sick.'

These R/T monitors often suffered the additional grief that they were aware of approaching disaster and could do nothing to stop it. They would hear a German leader yell the order to attack and know that he was diving on an unsuspecting RAF pilot below. 'I would often hear one of the WAAF operators murmuring "Oh God, oh God, please . . . *please* look up," and I knew how helpless she felt.'[47]

All reports of the WAAF under fire during the Battle speak of their courage, and none more so than those of the ubiquitous Inspector-General. On 20 August, after visiting Tangmere and finding 'an enormous amount of damage', Ludlow-Hewitt wrote:

As usual the WAAF have been quite exceptionally good. . . . The CO reported that the Ops Room was rocking with the bombing, and that the girls stood to their work with admirable coolness, setting an excellent example to everyone. . . . The really admirable behaviour of the WAAF under the stress of bombardment at very exposed stations such as RDF [radar] stations and aerodromes in the South is beyond all praise. . . .

Three days later, after visiting recently bombed Middle Wallop, he again reported: 'Everywhere the same story is told of the remarkable calm and courage displayed by the WAAF.'[48] Such virtues, taken for granted nowadays in a world of greater sexual equality, made a deep impression in the Service in 1940, and not only on elderly air marshals.

These bare references illustrate the immense contribution to the Battle made by literally millions outside the RAF. And within the RAF itself, the Battle was by no means only the work, as is so often thought, of Fighter Command. Coastal Command, by its reconnaissance, anti-invasion patrols and bombing, played a vital part: Coastal aircraft photographed the assembly and dispersal of the invasion craft, and it was a Coastal stripped-Spitfire which at length, on 29 October, reached out to cover the farthest Baltic ports and bring back the evidence that no invasion fleet was hiding there.[49] No less involved was Bomber Command, with its attacks on Berlin, German communications and airfields, and the invasion ports.

In its passive role, Balloon Command also played a most useful part. The balloons could not rise high, but they made it difficult for the enemy to come down below 5,000 feet, where he could bomb more accurately, and they were a death-trap to dive-bombers. They continually suffered losses from enemy pilots and the weather, and probably brought down more British than German aircraft, but the deterrent effect of their cables was considerable and, like the guns, they had a secondary value in cheering up the local civilians. Hanging over the cities or 'vulnerable points', the balloons were a brave and reassuring sight.

Within Fighter Command itself, Britain's shield and sword against aerial invasion, the victory was of course far from being only the work of Dowding and the pilots. Keith Park fought most of the tactical battle and surely deserves a statue too – at the Auckland airport which bears his name, or better still at Uxbridge. And the magnificent aircrews could have done nothing without the intelligent, well-trained and devoted ground crews, both groups alike recruited largely before the war. On these ground crews depended, among a host of other things, the signals traffic, the commissariat, the supply, distribution and fitting of equipment, the servicing of guns and radar, part of the ground defence, the servicing and minor repair of airframes as well as engines – and, usually flat out for speed, the refuelling and rearming of the aircraft after operations.

For months on end, many of these men were kept at the fullest possible stretch. The damage suffered by so many aircraft during the French campaign and the numerous modifications made between June and August 1940 to improve the performance or protection of the British fighters brought an enormous amount of work. One fitter recalled that during these months, in addition to the routine servicing, he had to make about ten modifications to each of his Hurricanes.[50]★

But when tribute is duly paid to the many contributors to the victory who are sometimes overlooked or forgotten, the mind rightly and inevitably comes back to those superb fighter pilots and their commander-in-chief. Perhaps more than any other victory in history, this one was achieved by a scientific system of defence built up over many years. But systems do not create themselves. In the building up of that system, though it could never have triumphed without the fruits of the genius of men like Camm, Mitchell and Watson-Watt, there was no one who

★P. O'Connor made the following modifications among others:
1) All Merlin engines removed, returned to Rolls-Royce for 'slipping clutch' and refitted.
2) Engine coolant changed to different glycol mixture.
3) Flare traps with coarser masks fitted, to prevent choking up.
4) Enlarged atomisers fitted in priming system.
5) Improved hand starter magneto gear fitted.
6) Propellers changed from two-bladed wooden to three-blade de Havilland two-speed type, to three-blade Rotol type with constant speed unit.
7) Carburettor linkings changed from stainless steel to phosphor-bronze.
8) Engine boost increased from 6¼ pounds psi to 9 pounds psi for 100 octane fuel.
9) Improved sparking-plugs fitted.
To these might have been added, at various times, the fitting of armour and later of self-sealing wing tanks.

played a greater part than the man whose duty it also was to operate it when the crisis came.

It would not be difficult to show that Dowding was by no means a ready champion of new ideas. His native caution, always demanding proof positive, precluded rapid acceptance. It had taken much to persuade him, for instance, that his fighters' guns would be far more effective 'harmonised' for converging fire at 250 yards instead of 400, and that attacks should be pressed home even closer than that. Even in the all-important field of radar there were several other RAF officers who, in Watson-Watt's opinion, grasped its possibilities and gave support more quickly than Dowding, who was not even in the radar pioneer's 'top four' for helpfulness. Among those with whom Watson-Watt found collaboration easier were Freeman – 'he believed in my little team from the first and fought many of its battles for it' – and, above all, Sholto Douglas, whom he found 'imaginative, enterprising, receptive and constructive . . . decisive and vigorous in action'.[51] Nevertheless, it was under Dowding as Air Member for Research and Development that radar first made its appearance, and under Dowding as AOC-in-C Fighter Command that it was successfully incorporated into the air defence system. He was a convinced, though far from uncritical, supporter from the early days, and without that support the radar chain would never have been in place to play its outstandingly important part in the Battle.

Similarly, it was under Dowding that the system of fighter control was evolved, without which early warning would have lost half its benefit. He had also supported from their earliest conception the development of the Hurricane and the Spitfire, and had put every ounce of his energy and authority into getting enough squadrons armed with them to win the Battle which he so clearly foresaw. And when, before the Battle, the danger arose that they would be wasted in vain efforts to save the reeling Allied armies in France, his was one of the two decisive voices which ensured that the wastage did not become fatal.

It was in what he did before the Battle, rather than in his conduct of it, that Dowding's prime achievement lay. In the Battle itself, since control of operations was delegated to Groups and sectors, it was Park, in command of the hardest pressed Group, who bore the main burden of responsibility: who had to decide which raids were important, and which were minor or feints, and what forces should be put up against them. Indeed, so completely did Park fight the tactical battle that Dowding was not even aware, in many respects, of how he was doing it.

On 13 October the Senior Air Staff Officer at Fighter Command, Air Vice-Marshal 'Strath' Evill, an officer of outstanding quality, found himself obliged to suggest to Dowding that they ought to have much fuller information about operations. The daily return from Groups gave a bare indication of sightings, interceptions and casualties, but provided no real picture of the fighting or the tactics. Evill wrote:

We do not know whether their squadrons are sent up singly or in twos or threes, or to what heights they are sent. We have no indication as to how squadrons in the air are disposed or whether factory areas are specifically covered. There is, in fact, no general statement of the action taken. . . . We have, I know, received – after calling for it – a report from 11 Group on their method of operation in the first six weeks of this battle. . . . We have also received from Leigh-Mallory reports as to why and how he employs his wing, and reports from Park as to why he does not. Apart from these communications we do not know a great deal about the way in which they conduct operations, and there is certainly no recognised routine for reports from Groups as to what they are doing. . . .[52]

Dowding's was in essence the strategic role, deciding among other things the forces to be kept in each Group. He can be criticised for not ensuring better co-ordination between 11 and 12 Groups, for being slow in assessing and disseminating the tactical lessons of the fighting, and for not insisting that new pilots who came to his squadrons during the Battle had at least some experience of air firing – many had never fired their guns at all, or only once or twice into a hill-side or the sea.[53] But his decision to retain squadrons in the north was brilliantly vindicated when the Luftwaffe struck there on 15 August; and his broad dispositions and his reinforcing and replacement arrangements, as did Park's use of single and paired squadrons, passed the acid test: they achieved victory. Throughout all his period of command, too, there was his splendid example of devotion, determination and integrity. Whatever laurels were withheld from him by the Air Ministry, he has posterity's.

And the aircrew, Dowding's 'chicks' – a term which delighted him when Churchill used it,[54] though one he would have been far too reserved to coin for himself – what more should be said of them? Nothing, perhaps, except that without their skill, their transcendent courage, their devotion and their sacrifice, the scientific system would have been devised in vain. Together, they enabled Britain to escape the devastating clash of armies and the horrors of Nazi occupation.

As the daylight Battle faded, and the bombs descended in full force by night, a new phase of Britain's resistance began. In the words of

Angus Calder, 'it was the battle of an unarmed civilian population against incendiaries and high explosive: the battle of firemen, wardens, policemen, nurses and rescue workers against the enemy they could not hurt. The front-line troops were doctors, parsons, telephonists. . . . Where the bombs fell, heroes would spring up by accident. . . .'[55]

Many of the heroes, as is so often the case, were heroes by force of example. This was a fact which the Prime Minister, himself a hero with a sense of humour even in the most difficult circumstances, tried to impress on Nelson, the black cat at No. 10 Downing Street. When Nelson showed fright at the sound of the guns, Churchill chided him for being unworthy of the name he bore, and added: 'Try to remember, Nelson, what those boys in the RAF are doing.'[56]

A week later, on 15 October, Churchill warned the War Cabinet that it would be two or three months before there could be any substantially better results against the night bombers. He added: 'The people of Britain must stick it out.'[57]

With no little inspiration from those who had saved them in the great air battles earlier, they did, to the enduring benefit of their country, and the world.

He 111, flying north over Millwall, London, the docks (*right centre*) and the Royal
Naval College, Greenwich (*bottom right*).

Sir Hugh Dowding with the King and Queen at Bentley Priory, 6 September 1940.

Peter Townsend with two of his ground crew, Kenley.

*Above:* James Nicolson of 249 Squadron, the only fighter VC.

*Above:* Five Czech sergeants of 310 Squadron.

*Right:* George Barclay of 249 Squadron.

*Above:* Douglas Bader, CO of 242 Squadron, who led the Duxford Wing.

*Right:* Roland 'Bee' Beamont of 87 Squadron.

Biggin Hill photographed by a German bomber during an evening raid on 30 August. German identification is accurate, except that (4) is the officers' mess.

Some of the pilots of 249 Squadron at North Weald in September. John Grandy, the CO (*third from right*), with George Barclay on his left.

Low-level Dornier attack on Kenley, 18 August 1940. Picture taken by a war photographer accompanying the raid.

The end for one more Dornier.

Two German crew survivors are marched off with heavy Army escort, 11 September 1940.

London's dockland burns, 7 September 1940.

'. . . to tend the wounded under fire': a heavy rescue team and helpers.

Shelterers in the London Underground, 1940 (painting by Joseph Bato).

The Battle fades; the 'blitz' continues, London, December 1940.
(Photograph by Cecil Beaton.)

# 23

*Scrambles*

## A MISCELLANY OF
## PERSONAL EXPERIENCES

*Aircrews' ranks are shown as
they were in the Battle.*

*Honours and decorations are
shown as they are today.*

*Flying Officer Paul Pitcher, 1 (Canadian) Squadron*
In the first Wing take-off at Northolt the three squadrons stationed
there – 303 Polish, 1 RAF and 1 Canadian, were lined up for take-off at
their respective dispersal areas in three different parts of the field. Due
to a confusion in take-off orders, all three squadrons opened throttle
simultaneously and headed towards the centre of the field where the
thirty-six aircraft met!

By some miracle, no aircraft collided with another or with the
ground, although the turbulence from slipstreams was unbelievable.
The station commander, who was witness to the scene, had to be helped
into the officers' mess for alcoholic resuscitation.

I seem to recall that part of the confusion arose from the fact that two
No. 1 Squadrons were involved. In any event, all Canadian squadrons
overseas were renumbered thereafter and given '400' numbers, 1
becoming 401.

## ACW Anne Turley-George

My sister Tig and I joined the WAAF before war was declared and we did not take it too seriously. Even when war was declared and we marched off to Tangmere, it was still a glorious game, and this illusion continued into the early summer of 1940.

That summer of 1940 found us round-eyed and very earnest indeed in the ops room manning the R/T sets. This was really exciting and we felt a part of things at last, transmitting directions to the fighter pilots and logging their messages.

Then one day the Stukas came howling down at us out of the sun and, after the first stunned disbelief, we tumbled into the shelters whilst they beat and hammered us into the ground. We ascended to chaos.

The squadrons thundered off the ground tirelessly. Off they pelted, day after day, those glorious, radiant boys. We were with them in sound and spirit. We heard their shouts of 'Tally Ho!' There was one boy who always burst into song as soon as he caught sight of the enemy and swung into the attack. We only heard these private war cries when they forgot to switch off their transmitters in the heat of battle, an awful yet uplifting experience. But that feeling of lead in the stomach when they failed to return was all too familiar. . . . There were so many. I remember when Caesar Hull was killed – we *all* admired him. The gay and gallant American Billy Fiske; the two Wood-Scawens, inseparable brothers, devout Catholics, charmers both – and all of them so young and so well endowed, and such a wicked, wicked waste. I mourned them then, now and for ever.

## Pilot Officer Harold Bird-Wilson CBE, DSO, DFC and Bar, AFC and Bar, 17 Squadron

The ground crew, RAF and WAAF, were just marvellous. All maintained our Hurricanes in a most professional manner. Dawn awakening in our beds at dispersal. The telephone rings to pass the States of Readiness to Sector ops at Debden – just across the aerodrome. If brought to readiness, then a quick change out of pyjamas into uniform and flying boots. Some pilots were known to scramble in their pyjamas. Not a recommended mode of dress for altitude or baling out!

Then the silence until the telephone rang again. 'Telephoneitis' became a norm, very worrying and to some 'twitching' on the nerves. The solid boredom and the rush of excitement. The scramble, the clear and steady voice of the controller giving us directions and height, the number of enemy aircraft, ever-growing, sometimes into hundreds.

And we were only twelve Hurricanes. We hoped and prayed that other squadrons had also been scrambled, but we never saw them. We just went ploughing in, picked our target and fought. Shots of adrenalin and dryness of mouth. The natural worry of life and death.

Soon, back to the aerodrome and the safe landing and the ground crew and armourers smiling a welcome, particularly when the guns had been fired. . . . The debriefing excitements, the casualties, the sorrow at the loss of a friend. Back on to Readiness. The wheel goes round and round, until dusk and stand-down. . . . There was no time for tears and only sorrow and off into the next scramble.

### LAC William Eslick, engine fitter, 19 Squadron

All through the Battle two brand new Spitfires stood collecting dust in the hangar. They were not even allotted squadron markings and *nothing could be touched*. These were the Command Reserve aircraft, Dowding's last gamble. No matter how desperate a spare skin-fitting became, to rob a Command Reserve aircraft was asking to be shot.

### Flight Sergeant George Unwin DSO, DFM and Bar, 19 Squadron

Flying Officer Jimmy Coward was shot down when Debden was attacked. One foot was shot away by a cannon shell. During the descent by parachute Jimmy removed his R/T leads from his helmet and made a tourniquet for his leg. He survived and I last saw him as an air commodore air attaché in one of the Scandinavian countries.

### W. Martin, anti-aircraft gunner, 43rd Regiment, Royal Artillery, Croydon aerodrome

We were fortunate to mess with the airmen, and would often be eating when the loud speakers would order 'Treble One come to Readiness' and, sometimes, 'Scramble'.

When the order 'Scramble' came over, the airmen belonging to that squadron did just that – they scrambled, leaving everything just where it was and running to the doors.

I remember marvelling at the alacrity and discipline of the Brylcreem Boys to a voice on the Tannoy.

Our orders to 'Stand To' came over with an almost apologetic air, it seemed to me, and our response was suitably slow and deliberate. Gathering up knife, fork, spoon and mug, perhaps a little hurriedly, we would walk to the exits, putting our gas masks to the 'Alert' position, and climbing up the stairways to our respective 'Gun-pits'. These were brick, square enclosures around a single gun mounted on a single strut. Here we would check the mechanism and load on a full drum – and wait wondering.

Time after time this happened, and the 'Stand Down' would be received with mixed feelings. We were never informed about what was going on. The aircraft would return and we would hear only rumours.

### Sergeant Edmund Walsh, air-gunner, 264 Squadron

When we were stationed at Gatwick, Flight Lieutenant Tuck shot down a Me 110 at the side of the airfield. It crashed only yards from where we were walking to our billet, and we had to dive for cover. Minutes later Tuck landed and taxied to the wreck and started to chop a piece off the tail for a memento. He had landed and got to the wreck before the station services could arrive!

Someone once said to me that an air-gunner would only have a total of seven minutes action before being killed. In consequence between July and October 1940 I knew that today may be my last, and I was in a very private world, but desperately proud and keen to do what I had been trained to do. Anyone who has experienced the firm throaty pull of a Merlin engine can imagine how a Defiant air-gunner felt with those blue exhaust flames snaking back past the turret and four air-cooled Brownings just waiting to protect your pilot, who was really at the mercy of how good you were when it came to it.

### Pilot Officer Peter Down, 56 Squadron

We were very young and crisis, gloom and doom never clouded our thoughts. We were also able to enjoy our private and social lives. When Victor Beamish became CO North Weald he stipulated that the squadrons should fly nine aircraft strong only. This meant each pilot had every fourth day free from duty. Blitz or no blitz, London entertainment and night life continued apace, and after a quick thirty-minute dash in our cars we were in central London with our girlfriends and enjoying life at our favourite haunts and night-clubs. The local hostelries at Epping and Harlow were very generous and accommodating, I seem to recall, and licensing hours usually discreetly stretched.

Returning to the mess at any hour of the night or early morning, there was to be found the ever smiling LACW (Leading Aircraftwoman) Carmichael to serve bacon and eggs and hot black coffee. An absolute gem, never to be forgotten. Nor 'Andy' the bar steward ('Gentlemen of

56 Squadron only drink the best, sir'), Innes Westmacott was duly handed a glass of Bostock & Kimptons 1922 port. We had every encouragement to remain sane.

### Pilot Officer John Greenwood, 253 Squadron
I was on my own in my Hurricane at 28,000 feet, full throttle and doing about 80 mph, just waffling along. Suddenly four 109s flew over me, about thirty yards away. How they didn't see me I really don't know. Anyway, I pulled my nose up and fired. At that height the recoil was too much for the old Hurricane, and I stalled and went into a spin. I never knew whether I hit them.

### Sergeant Pilot Sidney Holloway OBE, 25 Squadron
One day late in July a Swordfish landed at Martlesham, complete with torpedo. A highly excited Fleet Air Arm pilot jumped out, certain that he'd seen the German invasion fleet. 'They're coming, they're coming! There are hordes of them and my bloody tin fish is stuck!'

### D. Boots, armourer, 253 Squadron
It has been stated by [a well-known author] that the ground crews were cowardly. I never saw any evidence of this and only enjoyed the supreme comradeship and coolness of those around me. One occasion stands out, when a German bomber laid a stick of bombs across the airfield. A piece of metal had pierced the starboard wing of one of our fighters and set the ammo. exploding, about 1,200 rounds. One of the armourers dashed out to unload the guns while it was flashing around him and the Attack Alarm was still imminent.

The corporal of armourers was the calmest man I ever met. He looked as though his features were chiselled out like the figures at Mt Rushmore in America. Nothing perturbed him.

### J. T. Ryder, instrument repairer, 257 Squadron
At one time we were a very demoralised squadron until Wing Commander Tuck came, and then things changed. He vitalised the squadron, and we soon went to the top. It was not long before we built up a good score.

But alas many pilots were killed and this as ground crew we felt deeply. The bond on a squadron is very deep, and it was like having a brother killed when one of the pilots bought it.

Who can ever forget Wing Commander Tuck, 'Cowboy' Blachford or

CO Maffett, whose aircraft P3175 is in the Battle of Britain museum? I serviced this aircraft on 'B' flight. It was very nostalgic to see and touch this Hurricane after so many years.

## Pilot Officer W. D. David CBE, DFC, AFC
The standard officer's Van Heusen collar shrank in contact with sea water and was, therefore, very dangerous if you went in the drink. Several pilots were throttled and drowned. The silk scarf was the answer.

The ten days of fighting in France was hell, a real killer. The Battle of Britain was a picnic compared.

I used to pass on the lessons we learned in France. 'Get in close!' was probably the most important. 'You must get right in close to kill.' Another was, 'Make sure your cockpit is ready. Check everything, especially the hood runners.'

I wasn't happy with just the reflector gunsight. In certain light it was awkward. So I had a ring-and-bead fitted as well.

## Flight Lieutenant Dennis Armitage DFC, 266 Squadron
It was less than a month from that early morning on which we departed from Wittering that we got our orders to go back North and reform. I think it was about time. We were now reduced to only five serviceable pilots and our ground staff were ready for a rest, too. After almost a month of almost continuous sunshine, the day of our departure dawned overcast and drizzling, with a solid cloud base at about 3,000 feet.

It seemed unlikely that there would be much doing on such a day but we had to remain at fifteen minutes notice to take off until the new squadron arrived to relieve us at midday. It was just after 11 a.m. when we were told to scramble. The five of us piled into our Spitfires and took off. We were then told to orbit the aerodrome below cloud: there were about 200 enemy aircraft approaching above the cloud but we were not to engage them unless it appeared they were actually going to attack Hornchurch.

For some ten or fifteen long minutes we circled around in the rain, and then the order came. We were to climb through the cloud and try to split up the enemy bombers before they reached the aerodrome. I signalled the lads to close up and nosed my way up into the clouds with two Spitfires in tight formation on either side. . . .

## Flying Officer Jeffrey Quill OBE, AFC, 65 Squadron

Generally speaking, ex-Battle of Britain pilots often become a bit partisan on the relative merits of the Hurricane and the Spitfire. The Spitfire achieved, in the eyes of the public, a distinct aura of romance because of its great beauty of line and the ease of recognition in the air, and partly on account of its Schneider ancestry. After many years of reflection I take the view that it took both of them to win the Battle of Britain and neither would have achieved it on its own. The Hurricane achieved the greater damage to the enemy (as has often been pointed out), but without the Spitfire squadrons to fight the 109s their casualties might well have led to the losing of the battle.

As a man intimately involved with the Spitfire from its early stage in our own flight trials, the above is the most objective view I can take. I would not like to have been a Hurricane pilot in 1940 and greatly respect the courage and achievements of those who were.

## Sergeant Pilot Robert Beardsley DFC, 41 Squadron

On 30 September, having intercepted Do 17s and Me 109 escorts returning to the Pas de Calais over west Kent, I had attacked a 17 from beam and astern. I left it at 2,000 feet when it was smoking to attack a 109 which was returning to base alone. I followed this aircraft and expended my remaining ammunition, seeing it in an inverted dive smoking badly at 1,000 feet.

By this time I was well out to sea and alarmed to find that I was now the hunted – by six 109s in line astern behind me, queuing up for a chance to shoot.

At this stage I was out of ammunition and extremely frightened. I turned for 'home' coastline and headed for the Hythe area, hoping to find a cloud or two on the way. The Messerschmitts decided to accompany me and took turns in having a go, with me evading violently and praying as I had never done before.

One by one they departed as their fuel ran low and I was left with the leader, a most persistent fellow, who finally hit me with cannon and machine-gun fire. This attack jammed the throttle in the wide-open position, where it had been, I assure you, for some time!

Finally, as I identified the rising land towards Hawkinge, I was hit in the engine and glycol tank, fumes from which filled the cockpit. Side-slipping, I spotted Hawkinge, made it over the boundary, blew the wheels down and dropped the aircraft on to the grass. I was flaming and smoking and was hotly anxious to get out. The station fire-engine was tearing alongside as I stepped out and left the Spitfire to roll on whilst they sprayed it with foam – having ignored one of the principal rules of air combat: Don't follow the enemy back home.

### Nurse Ann Standen, Queen Victoria Hospital (Burns Unit)

It would be wrong to say we weren't horrified. Inwardly, you'd say, 'Oh my God, what will they do with them?' You didn't recoil in horror but you wondered what could be done. Faces were just horrible – even the man I would later marry. . . . By the time he called a halt to the treatment and said enough was enough, he had new eyelids, a new nose, new lips. They couldn't do much for his hands because they were too badly burned. It was amazing what they did do. He had sixty operations.

Relatives of the patients would come to the hospital to see the men. Some took it well. Some didn't. It was a shock.

### Corporal Claire Legge, WAAF plotter

Behind the controller's dais in the ops room there were four cabins which were monitoring the four radio channels. For reasons I've never understood, these were jobs they gave to girls. They monitored those channels and recorded what was said by the pilots in the air. The doors of these cabins were open most of the time. That's how the controller sitting in front of them found out how the battle was going. Once he'd got the men on to the enemy with his directions, it was up to them. What they heard often distressed the girls very badly. They knew the pilots and they heard them screaming and going down.

### Paul Smith, field artillery surveyor with the West Sussex Yeomanry

Within days we had the maps prepared for the New Romney area with range and bearings to all the possible targets should there be an enemy invasion. The guns were laid to fire 100 yards out to sea during darkness. There was to be no retreat so that the guns had to be targeted in all directions. This entailed my drawing panoramic sketches from all local church towers and possible vantage-points. I did this job because it was discovered that I had been to art school. No one knew why I always had to have an armed guard during these sessions. We thought it was perhaps to pacify angry vicars, to protect me from the Local Defence Volunteers or just to see I did not call off my war and go back home to my Somerset farm.

Now every day would see enemy planes flying inland or skirting the coast. We had a Lewis gun near New Romney Church and our lad would open up to add to the general noise. He was, we knew, a rather impatient character who, after a few weeks, claimed to have shot the hands off the church clock as he said they moved too slowly.

### Pilot Officer George Nelson-Edwards DFC, 79 Squadron
On 5 September 1940, after taking off in the middle of a bombing raid, my throttle lever jammed at full boost, it just wouldn't budge. There was nothing for it but to turn back and attempt a landing by blipping the switches. On touch-down I cut the engine, at the same time trying to avoid the bomb craters as the aircraft rolled on. At last I stopped and jumped out, dashing towards an air-raid shelter. Then a corporal popped up from nowhere. Realising that the Hurricane could be written off by a direct hit, he jumped into a nearby 15-cwt truck, pulling me in with him, and then drove on to the field at full speed. There was a tow-bar at the back and with my help he hitched it to the tail-wheel and towed the Hurricane clear, heading for the squadron dispersal. Having parked it safely, he drove away.

### Sergeant Pilot George Johns DSO, DFC, AFC, 229 Squadron
My log book tells me that on twenty-two occasions I dispersed my aircraft. Usually the squadron would rearm and refuel at Northolt and land at last-light on a small grass airfield, called Heathrow, used by Faireys for experimental flying and testing. There was no fuel, ammunition, communications nor lighting. Pilots in turn were dispersed to farm houses, the lucky ones to local pubs, where we were fed and packed off to bed with a thermos of coffee and collected about 3 a.m. for a first-light take-off.

### Pilot Officer Geoffrey Page DSO, DFC and Bar, 56 Squadron
On returning to the officers' mess at North Weald one evening, I was told by the duty orderly that my mother had phoned and wanted me to call her back as soon as possible. Getting through was not easy in those days, but eventually I made contact with her. 'I'm very worried about you, darling,' she informed me. As I had probably had several thousand rounds of enemy bullets fired at me during the day, I too had been a trifle worried about myself. She continued, 'I don't think your batman is drying your socks out properly, and you might catch a nasty cold.'

## *Pilot Officer George Welford, 607 Squadron*

After being shot down, I was in Ashford Hospital, Kent. Another inmate was Squadron Leader John Badger DFC of 43 Squadron. He had landed on an upturned branch of a tree after baling out. His pelvis was split apart and there was nothing that could be done, but, during the whole time until he died, he laughed and joked with the nurses and visitors as though his life expectancy was for ever.

## *Pilot Officer W. L. B. Walker, 616 Squadron*

On 1 July 1940 I took off with another trainee pilot and an operational pilot to practise a 'battle climb'. I was flying a Mark 1 Spitfire which had a hand pump for raising the undercarriage and was noticeably slower than the other two planes. We were flying in formation at 20,000 feet when suddenly a message from the ops room advised us that a 'bandit' was in the area. Almost immediately we spotted a Do 215 in the distance. Our leader and the other pilot opened throttle and set off in pursuit, but my plane being slower left me well behind. I had never previously fired the guns of a Spitfire, but I turned the switch on the control column to 'fire'.

When I reached the Dornier the other two planes were not to be seen and I closed within range and pressed the button. My first reaction was that there seemed to be very little vibration but the air was alive with tracer bullets, which was reassuring. After only seconds the Dornier caught fire and plunged earthwards.

With a feeling of considerable excitement, I returned to the airfield to be greeted with some envy by the rest of the squadron who had yet to see a German plane. Very soon I was describing the momentous event to the intelligence officer when the flight sergeant came into the office and said, 'Excuse me, sir, did you know that your guns were not loaded?'

The tracer bullets were not mine but the Dornier's, and when I arrived the other two had already done enough to start a delayed fire in the enemy. . . .

## *A. W. Dixon, New Zealander with 5th Field Regiment at Maidstone*

What was saddening in those days was the fact that the civilians in the area used to think that only RAF planes were being shot down because the recovery wagons were going by with only RAF planes on them. They didn't realise it was our materials that were needed, while the German planes were just left where they were shot down.

*J. R. Hearn, flight mechanic (engines), Coastal Army Co-operation Unit*

I recall going to collect a Hurricane pilot who had force-landed in a small field just outside Sittingbourne. When we eventually found him he was sitting in the middle of the field in a huge armchair that the local villagers had carried out to him; at his feet were two crates of Brown Ale, by courtesy of a nearby inn. He was blond, broad shouldered, well built and had the neck of a young bull. He looked like a king on his throne, the monarch of all he surveyed, and I'm not so sure that he wasn't!! Plates of sandwiches put at his feet were enjoyed by us all!! The size of the field raised doubts as to a safe take-off distance, but he would not consider for a moment dismantling the undamaged aircraft. He asked us to refuel just enough to enable him to reach North Weald. Eventually with the tail of the Hurricane touching the hedge on the downwind side of the field and the chocks firmly in place, the throttles were opened to almost full revs, and on the pilot's signal the chocks were whipped away and a perfect aircraft-carrier take-off was achieved. A 'piece of cake' as we said at the time!! A flick roll over the top of us and he faded into memory!

For myself the days in the RAF were perhaps the highlight of a working life spanning fifty-one years. During the darkest days my admiration and respect for aircrew never wavered, their courage proving, and acting, as a true spur and incentive to all ground crews. A bond of friendship and mutual respect was formed, something I have never experienced in any other walk of life. I feel proud and privileged to have served with the men that I did.

*Sergeant Pilot Frederick Perkin, 600 Squadron*

We were given only about twelve days flying at OTU, the turnover of pupils being suddenly very rapid, and the first time I fired my guns was at the enemy. At Manston we were repeatedly dive-bombed and strafed by 109s which seemed to be almost on standing patrol overhead. What a Blenheim squadron was doing there I cannot think. One Blenheim was once serviceable for an hour or two, so it was hardly surprising that the airfield was then evacuated and 600 Squadron moved to Hornchurch. Here we arrived in time for the first of two consecutive Saturday afternoon raids, when having parked my Blenheim in a shelter bay, a stick of bombs from nine Ju 88s fell across the field, destroying my aircraft and one landing about ten yards away from me.

*Squadron Leader Henry Hogan CB, DFC, CO 501 Squadron*
I was posted to 501 to command when the squadron was in France. I went to Southampton only to find that the last boat had sailed. The Air Ministry could not arrange an air passage. I eventually met the returning remnants at Croydon, seven in all and not one Hurricane serviceable, so I sent the pilots on forty-eight hours leave. I was asked how long it would take to be ready and I said three weeks. Instead, we were given one week, and the new Hurricanes began to arrive at once, now with Rotol variable-pitch props.

Meanwhile, as John Thompson was there with 111 Squadron, I did one or two ops with him, escorting Fleet Air Arm Swordfish with 250 pound bombs for the German gun emplacements above Calais. Then we were sent to Middle Wallop, where there were already two squadrons. We used Warmwell as a forward base. It wasn't really ready and the troops lived under canvas while we dropped in at dawn and left at dusk.

We were a very international squadron with two Czechs, four or five Poles, a Belgian, as well as two or three Fleet Air Arm. On 26 July we moved to Gravesend.

I think I was the only CO to serve throughout with the same squadron, and 501 was the only squadron to serve throughout the Battle without a break. It was quite a load for a CO. We had fifteen killed and many more injured who didn't come back to us, and all that led to a lot of residual responsibilities – letters to next-of-kin, funerals and burials, disposal of belongings, etc. As usual, COs were beset by form-filling, and there were sector meetings, Group meetings and so on. As I was also station commander at Gravesend, this was an added responsibility. I had to meet visitors and next-of-kin as well as deal with supply problems, damage to the station as well as our aircraft. Then there was the constant pilot supply problem. Some replacement pilots were straight from OTU, and these we just got into the air as soon as possible to give them some experience, but we were too tired to give them any dogfighting practice. They were very green, let's face it, youngsters who were completely bewildered and lost in action. Some of them had fired their guns into the sea at OTU. Others had never fired them.

On top of all that there was leading the squadron, which I did whenever I could, and got shot down four times, baled out once and force-landed three times, always with wheels down, once into a large field which was fully obstructed with poles and wires.

But my everlasting impression of the Battle was that the organisation for replacing aircraft and the supply of equipment was marvellous, as indeed was the spirit displayed by the pilots and ground crews. 'Chiefy', Flight Sergeant White, did wonders and his troops were absolutely marvellous.

Almost none of 501's Hurricanes reached their service, they got clobbered so often and so badly. But the delivery of replacements was amazing. Incidentally, we all had cine-cameras but they never worked – vibration, I think.

Among the fifteen killed on 501 I think I missed most my two original flight commanders, George Stoney and Philip 'PAN' Cox, both absolutely first rate; both would certainly have gone on to command their own squadrons.

### *Arthur G. Ethridge, cook and butcher, Eastchurch*

One thing for sure I can tell you is that when I left Eastchurch there was hardly a foot of ground that had not been hit by a bomb and filled in. I would just like to mention one other thing. We received most of our food supplies via a light railway, that ran from Sheerness to Leysdown. It also brought in new airmen and took out those who were leaving on postings, etc. We called it 'Puffing Billy'. The railway was single gauge, so it ran down, then back again, and during the whole time I was there that train always ran on time, raid or no raid, and to see the driver carrying on as if nothing was happening cheered us up no end. That man deserved a medal, if anyone did.

After my stint at Eastchurch, I was posted to Upper Heyford, Bomber Command, where I remustered to aircrew, then proceeded in a way to give Jerry some of the stick he had given me in the past.

### *Stephen Brown, flight mechanic, 152 Squadron*

We lost three good pilots, all Cranwell boys, Shepley, Jones, Wildblood, very early in the action off Portland and Weymouth. Then Beaumont and Border, all really good fellows. I often think of them. Marrs was the ace, 'Boy' Marrs, only nineteen when he was killed over Brest in 1941, just a kid. When the kites landed after being in action we used to know because the gun patches had been blown away. Then it was a mad dash to get them ready again, fuel and oil checked, oxygen bottle changed, R/T batteries charged, ammo. tanks changed and a thorough check over – everyone helped each other. If a tyre had to be changed we didn't use jacks, ten men under the main plane would lift the kite until the rigger changed the wheel.

*F. P. O'Connor, flight mechanic (engines), 601 Squadron*
One incident which always sticks in my mind is that one morning in a lull between the flaps, a Hurricane landed and taxied up to the watch office.

The pilot switched off the engine and got down from the cockpit, and while walking to the watch office took off the flying helmet and patted up *her* hair – a young 'flapper' – couldn't have been more than nineteen – delivering a Hurricane to replace one of our losses. I couldn't believe it.

At times I didn't know whether to be sick, or cry – the pressure was really a bit too much – to change a Hurricane radiator in a blacked-out hangar with just a couple of miserable inspection lamps, oil and glycol running up your sleeve, not being able to see properly – I sometimes have a nightmare about it now. . . .

Now the pilots, you could see that they had enough of it at times, as some started to stutter, and others got a twitch; it didn't matter if you were a damn good pilot, it was pure luck if you came through it all.

*Eric Hymer, flight mechanic, 72 Squadron*
Biggin Hill became for a while untenable. We moved to Croydon. We lost a lot of aircrew. For a time the senior officer was a boyish-looking pilot officer. His name I have forgotten, but he flew an extremely dirty aircraft which he appropriately called 'Black Bess' or 'Black Beauty'. He would not let us wash the Spitfire down lest we wash away his luck.

I don't think there was a great deal of intimacy between the pilots of 72 and the ground crews, or it may be at the time these young men were not around long enough for their names and faces to be printed indelibly on the mind. One did have an affection, though, or something of that sort, and most of us were affected by a hidden grieving.

One face and name I do remember. He was Tom Gray, a York lad only a year or so older than I. His home was near to mine and I had, in better times, seen him around. He came to us as a replacement pilot and I recognised him but do not know whether he recognised me. I saw his aircraft off on his first op. I remember saying something like, 'Good luck Sgt Tom,' and I seemed to know he was not coming back. Oddly enough I would have given my eye teeth to have been in his shoes at that time. Tom, I thought, was too gentle a chap for this kind of thing.

We moved back to Biggin Hill – 72's biggest day was still to come. It was a privilege to have served with the squadron even in so humble a manner. I was posted to a course before the last shots were fired. I regret not being there at the end.

*(Mrs) Chris Poole, cook, Warmwell*

It was lunchtime. Our squadron (234) was coming in after a fight and were going to refuel when two Jerries came in behind them and all hell was let loose, machine-gun firing, bombing, you name it we had it. I happened to be a waitress at the time in the mess serving those who came in. I had the plates in my hand – the next I knew I was in a corner of what was left of the mess standing up still, but on top of me was a young pilot, Harry Newman, only twenty-one, that was shot to pieces; me I was not touched. . . . After the bombing our toilets were two bins with a board across them and sacking around it. Two of us were on the toilets when our spotter planes saw us and, well, were our faces red, you can imagine. Well, you see, there was no roof on the top, and jokes were great for our morale.

*T. E. Soar, 504 Squadron, Hendon*

The cookhouse did something the Germans could not do. They put us out of action for twenty-four hours with some suspect minced beef stew. Oh how the dispersal hut rang with groans and moans of the departed ones and stank for days in the hot summer sunshine.

During an air-raid in Bristol a naked form burst through the hessian sacking of the shower tent and raced madly towards us exhorting us to jump into the slit trenches. As if to emphasise his commands, he leapt in and emerged covered from head to toe in thick red mud. But it wasn't as red as our CO's face when he faced us later.

*Donald Samson, flight mechanic (engines), 615 Squadron*

One intense recollection is of the day one of our Auxiliary Air Force pilots was awarded the DFC (announced over the Tannoy). This lad was in the cockpit of 'my' aircraft and about two nods away from being fast asleep at the controls – he was on readiness. This was 12 August. He was killed on the 14th! One wonders how many more died due to utter exhaustion.

I feel I should also mention that services on flights by both the NAAFI staff via vans, and the provision of food despite the raids – particularly on 18 August – by the 'cookhouse' staff were excellent and often unremarked upon – the 'Sally Army' were also gems.

*Sergeant Pilot Robert Plenderleith DFC, 73 Squadron*

Having come to after baling out of a burning Hurricane, I landed in an orchard occupied by an Army anti-aircraft unit and, lying helpless on

349

the ground with burns and leg injuries, was surrounded by an extremely friendly bunch of Squaddies. Then from outside the group came a frightening bellow – 'Stand back, men!' And there, on looking up from my somewhat infra-dig position on the ground, was the biggest regimental sergeant major I had ever seen.

'Well now, young man,' he said, thrusting towards me a flask in one hand and a steaming mug in the other. 'For shock you should have some hot sweet tea or a good slug of whisky.'

However, before being allowed any option on the choice of pick-up, he hastily shoved the flask back in his hip pocket with the resolute injunction, 'No, you'd better have the tea!'

### H. V. Cossons, ground defence, Royal East Kent Regiment, Hawkinge airfield

On probably 22 August we were on guard duties when some terribly loud explosions and brilliant flashes rent the darkness. We thought of invasion and became, once again, extremely tense. Our sergeant, a veteran of the Great War, said, 'Don't worry lads – it's our big guns shelling the French coast.' The result was that each terrific crash and flash caused us to cheer at the top of our voices and yell, 'Let 'em have it! Hit 'em for six!'

After a long spell all went quiet and the night passed by. The morning's papers carried the headlines, 'Kent Coast Shelled from France!'

### A. E. Jones, armourer, 609 Squadron

609 Squadron took over the defence of Portsmouth, operating from Middle Wallop and refuelling and rearming at Warmwell. . . .

During the Portsmouth raids many pilots used to tell the ground crew how things were going, and a pilot I spoke to told me how he dived on a bomber but realised he was going to miss. So he looped and came straight down on the enemy aircraft with just enough time for a quick touch on the firing button and pulling away. He said, 'I must have killed the pilot because the aircraft dropped down to earth. I don't think I have used much ammo.'

I took one ammunition tank from the aircraft and counted the rounds left. Out of 350 rounds there were 342 left. What a pilot!

### D. G. Williams, flight mechanic (airframes), 25 Squadron, North Weald

Our station commander was Group Captain Victor Beamish, one of three brothers who all held senior posts in the RAF. He was one of the finest men I have ever met. After an attack on the airfield he always came and had a chat with the ground crews, and visited us in our makeshift cookhouse at mealtimes. He was firm and he didn't allow standards to drop. I remember once he called a snap parade and told everyone how scruffy they looked. He then arranged a clothing parade with a warning to the Stores staff not to refuse any item of clothing which was handed in for exchange. As a rule it was very difficult to exchange clothing unless it was in shreds.

*J. Wynn, flight mechanic (engines), 501 Squadron, Kenley*
Douggie and I arrived at Whyteleaf after travelling from Gravesend around the last week of September 1940. . . .

Our first night at Kenley is not easily forgotten. We turned in for the night and I fell into a deep sleep. I thought that I was having a nightmare until I realised that I was waking to the sounds of heavy explosions. The lads were donning greatcoats and gumboots and dashing out of the billet. Being newly arrived 'Sprogs', Doug and I were somewhat confused by it all, so we did likewise. On reaching the entrance we were amazed to find that the camp was illuminated as though by giant searchlights and we felt the concussion from bombs and anti-aircraft guns. It was then that I realised that the Luftwaffe was paying us a visit and had straddled the barrack area with incendiaries. Light anti-aircraft guns were firing at parachute flares that had been released by the attacking aircraft and I remember thinking how the tracer ammunition which appeared to be floating so gracefully in an arc through the night sky could be so destructive. From a pile by the billet wall the lads were taking sandbags and dropping them on the incendiaries which were then quickly extinguished. Taking our cue from them we both joined in and dealt with quite a few. . . .

Returning to the billet I found that my hands were shaking and it wasn't till my mate Douggie said in his broad Scots accent, 'Yon bugger Hitler must have known that we had just arrived,' that things returned to normal.

*N. Robinson, AA gunner, Royal Marines*
I was one of a team of men manning a 2 pound Pompom gun on top of the Admiralty flat roof. We used the gun during all air raids, I do not think we ever hit anything. . . . Sometimes our duty went on for as long as sixteen hours at a time. . . . There was relief off duty at the Beaver

Club where the Canadians, whose club it was, made us welcome. The music and singing in the crypt at St Martin-in-the-Fields was a delight.

We all fought together, worked together, and a lot of people died together. I was a Northerner, nineteen years old in a place I had only read about, and I will always remember the people of London at that time with affection.

### Edith Kup, plotter, Debden

I was never called by my surname by anyone, except the WAAF officers, from the CO down. One was treated as a lady, saluted, had doors opened for one, etc., in the manners of the time. . . .

Then the CO sent for the MT girls – we were to be plotters, no one knew what *they* did. . . . So, into the ops room and its mysteries. Surrounded by earthworks, like a Roman fort, but the roof level with the top of the banks, and unprotected except by thick reinforced concrete, it was a big room with a table in the centre, tilted towards a balcony. The table was covered by a gridded map with phone points round it, four along the top and bottom. The controller, 'ops B' and various others were on the balcony, and we sat down round the table just anywhere, put on our headsets and were initiated into plotting. A clock with coloured five-minute sized triangles on it, and arrows to match on the table and blocks of wood with a place for raid number, height, and number of aircraft. Quite simple really. . . .

I only remember one girl having hysterics – we were all shocked, for we had been brought up not to show our feelings and keep control. Another girl, who just sat through our first attack struck dumb (I glanced along the faces), went on leave to Ireland and never came back. Calmness reigned amongst the frenzied activity, the controller gave the squadrons vectors to the enemy – we heard shouts of 'Tally Ho!' over the R/T and a running commentary followed, grim and tense. We always managed to hear it all, even though we were busy being told to all the time – anxious eyes on the clock with fuel states in mind, and desperate moments as one heard 'Blue two going down in flames' and whether or not he had managed to bale out, not always possible to see. Then 'Who's Blue two?', for we didn't know which pilot in a flight flew what in a sortie, it changed every time. Then anxious waits for the squadrons to pancake, only to be refuelled and rearmed, and up again as quickly as possible. The pilots got so tired that it was not unknown for them to fall asleep over the controls on landing, or stagger off to the dispersal hut or deck chair and flat out. . . .

It must be said the ground crews were fantastic, working round the clock throughout the battle to keep the aircraft in the air and looking after their pilots like fathers. . . .

The history books have it that the Battle ended on 31 October but not to us; certainly the aerodromes were not being attacked so regularly, but the boys were always in the air.

Contrary to present-day beliefs, and in spite of the grimness of the situation, everyone was lighthearted, and there was endless laughter. It was never going to happen to you, and if it did there was staunch support, as I found when Denis was killed. The fighter boys were a breed apart, sadly lost, in those days, for ever; and I and all who knew them were very privileged.

# APPENDICES

# I

# *Chronology of the Battle*

| Date | Weather | Main Targets and Events | LOSSES* L'waffe | RAF |
|---|---|---|---|---|
| July | | | | |
| 10 | Cloudy, clearing | Channel convoy. *First dogfight of over 100 aircraft.* | 13 | 6 |
| 11 | Cloudy | East-coast shipping. Portland, Portsmouth. | 20 | 4 |
| 12 | Fog, then thundery | East- and south-coast shipping. Aberdeen, Portland. (Night) Bristol, S. Wales. | 7 | 6 |
| 13 | Fog, cloudy | Shipping off Dover and Portland. *HQ 10 Group opens at Box.* | 7 | 1 |
| 14 | Light cloud, clear | Shipping off Dover and Swanage. | 2 | 4 |
| 15 | Cloudy | Shipping off Norfolk coast. | 3 | 1 |
| 16 | Fog and cloud | Little activity. *Hitler directive (No. 16) formally orders invasion preparations.* | 3 | 2 |
| 17 | Light rain | Shipping off Dundee and Beachy Head. | 2 | 1 |
| 18 | Light rain | Shipping off south-east coasts. South-coast ports. Some French and British airfields waterlogged. | 4 | 3 |
| 19 | Clear, showers | Dover. Bad day for Defiants of 141 Sqdn. *Hitler's 'peace-offer' in Reichstag speech.* | 2 | 8 |
| 20 | Cloudy, clearing | Heavy raids on shipping at Dover and Lyme Bay. Me 110 appears as a fighter-bomber. (Night) Merseyside. | 9 | 3 |
| 21 | Clear, showers | Heavy raids on shipping in Channel and Straits. | 9 | 6 |

357

| Date | Weather | Main Targets and Events | LOSSES* L'waffe | RAF |
|---|---|---|---|---|
| **July** | | | | |
| 22 | Clear, few showers | Shipping off south coast. *British rejection of 'peace-offer'.* | 1 | 0 |
| 23 | Cloudy, rain | A few attacks on east-coast shipping. | 3 | 0 |
| 24 | Cloudy, rain | Convoys in Channel. | 8 | 3 |
| 25 | Fine | Very heavy attacks on Channel convoy in co-operation with E-boats. 11 of 21 ships sunk or badly damaged. | 18 | 7 |
| 26 | Rain | South-coast shipping. *Channel convoys suspended in daylight hours.* | 4 | 2 |
| 27 | Clear, then stormy | Shipping. Two destroyers sunk and one damaged. | 4 | 1 |
| 28 | Fine | Shipping off Dover. South-coast ports. *Destroyers withdraw from Dover to Portsmouth.* Malan's 74 Sqdn in heavy combat, the CO forcing Moelders into crash-landing. | 18 | 5 |
| 29 | Fine | Heavy attacks on Dover harbour and convoy: one destroyer sunk. | 8 | 3 |
| 30 | Cloud, light rain | Shipping off east coast. *Hitler instructs Goering to be ready for intensive operations at 12 hours notice.* | 5 | 0 |
| 31 | Fine | Dover balloon barrage. Shipping off south-east and south-west coasts. | 5 | 3 |
| **August** | | | | |
| 1 | Fine, haze | Shipping off south and east coasts. Norwich (aircraft factory). (Night) S. Wales, Midlands. *Hitler directive (No. 17) to Luftwaffe to 'overpower the English air force with all the forces at its command, in the shortest possible time'. Invasion preparations to be complete by 15 September.* | 9 | 1 |
| 2 | Fine, drizzle over sea | Shipping off south-east coasts. (Night) S. Wales, Midlands. *Goering's Adlerangriff directive to Luftwaffe.* | 4 | 0 |

| Date | Weather | Main Targets and Events | LOSSES* L'waffe | RAF |
|------|---------|-------------------------|-----------------|-----|
| 3 | Cloudy, bright intervals | Shipping. (Night) S. Wales, Crewe, Liverpool. | 4 | 0 |
| 4 | Mainly fine | Little activity. | 0 | 0 |
| 5 | Fine | Shipping in Straits. | 6 | 1 |
| 6 | Cloudy, windy | Little activity. Shipping. *Goering orders* Adlertag *for 10 August.* | 1 | 1 |
| 7 | Cloudy | Convoy off east coast. | 2 | 0 |
| 8 | Cloudy, bright intervals | Heavy attacks on Channel convoy (the first westbound since 25 July) off Dover and Wight. Heaviest air fighting so far, involving 150+ aircraft. Ju 87s prove very vulnerable. (Night) Liverpool, Leeds, Bristol, Birmingham. | 31 | 20 |
| 9 | Cloud and rain | East-coast shipping. Dover balloons. Adlertag *postponed.* | 5 | 4 |
| 10 | Cloud and rain | Little activity. | 0 | 0 |
| 11 | Fine | Dover and Portland heavily attacked. Several senior Luftwaffe officers killed or captured. Convoys off east coast. (Night) Merseyside, Bristol Channel. | 38 | 32 |
| 12 | Fine | Several RAF airfields (Manston, Lympne, Hawkinge) and radar stations (Dover, Rye, Dunkirk, Ventnor) attacked in preparation for *Adlertag* next day. | 31 | 22 |

During this preparatory phase of the Battle the Luftwaffe attacked shipping on most days and laid mines on most nights, but sank only 30,000 tons out of the nearly 5 million tons which passed round the coasts. It lost 286 aircraft as against Fighter Command's 148 (plus two at night). Except on five days, most raids were undertaken by small forces. The widespread raiding at night was mainly by very small numbers of aircraft.

| Date | Weather | Main Targets and Events | LOSSES* L'waffe | RAF |
|---|---|---|---|---|
| August | | | | |
| 13 | Fine | *Adlertag* postponement to afternoon causes confusion in Luftwaffe, which nevertheless flies almost 1,500 sorties in 24 hours. Attacks on Southampton, Portland, airfields (Detling, Andover, Eastchurch, Lympne). (Night) Castle Bromwich (aircraft factory). | 45 | 13 |
| 14 | Cloudy, bright intervals | Dover, airfields (Manston, Middle Wallop, Sealand). | 19 | 8 |
| 15 | Fine | *Heaviest day's fighting so far, with* Luftflotte *5 joining in from Scandinavia at heavy cost to its bombers and* Me *110s.* Many airfields damaged (Lympne, Hawkinge, Middle Wallop, West Malling, Eastchurch, Croydon, Martlesham, Driffield), but north of England never attacked in strength by day again. Fighter Command flies 974 sorties. *Germans more strongly escorted. Hitler confirms invasion preparations to be completed by 15 September.* | 75 | 34 |
| 16 | Fine | Heavy raids on airfields (in Kent, and at Gosport, Tangmere, Brize Norton). Ventnor radar station. Luftwaffe flies over 1,700 sorties. (Night) Home Counties, Bristol Channel, East Anglia. | 45 | 21 |
| 17 | Fine | Lympne, otherwise mysterious silence from Luftwaffe. *Shorter courses introduced for British fighter pilots.* (Night) Mersey, S. Wales, Midlands. | 3 | 0 |
| 18 | Fine at first | Heavy fighting in course of intensive bombing of airfields in south and south-east (Croydon, Gosport, Ford, Thorney Island). Portsmouth. Big damage at Kenley airfield | 71 | 27 |

| Date | Weather | Main Targets and Events | LOSSES* L'waffe | RAF |
|------|---------|-------------------------|-----------------|-----|
| | | and Poling radar station. No. 1 (Royal Canadian Air Force) Sqdn's first operations. | | |
| 19 | Cloudy | Southampton area, Pembroke docks. *Goering issues orders for renewed attacks on Fighter Command. He orders stronger escort to Luftflotte 2's bombers, and transfers single-engined fighters for this purpose from Luftflotte 3, which is to concentrate more on night bombing. Ju 87s to be conserved for the invasion and special tasks.* | 6 | 3 |
| 20 | Cloudy, windy over land, becoming rainy | Weather restricts German activities. Manston, Martlesham. Polish 302 Sqdn in action for first time, vengeful and effective. Churchill's 'Never . . . has so much been owed by so many to so few.' | 7 | 2 |
| 21 | Cloudy, rainy | Enemy operations mainly limited to fighter 'tip and run' raids. Airfields in East Anglia, south and south-west attacked lightly. | 14 | 1 |
| 22 | Cloudy | Convoys in Dover Straits. Manston. (Night) Aberdeen, Yorkshire, Hampshire, S. Wales, Bristol, Filton (airfield and Bristol Co.'s works). | 3 | 5 |
| 23 | Cloudy, showers | Minor activity. (Night) Bristol, S. Wales, Cardiff. | 2 | 0 |
| 24 | Fine | Violent increase in Luftwaffe activity. Ramsgate, Dover, Portsmouth, and airfields (Manston five times, Hornchurch, N. Weald). (Night) S. Wales, Birmingham (aircraft factory), north-east coast and *unintentional bombs on central London.* | 38 | 22 |
| 25 | Fine, then cloudy | Driffield. Airfields in south-east, south and | 20 | 16 |

| Date | Weather | Main Targets and Events | LOSSES* L'waffe | RAF |
|---|---|---|---|---|
| **August** | | | | |
| | | south-west (Warmwell), the bombers heavily escorted. (Night) *RAF bomb Berlin in retaliation for bombs on London.* | | |
| 26 | Cloudy, brighter later | *Fierce and effective raids on airfields (especially Debden) mark the period of Fighter Command's greatest strain.* Dover, Folkestone. Ineffective attacks on Hornchurch and Portsmouth. (Night) Coventry, Birmingham, Plymouth. | 41 | 31 |
| 27 | Cloudy, rain | Weather restricts enemy action. (Night) Widely scattered raids on airfields and industrial areas. *German army invasion plan settled.* | 9 | 1 |
| 28 | Fair over land, cloudy over sea | Airfields (Eastchurch, Rochford). Luftwaffe fighters in sweeps. After further heavy losses the Defiant fighter is pulled out of the daylight battle. (Night) *Much heavier night raiding begins* – c.160 bombers against Merseyside, 180 elsewhere. In 600 sorties by night, *Luftflotte* 3 has lost only 7 aircraft. | 30 | 20 |
| 29 | Cloudy, clearing later | Some 700 Luftwaffe fighters in provocative sweeps to which RAF do not respond. The Chief of Kesselring's fighter organisation claims unlimited fighter superiority has been achieved. South and south-east airfields. (Night) Heavy raiding continues against Merseyside (176 sorties) and elsewhere (44 sorties). | 17 | 9 |
| 30 | Fine | Very heavy bombing of airfields (Lympne, Biggin Hill twice, Detling). Vauxhall works at Luton. (Night) Heavy bombing again on Merseyside. | 36 | 26 |

| Date | Weather | Main Targets and Events | LOSSES* L'waffe | RAF |
|---|---|---|---|---|
| 31 | Fine | Very heavy bombing of airfields (Detling, Eastchurch, Croydon, and sector stations Biggin Hill, Hornchurch twice, and Debden). Some close to unserviceability. Radar stations also attacked. (Night) Merseyside heavily, Midlands. | 41 | 39 |
| September 1 | Fine | Tilbury, Chatham. South-east airfields (Debden, and severe damage at Biggin Hill, Eastchurch, Detling). (Night) Bristol, S. Wales, Midlands, Merseyside. | 14 | 15 |
| 2 | Fine | Several airfields (including Biggin Hill, Lympne, Detling, Eastchurch three times, Hornchurch twice, Gravesend). Rochester (aircraft factory). (Night) Merseyside, Midlands, Manchester, Sheffield. | 35 | 31 |
| 3 | Fine | Airfields again (Manston, West Malling, much damage at North Weald) and heavy fighting. (Night) Merseyside, S. Wales, south-east England. *Hitler moves target date for invasion from 15 to 21 September. Decision to be taken ten days beforehand.* | 16 | 16 |
| 4 | Fine | Airfields (Bradwell, Lympne, Eastchurch twice). Medway towns (aircraft factory at Rochester), Weybridge (aircraft factory). (Night) Liverpool, Bristol, south-east England. *Hitler publicly threatens invasion, also reprisals for British bombing of German towns.* | 25 | 17 |
| 5 | Fine | Biggin Hill yet again, and Detling. Thameshaven oiltanks set on fire (extinguished). | 23 | 20 |
| 6 | Fine | Airfields in south-east including Biggin Hill. | 35 | 23 |

| Date | Weather | Main Targets and Events | LOSSES* L'waffe | RAF |
|------|---------|-------------------------|-----------------|-----|
| September | | | | |
| | | Rochester and Weybridge (aircraft factories). A few Ju 87s employed again, and roughly handled, as were the Poles of 303 Sqdn. Heavy and accurate attack on oil targets at Thameshaven: fires not extinguished attract further attack during the night. Coastal Command's Photographic Reconnaissance Unit during the week has photographed steadily growing numbers of invasion craft in the Dutch, Belgian and French Channel ports, which from 5 September have come under attack from Bomber Command. *British order Invasion Alert No. 2 – attack probable within three days.* | | |
| | | In the period from *Adlertag* on 13 August to 6 September, characterised by repeated attacks on the British airfields, the Luftwaffe has lost about 670 aircraft, Fighter Command 400. Fighter Command is holding its own, but is running down. The danger-points are that wastage of fighters is exceeding production, that a shortage of skilled pilots has developed, and that there has been much damage to the sector stations. Fortunately the Germans are about to switch to a different main objective. | | |
| 7 | Fine | *The Luftwaffe switches to London,* granting relief to the airfields: the turning-point in the Battle. Some 1,000 enemy aircraft over and around the capital | 41 | 28 |

| Date | Weather | Main Targets and Events | LOSSES* L'waffe | RAF |
|------|---------|-------------------------|-----------------|-----|
|      |         | by day, followed by heavy night raid. Thameshaven and the London docks the main objective in both cases. *Code-word 'Cromwell' brings British forces to highest pitch of readiness and action stations.* | | |
| 8 | Fine | Lull by day. London bombed heavily by night. Dowding's 'Squadron Stabilization' scheme introduced. | 15 | 2 |
| 9 | Fine | Thames Estuary, Southampton. Major attack with some 200 bombers on London frustrated by 11 and 12 Groups, jettisoned bombs damaging suburbs widely. | 28 | 19 |
| 10 | Cloudy, rain | Slight activity. (Night) London, S. Wales, Merseyside. Bomber Command raid on Eindhoven airfield knocks out ten He 111s. *Hitler postpones taking decision on the invasion until 14 September.* | 4 | 1 |
| 11 | Cloudy, then fine | Four airfields. London, Southampton, Portsmouth. (Night) London, Merseyside. | 25 | 29 |
| 12 | Rain | Slight activity. The German barge concentrations still growing. (Night) London, S. Wales, Midlands, Merseyside. | 4 | 0 |
| 13 | Showers, bright intervals | Small raids only on London – little damage. (Night) London. All forces of Bomber Command, day and night, attack invasion ports and continue during next fortnight. | 4 | 1 |
| 14 | Showers, bright intervals | South London and radar stations. (Night) London, S. Wales. *Hitler still pinning his faith on the Luftwaffe postpones invasion decision for* | 14 | 14 |

| Date | Weather | Main Targets and Events | LOSSES* L'waffe | RAF |
|---|---|---|---|---|
| September | | | | |
| | | *three more days, i.e. until 17 September*. Earliest date for invasion would then be 27 September. | | |
| 15 | Fine | Largest ever German formations over London and south-east, in two big raids, but mainly broken up by the 24 Fighter Command squadrons operating on this day, since known as Battle of Britain Day. An undisputed victory. Attacks also on Portland and Southampton. (Night) London, Midlands. | 60 | 26 |
| 16 | Cloudy, rain | Slight activity, mainly in south-east and East Anglia. (Night) London, Midlands, Merseyside. | 9 | 1 |
| 17 | Cloudy, showers | Activity as for the previous day, few bombers but fighter sweeps. British bombers sink 84 barges at Dunkirk. (Night) London, Merseyside. *Hitler postpones invasion indefinitely*, but orders preparations to continue. | 8 | 5 |
| 18 | Showers | The few daylight bombers, some attacking oil targets in the Estuary, suffer badly, nine Ju 88s of III/KG77 being shot down in 2 or 3 minutes. (Night) London, Merseyside. *Germans begin to disperse invasion fleet to avoid further damage from bombing.* | 19 | 12 |
| 19 | Showers | Little daylight activity. (Night) London, Merseyside and routine minelaying. | 0 | 0 |
| 20 | Showers | Heavy fighter-sweep towards London leads to dogfights, the outcome favouring the Luftwaffe more than usual. (Night) London. | 7 | 7 |
| 21 | Fine later | Fighter-sweeps in east Kent. (Night) London, Merseyside. | 0 | 0 |

| Date | Weather | Main Targets and Events | LOSSES* L'waffe | RAF |
|------|---------|------------------------|-----------------|-----|
| 22 | Fog, showers | Slight activity. (Night) London, Merseyside. | 1 | 0 |
| 23 | Fine | Sweeps towards London. (Night) London, Merseyside. | 9 | 11 |
| 24 | Fine | Tilbury, Southampton (Woolston Spitfire factory damaged by fighter-bombers). (Night) London, Merseyside. | 11 | 4 |
| 25 | Fine | Plymouth, Portland, Bristol (Filton). Further attack by heavily escorted bombers on aircraft factories. (Night) London, S. Wales, Lancashire. | 13 | 4 |
| 26 | Fine | Southampton. Woolston factory gutted but Spitfire production now well dispersed. | 9 | 9 |
| 27 | Fine | London, Bristol. Heavily escorted bomber raids on London and Filton largely frustrated, with big losses to Ju 88s and Kesselring's fighters. (Night) London, Midlands, Merseyside. | 55 | 28 |
| 28 | Fine | London, Solent. Scattered bomber raids massively escorted, with inevitable consequences. Hurricanes particularly suffering. (Night) London. | 16 | 16 |
| 29 | Fine | Some activity, reduced, in south-east and E. Anglia. Liverpool bombed in daylight from the west, but raid intercepted. (Night) London, Merseyside. | 5 | 5 |
| 30 | Fine | London, Westland factory at Yeovil (attack defeated). On this last day of mass daylight bomber raids the Luftwaffe reintroduces expensively discredited tactics and pays a heavy price in bombers and fighters for negligible damage. (Night) London. | 48 | 20 |

| Date | Weather | Main Targets and Events | LOSSES* L'waffe | RAF |
|---|---|---|---|---|
| October | | | | |
| 1 | Fair | A new phase opens in which the Germans use their main bomber force almost entirely under cover of darkness. In daylight they send over only small numbers of fast Ju 88s together with Messerschmitt fighters at high altitude carrying bombs, protected by further fighters above. This activity occurs every day and proves extremely difficult to deal with, but strategically is of little benefit to the Germans. At night London is bombed heavily (by an average of 150 bombers) every night of the month except one. 'Fighter-bomber sweeps' and 'London' are the entries to be understood for each date in this month. | 6 | 4 |
| 2 | Fine | | 10 | 1 |
| 3 | Rain | Within the standard activity, a single Ju 88 hits the de Havilland factory at Hatfield. | 9 | 1 |
| 4 | Fog, rain | At their meeting Hitler informs Mussolini that only the lack of five days of consecutively good weather has frustrated his invasion plans. | 12 | 3 |
| 5 | Showers, bright periods | West Malling and Detling airfields. Southampton bombed without opposition in the air. | 13 | 8 |
| 6 | Rain | Small raids penetrate to several airfields (Middle Wallop, Northolt, Biggin Hill). | 6 | 1 |
| 7 | Cloud, showers | Heavier raid by escorted Ju 88s on Westland factory at Yeovil. Little damage and 7 of the enemy shot down. | 21 | 17 |
| 8 | Fair | Attack on Rootes' works at Speke. | 14 | 4 |

| Date | Weather | Main Targets and Events | LOSSES* | |
| | | | L'waffe | RAF |
|---|---|---|---|---|
| 9 | Cloud, rain | Airfields in the south-east. | 9 | 3 |
| 10 | Showers, bright intervals | Fighter-bombers in streams, great difficulty in intercepting. | 4 | 4 |
| 11 | Fair | | 7 | 9 |
| 12 | Fog, clearing | Biggin Hill, Kenley. *Hitler postpones invasion until – if then thought advisable – the spring of 1941.* | 11 | 10 |
| 13 | Fog, clearing | | 5 | 2 |
| 14 | Rain | (Night) Heaviest raid on London thus far. Coventry also bombed. | 4 | 0 |
| 15 | Fair | For once, RAF fighters bounce high-flying Me 109s out of the sun, shooting down 4. (Night) Heavier still on London – 400+ bombers. Much damage and many railway termini out of action. | 14 | 15 |
| 16 | Cloudy | With the autumn weather, accident casualties on both sides from now on often exceed combat casualties. | 13 | 1 |
| 17 | Showery, bright intervals | | 15 | 3 |
| 18 | Fog | Goering praises his fighter pilots for inflicting such terrible losses on Fighter Command, and his bomber pilots for having 'reduced the British plutocracy to fear and terror'. | 15 | 4 |
| 19 | Cloud | | 5 | 2 |
| 20 | Cloud | High-flying fighter-bombers revert to mass attacks in place of streams. | 14 | 4 |
| 21 | Fog | | 6 | 0 |
| 22 | Fog | Five German crashes lead to loss of several senior officers. | 11 | 5 |
| 23 | Cloudy | (Night) Glasgow as well as London. | 3 | 1 |
| 24 | Cloudy | | 8 | 4 |
| 25 | Cloudy | Airfield at Montrose. (Night) Italians reluctantly allowed by the Germans to join in the bombing (Harwich), but with dismal results. | 20 | 10 |

| Date | Weather | Main Targets and Events | LOSSES* L'waffe | RAF |
|------|---------|-------------------------|-----------------|-----|
| October | | | | |
| 26 | Cloudy, showers | | 10 | 4 |
| 27 | Cloudy | Seven airfields attacked. Continuing fighter-bomber raids and individual tip-and-run bomber attacks force Fighter Command to fly over 1,000 sorties. That it can do so is proof of its continuing strength. | 15 | 10 |
| 28 | Cloudy | | 11 | 2 |
| 29 | Fair | Portsmouth, Ramsgate, N. Weald. Tactical foresight leads to the shooting down of 11 high-flying Me 109s in 6 minutes. The Italians reappear briefly by day with 15 bombers and 73 fighters, the CR42 biplanes causing more puzzlement than anxiety. | 19 | 7 |
| 30 | Rain | Unsuccessful attempt to penetrate to London by day. | 8 | 5 |
| 31 | Rain | The great Battle fizzles out damply, the Germans having exhausted every tactical alternative after being deprived of their best chance of victory by the inept decision of their Supreme Command to attack London rather than continue with the direct offensive against Fighter Command and its ground installations. | 0 | 0 |

* The losses are basically as given in the official history, *The Defence of the United Kingdom* (HMSO, London, 1957). They were compiled from Fighter Command sources on the British side, Luftwaffe Quartermaster-General sources on the German. Since then further work has been done, notably by Francis K. Mason in his *Battle over Britain* (McWhirter Twins, London, 1969) and by researchers for the *After the Battle* publications, to refine and correct these figures, in particular by distinguishing losses in combat from those arising from other causes. However, no other set of figures has yet been given official status, and these from the official history, if not unchallengeable in detail, give a sufficiently clear indication of the scale of activity and the ratio of success.

# II

# *Basic Statistics of Fighter Command and Luftwaffe Aircraft Engaged in the Battle of Britain*

## *British*

Fighters:

| | MAX. SPEED | CEILING IN FT | ARMAMENT |
|---|---|---|---|
| Hurricane I | 316 mph @ 17,500 ft | 32,000 | 8 × .303 mg |
| Spitfire I | 355 mph @ 19,000 ft | 34,000 | 8 × .303 mg |
| Defiant | 304 mph @ 17,000 ft | 30,000 | 4 × .303 mg |
| Blenheim IV | 266 mph @ 11,000 ft | 26,000 | 7 × .303 mg |

## *German*

| | | | |
|---|---|---|---|
| Messerschmitt 109E | 355 mph @ 18,000 ft | 35,000 | 2 × 7.9 mm mg<br>2 × 20 mm cannon (variable) |
| Messerschmitt 110 | 345 mph @ 23,000 ft | 33,000 | 6 × 7.9 mm mg<br>2 × 20 mm cannon |

Bombers:

| | | | |
|---|---|---|---|
| Junkers 87B | 245 mph @ 15,000 ft | 23,000 | 3 × 7.9 mm mg |
| Junkers 88 | 287 mph @ 14,000 ft | 23,000 | 3 × 7.9 mm mg |
| Dornier 17 | 255 mph @ 21,000 ft | 21,000 | 7 × 7.9 mm mg |

(Dornier 215 slightly enhanced performance)

| | | | |
|---|---|---|---|
| Heinkel 111 | 240 mph @ 14,000 ft | 26,000 | 7 × 7.9 mm mg |

# III

# *Higher Command*

## SUMMER 1940

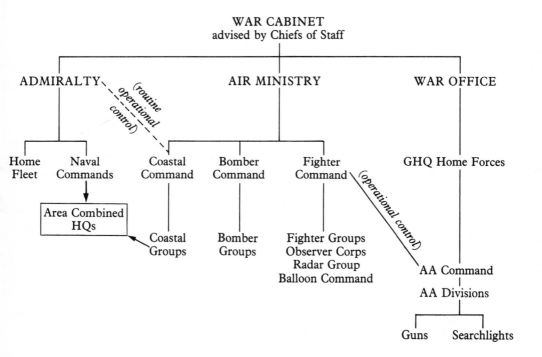

WAR CABINET
advised by Chiefs of Staff

ADMIRALTY     *(routine operational control)*     AIR MINISTRY     WAR OFFICE

Home Fleet    Naval Commands    Coastal Command    Bomber Command    Fighter Command *(operational control)*    GHQ Home Forces

Area Combined HQs

Coastal Groups    Bomber Groups    Fighter Groups Observer Corps Radar Group Balloon Command    AA Command

AA Divisions

Guns    Searchlights

# IV

# Air Defence Higher Formations

## JULY–SEPTEMBER 1940

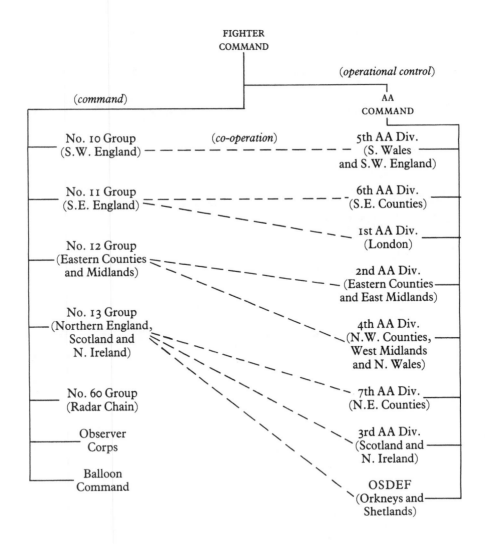

# V

# *Operational Chain of Command in the Luftwaffe*

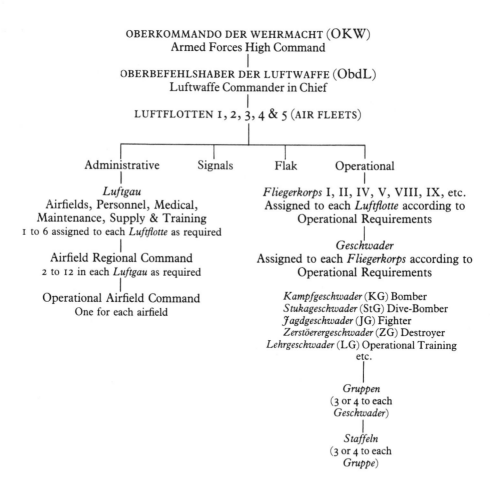

OBERKOMMANDO DER WEHRMACHT (OKW)
Armed Forces High Command

OBERBEFEHLSHABER DER LUFTWAFFE (ObdL)
Luftwaffe Commander in Chief

LUFTFLOTTEN 1, 2, 3, 4 & 5 (AIR FLEETS)

Administrative      Signals      Flak      Operational

*Luftgau*
Airfields, Personnel, Medical,
Maintenance, Supply & Training
1 to 6 assigned to each *Luftflotte* as required

*Fliegerkorps* I, II, IV, V, VIII, IX, etc.
Assigned to each *Luftflotte* according to
Operational Requirements

Airfield Regional Command
2 to 12 in each *Luftgau* as required

*Geschwader*
Assigned to each *Fliegerkorps* according to
Operational Requirements

Operational Airfield Command
One for each airfield

*Kampfgeschwader* (KG) Bomber
*Stukageschwader* (StG) Dive-Bomber
*Jagdgeschwader* (JG) Fighter
*Zerstöerergeschwader* (ZG) Destroyer
*Lehrgeschwader* (LG) Operational Training
etc.

*Gruppen*
(3 or 4 to each
*Geschwader*)

*Staffeln*
(3 or 4 to each
*Gruppe*)

Nearest RAF equivalents: *Geschwader* = Group; *Gruppe* = Wing; *Staffel* = Squadron

374

# VI

# Equivalent Commissioned Ranks: RAF and Luftwaffe

Air Chief Marshal
Air Marshal
Air Vice-Marshal
Air Commodore

Generalfeldmarschall and Generaloberst
General der Flieger
Generalleutnant
Generalmajor

---

Group Captain
Wing Commander
Squadron Leader
Flight Lieutenant
Flying Officer
Pilot Officer

Oberst
Oberstleutnant
Major
Hauptmann
Oberleutnant
Leutnant

# VII

# *Fighter Command Order of Battle*

## 8 AUGUST 1940

*HQ Bentley Priory, Stanmore*
*(Air Chief Marshal Sir Hugh Dowding)*

### NO. 10 GROUP, BOX, WILTS.
### (Air Vice-Marshal Sir Quintin Brand)

| Squadron | Aircraft | Station |
|---|---|---|
| | *Pembrey Sector* | |
| 92 | Spitfire | Pembrey |
| | *Filton Sector* | |
| 87 | Hurricane | Exeter |
| 213 | Hurricane | Exeter |
| | *St Eval Sector* | |
| 234 | Spitfire | St Eval |
| 247 (one flight) | Gladiator | Roborough |
| | *Middle Wallop Sector* | |
| 238 | Hurricane | Middle Wallop |
| 609 (West Riding) | Spitfire | Middle Wallop |
| 604 (County of Middlesex) | Blenheim | Middle Wallop |
| 152 | Spitfire | Warmwell |

### NO. 11 GROUP, UXBRIDGE
### (Air Vice-Marshal K. R. Park)

| Squadron | Aircraft | Station |
|---|---|---|
| | *Tangmere Sector* | |
| 43 | Hurricane | Tangmere |
| 601 (County of London) | Hurricane | Tangmere |
| 145 | Hurricane | Westhampnett |

| Squadron | Aircraft | Station |
|---|---|---|
| | *Kenley Sector* | |
| 615 | Hurricane | Kenley |
| 64 | Spitfire | Kenley |
| 111 | Hurricane | Croydon |
| | *Biggin Hill Sector* | |
| 32 | Hurricane | Biggin Hill |
| 610 (County of Chester) | Spitfire | Biggin Hill |
| 501 (County of Gloucester) | Hurricane | Gravesend |
| 600 (City of London) | Blenheim | Manston |
| | *Hornchurch Sector* | |
| 54 | Spitfire | Hornchurch |
| 65 | Spitfire | Hornchurch |
| 74 | Spitfire | Hornchurch |
| 41 | Spitfire | Hornchurch |
| | *Northolt Sector* | |
| 1 | Hurricane | Northolt |
| 257 | Hurricane | Northolt |
| | *North Weald Sector* | |
| 151 | Hurricane | North Weald |
| 56 | Hurricane | Rochford |
| 25 | Blenheim | Martlesham |
| | *Debden Sector* | |
| 17 | Hurricane | Debden |
| 85 | Hurricane | Martlesham |

### NO. 12 GROUP, WATNALL, NOTTS.
### (Air Vice-Marshal T. L. Leigh-Mallory)

| Squadron | Aircraft | Station |
|---|---|---|
| | *Duxford Sector* | |
| 19 | Spitfire | Duxford |
| | *Coltishall Sector* | |
| 242 | Hurricane | Coltishall |
| 66 | Spitfire | Coltishall |
| | *Wittering Sector* | |
| 229 | Hurricane | Wittering |
| 266 | Spitfire | Wittering |
| 23 | Blenheim | Colly Weston |

| Squadron | Aircraft | Station |
|---|---|---|
| | *Digby Sector* | |
| 46 | Hurricane | Digby |
| 611 (West Lancashire) | Spitfire | Digby |
| 29 | Blenheim | Digby |
| | *Kirton-in-Lindsey Sector* | |
| 222 | Spitfire | Kirton-in-Lindsey |
| 264 | Defiant | Kirton-in-Lindsey and Ringway |
| | *Church Fenton Sector* | |
| 73 | Hurricane | Church Fenton |
| 249 | Hurricane | Church Fenton |
| 616 (South Yorkshire) | Spitfire | Leconfield |

NO. 13 GROUP, NEWCASTLE UPON TYNE
(Air Vice-Marshal R. E. Saul)

| Squadron | Aircraft | Station |
|---|---|---|
| | *Catterick Sector* | |
| 219 | Blenheim | Catterick |
| | *Usworth Sector* | |
| 607 | Hurricane | Usworth |
| 72 | Spitfire | Acklington |
| 79 | Spitfire | Acklington |
| | *Turnhouse Sector* | |
| 232 (one flight) | Hurricane | Turnhouse |
| 253 | Hurricane | Turnhouse |
| 605 (County of Warwick) | Hurricane | Drem |
| 141 | Defiant | Prestwick |
| | *Dyce Sector* | |
| 603 (City of Edinburgh) | Spitfire | Dyce and Montrose |
| | *Wick Sector* | |
| 3 | Hurricane | Wick |
| 504 (County of Nottingham) | Hurricane | Castletown |
| 232 (one flight) | Hurricane | Sumburgh |
| | *Aldergrove Sector* | |
| 245 | Hurricane | Aldergrove |

*Total* 55½ squadrons (28 Hurricane, 19 Spitfire, 6 Blenheim [night], 2 Defiant, ½ Gladiator).

# VIII

# *Luftwaffe Order of Battle against Britain*

## 13 AUGUST 1940

### HIGH COMMAND
Berlin
(Reichsmarschall H. Goering)

LUFTFLOTTE 2
HQ Brussels
(Generalfeldmarschall
A. Kesselring)

*Fliegerkorps* I
HQ Beauvais
KG1 (He 111)
KG76 (Do 17 and Ju 88)

*Fliegerkorps* II
HQ Ghent
KG2 (Do 17)
KG3 (Do 17)
KG53 (He 111)
II/StG1 (Ju 87)
IV/StLG1 (Ju 87)
*Erprobungsgruppe* 210
(Me 109 & 110)

*Fliegerdivision* 9
HQ Soesterberg
KG4 (He 111 and Ju 88)
I/KG40 (FW 200)
KGr100 (He 111)

*Jagdfliegerfuehrer* 2
HQ Wissant
JG3 (Me 109)
JG26 (Me 109)
JG51 (Me 109)
I & II/JG52 (Me 109)
JG54 (Me 109)
ZG26 (Me 110)
II & III/ZG76 (Me 110)
I/LG2 (Me 109)

LUFTFLOTTE 5
HQ Oslo
(Generaloberst H.-J. Stumpff)

*Fliegerkorps* X
HQ Stavanger
I and III/KG26 (He 111)
I and III/KG30 (Ju 88)
I/ZG76 (Me 110)

LUFTFLOTTE 3
HQ Paris
(Generalfeldmarschall
H. Sperrle)

*Fliegerkorps* IV
HQ Dinard
LG1 (Ju 88)
KG27 (He 111)
StG3 (Ju 87)

*Fliegerkorps* V
HQ Villacoublay
KG51 (Ju 88)
I & II/KG54 (Ju 88)
KG55 (He 111)

*Fliegerkorps* VIII
HQ Deauville
I & III/StG1 (Ju 87)
I & II/StG2 (Ju 87)
StG77 (Ju 87)
V/LG1 (Me 109)

*Jagdfliegerfuehrer* 3
HQ Cherbourg
JG2 (Me 109)
JG27 (Me 109)
JG53 (Me 109)
I & II/ZG2 (Me 110)

Plus reconnaissance aircraft in all *Luftflotten*

| TOTAL STRENGTH AND SERVICEABILITY 10 AUGUST 1940 | | |
|---|---|---|
| Long-range bombers | 1,360 | 998 |
| Dive-bombers | 406 | 316 |
| Single-engined fighters | 813 | 702 |
| Twin-engined fighters | 319 | 261 |
| Long-range reconnaissance | 113 | 78 |

# IX

# *Anti-Aircraft Defences*

Number and Location of Heavy Guns
21 August 1940
(in brackets, number at 11 September)

HQ ANTI-AIRCRAFT COMMAND, STANMORE
(Lieutenant-General Sir Frederick Pile)

### 1ST AA DIVISION
(Major-General F. L. M. Crossman)

| | |
|---|---|
| London | 92 (+107) |
| Langley | 28 |
| Hounslow | 4 |
| Stanmore | 4 |
| | 128 (+107) |

### 2ND AA DIVISION
(Major-General M. F. Grove-White)

| | |
|---|---|
| Leighton Buzzard | 4 |
| Norwich | — (+4) |
| Nottingham | 16 |
| Derby | 40 (−8) |
| Sheffield | 27 |
| Scunthorpe | 24 (−24) |
| Humber | 38 (−12) |
| Mobile battery | 8 |
| Aerodromes | 22 |
| | 179 (−40) |

### 3RD AA DIVISION AND OSDEF
(Major-General L. R. Hill)

| | |
|---|---|
| Belfast | 7 |
| Londonderry | — (+4) |
| Clyde | 27 (+7) |
| Ardeer | 8 |
| Kyle of Lochalsh | 4 |
| Aberdeen | 4 |
| Scapa Flow | 88 |
| Shetlands | 12 |
| Aerodromes | 8 |
| | 158 (+11) |

### 4TH AA DIVISION
(Major-General C. A. E. Cadell)

| | |
|---|---|
| Barrow | — (+8) |
| Liverpool | 56 (+2) |
| Manchester | 20 |
| Crewe | 16 (−8) |
| Birmingham | 71 (−7) |
| Coventry | 32 (−12) |
| Ringway Aerodrome | 4 |
| | 199 (−17) |

### 5TH AA DIVISION
(Major-General R. H. Allen)

| | |
|---|---|
| Milford Haven | — (+4) |
| Swansea | 16 (+8) |
| Cardiff | 26 |
| Newport | 16 (+4) |
| Brockworth | 24 |
| Bristol | 32 |
| Falmouth | 12 |
| Plymouth | 46 (−20) |
| Yeovil | 4 |
| Portland | 14 |
| Holton Heath | 8 |
| Southampton | 39 (−8) |
| Portsmouth | 44 (−4) |
| Bramley | 8 |
| Aerodromes (including Brooklands) | 20 |
| | 309 (−16) |

|  |  |  |  |
|---|---|---|---|
| **6TH AA DIVISION** | | **7TH AA DIVISION** | |
| (Major-General F. G. Hyland) | | (Major-General R. B. Pargiter) | |
| Dover | 18 (−4) | Leeds | 20 |
| Thames and | | Tees | 30 |
| Medway South | 72 | Tyne | 50 |
| Thames and | | Mobile guns | 4 (−4) |
| Medway North | 48 | Aerodromes | 14 |
| Harwich | 15 (−7) | | 118 (−4) |
| Aerodromes | 35 (+8) | | |
| | 188 (−3) | | |

*Total* 1,279 (+38) heavy guns, mainly 3.7″, 4.5″ and old 3″. In addition to the heavy guns there were approximately 700 light anti-aircraft guns (2 pounders, and Bofors 40 mm) and just under 3,000 light machine-guns and 20 mm Hispano, mostly disposed for the protection of airfields, factories and other vital points.

# X

# *The Balloon Defences*

## 31 AUGUST 1940

### HQ BALLOON COMMAND
(Air Vice-Marshal O. T. Boyd)

NO. 30 (BALLOON BARRAGE) GROUP, LONDON
(Group Captain W. J. Y. Guilfoyle)

*No. 1 Balloon Centre, Kidbrooke*
154 balloons
(40 waterborne)
*No. 2 Balloon Centre, Hook, Surrey*
135 balloons
*No. 3 Balloon Centre, Stanmore*
114 balloons
*No. 4 Balloon Centre, Chigwell*
159 balloons
(13 waterborne)

*Total 562*

NO. 31 (BALLOON BARRAGE) GROUP, BIRMINGHAM
(Air Commodore J. C. Quinnell)

*No. 5 Balloon Centre, Sutton Coldfield*
112 balloons
(9 waterborne)
*No. 6 Balloon Centre, Wythall*
136 balloons
*No. 7 Balloon Centre, Alvaston, Derby*
32 balloons
*No. 8 Balloon Centre, Fazakerley*
100 balloons
(12 waterborne)
*No. 9 Balloon Centre, Warrington*
96 balloons
*No. 10 Balloon Centre, Manchester*
80 balloons

*Total 556*

NO. 32 (BALLOON BARRAGE) GROUP, ROMSEY
(Air Commodore A. A. Walker)

*No. 11 Balloon Centre, Bristol*
144 balloons
*No. 12 Balloon Centre, Fareham*
130 balloons
(10 waterborne)
*No. 13 Balloon Centre, Plymouth*
72 balloons
(14 waterborne)
*No. 14 Balloon Centre, Cardiff*
146 balloons
(10 waterborne)

*Total* 492

NO. 33 (BALLOON BARRAGE) GROUP, SHEFFIELD
(Air Commodore S. W. Smith)

*No. 15 Balloon Centre, Newcastle*
120 balloons
(7 waterborne)
*No. 16 Balloon Centre, Sheffield*
72 balloons
*No. 17 Balloon Centre, Sutton-on-Hull*
74 balloons
(24 waterborne)

*Total* 266

NO. 34 (BALLOON BARRAGE) GROUP, EDINBURGH
(Group Captain H. R. Busteed)

*No. 18 Balloon Centre, Glasgow*
256 balloons
(15 waterborne)
*No. 20 Balloon Centre, Lyness*
56 balloons
(16 waterborne)

*Total* 312

*Under Group Command (Kyle of Lochalsh)*
16 balloons
(11 waterborne)

*Total* 2,204 balloons (181 waterborne)

# XI

# Fighter Command Order of Battle

## 7 SEPTEMBER 1940

*HQ Bentley Priory, Stanmore*
*(Air Chief Marshal Sir Hugh Dowding)*

### NO. 10 GROUP, BOX, WILTS.
(Air Vice-Marshal Sir Quintin Brand)

| Squadron | Aircraft | Station |
|---|---|---|
| | *Pembrey Sector* | |
| 92 | Spitfire | Pembrey |
| | *Filton Sector* | |
| 87 | Hurricane | Exeter and Bibury |
| 213 | Hurricane | Exeter |
| | *St Eval Sector* | |
| 238 | Hurricane | St Eval |
| 247 (one flight) | Gladiator | Roborough |
| | *Middle Wallop Sector* | |
| 234 | Spitfire | Middle Wallop |
| 609 (West Riding) | Spitfire | Middle Wallop |
| 604 (County of Middlesex) | Blenheim | Middle Wallop |
| 56 | Hurricane | Boscombe Down |
| 152 | Spitfire | Warmwell |

### NO. 11 GROUP, UXBRIDGE
(Air Vice-Marshal K. R. Park)

| Squadron | Aircraft | Station |
|---|---|---|
| | *Tangmere Sector* | |
| 43 | Hurricane | Tangmere |
| 601 (County of London) | Hurricane | Tangmere |
| 602 (City of Glasgow) | Spitfire | Westhampnett |

| Squadron | Aircraft | Station |
|---|---|---|
| | *Kenley Sector* | |
| 66 | Spitfire | Kenley |
| 253 | Hurricane | Kenley |
| 72 | Spitfire | Croydon |
| 111 | Hurricane | Croydon |
| | *Biggin Hill Sector* | |
| 79 | Spitfire | Biggin Hill |
| 501 (County of Gloucester) | Hurricane | Gravesend |
| | *Hornchurch Sector* | |
| 222 | Spitfire | Hornchurch |
| 603 (City of Edinburgh) | Spitfire | Hornchurch |
| 600 (City of London) | Blenheim | Hornchurch |
| 41 | Spitfire | Rochford |
| | *Northolt Sector* | |
| 1 (Royal Canadian Air Force) | Hurricane | Northolt |
| 303 (Polish) | Hurricane | Northolt |
| 504 (County of Nottingham) | Hurricane | Northolt |
| 1 | Hurricane | Heath Row |
| | *North Weald Sector* | |
| 249 | Hurricane | North Weald |
| 46 | Hurricane | Stapleford Abbots |
| | *Debden Sector* | |
| 17 | Hurricane | Debden |
| 257 | Hurricane | Martlesham and North Weald |
| 25 | Blenheim | Martlesham |
| 73 | Hurricane | Castle Camps |

### NO. 12 GROUP, WATNALL, NOTTS.
### (Air Vice-Marshal T. L. Leigh-Mallory)

| Squadron | Aircraft | Station |
|---|---|---|
| | *Duxford Sector* | |
| 19 | Spitfire | Duxford |
| 310 (Czechoslovak) | Hurricane | Duxford |
| | *Coltishall Sector* | |
| 242 | Hurricane | Coltishall |
| 616 (South Yorkshire) | Spitfire | Coltishall |
| 266 | Spitfire | Coltishall and Wittering |
| | *Wittering Sector* | |
| 23 | Blenheim | Wittering |
| 229 | Hurricane | Wittering and Bircham Newton |

| Squadron | Aircraft | Station |
|---|---|---|
| | *Digby Sector* | |
| 151 | Hurricane | Digby |
| 611 (West Lancashire) | Spitfire | Digby |
| 29 | Blenheim | Digby |
| | *Kirton-in-Lindsey Sector* | |
| 74 | Spitfire | Kirton-in-Lindsey |
| 264 | Defiant | Kirton-in-Lindsey |
| | *Church Fenton Sector* | |
| 85 | Hurricane | Church Fenton |
| 302 (Polish) | Hurricane | Church Fenton |
| 64 | Spitfire | Church Fenton and Ringway |

### NO. 13 GROUP, NEWCASTLE UPON TYNE
#### (Air Vice-Marshal R. E. Saul)

| Squadron | Aircraft | Station |
|---|---|---|
| | *Catterick Sector* | |
| 54 | Spitfire | Catterick |
| 219 | Blenheim | Catterick |
| | *Usworth Sector* | |
| 607 | Hurricane | Usworth |
| 610 (County of Chester) | Spitfire | Acklington |
| 32 | Hurricane | Acklington |
| | *Turnhouse Sector* | |
| 65 | Spitfire | Turnhouse |
| 141 | Defiant | Turnhouse |
| 605 (County of Warwick) | Hurricane | Drem |
| 615 | Hurricane | Prestwick |
| | *Dyce Sector* | |
| 145 | Hurricane | Dyce and Montrose |
| | *Wick Sector* | |
| 3 | Hurricane | Castletown |
| 232 (one flight) | Hurricane | Sumburgh |
| | *Aldergrove Sector* | |
| 245 | Hurricane | Aldergrove |

*Total* 59½ squadrons (31 Hurricane, 20 Spitfire, 6 Blenheim [night], 2 Defiant, ½ Gladiator).

# XII

# *100 Octane Fuel*

At around the time of the fall of France in May 1940, RAF pilots flying Merlin-engined fighters (i.e. the Hurricane and Spitfire) were at once gratified and mystified that the power rating of their aircraft enjoyed a (literally) sudden boost in power. The standard aviation fuel of the Luftwaffe and the RAF at the outbreak of the war was 87 (or there-abouts) octane. Jeffrey Quill, the notable Spitfire test pilot, wrote to the authors on 15 August 1988, in response to an enquiry about the introduction of 100 octane fuel:

I think it virtually certain that the Hurricane operated in France on 87 octane because I think it was only shortly before the Battle of Britain that we changed over to 100 octane. It had the effect of increasing the combat rating of the Merlin from 3,000 rpm at 6½ lb boost or 9 lb boost to 3,000 rpm at 12 lb boost. This, of course, had a significant effect upon the rate of climb, particularly as the constant speed propellers (also introduced just before the Battle) ensured that 3,000 rpm was obtainable from the ground upwards whereas previously it had been restricted by the two-pitch propellers. It also had an effect upon the maximum speed but this was not so significant as the effect upon rate of climb.

This increase of power in the British front-line fighters in the brief period between the Battle of France and the Battle of Britain came as an unpleasant surprise to Luftwaffe fighter pilots. It was not until late August that a force-landed Spitfire was analysed in detail, and the fuel was discovered to be 'green' and of much higher octane than the standard 'blue' 87 octane.

This 'rich mixture response' 100 octane fuel had been in regular use by the US Army Air Corps since 1938, on a top-secret basis. Under a cloak of security, the British Air Ministry began negotiations with the Anglo-American Oil Company (i.e. Esso) for the supply of this fuel, which became known in the trade as BAM 100, and a long-term contract was concluded between the Air Ministry and International Aviation Associates.

Unfortunately, with the outbreak of war in September 1939, the US Congress invoked the Neutrality Act, prohibiting the supply of this life-saving fuel. Several anxious months passed before a compromise was reached by the Roosevelt Administration and the British Government whereby the supply of this fuel could be renewed on a 'dollar on the barrel-head' basis.

# Source References

## 1: No Longer an Island

1 *The Times*, 2 October 1916
2 *Ibid.*
3 Alfred Gollin, *No Longer an Island* (Heinemann, London, 1984), p. 1
4 *Ibid.*, p. 193
5 W. S. Churchill, *The World Crisis*, vol. I: 1911–14 (Thornton Butterworth, London, 1923), p. 312
6 H. A. Jones, *The War in the Air*, vol. III (OUP, Oxford, 1931), pp. 382–3
7 C. Cole and E. F. Cheeseman, *The Air Defence of Britain: 1914–18* (Putnam, New York, 1983), pp. 232–72
8 Jones, *op. cit.*, vol. V, pp. 487–91
9 E. B. Ashmore, *Air Defence* (Longmans Green, London, 1929), p. 39
10 Cole and Cheeseman, *op. cit.*, pp. 288–30
11 Ashmore, *op. cit.*, pp. 53–6
12 Jones, *op. cit.*, Appendices, pp. 8–14
13 *Ibid.*, vol. III, pp. 243–8
14 *Ibid.*, Appendices, pp. 165–71
15 Ashmore, *op. cit.*, p. 92
16 R. M. Fredatte, *The First Battle of Britain, 1917–18* (Cassell, London, 1966), p. 165
17 Cecil Lewis, *Sagittarius Rising* (Peter Davies, London, 1936), pp. 181–2
18 Ashmore, *op. cit.*, pp. 92–4

## 2: Groundwork

1 CAB 23/3 (WC233 – Appendix II). The Report is printed in Jones, *op. cit.*, vol. VI, Appendix II.
2 RAF List, 1920
3 *Ibid.*
4 H. Montgomery Hyde, *British Air Policy between the Wars* (Heinemann, London, 1976), chapter 2 *passim*, which also gives references to the relevant CID and Cabinet papers; also see A. Boyle, *Trenchard* (Collins, London, 1962), pp. 331–50
5 General Lord Ismay, *Memoirs* (Heinemann, London, 1960), p. 34
6 Montgomery Hyde, *op. cit.*, pp. 63–8; Cmd 467, CAB 27/71/FC (3)
7 Viscount Templewood, *Empire of the Air* (Collins, London, 1957), pp. 36–7
8 *Ibid.*, pp. 69–70
9 Montgomery Hyde, *op. cit.*, pp. 111–12
10 CP 270 (23)
11 Montgomery Hyde, *op. cit.*, pp. 142–8; Cmd 2029, CAB 23/46
12 Montgomery Hyde, *ibid.*, pp. 140–41; Baldwin Papers, 1 fl 3–4A
13 CP 270 (23)
14 Hansard HC 5th series vol. 165: col. 2141
15 Templewood, *op. cit.*, p. 199
16 CID 118A (Steel–Bartholomew Report) and CID 120
17 N. H. Gibbs, *Grand Strategy*, vol. I: *Rearmament Policy* (HMSO, London, 1976), p. 49; CAB Cons. 52(29)3
18 E. B. Haslam, *The History of RAF Cranwell* (HMSO, London, 1982), chapter 7
19 AIR I, Box 209, File 16030 7/21
20 Montgomery Hyde, *op. cit.*, p. 306 and Appendix VII; CP 193 (34); Gibbs, *op. cit.*, pp. 106 and 563; J. M. Spaight, *The Expansion of the Royal Air Force, 1934–9* (Air Historical Branch Narrative, Ministry of Defence); CAB Cons. 29(34)3, Hansard HC 5s vol. 292:1275

21 Montgomery Hyde, *ibid.*, Appendix VII; Gibbs, *ibid.*, pp. 176–7, 561 and 563; Spaight, *ibid.*; DC(M) 32, 141 and 143; Hansard HC 5s vol. 302:367

22 Montgomery Hyde, *ibid.*, pp. 363–5 and Appendix VII; Gibbs, *ibid.*, pp. 362–5; Spaight, *ibid.*; Cmd 5107, CAB Cons. 10(36)

23 T. C. G. James, *The Origins and Pre-War Growth of Fighter Command* (AHB Narrative), pp. 15–23

24 *Ibid.*, pp. 26–37

25 Details of Dowding's career from B. Collier, *Leader of the Few* (Jarrolds, Norwich, 1957) and R. Wright, *Dowding and the Battle of Britain* (Macdonald, London, 1969)

*3: The Bomber Won't Always Get Through*

1 Herbert Molloy Mason, *The Rise of the Luftwaffe* (Cassell, London, 1975), p. 158; for Lipetsk generally, see chapter 8 of this work and Hanfried Schliephake, *The Birth of the Luftwaffe* (Ian Allen, London, 1971), pp. 13–22

2 Francis K. Mason, *Battle over Britain* (McWhirter Twins, London, 1969), p. 57

3 H. M. Mason, *op. cit.*, pp. 160–62

4 *The Rise and Fall of the German Air Force* (Restricted Air Ministry Paper No. 248, London, 1948), pp. 4–11

5 H. M. Mason, *op. cit.*, pp. 248–51

6 Denis Richards, *Royal Air Force 1939–45:*, vol. I: *The Fight at Odds* (HMSO, London, 1953), p. 7

7 *Ibid.*, p. 410

8 F. H. Hinsley, *British Intelligence in the Second World War*, vol. I (HMSO, London, 1979), p. 60

9 A. Galland, *The First and The Last* (Methuen, London, 1955), pp. 1–40

10 R. Beamont, *Fighter Test Pilot* (PSL, London, 1986), p. 11

11 J. Quill, *Spitfire – A Test Pilot's*

*Story* (John Murray, London, 1983), p. 58

12 *Ibid.*, p. 76

13 L. Forrester, *Fly for Your Life* (Muller, London, 1956), p. 75

14 W. Green, *Famous Fighters of the Second World War* (Macdonald, London, second series, 1962), p. 26

15 Hansard HC 5s vol. 270:632

16 Richards, *op. cit.*, p. 24

*4: Late Spurt*

1 Gibbs, *op. cit.*, p. 595

2 Montgomery Hyde, *op. cit.*, p. 408

3 Gibbs, *op. cit.*, pp. 308–10

4 *Ibid.* pp. 313–14; COS 698

5 Gibbs, *ibid.*, p. 315; CAB Cons. 15(38)

6 Gibbs, *ibid.*, p. 385; CAB Cons. 21(38)6

7 AHB Narrative, *The Origins and Pre-War Growth of Fighter Command*, p. 44

8 *Ibid.*, pp. 45–7

9 *Ibid.*, p. 67

10 Gibbs, *op. cit.*, p. 583

11 AHB Narrative, *op. cit.*, p. 69

12 *Ibid.*, p. 74

13 Gibbs, *op. cit.*, pp. 387–9

14 *Ibid.*, p. 518

15 AHB Narrative, *op. cit.*, p. 85

16 *Ibid.*, p. 86

17 *Ibid.*, pp. 80–82

18 B. Collier, *The Battle of Britain* (Batsford, London, 1962), p. 163

19 *Ibid.*

*5: Bonus of Time*

1 Fuehrer Directive No. 2, 3 September 1939, quoted in H. R. Trevor-Roper (ed.), *Hitler's War Directives* (Sidgwick & Jackson, London, 1964), p. 6

2 W. G. Ramsey (ed.), *The Blitz Then and Now* (After the Battle Publications, London, 1987), p. 27

3 A. C. Deere, *Nine Lives* (Hodder & Stoughton, London, 1959), p. 39

4 Fuehrer Directive No. 5, 30 September 1939, quoted in Trevor-Roper, *op. cit.*, p. 12
5 Quoted in Ramsey (ed.), *op. cit.*, p. 38
6 *Ibid.*, pp. 73–6
7 AM file S2116 Enc. 1<sup>A</sup>; AHB Narrative, *Air Defence of Great Britain*, vol. I, p. 112
8 *Ibid.*, p. 113
9 *Ibid.*, p. 117

6: *Surviving the Storm*

1 The events in Norway are described in AHB Narrative, *The Campaign in Norway*; T. K. Derry, *The Campaign in Norway* (HMSO, London, 1950); Richards, *op. cit.*, chapter 4; P. B. Lucas, *Wings of War* (Hutchinson, London, 1983), pp. 56–61
2 Developments in France from September 1939 to May 1940 are described in AHB Narrative, *The Campaign in France and the Low Countries*
3 *Ibid.*, for opening days of German attack
4 COS (40) 123rd meeting
5 W. S. Churchill, *The History of the Second World War*, vol. II: *Their Finest Hour* (Cassell, London, 1949), pp. 38–9
6 Paul Richey, *Fighter Pilot* (Jane's, London, 1980), pp. 108–9
7 Fighter Command file S315, quoted in AHB Narrative, *The Air Defence of Great Britain*, vol. I, Appendix 10
8 A. J. P. Taylor, *English History, 1914–45* (OUP, Oxford, 1965), p. 485
9 Wright, *op. cit.*, p. 105
10 COS (40) 133rd meeting
11 *Ibid.*, 134th meeting
12 Churchill, *op. cit.*, p. 38
13 Wright, *op. cit.*, pp. 118–20
14 WM (40) 125
15 Norman Franks, *Fighter Leader*

(William Kimber, London, 1978), pp. 57–64
16 Lucas, *op. cit.*, p. 47
17 Fighter Command file S19048, quoted in AHB Narrative, *op. cit.*, Appendix 11
18 WP (40) 159
19 Quoted in AHB Narrative, *op. cit.*, Appendix 13
20 SWC (39/40) 11th meeting
21 Quoted in H. M. Mason, *op. cit.*, p. 340
22 Hinsley, *op. cit.*, pp. 144–9
23 David Irving, *The Rise and Fall of the Luftwaffe* (Weidenfeld & Nicolson, London, 1973), p. 90
24 Mason, *op. cit.*, p. 356
25 Churchill, *op. cit.*, p. 103
26 Mason, *op. cit.*, p. 258; Matthew Cooper, *The German Air Force 1939–45* (Jane's, London, 1981), p. 119
27 Galland, *op. cit.*, p. 49
28 Churchill, *op. cit.*, p. 103
29 AM Sir Victor Goddard, *Skies to Dunkirk* (William Kimber, London, 1982), p. 207
30 Deere, *op. cit.*, pp. 44–71
31 AHB Narrative, *The Campaign in France . . .* , p. 364
32 *Ibid.*, p. 366; COS (40) 421
33 WM (40) 153
34 *Ibid.*, 158
35 SWC 16th meeting
36 AHB Narrative, *The Campaign in France . . .* , pp. 474–5
37 Richey, *op. cit.*, p. 133
38 *Ibid.*, p. 135

7: *Battle Order*

1 J. R. M. Butler, *Grand Strategy*, vol. II (HMSO, London, 1957), pp. 172–3
2 *Ibid.*, p. 183
3 B. Collier, *The Defence of the United Kingdom* (HMSO, London, 1957), pp. 106–7
4 M. M. Postan, *British War*

*Production* (HMSO, London, 1952), p. 116
5 *Ibid.*, p. 484
6 AHB Narrative, *ADGB*, vol. II, p. 8
7 Hansard HC 5s vol. 361:152
8 D. Richards, *Portal of Hungerford* (Heinemann, London, 1978), p. 195
9 COS (40) 390; WP (40) 168
10 A. Calder, *The People's War* (Cape, London, 1969), p. 113
11 Telford Taylor, *The Breaking Wave* (Weidenfeld & Nicolson, London, 1967), p. 47
12 *Ibid.*, p. 48
13 T. Taylor, *op. cit.*, p. 49; Fuehrer Directive No. 9, quoted in Trevor-Roper, *op. cit.*, p. 18
14 *Ibid.*, p. 54; Fuehrer Directive No. 13, quoted in *ibid.*, p. 27
15 Asher Lee, *Goering, Air Leader* (Duckworth, London, 1972), pp. 91–2
16 T. Taylor, *op. cit.*, p. 64
17 *Ibid.*, pp. 66–7; Fuehrer Directive No. 16, quoted in Trevor-Roper, *op. cit.*, pp. 34–7
18 *Ibid.*, pp. 60–61
19 Cooper, *op. cit.*, p. 133
20 Sir Frederick Pile, *Ack-Ack* (Harrap, London, 1949, paperback edn), pp. 88–9

*8: British Day One, 10 July 1940*

1 Robert Rhodes James (ed.), *'Chips': The Diaries of Sir Henry Channon* (Weidenfeld & Nicolson, London, 1970), p. 319
2 I. Jones, *Tiger Squadron* (W. H. Allen, London, 1954), p. 225

*9: Channel Fight, 11 July–11 August*

1 T. Taylor, *op. cit.*, p. 127
2 *ICARE* magazine 35/36 (Orly Airport, Paris, 1965), p. 129

3 *Daily Herald*, 8 July 1940
4 In family possession and supplied to authors
5 AHB Narrative: *The Air Defence of Great Britain*, vol. II: *The Battle of Britain* (unpublished), hereafter cited as *Narrative*, p. 215
6 T. Taylor, *op. cit.*, pp. 225–38
7 *Fuehrer Conferences on Naval Affairs* (Admiralty, London, 1947), p. 80
8 T. Taylor, *op. cit.*, pp. 72–4, based *inter alia* on Halder diary, 31 July 1940
9 Trevor-Roper (ed.), *op. cit.*, pp. 37–8
10 T. Taylor, *op. cit.*, pp. 130–32
11 *Ibid.*

*10: Clearing the Way, 12 August*

1 D. Knight, *Harvest of Messerschmitts* (Warne, London, 1981), p. 89
2 *Narrative*, p. 113
3 Knight, *op. cit.*, p. 88
4 *Ibid.*, p. 91
5 Quill, *op. cit.*, p. 167
6 56 Squadron combat report, *Narrative*, p. 122

*11: Eagle Day – and After, 13/14 August*

1 Sybil Eccles (ed.), *By Safe Hand: Letters of Sybil and David Eccles 1939–42* (Bodley Head, London, 1983), p. 144
2 Quoted in N. Gelb (ed.), *Scramble* (Michael Joseph, London, 1986), p. 116
3 *Ibid.*
4 F. Partridge, *A Pacifist's War* (Hogarth Press, London, 1978), pp. 53–4
5 A. Bryant (ed.), *The Alanbrooke War Diaries*, vol. I: *The Turn of the Tide* (Fontana, London, 1965), p. 170
6 AIR/2, Inspector-General's Reports, 1940
7 Pile, *op. cit.*, p. 122

## 12: Enter – and Exit – Luftflotte 5, 15 August

1 ICARE, op. cit., p. 53
2 C. Bekker, The Luftwaffe War Diaries (Macdonald, London, 1967), p. 158
3 Gelb (ed.), op. cit., p. 118
4 Narrative, p. 163
5 Beamont, op. cit., pp. 29–30
6 Deere, op. cit., p. 112
7 Narrative, p. 176
8 The Earl of Avon, The Eden Memoirs: The Reckoning (Cassell, London, 1965), p. 137
9 Churchill, op. cit., p. 286
10 J. Colville, The Fringes of Power: Downing Street Diaries 1939–45 (Hodder & Stoughton, London, 1985), pp. 223–4

## 13: The Assault Continues, 16 August

1 Gelb (ed.), op. cit., p. 155
2 Ibid., p. 143
3 Rhodes James (ed.), op. cit., p. 323
4 Gelb (ed.), op. cit., p. 143

## 14: Respite and Re-engagement, 17–18 August

1 Quoted in A. Price, Battle of Britain: The Hardest Day (Macdonald, London, 1979), p. 19
2 Galland, op. cit., p. 73
3 Richard Jones to authors, 1988
4 Quoted in M. Gilbert, Finest Hour (Heinemann, London, 1983), p. 761
5 ICARE, op. cit., p. 59
6 Ibid., p. 111
7 Ibid., p. 71
8 Quoted in Price, op. cit., p. 71
9 Ibid., p. 72
10 Ibid., p. 73
11 Ibid.
12 Ibid., pp. 76–7
13 Knight, op. cit., p. 100
14 Quoted in Price, op. cit., p. 109
15 Ibid., p. 95
16 N. Nicolson (ed.), Harold Nicolson: Diaries and Letters 1939–45 (Collins, London, 1973), p. 108
17 Earl of Birkenhead, The Life of Lord Halifax (Hamish Hamilton, London, 1965), p. 461
18 Avon, op. cit., p. 136
19 Narrative, p. 207
20 Price, op. cit., p. 136
21 Bekker, op. cit., p. 165
22 Colville, op. cit., p. 225

## 15: Desperate Days, 19 August–6 September

1 Bekker, op. cit., p. 166
2 Narrative, p. 219
3 Ibid., pp. 237–8
4 Bekker, op. cit., p. 46
5 Narrative, p. 239
6 Gelb (ed.), op. cit., p. 120
7 Knight, op. cit., p. 116
8 Narrative, p. 391
9 Ibid., p. 382, quoting 11 Group/S.493, 12 September
10 Bekker, op. cit., p. 169
11 Ibid., p. 170
12 Deere, op. cit., p. 142
13 Ben Pimlott (ed.), The Second World War Diary of Hugh Dalton 1940–45 (Cape, London, 1986), p. 86
14 K. Burt and J. Leasor, The One that Got Away (Collins, London, 1956), p. 15

## 16: Strategic Turning-Point

1 Webster and Frankland, Strategic Air Offensive against Germany, vol. I (HMSO, London, 1951), pp. 178–80
2 W. Shirer, Berlin Diary, quoted in T. Taylor, op. cit., pp. 156–8
3 Ibid.
4 Ibid.
5 Bekker, op. cit., pp. 171–2
6 A. Kesselring, Soldat bis zum Letzten Tag (Athenaeum-Verlag, Bonn, 1953), p. 95
7 Galland interview with D. Richards, 7 June 1945, Appendix to Narrative

8 T. Taylor, *op. cit.*, pp. 72–3
9 Sir Hugh Dowding, *Despatch*
   (HMSO, London, 1946)

### 17: *The New Target, 7 September*

1 *Narrative*, pp. 408–9
2 Gelb (ed.), *op. cit.*, p. 230
3 D. Wood and D. Dempster, *The Narrow Margin* (Hutchinson, London, 1961), p. 337
4 Gelb (ed.), *op. cit.*
5 *Narrative*, p. 411
6 G. Barclay, *Fighter Pilot* (William Kimber, London, 1976), p. 50
7 A. McKee, *Strike from the Sky* (Souvenir Press, London, 1960), p. 217
8 *Ibid.*, p. 218
9 Nicolson (ed.), *op. cit.*, p. 111
10 Barclay, *op. cit.*, p. 51
11 I. Maisky, *Memoirs of a Soviet Ambassador* (Hutchinson, London, 1967), p. 107
12 Bryant (ed.), *op. cit.*, p. 174
13 Churchill, *op. cit.*, p. 276

### 18: *'Ominous Quiet!', 8–14 September*

1 *Narrative*, p. 525
2 J. Wheeler-Bennett, *King George VI* (Macmillan, London, 1958), p. 468
3 RAF Casualty (Tom Gleave), *I Had a Row with a German* (Macmillan, London, 1941), p. 68
4 *Ibid.*, p. 75
5 *Narrative*, p. 527
6 Bryant (ed.), *op. cit.*, p. 174
7 Trevor-Roper (ed.), *op. cit.*, p. 38
8 *Fuehrer Conferences . . .* , pp. 98–100

### 19: *'The odds were great . . .', 15 September*

1 Churchill, *op. cit.*, p. 293
2 Galland, *op. cit.*, p. 73
3 *Narrative*, p. 454

4 Barclay, *op. cit.*, p. 56
5 Eccles (ed.), *op. cit.*, p. 151
6 Knight, *op. cit.*, p. 134
7 Gelb (ed.), *op. cit.*, p. 247
8 *Ibid.*, p. 246
9 Churchill, *op. cit.*, p. 296

### 20: *The Scent of Victory, 16–30 September*

1 Gelb (ed.), *op. cit.*, p. 250
2 Cecil Beaton, *The Years Between: Diaries 1939–44* (Weidenfeld & Nicolson, London, 1965), pp. 42–3
3 Gelb (ed.), *op. cit.*, p. 248
4 *Fuehrer Conferences . . .* , p. 97
5 *Narrative*, p. 491

### 21: *The Battle Fades, October*

1 Gelb, *op. cit.*, p. 255
2 *Ibid.*, p. 256
3 Knight, *op. cit.*, p. 115
4 *Fuehrer Conferences . . .* , p. 103
5 Churchill, *op. cit.*, p. 482

### 22: *Retrospect*

1 AIR 2/7281 (Park's reports); AIR 20/5202 (Dowding's *Despatch*)
2 Hansard HC 5s vol. 292:2526
3 Bekker, *op. cit.*, pp. 171–3
4 Hinsley, *op. cit.*, pp. 186–90
5 'Sealion' directive, 1 August 1940, *Fuehrer Conferences . . .* , p. 81
6 *Rise and Fall of the German Air Force*, p. 17
7 Galland interview with D. Richards, 7 June 1945
8 Richards, *The Fight at Odds*, p. 190n
9 AIR 16/659, 18 August 1940
10 AIR 20/5202
11 AIR 16/131, Dowding's memo to Under-Secretary of State on 'Tactics v. Massed Bomber Formations', 19 September 1939
12 AIR 2/360
13 Letter to authors

14 Letter to authors
15 J. E. Johnson, *Wing Leader* (Chatto & Windus, London, 1956), p. 52
16 AIR 16/131 115719
17 AIR 2/7281, 11 Group Op. Instr. No. 10, 5 September 1940, *Narrative*, pp. 352–4, Appendix 11
18 P. B. Lucas, *Flying Colours* (Panther, London, 1983), p. 170
19 AIR 2/7281, *Narrative*, p. 346
20 *Ibid.*, Appendix 10: 11 Group Op. Instr. No. 7, 28 August 1940
21 AIR 2/7281 Enc. 6$^B$
22 Lucas, *op. cit.*, pp. 182–4
23 AIR 16/375; AIR 2/7281, Enc. 16$^A$
24 AIR 2/7281, Enc. 17$^E$
25 *Ibid.*
26 *Ibid.*, Enc. 15$^C$
27 AIR 24/507, Fighter Command Form 540
28 Lucas, *op. cit.*, p. 180
29 AIR 16/282, 14 October 1940; AIR 2/7281, 24 September 1940
30 AIR 19/572, Enc. 10$^A$
31 Lucas, *op. cit.*, pp. 195–6
32 AIR 2/7337; CAB B1/22
33 AIR 16/677
34 W. Eslick, *Whacker's Air Force* (unpublished)
35 AIR 19/572, Enc. 13$^A$;

Slessor-Portal letter, at Christ Church, Oxford, Box C/4
36 Wright, *op. cit.*, p. 241
37 AIR 19/572
38 Wright, *op. cit.*, p. 242
39 Lucas, *op. cit.*, p. 217
40 *The Battle of Britain* (HMSO, London, 1941)
41 M. Gilbert, *op. cit.*, pp. 1060–61
42 *Ibid.*, p. 849
43 Hinsley, *op. cit.*, p. 178
44 Gilbert, *op. cit.*, p. 693; Ismay, *op. cit.*, pp. 188–9
45 Collier, *op. cit.*, pp. 137–8
46 Calder, *op. cit.*, p. 148
47 Aileen Clayton, *The Enemy is Listening* (Hutchinson, London, 1980), pp. 39–48
48 AIR 2/7316, 19 and 20 August 1940
49 Hinsley, *op. cit.*, pp. 186–90
50 Letter from P. O'Connor to authors
51 R. Watson-Watt, *Three Steps to Victory* (Odhams, London, 1957), p. 163
52 AIR 16/635
53 Letters to authors
54 Dowding, *op. cit.*
55 Calder, *op. cit.*, p. 156
56 Gilbert, *op. cit.*, p. 834
57 *Ibid.*, p. 844

# Acknowledgments

We are very grateful to the undermentioned members of the Battle of Britain Fighter Association for their generous contributions to this book and we apologise for any omissions or inaccuracies. The ranks listed are the highest attained.

Flt Lt Donald Anderson AE; Sqn Ldr John Anderson; Wg Cdr M. F. Anderson DFC; Flt Lt Michael Appleby; Sqn Ldr D. L. Armitage DFC; Sqn Ldr James Bailey DFC; Flt Lt John Bailey; Sqn Ldr Cyril Bamberger DFC and Bar; Sqn Ldr Robert Barber AFC; Flt Lt Eric Barnard AE; Sqn Ldr Patrick Barthropp DFC, AFC; Sqn Ldr Anthony Bartley DFC and Bar; Wg Cdr Eric Barwell DFC and Bar, AE; Flt Lt Gordon Batt; Sqn Ldr Percival Beake DFC; Wg Cdr Roland Beamont DSO and Bar, DFC and Bar, DFC (US); Sqn Ldr Robert Beardsley DFC; Gp Cpt. Stephen Beaumont OBE, AE; Sqn Ldr George Bennions DFC; Flt Lt Benjamin Bent DFC; Sqn Ldr M. Bentley-Beard DFM, AFC; A. Cdre Ronald Berry CBE, DSO, DFC and Bar; AV-M Harold Bird-Wilson CBE, DSO, DFC and Bar, AFC and Bar; Grp Cpt. John Bisdee DFC, OBE (Mil.); Wg Cdr William Blackadder DSO, OBE; Wg Cdr G. Douglas Blackwood; Flt Lt A. J. Blayney AFC; Wg Cdr Roger Boulding; Sqn Ldr Benjamin Bowring AE; Wg Cdr Francis Brinsden; A. Cdre Peter Brothers CBE, DSO, DFC and Bar; Wg Cdr Ronald Brown MBE; Grp Cpt. Geoffrey Brunner AFC and Bar; Flt Lt Alan Burdekin AE; Flt Lt J. H. B. Burgess; Sqn Ldr Lionel Casson DFC, AFC; Flt Lt William Clark DFM; Flt Lt A. W. Cook DFM; Wg Cdr Ivor Cosby DFC; A. Cdre James Coward AFC; Wg Cdr David Cox DFC and Bar, *Croix de Guerre avec Palme*; Sqn Ldr E. W. Cranwell DFC, AE; AV-M Edward Crew CB, DSO and Bar, DFC and Bar; AM Sir Denis Crowley-Milling KCB, CBE, DSO, DFC, AE; Flt Lt Wallace Cunningham DFC; Wg Cdr C. F. Currant DSO, DFC and Bar; Grp Cpt. H. S. Darley DSO; Grp Cpt. W. D. David CBE, DFC, AFC; AV-M Robert Deacon-Elliott CB, OBE, DFC, AE; Wg Cdr Christopher Deanesly DFC, AE; AV-M Alan Deere DSO, OBE, DFC and Bar, AFC, DFC (US), *Croix de Guerre avec Palme*; Flt Lt Jack Derbyshire DFC, DFM; Sqn Ldr R. H. Dibnah; Flt Lt John Down; Flg Off. Peter Down; Flt Lt G. G. F. Draper; Sqn Ldr B. H. Drobinski DFC, VM, KW and 3 Bars; Grp Cpt. Byron Duckenfield AFC; Grp Cpt. Sir Hugh ('Cocky') Dundas CBE, DSO and Bar, DFC; A. Cdre John Ellacombe CB, DFC and Bar; Grp Cpt. T. A. F. Elsdon OBE, DFC; Flt Lt W. R. Evans; Wg Cdr Jan Falkowski VM; A. Cdre Harold Fenton CBE, DSO, DFC; Sqn Ldr Antony Fisher AFC; Flt Lt Roy Ford; Flt Lt Terence Forshaw; Sqn Ldr Anthony Forster DFC; Flg Off. Ronald Forward; Sqn Ldr Robert Foster DFC, AE; Wg Cdr Peter Fox; Wg Cdr Fajtl Frantiĕk DFC; Sqn Ldr Charles Frizell DFC, Order of Cloud and Banner; Sqn Ldr C. M. Gibbons AE; Sqn Ldr John Gibson DSO, DFC; Grp Cpt. Edward Graham; Marshal of the RAF Sir John Grandy GCVO, KBE, DSO; Grp Cpt. Colin Gray DSO, DFC and 2 Bars; Flt Lt John Greenwood; Wg Cdr D. H. Grice MBE, DFC; Grp Cpt. Richard Haine OBE, DFC; Flt Lt Peter Hairs MBE;

Flt Lt Roger Hall DFC; Sqn Ldr Ronald Hamlyn AFC, DFM; Sqn Ldr D. J. Hammond; Flt Lt Cyril Hampshire; Sqn Ldr Norman Hancock DFC; Wg Cdr M. S. Harbourne CBE, DSO, DFC and Bar; Wg Cdr Ralph Havercroft AFC; Lt Col R. C. Hay DSO, DSC and Bar; Wg Cdr Thomas Hayes DFC; Wg Cdr George Hebron; Wg Cdr Hugh Heron AFC; Flt Lt Gordon Hewett; Sqn Ldr J. M. Hewson DFC; Wg Cdr Frederick Higginson OBE, DFC, DFM; AV-M Henry Hogan CB, DFC; Wg Cdr Eustace Holden DFC; Sqn Ldr Sidney Holloway OBE; Flt Lt D. H. Hone; Wg Cdr Geoffrey Howitt DFC and Bar; Flt Lt Henry Hoyle; AV-M Desmond Hughes CB, CBE, DSO, DFC and 2 Bars; Flt Lt William Hughes DFC, AE; Flt Lt Charles Hurry AFC; Sqn Ldr Iain Hutchinson TD; Wg Cdr Donald Jack; Wg Cdr Bernard Jennings DFM, AFC; Flt Lt Miroslav Jiroudek; Grp Cpt. George Johns DSO, DFC, AFC; AV-M James Edgar ('Johnnie') Johnson CB, CBE, DSO and 2 Bars, DFC and Bar; Flt Lt Reginald Johnson; Sqn Ldr William Johnson DFC and Bar; AV-M A. V. R. ('Sandy') Johnstone CB, DFC, DL; Flt Lt Richard Jones; Flt Lt Robert Jones; Wg Cdr Joseph Kayll DSO, DFC; Wg Cdr Ronald Kellett DSO, DFC, VM; Sqn Ldr Alan Kellow; Cpt. N. L. D. Kemp DFC; Wg Cdr Donald Kingaby DSO, DFM and 2 Bars, AFC; Flt Lt Jan Kowalski DFC, Cross of Valour and 2 Bars, VM; Sqn Ldr Taddeus Kumiega Cross of Valour and 2 Bars; Col Henry Lafont Cross of Liberation, *Commandeur Légion d'Honneur*; Flt Lt John Lauder; A. Cdre James Leathart CB, DSO; Sqn Ldr Kenneth Lee DFC; Wg Cdr Alan Lees DFC; Sqn Ldr Arthur Leigh DFC, DFM; Flt Lt M. E. Leng; Grp Cpt. R. C. F. Lister DFC; Flt Lt Alexander MacGregor AE and Bar; Sqn Ldr John Mackenzie; Wg Cdr Kenneth Mackenzie DFC, AFC, AE; Wg Cdr C. Hector Maclean AE and Bar; Wg Cdr Robin McNair DFC and Bar; Flt Lt Jan Malinski Cross of Valour and 3 Bars, VM; Flt Lt Jack Mann DFM, AE; Grp Cpt. Graham Manton MID (Burma); Flt Lt E. H. Marsh; Sqn Ldr Ludwik Martel VM, KW, KZ; Grp Cpt. Peter Matthews DFC; Wg Cdr Michael Constable Maxwell DSO, DFC; Grp Cpt. A. G. Miller; Wg Cdr Richard Mitchell DFC, MBE; Grp Cpt. the Hon. Hartland de M. Molson OBE; Grp Cpt. Arthur Montagu-Smith; Sqn Ldr Dulverton Moore DFC and Bar; Wg Cdr Roger Morewood; A. Cdre Edward Morris CB, CBE, DSO, DFC; Flt Lt Maurice Mounsdon; Wt Off. Robert Mowat; Wg Cdr George Nelson-Edwards DFC; Sqn Ldr Harry Snow Newton AFC; Plt Off. Hugh Niven; Sqn Ldr Norman Norfolk; Flt Lt John Norwell AFC, AE; Grp Cpt. S. G. Nunn OBE, DFC; Flt Lt R. C. Nutter DFC; Grp Cpt. Peter O'Brian OBE, DFC; Grp Cpt. Anthony O'Neill; Wg Cdr Geoffrey Page DSO, DFC and Bar; Sqn Ldr V. D. Page; Sqn Ldr Charles Palliser DFC; Wg Cdr Peter Parrott DFC and Bar; Flt Lt Frederick Perkin; Flt Lt James Pickering AFC, AE and Bar; Sqn Ldr Tony Pickering; Wg Cdr Paul Pitcher; Wg Cdr Richard Power; Flt Lt Robert Plenderleith DFC; Flt Lt Harry Prowse; Sqn Ldr Jeffrey Quill OBE, AFC; Flt Lt James Renvoize; Sqn Ldr Roland Richardson AFC; A. Cdre David Roberts; Flt Lt Ralph Roberts; Grp Cpt. Marcus Robinson AFC and Bar; Wg Cdr Jack Rose CMG, MBE, DFC; ACM Sir Frederick Rosier GCB, CBE, DSO; Wg Cdr James Sanders DFC; Wg Cdr Cecil Saunders DFC; Sqn Ldr Donald Scott; AV-M David Scott-Malden DSO, DFC; Flt Lt Karel Seda; Flt Lt Raymond Sellers AFC; Grp Cpt. Desmond Sheen DFC and Bar; Wg Cdr Edward Shipman; Wg Cdr F. M. Smith DFC; Wg Cdr Roddick Lee Smith OBE; Grp Cpt. D. G. H. Spencer CBE; Sqn Ldr Robert Spurdle DFC and Bar; Wg Cdr H. M. Stephen CBE, DSO, DFC and Bar; Sqn Ldr P. J. T. Stephenson DFC; Sqn Ldr Geoffrey Stevens; Sqn Ldr Donald Stones

DFC and Bar; Wg Cdr James Storrar DFC and Bar, AFC, AE; Flt Lt George Stroud AE and Bar; Wg Cdr Richard Summers OBE, AFM; Grp Cpt. Fraser ('Barry') Sutton DFC; Sqn Ldr Alexander Thom DFC; Wg Cdr Robert Thomas; Flt Lt A. R. F. Thompson DFC; Sqn Ldr Lawrence Thorogood DFC; Flt Lt R. E. Tongue; Sqn Ldr Douglas Turley-George DFC, King Haakon VII Medal and Bar; Flt Lt F. J. Twitchett; Wg Cdr Witold Urbanoicz DFC and Bar, US Air Medal; Wg Cdr George Unwin DSO, DFC; Sqn Ldr Frank Usmar; Flt Lt Josef Vopalecky, *Croix de Guerre*; Flt Lt A. Vrana *Chev. Légion d'Honneur*; Sqn Ldr H. K. Wakefield DFC; Flt Lt W. L. B. Walker; Flt Lt Edmund Walsh; Sqn Ldr T. A. Warren; A. Cdre Paul Webb CBE, DFC, AE; Flt Lt Jack Weber; Sqn Ldr George Welford; Grp Cpt. Edward Wells DSO, DFC and Bar; Sqn Ldr Patrick Wells DSO; Sqn Ldr Geoffrey Wellum DFC; Sqn Ldr A. Whitby DFM; Sqn Ldr D. C. Wilde DFC, AE; Flg Off. Kenneth Wilkinson; Wg Cdr R. C. Wilkinson OBE, DFM; Sqn Ldr Wilfred Wilkinson; Sqn Ldr Thomas Williams DFC; Wt Off. Norman Woodland; Grp Cpt. Allan Wright DFC and Bar, AFC.

Among other former officers we should like to thank are: The Rt Hon. The Earl of Selkirk KT, GCMG, OBE, AFC; Flt Lt Julian Bedcock; Sqn Ldr Jeremy Howard-Williams DFC; and Wg Cdr P. B. ('Laddie') Lucas CBE, DSO and Bar, DFC.

We are also much indebted to the following, who served on the ground: J. Addyman, R. Anderson, R. Anglo, R. A. Barber, S. Bennell, C. R. Blachford, P. V. Borrill, J. M. J. Booth, D. Boots, G. Bottomley, R. A. Boyce, S. Brown, C. Burridge, J. W. Carrington, J. Cary (Ms), M. Climshaw (Mrs), D. Coghlan, G. M. Cook (Mrs), C. A. Cooper, H. V. Cossons, S. Coventry, J. Crawshaw, B. Croft, A. Dann, R. Davies, L. Davis (Mrs), O. J. Dean, E. M. Denness (Mrs), A. W. Dixon, R. A. Dobson, J. Doherty, J. F. Egan, J. E. C. Ellard, J. D. Elliott, W. Eslick, A. G. Ethridge, H. A. Failes, S. Faulkner, D. Finn (Mrs), P. J. Foreman, E. G. Fox (Mrs), J. Frappel, T. Gledhill (Mrs), A. P. Gordon, G. E. Gumbrell, R. Harvey, J. R. Hearn, A. B. Hench, E. E. Hind (Mrs), A. Hitchinson (Miss), C. F. G. Holliday, E. F. Holmes, N. Howard (Mrs), Rev. E. Hymer, J. T. Ingle, G. A. Jackson, H. B. Jackson, J. N. James, H. P. Johns, A. E. Jones, P. Jones, R. W. Jones, V. M. Kirkwood (Mrs), R. E. J. Knight, E. Kup (Mrs), H. J. Lazenby, D. G. Lee, W. R. Lee, G. F. Lewin, L. E. Lockwood, F. Luke, A. H. McGillivray (Mrs), Col P. MacIver, S. A. J. Martin, W. Martin, C. H. May, G. E. Mayhew, D. R. Morris, A. N. Newman, W. M. Newton, O. J. Noble (Mrs), F. P. O'Connor, J. Oldham, R. W. Pett, J. Player, C. S. Poole (Mrs), H. W. Priestley, J. L. Rawlings (Miss), J. J. Regan, W. H. Rigby, G. Riley, F. Roberts, N. Robinson, D. Rodway (Mrs), R. S. Rogers, E. A. Russell, J. T. Ryder, D. R. Samson, G. Searle (Mrs), F. C. Shelley, J. R. V. Skelton, E. M. Skipper, I. M. Smith (Miss), P. Smith, T. E. Soar, J. Southwood, E. Walker, E. D. Webster (Mrs), H. Wheeler, R. C. Whinhurst, D. G. Williams, D. R. Wood, J. Wynn, T. M. Yates.

The poems at the start of Parts One and Two are taken from *Verses of a Fighter Pilot* by Flying Officer A. N. C. Weir DFC (Faber, London, 1941); the poem at the beginning of Part Three is from *Air Force Poetry* by John Pudney and Henry Treece (eds) (John Lane/The Bodley Head, London, 1944). They are reproduced by kind permission of the publishers.

# Index

Because of the numerous promotions on both sides during the Battle, the ranks are excluded except in the case of senior commanders.

Aalborg (Denmark), 171
Abenhausen, Oberleutnant, 270
Abyssinia, 25, 54
Acworth, Bernard, 199
*Adlerangriff* ('Eagle Attack'); strategy, 138–40, 144; begins, 154–5, 158, 307
*Adlertag* ('Eagle Day'), 138–9, 154
Admiralty: 1914 air defence of UK, 9; and formation of RAF, 13; and dismemberment of RAF, 18, 20; runs Fleet Air Arm, 20n; and air-sea rescue, 135; and deployment of capital ships, 328; *see also* Royal Navy
Advanced Air Striking Force (AASF), 83–4, 91, 99
Aeronautical Research Committee, 49
AI (radar air interception), 224–5, 322
Air Defence Committee, 50
Air Defence of Great Britain (ADGB), 23, 26–7
Air Defence of Great Britain Committee, 56
Air Fighting Development Unit, 313
Air Ministry: formed (1918), 13; and independent RAF, 19; responsibilities, 23; and command structure, 27; and scientific air defence, 49–50; and pre-war air strength, 52–3, 55, 57, 77; relations with Dowding, 77; and breaking of German codes, 92; and aircraft production, 102–3; Air Tactics, 313; and conduct of Battle, 325; *see also* Fighter Command; Royal Air Force
Air Ministry Experimental Stations (AMES), 51
air-sea rescue service: German, 134–5, 303; British, 135
Air Staff, 54, 76–9, 242–3
Air Transport Auxiliary, 62, 329
Aircraft Production, Ministry of, 102, 171
airfields (British): numbers, 64; attacked, 122, 148–53, 160–1, 169, 171, 175, 180–2, 191–2, 202, 223, 226, 230, 232, 248, 302; satellite, 135–6; crater

repairs, 200; concentrated attacks on, 203–7, 215; Germans misidentify, 215; effect of damage to, 236–7; *see also* individual airfields
airscrews (propellers), 83–4, 168
Albania: Italy invades, 60
Allard, Geoffrey, 232
Allen, James, 132
Allen, Johnny, 190, 285
Americans: form LDV units, 185; serve in RAF, 187–8, 191
Amery, L. S., 20
Anderson, AC2, 164
Anderson shelters, 63
Andover: Staff College, 21
Anti-Aircraft Command, 62–3, 113, 280
anti-aircraft guns (British): effectiveness, 48; pre-war strength, 56–8, 62, 113–14; at Portsmouth, 146; in defence of London, 263, 269; contribution to victory, 328
appeasement policy, 55, 65
Appleby, Michael, 199n
Arado company (Germany), 43
armament (aircraft), 36–7, 156
Armitage, Dennis ('Tage'), 157, 210, 231–2, 286, 340
armour-plating, 233–4
Army, British: contribution to victory, 328; *see also* British Expeditionary Force
Army Co-operation pilots, 221, 225
artillery bombardments: on Dover, 143–4, 350
Aschenbrenner, Friedrich, 162
Ashfield, Geoffrey, 224
Ashford (Kent), 210–11
Ashmore, Major-General E. B., 11–12, 14–15, 23
Atkinson, George, 156
Attlee, Clement, 60, 103
Australians, 191
Austria: Hitler occupies, 54–5
Auxiliary Air Force (AAF), 22, 58, 61
Axon, Peter, 143

Back Component, Hawkinge, 92n
Bader, Douglas: in action, 259, 276, 278, 280, 282; leadership, 289; in tactics controversy, 315–17, 319
Badger, John, 344
Baldwin, Stanley, 21, 25, 47–8, 53, 58, 108
Balfour, Arthur James, 19–20, 23
Balfour, Harold, 316, 321
balloon barrages, 57–8, 61–2, 114, 330–1
Balloon Command, 27, 61–2, 114, 330
Bamberger, Cyril, 288
Banbury (Oxfordshire): attacked, 272
Banks, Frank ('Rod'), 170
Barclay, George, 260, 262–3, 276
barges (invasion): bombed, 293–4
'Barking Creek, Battle of' (1939), 67
*Barn Hill*, SS, 69
Barran, Philip, 132
Barratt, Air Marshal A. S., 83, 85–7, 98
Barry, Norman, 190
Barthrop, Paddy, 198
Bartley, Tony, 290
Barton, R. A. ('Butch'), 289
Battle aircraft, 79, 91; losses, 100
Battle of Britain: official dating of, xvi, 8, 109, 121, 303, 353; British victory, 301; Dowding's *Despatch* on, 322; British pamphlet on, 324; myths of, 325–8
Battle of Britain Fighter Association, 121, 132n, 271, 325
Bawdsey Manor (Suffolk), 51, 59
Beamish, Victor, 233, 288–9, 338, 350–1
Beamont, Roland ('Bee'), 38, 176, 178
Beardsley, Robert, 341
Beaton, Cecil, 291
Beatty, Admiral David, 20
Beaufighter aircraft, 225, 322
Beaverbrook, William Maxwell Aitken, 76; as Minister of Aircraft Production, 102–3, 105, 325; Bevin on, 104n; requests aluminium utensils, 108; Dalton on, 239
Bekker, Cajus, 196
Beley, Robert, 145
Belfast: raid on, 163
Belgians: service in RAF, 191
Belgium, 91–2, 101
Bennions, George H., 292
Bent, Benjamin, 225
Bentley Priory: Fighter Command HQ at, 27, 117; filter room, 116

Berlin: bombed, 243–5
Bertram, Otto, 163
Bessborough family, 217
Bevan, Aneurin, 60
Bevin, Ernest, 104
Biggin Hill: and World War I ground control, 16; airfield attacked, 179, 182; concentrated attacks on, 203, 207–9, 214, 226, 238–9, 248; ops room destroyed, 236
Bird-Wilson, Harold, 202, 336
Birmingham: bombed, 163, 304
Bisdee, John D., 188
Blachford, C. R. ('Cowboy'), 165, 169, 339
'Black Thursday' (15 August), 191
Blackett, Professor P. M. S., 49
Blackwood, George, 230
Blake, Anthony, 290
Blenheim aircraft: qualities, 42–3; on coastal patrol, 61; and squadron strength, 78–9; losses, 91, 100; bomb Luftwaffe airfields, 122, 139; night flying, 224–6
Blériot, Louis, 8
Bletchley Park *see* Government Code and Cipher School
BMW engines (aircraft), 46
Bodie, C. A. W. ('Boggle'), 280, 282
Bomber Command: formed, 27; pre-war condition, 59; Dowding proposes offensive for, 86; and Dunkirk, 95; attacks Luftwaffe airfields, 106, 122, 139, 270, 292; attacks west Germany, 110; role in Battle of Britain, 112, 330; casualties, 132n; raids on Italy, 163, 303; pilots join Fighter Command, 201; offensive actions, 242–5; attacks German invasion ports, 265, 292–4; attacks Eindhoven, 270; *see also* Royal Air Force
Boots, D., 339
Bott, Oberleutnant, 124
Bouchier, Cecil Arthur ('Daddy'), 285–6
Boulogne: bombed, 293
Boulton and Paul company, 42; *see also* Defiant aircraft
Bowen, E. G., 224
Bowhill, Air Chief Marshal Sir Frederick, 21
Boyd, Air Vice-Marshal O. T., 114
Brancker, Sefton, 21
Brand, Air Vice-Marshal Sir Quintin: commands 10 Group, 115, 122, 165, 176, 195, 295–6; expects renewed

enemy attacks, 228; in tactics discussion, 316
Brandenburg, Ernst, 32
Brandenburg, Oberleutnant, 192
Brauchitsch, Walter von, 110, 161–2, 175
Brighton: attacked, 272
Bristol aircraft company, 42; see also Filton
Bristol Fighter (World War I), 42
Britain: pre-war defensive strategy, 53–6; German invasion threat against, 104, 106–10, 123, 136–7, 245, 247, 265–6, 272–3, 293–4, 308; conditions and morale in, 105, 107–8; Goering's air strategy against, 137–8; invasion postponed indefinitely, 283, 301
British Air Mission (in USA), 322–3
British Expeditionary Force (1914), 9
British Expeditionary Force (1939–40): fighter support for, 61, 71, 76–9, 82–8; retreat and evacuation, 88, 92–6, 99
British Intelligence in the Second World War (official history; by F. H. Hinsley), 327
Brize Norton: airfield attacked, 195–6
Broadhurst, Harry, 158
Brooke, Lieutenant General Sir Alan, 160, 265
Brooke-Popham, Air Chief Marshal Sir Robert, 21
Brooklands: aircraft factories attacked, 239–41
Brown, Stephen, 347
Browning machine-guns, 37, 41
Brzezina, S., 156
Brzozowski, M., 270
Buckingham Palace, 269, 277
Budig, Fritz, 148
Bulman, P. W. S. ('George'), 37, 43
Burton, Percy, 233
Butterweck, Friedrich, 149

Calais: docks bombed, 293
Calder, Angus, 334
Camm, Sydney, 35–6, 41, 331
Canadians, 189, 191; see also Royal Canadian Air Force
Canewdon radar station, 66
Cap Gris Nez: guns at, 131, 133
Carbury, Brian, 190
Carmichael, LACW, 338
Carver, Ken, 271
Castle, Rowlands, 217

casualties: RAF, 132, 214, 249–50; Luftwaffe, 214; civilian (British), 304; see also losses (aircraft)
'Catapult, Operation', 106
Chain Home (CH) stations, 51, 58, 142, 145; attacked, 142–3, 215–16; efficacy, 275; see also Ventnor
Chain Home Low (CHL) stations, 51, 71, 142, 145; attacked, 140; efficacy, 275
Chamberlain, Neville, 52–3, 55, 57–8, 60; announces war, 63, 65; resigns, 84; Churchill informs of Battle successes, 184
Chamier-Glisczinski, Wolfgang von, 179
Channel: German aircrew fear of, 198, 310
Channon, Sir Henry ('Chips'), 123, 193, 231
Cherbourg Peninsula: as Luftwaffe base, 122
Chiefs of Staff (British), 54, 89–91, 98, 104
Churchill, Winston S.: in World War I, 9; and retaliatory raids, 13; accepts independent RAF, 18–19; urges rearmament, 53, 55; on sirens, 66; and Finnish war, 81; as Prime Minister, 84; and supply of fighter support to France, 86–8, 90–1, 99; on Dunkirk, 95; forms Ministry of Aircraft Production, 102, 104n; gains emergency powers, 103; defiance, 105; Hitler abuses, 110; and fall of France, 123; and conduct of Battle of Britain, 182–4; contacts Chamberlain, 184; praises RAF, 199; minutes, 199–200; visits South-East, 230–1; and shooting of parachuting airmen, 231; and RAF bombing offensive, 243; on threatened invasion, 266; visits 11 Group HQ, 274, 282; Roosevelt warns of impending invasion, 294; on Italian air force raid, 304; on bombing of London, 308, 334; and enemy losses, 311; and fighter tactics controversy, 316; and Dowding's service, 320–4; on naval deployment, 327; names Dowding's 'chicks', 333
Civil Air Guard, 62
Civil Defence: system developed, 57, 62–3
Civilian Repair Organisation, 329
Clements, M., 181
Coastal Command: formed, 27; patrols, 69–70; absorbs Blenheim squadrons, 79; and Dunkirk, 95; and German invasion threat, 106, 292–3; role in Battle, 112; pilots join Fighter

Coastal Command – *cont.*
Command, 201; attacks German
airfields, 292; contribution to Battle,
330
Cobden, Donald G., 127
Cock, J. R., 176, 178, 231
Comely, Peter, 141
Committee for the Scientific Survey of Air
Defence, 49–51
communications: damage and repairs to,
236
Component Force (France), 83–5, 87–8,
90, 96
Connors, Stanley, 181
conscription: introduced in Britain, 60
controlled interception, 64; *see also* ground
control
convoys (British): attacked, 1, 125, 131,
133–4, 139, 144–5
Cooke, Charles, 124
Cooke, D., 132
Cooper, Charles, 181, 237–8
Cosby, Ivor H., 225
Cossons, H. V., 350
Couland, Alf, 181
Courtney, Christopher, 21
Coward, T. J. B., 337
Cox, David, 213
Cox, Philip ('PAN'), 133, 347
Cranwell Cadet College, 21, 24
Craven, Sir Charles, 103
'Cromwell' order, 266, 294
Crook, David, 159–60, 165
Cross, K. B., 82
Crossley, Mike, 150–1, 197, 206
Croydon: airfield attacked, 181–2, 184,
300
Cunningham, John ('Cat's Eyes'), 225
Curtiss D12 engine, 34
Czechoslovakia, 55, 57–8, 60
Czechs: serve with RAF, 186–7, 191, 230–
2, 239, 284
Czernin, Count Manfred Beckett, 229

Daimler-Benz company (Germany), 43
Dalton, Hugh, 239
Darley, George, 159, 228
David, W. Denis, 139, 231, 275, 340
Davis, Chris, 190
Davis, James, 187
Daw, William and Alice, 277
DB 600 engine (German), 47
DB 601 engine (German), 44–5
Danzig, 63
Deacon-Elliott, R., 174
'death-rays', 49

Debden: airfield attacked, 229
Deere, Alan: and 'Battle of Barking
Creek', 67; Dunkirk experiences,
96–8; in Battle, 139, 190–1; on
Malan's shooting, 156; shot down,
178; New Zealand origins, 190; on
exhaustion, 201; denies Manston's
breakdown of morale, 226; crash,
238–9; and new pilots, 285
Defence Regulation 18B, 108
Defiant aircraft, 42, 94, 130, 227–8
Deighton, Len, 226
Denmark: occupied, 80; as Luftwaffe
base, 171, 173, 307, 326
Derby, Edward George Villiers Stanley,
17th Earl of, 20
Detling (Kent): airfield attacked, 160–2
Development and Production, Department
of, 102
Dewar, John, 228, 231
Dill, Field Marshal Sir John, 96
Disarmament Conference, 1933, 24–5
Dixon, A. W., 344
Donahue, A. G., 150
Donaldson, E. M., 67
Donaldson, J. W. ('Baldy'), 81
Dornier Do 17 bomber: design and
performance, 45–6; in France,
83–4; Dunkirk losses, 93;
reconnaissances by, 123–4; attacked,
125–6; vulnerability, 150
Dornier Do 18 flying boats, 134
Dornier Do 215 aircraft, 123
Dortmund-Ems Canal, 245
Douglas, Air Vice-Marshal Sir W. Sholto,
36; and tactics controversy, 316–19;
replaces Dowding, 320, 322–3;
reproaches Dowding, 321; supports
Watson-Watt, 332
Dover: actions over, 126, 133, 163;
CH station at, 142–3, 256,
270
Dowding, Air Chief Marshal Sir Hugh
Caswall Tremenheere: calibre, 21;
heads Fighter Command, 28–9, 31;
career and achievements, 28–30, 332;
supports radar, 29, 50, 332; and
aircraft armament, 37; air defence
plan, 56, 58; and Fighter Command
strength, 60; resists sending fighters
to France, 61, 71, 76–8, 81, 84, 86–7,
89–91, 98–9, 325; controls Anti-
Aircraft Command, 62; increased
squadron requirements, 70, 76–80;
improvements to Command, 71;
relations with Air Ministry, 77–8; and

Norway campaign, 82; proposes bombing offensive, 86–7; letter to Air Ministry on minimum requirements, 89; and evacuation of BEF, 92–3, 95; and fighter production, 102–3; praises Beaverbrook, 103; optimism, 105; strength at start of Battle of Britain, 112; professionalism, 113; command and organisation, 113–14; in ops room, 117; deployment of squadrons and reinforcements, 138, 153, 230, 250, 268, 319; expects major attack, 166; and attacks on N.E. England, 173–4, 183–4; and conduct of Battle, 183; Churchill praises, 184; and damage to CH stations, 216; and head-on attacks, 233; high losses, 237; and pilot shortage, 249–51; 'Stabilisation Scheme', 251; and mass raids on London, 259, 265; leadership, 287, 309, 321; gains upper hand, 292; on phases of Battle, 307; and enemy losses, 311; and fighter tactics controversy, 313–17, 326; replaced, 319–23; opposes Salmond proposals, 321; rejects fighter nights, 322; heads British Air mission in USA, 322; later career and retirement, 322–5; peerage, 324; and Enigma decrypts, 326; assessed, 332–3

Down, Peter, 338
Driffield (Yorkshire): airfield attacked, 171
drop tanks, fuel (*Dackelbauch*), 198
Drummond-Hay, Peter, 132
Dumont, Alberto Santos, 8
Dundas, Hugh ('Cocky'), 160, 171, 174, 223
Dundas, John, 160, 165
Dungeness, 149
Dunkirk CH station (Canterbury), 142–3
Dunkirk: evacuation, 1940, 91–8, 105
Dunlop Fort rubber works: bombed, 224
Duxford Wing: in action, 259, 270, 275–6, 278, 280, 290; and tactics, 315–19; score claim, 319
'Dynamo, Operation' (Dunkirk), 93–4, 98

E-boats, 131
Eagle Squadrons, 290; *see also* Americans
early-warning system, 48–51, 140–2, 275
East Grinstead: Queen Victoria Hospital, 271, 342
Eastbourne: attacked, 272
Eastchurch, 157, 196, 226
Ebbighausen, Hauptmann, 193

Eccles, David, 159
Eccles, Sybil, 159, 277
Eckford, Alan F. ('Shag'), 206
Eden, Anthony, 25, 101, 183, 213, 294
Edmonds, Brigadier General Sir James, 21n
Edwards, George Nelson, 213
Eindhoven (Holland): bombed, 270
Elham (Kent), 157, 213
Elizabeth, Queen of George VI, 269
Ellington, Air Chief Marshal Sir Edward, 77
Elliot, A. G., 34
Ellis, John, 149, 207
*Englandgeschwader* (World War I), 10–11, 14
Enigma machine and decrypts, 92, 268, 308, 326–7
*Erprobungsgruppe* 210: 134, 142, 179–82, 238, 280, 294, 296–7, 300, 303; leadership, 289
Eslick, William, 168, 170, 234, 322n, 337
Esso oil company, 35
Ethridge, Arthur G., 347
Evill, Air Vice-Marshal (Sir) Douglas Claude Strathern, 319, 323
Ewald, Wolfgang, 210
Expansion Schemes (RAF), 25–6

Fairey, Richard, 34
Falkenstein, Freiherr von, 237
Faviell, Frances, 291
Fenton, H. A., 232
Fernsebner, Feldwebel, 133
Ferris, Henry M., 192
Field Force squadrons (with BEF), 76, 78
Fifth Column, 106–7
Fighter Command: formed, 27–9; pre-war state, 59–60; as support to BEF and French Army, 61, 71, 76–9, 82–8, 99; at outbreak of war, 63, 76; and ground control system, 64, 118; shipping protection patrols, 69, 70, 79; low early losses, 70; improvements and expansion, 70–1, 76–80; strength reduced by actions in France, 89–90; close support for bombers, 92; offensive sorties over Channel ports, 92; at Dunkirk, 94–5, 98; losses in France, 100; and German attacks on shipping, 111; strength at start of Battle of Britain, 112; operational direction and organisation, 114–17; operations

Fighter Command – *cont.*
rooms, 116–17; and 'Fighting Area
Attacks', 122; satellite airfields, 135;
international recruitment and
composition, 186–91; outnumbered,
220–1, 235; pilot shortage, 221;
damage to ground organisation and
communications, 235–6, 248; morale
and exhaustion in, 237–8, 310;
squadron movement, 250–1; strength
revived, 274; senses victory, 280, 282;
leadership in, 284–9; German attempt
to destroy, 308; superior information,
309; controversy over tactics, 311–17;
*see also* Battle of Britain; losses
(aircraft); Royal Air Force
GROUPS
no. 9 Fighter Group, 114n
no. 10 Fighter Group, 64, 70;
responsibility and strength,
115–16, 122; satellite airfields, 135;
actions, 145, 176, 193, 230;
attacked in *Adlerangriff*, 158; and
squadron deployment, 251;
combats mass bombers, 278;
tactics, 316
no. 11 Fighter Group, 28, 66–7, 89;
at Dunkirk, 92–4; responsibility
and strength, 115; pressure on, 122;
actions, 125, 131–2, 145, 152, 176,
193, 230, 232; report on Kenley
attack, 207; airfields attacked, 226;
damage to, 248, 250–1, 267; saved
by change of German tactics, 267;
Churchill visits HQ, 274; and early-
warning system, 275; combats mass
bombers, 278, 280; losses, 292;
tactics, 315–19
no. 12 Fighter Group, 27;
responsibility and HQ, 116, 122;
losses, 130; and squadron
deployment, 251; fighter tactics,
315–18
no. 13 Fighter Group, 64, 116, 173–4,
251
no. 14 Fighter Group, 70, 114n
Fighting Area (UK), 23, 26, 56
Fighting Area Attacks, 122
filter rooms, 116, 321
Filton (Bristol): factory bombed, 224,
294–5
Fink, Johannes, 154–7, 260–1
Finland, 81
Fisher, Basil, 127
Fiske, W. M. L., 188–9, 194, 336
Fisser, Dr, 146–8

Fleet Air Arm, 19n, 20n; pilots in Battle of
Britain, 193, 201, 284, 290
Flinders, John ('Polly'), 208
Flying Training Manual, 314
Focke-Wulf company (Germany), 43; 190
aircraft, 44
Forbes, Admiral of the Fleet Sir Charles,
327
Ford: airfield attacked, 215
Foreness CHL station, 144, 256
Fox light bomber, 34
France: Air Force strength, 25; and
German threat, 55, 64; and Czech
crisis, 57; 1940 collapse, 64, 90, 99,
104–5, 108; Germans invade, 84;
requests British air support, 85–7, 90,
98–9; Air Force losses, 90; Fleet
neutralised, 106; *see also* French
Franco, General Francisco, 34
Frantisek, Josef, 186–7, 301
Freeman, Air Chief Marshal Sir Wilfrid,
21, 102–3, 332
French: pilots serve in RAF, 191, 284
French 1st Army, 94
French 7th Army, 94
French, Field Marshal John Denton
Pinkstone, 9, 11
Froelich, Stefan, 276
fuels (aircraft), 35

Galland, Adolf: training, 33–4; and British
fighter performance, 35; on Dunkirk,
95; and *Adlertag*, 163; on drop tanks,
198; aggression, 219; favours
bombing of London,
244–5; and Luftwaffe failure, 275,
283; escorts mass bomber attacks,
278; leadership, 289; and aircraft
limitations, 310
Gassner, Alfred, 46
GCI (Ground Control Interception)
stations, 225
Geddes, Sir Eric, 19–20
George VI, King, 105, 164, 269, 323
Germany: bombed in World War I, 14; as
threat, 26; pre-war air power, 31–4,
52, 56; aircraft development and
design, 43–7; pre-war aggression, 54–
5, 60; bombing offensive against, 86–
7; advance in France and Low
Countries, 88, 91; invasion plan
against Britain, 104, 106, 108–10,
136–7, 245, 247,
265–6, 272–3, 283, 292–3, 308;
bombing offensive against, 242–5
Gilbert, Martin, 326

Gillam, Denys, 171
Gillan, John, 38
Gladiator aircraft, 36, 79, 81–2
Gleave, Tom, 271
Gleed, Ian ('Widge'), 88, 176
*Glorious*, HMS, 81–2
*Gneisenau* (German warship), 82
Gobeil, F. M., 189
Goddard, Victor, 96
Goebbels, Joseph, 45, 135, 272, 324
Goering, Hermann: heads German Air Ministry, 32–3; on Me 110, 45; claims destruction of BEF, 93; and air offensive against Britain, 109; as C. in C., 111; and British recalcitrance, 129; and invasion plans, 131, 136; *Adlerangriff* strategy, 137–40, 154–5, 158, 163, 175, 191; visits High Command, 141; and RAF recruitment, 186; tactics, 202; and Stuka losses, 216; criticises Luftwaffe fighter pilots, 219; changes plans at Karinhall, 220, 223–4; and bombing of Berlin, 243; and bombing of London, 244–5, 267; assesses progress of Battle of Britain, 247–8; at St Omer, 254; personal command, 254; observes bombing armada, 255–6, 261; underestimates RAF fighter strength, 280; poor leadership, 309; in British pamphlet on Battle of Britain, 324
Goetz, Ferdy, 255, 261
Gollin, Alfred, 8
Gordon, John, 156
Gort, Field Marshal John Vereker, 85–6, 91
Gosport, 194; airfield attacked, 215
Government Code and Cipher School, Bletchley Park, 92, 326
GPO (War Group) *see* Post Office War Group
Graham, E., 174, 238
Grandy, John, 195, 289
Gravesend, 252, 300
Gray, Colin F., 190, 192, 201, 285
Gray, Tom, 348
Great Yarmouth, 226
Greenshields, Henry la Fore, 193, 196
Greenwood, John, 339
Gribble, George D., 201
Grice, Richard, 175, 208, 288
ground control: developed in World War I, 11, 14–16; system at outbreak of World War II, 64, 118; in operation,

276; and night fighters, 322; *see also* GCI
ground staff and maintenance, 167–70, 331
Guderian, General Heinz, 88, 91, 108

Haamstede: bombed, 139
Hahn, Hans von, 237, 289
Halder, Franz, 110
Halifax bombers, 59
Halifax, Edward Frederick Lindley Wood, 1st Earl of, 110, 212, 322
Hallings-Pott, John, 164
Halton: Apprentices' School, 21
Hanbury, Felicity, 239
Handrick, Gotthart, 161
Hannah, John, VC, 293
Hardinge of Penshurst, Alexander Henry Louis, 2nd Baron, 269
Hardy, Richard, 178, 182
Harland and Wolff works, London; bombed, 259
Harrier jump-jets, 42
Harris, Air Chief Marshal Sir Arthur, 21, 323
Harrogate: attacked, 272
Hart bomber, 35–6
Hatfield: de Havilland works attacked, 298
Haviland, J. K., 188
Hawker Engineering Company, 35–7; *see also* Hurricane fighter
Hawkinge: airfield attacked, 148, 150–1, 175, 236n; Back Component, 92n
Haysom, G. D. L., 190
head-on attacks, 232–3
Hearn, J. R., 161, 345
Heinkel company (Germany), 43
Heinkel He 51 fighter, 34
Heinkel He 59 seaplane, 134–5
Heinkel He 111 bomber: design and performance, 45–7; uses Lorenz blind-landing set, 69; examined by British, 69; activities, 141; vulnerability, 150
Heinkel He 112 fighter, 43
Henderson, Elspeth, 239
Hendon: airshows, 22, 28; aircraft reserves at, 199
Hendon Borough Council, 157
Heyworth, J., 312
Higgins, Air Chief Marshal John, 21
Higgs, Tom, 126
Hill, Professor A. V., 49
Hillary, Richard, 271
Hillingdon House, Uxbridge, 27
Hintze, Otto, 143, 303

Hitler, Adolf: rise to power, 25, 31; and development of German air power, 32–3; strategic initiative, 54; aggressive actions, 54–5, 57–8, 60, 63, 65; meets Chamberlain, 58; attacks France, 68, 101; and outbreak of war, 76; occupies Denmark and Norway, 80; and elimination of BEF, 93, 95; attacks Low Countries, 101; and plans for invasion of Britain, 109–10, 136–7, 245, 273, 294, 304; orders bombing offensive against Britain, 109; hopes for peace settlement, 110, 131; halted by Battle of Britain, 118; and British recalcitrance, 129; and attack on Croydon, 182; reprisal bombings of London, 243–5, 308; postpones invasion indefinitely, 283, 301, 308; see also Germany

Hives, Ernest Walter, 34
Hoare, Sir Samuel, 19
Hogan, Henry A. V., 133, 150, 299, 346
Holland, 101
Holloway, Sidney, 225, 339
Holmes, G. M., 277
Home Defence Force, 11, 21–5; command, 26–7
Home Fleet (British), 68
Home Guard (formerly Local Defence Volunteers), 101, 106, 185, 266, 328
Hood, HMS, 68
Hooker, Stanley, 35
Hope, Sir Archibald, 188, 194
Hornchurch: airfield attacked, 170, 217, 226
Houston, Dame Lucy, 39n
Hughes, Desmond, 228
Hughes, Paterson, 241
Hugo, Petrus Hendrink ('Dutch'), 190, 206
Hull, Caesar, 262, 268, 336
Hurricane fighter: engine, 35; design and performance, 36–8, 41, 45, 48; pre-war supply, 38; modifications, 71, 83–4, 234, 331; in France, 76–8, 83–6, 89, 99; in squadron service, 79–80, 84; in Norway campaign, 82–3; losses at Dunkirk, 94–5; losses in France, 100; as production priority, 102; numbers at start of Battle of Britain, 112–13; qualities, 136, 341; cannon-equipped, 156; night-fighting, 224; counters escorted bombers, 235; production, 307–8; Dowding supports, 332

Hutchinson, Iain, 170, 234–5, 290–1
Huth, Joachim Friedrich, 125, 155, 289
Hymer, Eric, 348

IFF (identification friend or foe), 51, 67n, 71
Imperial Airways, 22
India: RAF role in, 20
Ingle, J. J., 193
Inner Artillery Zone (British), 23, 26, 263, 269
Inskip, Sir Thomas, 53–4
invasion of Britain see Britain; also 'Sealion'
Ismay, General Hastings Lionel, 18, 90
Israelis: in RAF, 191
Italy: invades Abyssinia, 25; invades Albania, 60; joins Germany, 104; air attacks on Malta and Sidi Barrani, 123, 127; bombed, 163, 303; air force attacks Britain, 303–4

Jamaicans: in RAF, 191
Jameson, P. G., 82
Jay, D. Trevor, 275
Johns, George, 234, 343
Johnson, Air Vice-Marshal John E., 313
Johnstone, A. V. R. ('Sandy'), 258
Jones, A. E., 350
Jones, H. A., 14
Jones, Ira ('Grandpa Tiger'), 127
Jones, Peter, 194
Jones, R. V., 69, 269
Jones, Richard, 287
Josclin, John, 132
Jumo engines (German), 47
Junkers 86P aircraft, 214
Junkers Ju 87 (Stuka) dive bomber, 47; at Dunkirk, 94; efficacy, 121, 161; raids by, 129–30, 133, 144; vulnerability, 130, 136, 139, 187, 193; losses, 216; withdrawn, 220
Junkers Ju 88 bomber, 46–7, 123, 134, 136, 145, 150

Karinhall, 220, 224
Keil, Anton, 175
Keitel, Feldmarschall Wilhelm, 109, 245, 301
Kelley, Frank, 128
Kenley: early attacks on airfield, 179, 181–2, 351; concentrated attacks on, 203–7, 214, 226, 236, 248
Kennedy, Joseph P., 185
Kent, HRH George, Duke of, 123
Kent, J. A., 189

Keogh, V. C. ('Shorty'), 187–8
Kesselring, Feldmarschall Albert: and
    destruction of BEF, 93; supports
    assault on Britain, 108; commands
    *Luftflotte* 2: 111, 125; and weather
    conditions, 123; actions, 130–1, 153;
    on strength of bomber force, 138;
    underestimates British fighter
    numbers, 140; and Goering, 141, 175,
    202, 254; and Rubensdoerffer's
    attacks on radar, 144; attacks south-
    coast radar stations, 145, 148; and
    *Adlerangriff*, 160–1, 164, 195, 227;
    and raid on Detling, 162; and raid on
    Croydon, 182; concentrated raids,
    202, 207; Sperrle forces transferred
    to, 219, 229; tactics, 232; favours
    bombing of London, 244–5; assesses
    progress of Battle, 247–8; and KG26,
    270; and strength of Fighter
    Command, 272; misunderstands
    RAF early-warning system, 275;
    pilots' experience, 289; sends lone
    bombers, 290; and Hitler directive,
    302
Kestrel engine (Rolls-Royce), 34, 36,
    43
King, Eric, 195
Kingsley, John, 210
Kleyenstueber, Arno, 173
'Knickebein' system, 69, 268–9
Knoetsch, 'Bubi', 43
Kreiger, Hauptmann, 126
Kreipe, Major, 93
Kretzer, Obergefreiter, 182
Kuenstler, Hauptmann, 270
Kup, Edith, 352

Labour and National Service, Ministry of,
    103–4
Lacey, J. M. ('Ginger'), 202
Lamberty, Rudolf, 209
*Lancastria*, SS, 99
Law, Andrew Bonar, 19, 21
Lawrence, K. A., 190
leadership: in RAF, 284–9; in Luftwaffe,
    289
League of Nations, 24
Learoyd, R. A. B., VC, 245n, 293
Leathart, James, 132, 190, 192, 201, 226,
    284–6, 301
Leckrone, Phil, 290
Lee, D. G., 150–1
Lee, Kenneth, 211
Lee-on-Solent, 194
Legge, Claire, 342

*Legion Kondor* (Spanish Civil War), 34,
    111
Leigh, Rupert, 123
Leigh-Mallory, Air Vice-Marshal (Sir)
    Trafford: commands 12 Group, 116,
    295; aids 11 Group, 226; criticised,
    287; in tactics controversy, 315–19,
    326; replaces Park, 320; and conduct
    of Battle, 333
Lemon, (Sir) Ernest, 103
Lewin, Ronald: *Ultra Goes to War*,
    326
Lewis, Cecil: *Sagittarius Rising*, 15
Lipetsk (USSR), 31–2
Liverpool: bombed, 224, 291, 304
Llanreath, 223
Lloyd George, David, 11, 17, 239
Local Defence Volunteers *see* Home Guard
Loerzer, Bruno, 254
London: bombing and defence in World
    War I, 10–15; inter-war defences, 23,
    26; World War II bombing, 122, 224,
    227, 243–5; mass attacks on, 258–63,
    267–70, 276–8, 290–1, 304, 308;
    damage, 262, 264, 268; Me 109s
    bomb, 298–9
Londonderry, Charles Stewart Henry
    Vane-Tempest-Stewart, 7th Marquess
    of, 50
losses (aircraft): RAF, 127, 136, 153, 160,
    162, 183, 214, 229, 237, 247–8, 271,
    282–3, 291, 310–11; Luftwaffe, 70,
    100, 136, 139, 153, 160, 162, 182–3,
    191, 214, 229, 247, 271, 282–3, 291,
    310–11; controversy over, 310–11
Lucas, P. B. ('Laddie'), 319
Ludlow-Hewitt, Air Chief Marshal Sir
    Edgar, 21, 149–50, 164, 175, 330
Luederitz, Oberleutnant, 147
Luetzow, 289
*Luftflotten see* Luftwaffe
Lufthansa (air line), 32–3
*Luftsportverband*, 32
Luftwaffe: 1930s development and
    expansion, 25, 31–4, 56; aircraft
    development, 43–7; support role for
    Army, 63, 309; attacks on British
    Fleet, 68–9; coastal attacks, 70;
    calculated loss rate, 76; actions in
    France, 82–6, 91; code broken, 92–3;
    at Dunkirk, 93–6; reconnaissance
    flights over England, 99, 123; losses
    in France, 100; regroups before
    proposed invasion of Britain, 108;
    bombing offensive against Britain,
    109, 137–8; and German invasion

Luftwaffe – *cont.*
plans, 110, 136–7; strength at start of Battle of Britain, 111–12, 117; high morale, 117–18, 162; airfields bombed, 106, 122, 139, 270, 292; air-sea rescue service, 134–5, 303; bomber strength, 138; early optimism, 140; attacks N.E. England and Scotland, 171, 173–4; high-altitude photo-reconnaissance, 214; command changes, 219; numerical superiority, 220–2, 235; night attacks, 224–7; heavy armour-plate, 233–4; declining morale, 236–7, 275, 282, 310; mass bombing attacks on London, 255–6, 258–65, 267–70, 276–8, 304; manoeuvres to confuse tracking, 256; leadership qualities in, 289; ceases daylight bombing, 297; poor information, 309; organisation and fighting role, 309; weakness, 310; fighting tactics, 313; *War Diaries*, 237; *see also* losses (aircraft)
FORMATIONS
*Luftflotte* 1: 111, 154
*Luftflotte* 2: and Dunkirk, 93; command and responsibility, 111–12, 115; preparation, 129; and *Adlerangriff*, 154, 193, 196, 217; losses, 182, 216; concentrates attacks, 203; increased Me 109s in, 229; mass formations, 276
*Luftflotte* 3: command and responsibility, 111–12, 115; over West Country, 126; preparation, 129; and convoy 'Peewit', 139; mistakes front-line airfields, 215; night raids, 263; low morale, 275; attacks Filton, 295
*Luftflotte* 5: 111, 154, 171, 173–4
UNITS
I/JG2, 255
III/JG2, 163
JG3, 276
II/JG3, 241
JG26 ('Schlageter'), 149, 161, 163–4, 179, 219, 278
I/JG27, 133
I/JG51, 125, 138, 219, 303
JG52, 164, 303
JG53, 145
JG54, 278
KG2, 154–5, 192, 260–1, 278
KG3, 179, 191
KG26, 182, 191, 270
II/KG27, 141

KG30, 171
KG51 (*Edelweissgeschwader*), 145–6
KG53, 278
KG55, 165, 296
KG56, 278
KG76, 203
III/KG76, 276
KG77, 296
III/KG77, 290
KG100, 162–3, 224
LG1, 158, 161, 191
I/StG2, 194
II/StG2, 163
I/StG77, 216
ZG2, 145
I/ZG2, 239
ZG26, 125, 155
ZG76, 145
OTHER FORMATIONS *see Erprobungsgruppe* 210
Lukaszwickz, K., 145
Lutz, Martin, 142, 294, 296–7
Lympne: airfield attacked, 148–50, 175, 236n; Ludlow-Hewitt visits, 164

McArthur, James, 258, 262
Macdonald, A. R. D., 288
Macdonald, Peter, 316–17
MacDonald, Ramsay, 39n
Macfie, F. Colin, 290
McGregor, Hector, 146–8
McIndoe, Sir Archibald, 271
Mackenzie, Kenneth, 300–1
McKnight, Willie, 189
MacLean, C. Hector, 201
McNab, E. A., 189
Maffett, G. H., 340
Maintenance Command, 27, 62, 100
Maisky, Ivan, 264
Malan, A. G. ('Sailor'), 92, 139, 156, 166, 190, 206
Malta, 123, 127
Mamedoff, Andrew, 187, 227
Manchester: bombed, 304
Manchester aircraft, 59
Manston airfield ('Charlie 3'): attacked, 122, 148, 151–3, 164, 175, 210, 223, 226, 236n; Churchill on slow repairs to, 200
Marrs, Eric ('Boy'), 296, 347
Martin, W., 337
Martini, General Wolfgang, 144, 157
Martlesham Heath: airfield attacked, 175, 180, 236
Mary, Queen Mother, 105
Meisel, Captain, 216

Merlin engine (Rolls-Royce), 34–5, 38–9, 42, 44

Mers-el-Kebir, 106

Messerschmitt company (*formerly* BFW), 43

Messerschmitt Me 109 fighter: in Spanish Civil War, 34; development, design and performance, 43–5, 168; in action in France, 83–4; numbers at start of Battle of Britain, 112–13; 'free-chase' activities, 121, 125, 141, 158, 202, 223; on escort, 124–5; qualities, 136, 291, 309–10; as bomber, 142; as close escort, 235; high-flying, 292, 298–300, 302–3; E7 and E4/N models, 298; range limitations, 309–10

Messerschmitt Me 110 aircraft: design, development and performance, 45; in action in France, 83–4; numbers at start of Battle of Britain, 112–13; inadequacy and vulnerability, 125, 136, 178, 220, 229; as bomber, 142, 300; drop tanks fitted, 198

Messerschmitt, Willy, 43, 45

Metropolitan Air Force, 21n, 53

Middle Wallop, 158–9, 165, 179; WAAFs at, 330

Milch, Feldmarschall Erhard, 32–3, 108

Mills, Bernard, 181

Mills, Stuart, 81

Mitchell, Reginald Joseph, 35, 38–9, 41, 331

Mitchell, Tom, 176

Moelders, Werner, 34, 163, 219, 313

Mola Vidal, General Emilio, 107n

Montgomery, R., 150

Morris, Edward, 233, 288

Mortimer, Joan, 209

Mosley, Sir Oswald, 108

Mosquito aircraft, 298

Mungo-Park, J. C., 126

Munich agreement, 1938, 58–9, 64

Mussolini, Benito, 54, 163, 303

Mustang aircraft (P51), 35, 46n

Narvik (Norway), 82

Nelson-Edwards, George, 343

*New York Herald Tribune*, 128, 187

*New York Times*, 130, 184–5

*New Yorker* magazine, 196

New Zealanders: in RAF, 190–1

Newall, Air Chief Marshal Sir Cyril, 21, 78, 86–91, 316

Newman, Harry, 349

Nicolson, Harold, 212, 261

Nicolson, James, VC, 195

Night Air Defence Committee, 321

night raids, 224–7, 263, 268–80, 290–1

Noble, Olive, 271

Norfolk, Norman, 288

North Sea: shipping protection in, 76

North Weald: airfield attacked, 226, 303

Northcliffe, Alfred Charles William Harmsworth, Viscount, 8

Northern Ireland, 76

Northolt, 236n, 248, 252

Norway, 80–2; as bomber base, 173, 307, 326

Observation Corps (World War I), 11

Observer Corps (*later* Royal Observer Corps): development of, 26, 57; mobilised, 58; training, 67; HQ, 114; standards, 114; in action, 145, 195, 232, 256; misses KG2 on *Adlertag*, 155; and KG76 concentrated attack, 203; and mass raids, 269; contribution to victory, 328

O'Connor, F. P., 331n, 348

octane rating (petrol), 35

Oeusan, Walter, 289

Oldham, Jack, 168–9

Operational Training Units (OTUs), 221

operations rooms, 15–16, 23, 116–17; damaged, 236; WAAFs in, 329, 352–3

Orwell, George, 106

Ostend: docks bombed, 293

Osterkamp, Major General Theo, 138, 219

Osterman, Hellmuth, 237

Outer Artillery Zone (British), 23, 26, 56

Oxspring, R. W., 280

Packard company (USA), 35

Page, Geoffrey, 343

Palliser, Charles C., 233, 288–9

Panter-Downes, Mollie, 196

Parachute and Cable (PAC), 204–5, 208

Park, Air Vice-Marshal (Sir) Keith Rodney: and fighters in France, 89; and Dunkirk, 93–5, 115; commands 11 Group, 115; and conduct of Battle, 153, 163, 175–6, 192, 195, 217, 230, 235, 295–6, 333; on pilot shortage, 200, 250; and damage to CH stations, 216; reappraisal by, 222; requests help from Leigh-Mallory, 226; on effect of ground damage, 236; and mass attacks on London, 258–9, 265; orders squadrons to work in pairs, 272; and Churchill's visit, 282; dissatisfied with Group's success, 284;

Park, Air Vice-Marshal – *cont.*
  as leader, 288; and high-flying Me 109
    bombers, 299–300; on phases of
    Battle, 307; and aircraft losses, 311;
    and fighter tactics controversy, 315–
    19, 323; replaced, 320; importance
    and achievements, 331–3
Partridge, Frances, 160
Peel, John, 2–3
Pembroke docks, 222
Perkin, Frederick, 345
Perthes, Oberleutnant von, 232
Petersen, Feldwebel, 205
Pevensey (Sussex), 142
'Phoney War', 68, 80
photoreconnaissance: by Luftwaffe, 214
Pile, Lieutenant General Sir Frederick
    ('Tim'), 113, 164, 186–7
pilots (RAF): shortage of, 102, 221, 307;
    skill and quality of, 118, 333; attitude
    to fighting, 162, 325; international
    origins, 186–91; casualties and
    replacements, 200–2, 249–50;
    Luftwaffe shoot while parachuting,
    231; morale, 237–8; training, 285–6;
    exhaustion and relief, 286; and fighter
    tactics, 312–13
'Pipsqueak' (signal system), 64
Pitcher, Paul, 335
Plenderleith, Robert, 349
Pobjoys aircraft works, Rochester, 179
Poland, 60, 63
Poles: service in RAF, 186–7, 191, 217,
    284, 302; shoot at parachuting enemy,
    231–2
Poling: CH station, 145, 193, 215–16
Pond, Bill, 216
Poole, Mrs Chris, 349
Portal, Air Marshal Sir Charles, 21–2,
    317–18, 322
Portland, 130, 139, 142, 145, 176, 178–9,
    280
Portsmouth, 145–6, 148, 176, 178–9, 227
Post Office War Group, 236, 328
Prime Minister's Committee on Air
    Organisation and Home Defence
    against Air Raids (World War I), 11

Queen Victoria Hospital *see* East Grinstead
Quill, Jeffrey, 40–1, 152, 168, 341

R 101 (airship), 29
Raab, Wilhelm, 204
radar (radio-location): Dowding supports,
    29, 332; development of, 50–1; chain
    of stations in Britain, 52, 58, 64; for

gun-laying, 113; stations attacked,
    138–9, 141–3, 146, 148, 153; stations
    restored, 145; attacks discontinued,
    220
radio telephones, 14, 64
Raeder, Grand Admiral Erich, 108, 110,
    137, 245
RDF (radio direction finding), 51; *see also*
    radar
Reading (Berkshire), 272
rear-view mirrors (aircraft), 234
Red Cross markings, 134–5
Regia Aeronautica (Italy), 33; *see also* Italy
Reserve Command, 27
Restemeyer, Werner, 173–4
Reynaud, Paul, 85, 99
Reynell, R. C., 262
Rhodesians: in RAF, 191
Richey, Paul, 85, 100
Richthofen, General Wolfram, Freiherr
    von, 2, 216
Riegel, Kurt, 133
Roach, R. J. B., 252–4
Roberts, David, 158
Robinson, N., 351
Rochester (Kent), 160–1, 179
Roessiger, Wilhelm-Richard, 143
Rolls-Royce company, 34–5, 39, 113
Roosevelt, Franklin Delano, 185, 294
Rosier, Air Chief Marshal Sir Frederick,
    312
Rosyth (Scotland), 68
Roth, Joachim, 203, 205, 209
Rotterdam: bombed, 122
Rowe, A. P., 49–50
Rowledge, A. J., 34
Royal Air Force: formed (1918), 13;
    strength reduced, 17–18; maintains
    independence, 18–20; and Middle
    East air control, 19; 1930s expansion,
    25, 34, 36, 52, 55–6, 59; command
    structure, 27; aircraft development,
    34–6; overseas strength, 52–3; pre-
    war deficiencies, 59; losses in France,
    100; and prevention of invasion, 104;
    and enemy Red-Cross marked
    aircraft, 134; air-sea rescue, 134–5;
    German aim to destroy, 308–9; *see*
    *also* Bomber Command; Coastal
    Command; Fighter Command; losses
    (aircraft)
SQUADRONS
    1 Squadron, 76, 83–5, 99, 256, 259,
      335
    3 Squadron, 84, 88, 99, 190
    17 Squadron, 99, 228

19 Squadron, 168, 170, 198, 259, 319
25 Squadron, 225
32 Squadron, 125–6, 150, 163, 181, 192, 206, 208–9
41 Squadron, 70, 97, 174, 241, 285, 288, 292
43 Squadron, 69, 158, 194, 215–16, 256; relieved, 268
46 Squadron, 69, 82
54 Squadron, 92, 96–7, 132, 144, 152, 175, 190, 192, 201, 286, 301; relieved, 239
56 Squadron, 66, 123, 152, 161, 210, 238
64 Squadron, 150, 179, 199, 287; relieved, 222
65 Squadron, 121, 144, 151–2
66 Squadron, 123–4, 259, 280
72 Squadron, 94, 174, 238, 288, 348
73 Squadron, 76, 83–4, 99, 171, 259
74 Squadron, 67, 96, 124–7, 156, 166; relieved, 222
79 Squadron, 84, 174, 187, 190, 233, 256, 288
85 Squadron, 76, 153, 230, 232
87 Squadron, 76, 88, 141, 176, 228, 275
92 Squadron, 127, 189, 268, 270, 290, 296
107 Squadron, 122
111 Squadron, 125, 144, 156, 179–81, 189, 192, 205, 232, 256, 300; relieved, 222, 237, 268
141 Squadron, 130–1, 228
145 Squadron, 1–3, 166, 202; relieved, 222
151 Squadron, 67, 130, 145, 256, 279
152 Squadron, 147, 216, 296
213 Squadron, 94, 146, 263
222 Squadron, 170, 234, 270, 290, 292
229 Squadron, 271
234 Squadron, 165, 241
238 Squadron, 166, 232
242 Squadron, 99, 189, 259, 316, 319
249 Squadron, 195, 233, 256, 258, 260, 276, 303
253 Squadron, 168, 240, 250, 256, 276
257 Squadron, 1, 158, 238, 289, 303
263 Squadron, 81–2
264 Squadron, 94, 228, 230
266 Squadron, 157, 192–3, 210, 232, 252, 286; relieved, 222
302 Squadron, 223, 302

303 Squadron, 189, 256, 259, 270, 300–1, 335
310 Squadron, 230, 319
501 Squadron, 84, 99, 133, 144–5, 150, 175, 190, 217, 241, 250, 256, 258, 299, 346
504 Squadron, 84, 256, 276–7
600 Squadron, 85, 263
601 Squadron, 130, 198, 215–16; relieved, 222
602 Squadron, 68, 216, 258, 299, 303
603 Squadron, 68, 123, 190, 259
605 Squadron, 174
607 Squadron, 68, 79, 84, 300
609 Squadron, 1, 122, 129, 159–60, 165, 187–8, 227–8, 258, 262, 277
610 Squadron, 149, 207–9, 288
615 Squadron, 79, 163, 190, 205–6
616 Squadron, 171, 173–4, 223, 230, 250, 290
Royal Air Force *Narrative*, 220, 222
Royal Air Force Volunteer Reserve, 62
Royal Canadian Air Force, 189; no. 1 Squadron (*later* 401), 189, 230, 335
Royal Corps of Signals, 236
Royal Flying Corps (RFC), 8–9, 13
Royal National Lifeboat Institution, 135
Royal Naval Air Service, 13
Royal Navy: and RFC, 9; air arm, 19; mobilised, 58; and prevention of invasion, 104, 106, 327; and neutralisation of French fleet, 106
*Royal Oak*, HMS, 68
Royce, Sir Henry, 34
Rubensdoerffer, Walter: operations, 142, 144, 146, 162–4, 175, 179–81, 203; killed, 182, 289
Rundstedt, Feldmarschall Karl Rudolf Gerd von, 95
Ryder, J. T., 167, 238, 339
Rye (Sussex), 143

S.6 aircraft (British), 39
St Exupéry, Antoine de, 90
Sackville-West, Vita, 153
Salisbury, James Edward Hubert Gascoyne-Cecil, 4th Marquess of, 19–21
Salmond, Geoffrey, 21
Salmond, Marshal of the RAF Sir John, 21, 321
Samson, David, 207
Samson, Donald, 349
Satchell, W., 223
Saul, Air Vice-Marshal Richard, 116

Saunders, S., 151–2
Scapa Flow: defence of, 61, 68–9, 76; U-boat penetrates, 68
Schad, Leutnant, 147
*Scharnhorst* (German warship), 82
Schellmann, 289
Schlichting, F.-K., 141
Schmidt, Josef ('Beppo'), 173, 179, 186
Schmued, Edgar, 46n
Schneider Trophy races, 22, 38
Schroeder, Leutnant, 124
*Schwarme* formation, 313
Scott, E., 270
Sealand (Cheshire), 164
'Sealion' (*Seeloewe*; German invasion plan), 110, 137, 140, 245, 265; and *Adlerangriff*, 154; postponed, 301, 308
searchlights (British), 56, 62
Seekt, General Hans von, 31–2
Selle, Erich von, 241
Seversky, Alexander, 184
Shallard, Pat, 285
Sheffield: Vickers works, 248
Shell oil (company), 35
Shirer, William L., 243
Short Brothers works, Rochester, 179, 239
Sidi Barrani, 123, 127
Silvertown, 264
Simon, Sir John, 25
Simpson, Peter, 211–13
Sinclair, Sir Archibald, 199–200, 239, 311, 320–1, 323–4
Slessor, Air Commodore (Sir) Jack, 21, 322
Smith, Sub-Lieutenant, 2–3
Smith, Andrew ('Big Bill'), 125
Smith, Paul, 342
Smith, Roddick Lee, 156
Smith, Wynford, 132
Smuts, Field Marshal Jan Christian, 11, 13, 17
Soar, T. E., 349
Sombern, Oberleutnant, 124–5
Sommer, Otto, 205
Sopwith, Thomas O. M., 37
Sorley, Ralph, 37
South Africans: in RAF, 190–1, 206
Southampton, 145, 158, 176, 222; *see also* Woolston
Spanish Civil War, 34, 46, 107n
Spencer, D. G. H., 221n
Spencer, Desmond, 210
Sperrle, Feldmarschall Hugo von: at Lipetsk, 31; commands *Luftflotte 3*, 111, 122, 126; and weather conditions, 123; on strength of bomber force, 138; underestimates British fighter numbers, 140; and Goering, 141, 175, 182; attacks south-coast radar stations, 145, 148; uses 'free-chase' Me 109s, 158; and *Adlerangriff*, 161, 164, 195, 227, 230; forces transferred to Kesselring, 219, 229; night raids, 229; escort tactics, 235; opposes bombing of London, 244; raids Portland, 280; pilots' experience, 289; sends lone bombers, 290; attacks aircraft factories, 296; and Hitler directive, 302
Spitfire aircraft: engine, 35; design, development and performance, 38–41, 45, 48, 168; pre-war production and supply, 41; modifications, 71, 167–8, 234; in squadron service, 79–80; and BEF evacuation, 92, 94; losses at Dunkirk, 94–5; losses in France, 100; as production priority, 102; numbers at start of Battle of Britain, 112–13; qualities, 136, 341; counter-measures against escorted bombers, 235; Mark 2, 252; high-flying patrols, 292, 299, 302–3; production, 307–8; Dowding supports, 332; *see also* Supermarine company
Staff College *see* Andover: Staff College
Standen, Ann, 342
Stanmore: HQs at, 113–14
Steel, John, 21
Stephens, M. M., 88
Stirling bomber, 59
Stones, Donald, 156n, 187, 233–4
Stoney, George, 217, 347
Storckl, Alois, 165
Storrar, James, 1–2
Student, Jurt, 31
Stumpff, General Hans-Juergen, 111, 173–4, 326
Summers, J. ('Mutt'), 39
Supermarine company, 38, 41; *see also* Woolston
Supply, Ministry of, 53
Swinton, Sir Philip Cunliffe-Lister, 50, 55
Sword of Honour (Cranwell), 24–5
Sykes, Sir Frederick, 18

tactics (fighter): RAF controversy over, 311–17, 326
Tangmere: airfield attacked, 193–4; losses, 252; WAAFs at, 330
Taranto (Italy), 304
Taylor, A. J. P., 60, 86
Tedder, Arthur, 21

Tempest aircraft, 41
Ten Year Rule (British), 24
Thalman, Willy, 126
Thameshaven: oil storage tanks attacked, 241, 260
Thompson, John, 125–6, 131, 156, 180–2, 192, 237, 268, 346
Thornaby, 223
Thorney Island: airfield attacked, 215
Tietzen, Horst, 218
Times, The, 162
Tizard, Sir Henry, 49, 51
Tobin, E. Q. ('Red'), 187
Townsend, Peter, 69, 139, 153, 230, 238
Training Command (RAF), 27
Trautloft, Hannes, 278, 283, 289
Trenchard, Sir Hugh: maintains RAF independence, 18–21; develops RAF, 21–2; and Home Defence, 24; and Dowding, 28; peerage, 324
Trousdale, Richard, 210, 252–3
Tuck, Robert Stanford, 40–1, 92, 202, 211, 238, 289, 338, 339
Turley-George, Anne, 336
Turley-George, Douglas R. ('Dickie'), 132, 301
Turner, Helen, 239
Typhoon aircraft, 41

U-47 (submarine), 68
Ultra, 326–7; see also Enigma machine
Union of Soviet Socialist Republics (USSR): pre-war Luftwaffe flying school in, 31; and threat to Czechoslovakia, 57; and division of Poland, 63; winter war with Finland, 81; in Chiefs of Staff paper, 104; occupies Baltic states, 110; Hitler attacks, 137, 245
United States of America: Neutrality Act, 35; economic support for Britain, 104; and British morale, 106; press reports in, 128, 184; Dowding mission in, 322
University Air Squadrons, 22
Unwin, George, 337
Urie, J. Dunlop, 201

Ventnor (Isle of Wight), 145; CH station attacked and damaged, 146–8, 153, 194, 227; repaired, 197; operations, 228
Vickers aircraft company, 39, 248
Vincent, Clifford, 143
Vincent, Stanley, 280–2
Vuillemin, General Joseph, 98

Waalhaven (Netherlands), 85
Walker, Johnny, 238
Walker, W. L. B., 344
Walsh, Edmund, 338
Wapiti aircraft, 221 & n
War Cabinet (British), 86–90, 98
War Office, 9, 13, 18, 20
Ward, Derek, 176
Warmwell airfield, 135, 229
Watnall (Nottinghamshire), 27
Watson-Watt, Sir Robert, 49–51, 67n, 331–2
Way, B. H. ('Wonkey'), 132
Webb, Paul, 201–2
Wedel, Professor Hassel von, 276–8
Weir, A. N. C.: quoted, 5, 119
Weitkus, Paul, 260–1
Welford, George, 344
Werra, Oberleutnant von, 241
West Malling: airfield attacked, 182, 192, 300
Westmacott, Innes, 339
Weygand, General Maxime, 99, 105
Weymouth (Dorset), 2, 139, 142, 176
White, Flight Sergeant, 347
Wieck, Helmut, 160n
Wilcox, Ronald: quoted, 305
Wilkins, A. F., 49–50
Wilkinson, Rodney ('Wilkie'), 192–3, 209, 231, 286
Williams, Billy, 190
Williams, Cedric, 228
Williams, D. G., 350
Williams, Wycliff, 252–4
Wimperis, H. E., 49–50
Winant, John G., 194n
Winterbotham, F. W., 325–6
Wittering, 252
Women's Auxiliary Air Force (WAAF): formed, 62; actions, 235; importance, 329–30
Women's Voluntary Service, 328
Wood, Sir Kingsley, 59
Wood-Scawen, P. P. and C. A., 336
Woolston (near Southampton): Supermarine works, 113, 145, 158, 280, 294–5
Woolwich arsenal: bombed, 259
World War I, 10–12
Wright, Robert, 86–7, 323
Wynn, J., 351

Y (Interception) Service, 329

Zeppelin, Count Ferdinand von, 8
Zeppelins (German), 7–10, 14